bd PRINTED IN U.S.A.

ESSAYS *of Our Time I*

ESSAYS *of*

Our Time I

Edited by **Leo Hamalian**
and **Edmond L. Volpe**
The City College of New York

McGraw-Hill *Book Company*
New York   Toronto   London

1960

ESSAYS OF OUR TIME I

This book was set in Linotype Fairfield, a modern type face designed by Rudolph Ruzicka. The display type is Lining Cairo Bold and Caledonia Italic. Drawings are by Albert H. Sugimoto.

We wish to express our gratitude to the writers, agents, and publishers listed below for their kind cooperation in granting permission to reprint copyrighted material.

William Barrett, "Modern Art," from *The Irrational Man*, copyright 1958 by the author. By permission of Doubleday & Company, Inc.

William Warren Bartley, III, "I Call Myself a Protestant," *Harper's Magazine*, May, 1959. By permission of the author.

Bruno Bettelheim, "Joey: A 'Mechanical Boy,'" *Scientific American*, March, 1959. By permission of the author and the publisher.

Percy W. Bridgman, "Science and Common Sense," *Scientific Monthly*, June, 1954. By permission of the publisher.

Roger Burlingame, "The Analyst's Couch," *Harper's Magazine*, April, 1959. By permission of Littauer and Wilkinson and the author.

Preface

EXAMINING the many essay collections fresh off the presses, no teacher can be blamed for feeling like the Mark Twain character who didn't "see no p'ints about that frog that's any better'n any other frog." Yet, we hope that *Essays of Our Time,* though it may be another frog in a large puddle, does have outstanding "p'ints."

Over a number of teaching years we have discovered that students respond most readily to essays dealing with the world in which they are maturing. Our purpose in this collection, therefore, has been to bring together contemporary essays by outstanding artists, thinkers, and scientists of our time. Two basic criteria have guided our choice of an essay: (1) its interest for students and (2) the quality of the thinking and writing.

The aim of any collection of essays for college students is to stimulate their thinking and to provide them with examples of good writing. Good writing is, of course, available from any period, but an essay devoted to the concerns of another era, or even of another generation, no matter how well written, seems to engage the interest of the student far less effectively than one that relates to and illumines the world in which he lives. Deeply involved though he may be in the personal perplexities of maturing, the college student is aware that his is an age of political, cultural, and intellectual upheaval.

The student of the present decade has been described—perhaps unjustly—as apathetic, uncommitted, withdrawn into a private dream of personal security. And in contrast to the student of the thirties and forties he may seem to be. But his withdrawal, we have concluded, is not deliberate, conscious. Without fully comprehending what is occurring in his world, he senses the tensions and often buries his head in a vision of a suburban home from which he can commute each morning to his organization.

Beneath this protective surface of indifference, however, the student today is eager for understanding and knowledge. Essays dealing with the world he faces do interest him. It is our conviction that the interested student will learn, and we have therefore chosen essays that describe and analyze the conditions and the forces that make

his world what it is. Louis Finkelstein considers the moral responsibility of the businessman, and Jerome Ellison examines the activities of college students; Robert Lowry and Bruce Catton describe
what we do with our leisure time. Ian Stevenson and Bruno Bettelheim explore the expanding frontiers of mind and medicine; William
Barrett discusses the forces at work in modern art, and Agnes DeMille
explains the plight of the female artist in our society; Russell Lynes
analyzes the teenager; and four young thinkers, Walter Kaufmann,
Philip Scharper, Arthur Cohen, and William Warren Bartley III,
present four views of religious faith in the modern world.

Of course, we do not for a moment think that the student should
be cut off from the past or be persuaded that sound thinking and
good writing are confined to his own time. We do believe, however,
that the introductory courses in college English can influence the
student's future attitude toward writing and literature, and that a
collection of outstanding essays couched in his own idiom can help
him to recognize the power and beauty of clear thought and
expression.

Selecting the essays for this collection was a pleasant and rewarding task. We were forced to find the time—which should be available
for teachers but seldom is—to read extensively in contemporary
periodicals and books. Organizing our selections, however, proved
difficult. Most anthologies group essays thematically or by types, and
accepting this convention, we considered several thematic categories.
But we soon discovered that with our basic aim—to collect the best
written, most stimulating contemporary essays—our categories forced
us to exclude selections we wanted to include. We juggled our
themes, broadened them, narrowed them, increased the number.
Finally, we decided that our aim could best be served if we abandoned the idea of predetermined categories, made our selections, and
then arranged those that were in some way thematically related into
groups. Thus we have not included essays merely to fill in a category;
at the same time, though we have not titled our groupings, the divisions indicated in the table of contents constitute thematic units. The
teacher who works with themes may find the following descriptions
useful: (1) informal humorous essays, (2) language and reading,
(3) leisure in our time, (4) views of our society, (5) values of our
time, (6) the inner world, (7) art and artist, (8) science, and
(9) religion.

The groups have been arranged in order of increasing complexity of idea, and though none of the essays is difficult, there might
be obvious advantages in following the suggested order.

This book was inspired by our experience in the classroom. Our students have reacted with enthusiasm to essays of their own time, and it is our hope that students will also be stimulated by this collection to think and to write.

Leo Hamalian
Edmond L. Volpe

Contents

Essays of Our Time I ● *Part* 1

JAMES THURBER, *internationally known for the irony, satire, and fantastic humor of his drawings and prose sketches of twentieth-century American life, was associated with the* New Yorker *for many years. Born and educated in Ohio, he made his home in Connecticut, and despite failing eyesight, continued to produce his witty essays and stories until his death in 1962.*

LAWRENCE DURRELL, *British poet, novelist, and diplomat in the Near East, has written a fine study of the Cyprus situation,* Bitter Lemons, *and his recent quartet set in Egypt,* Justine, Balthazar, Mountolive, *and* Clea, *has gained him international fame. "La Valise" is from a second volume of impressions about the diplomatic corps.*

DYLAN THOMAS, *often described as the Byron of the twentieth century, was born in Wales. Primarily a poet, his prose captures the brilliant sensuous word play that characterizes his poetry. His poetry and his personality won a wide American following, and he travelled through the country on reading tours. His death in New York at the age of thirty-nine cut short a remarkable and original poetic voice.*

JAMES THURBER

If Grant Had Been Drinking
at Appomattox

THE MORNING OF THE NINTH of April, 1865, dawned beautifully. General Meade was up with the first streaks of crimson in the eastern sky. General Hooker and General Burnside were up, and had breakfasted, by a quarter after eight. The day continued beautiful. It drew on toward eleven o'clock. General Ulysses S. Grant was still not up. He was asleep in his famous old navy hammock, swung high above the floor of his headquarters' bedroom. Headquarters was distressingly disarranged: papers were strewn on the floor; confidential notes from spies scurried here and there in the breeze from an open window; the dregs of an overturned bottle of wine flowed pinkly across an important military map.

Corporal Shultz, of the Sixty-fifth Ohio Volunteer Infantry, aide to General Grant, came into the outer room, looked around him, and sighed. He entered the bedroom and shook the General's hammock roughly. General Ulysses S. Grant opened one eye.

"Pardon, sir," said Corporal Shultz, "but this is the day of surrender. You ought to be up, sir."

"Don't swing me," said Grant sharply, for his aide was making the hammock sway gently. "I feel terrible," he added, and he turned over and closed his eye again.

"General Lee will be here any minute now," said the Corporal firmly, swinging the hammock again.

"Will you cut that out?" roared Grant. "D'ya want to make me sick or what?" Shultz clicked his heels and saluted. "What's he coming here for?" asked the General.

"This is the day of surrender, sir," said Shultz. Grant grunted bitterly.

"Three hundred and fifty generals in the Northern armies," said Grant, "and he has to come to *me* about this. What time is it?"

"You're the Commander-in-Chief, that's why," said Corporal Shultz. "It's eleven twenty-five, sir."

"Don't be crazy," said Grant. "Lincoln is the Commander-in-Chief. Nobody in the history of the world ever surrendered before lunch.

Doesn't he know that an army surrenders on its stomach?" He pulled a blanket up over his head and settled himself again.

"The generals of the Confederacy will be here any minute now," said the Corporal. "You really ought to be up, sir."

Grant stretched his arms above his head and yawned.

"All right, all right," he said. He rose to a sitting position and stared about the room. "This place looks awful," he growled.

"You must have had quite a time of it last night, sir," ventured Shultz.

"Yeh," said General Grant, looking around for his clothes. "I was wrassling some general. Some general with a beard."

Shultz helped the commander of the Northern armies in the field to find his clothes.

"Where's my other sock?" demanded Grant. Shultz began to look around for it. The General walked uncertainly to a table and poured a drink from a bottle.

"I don't think it wise to drink, sir," said Shultz.

"Nev' mind about me," said Grant, helping himself to a second, "I can take it or let it alone. Didn' ya ever hear the story about the fella went to Lincoln to complain about me drinking too much? 'So-and-So says Grant drinks too much,' this fella said. 'So-and-So is a fool,' said Lincoln. So this fella went to What's-His-Name and told him what Lincoln said and he came roarin' to Lincoln about it. 'Did you tell So-and-So I was a fool?' he said. 'No,' said Lincoln, 'I thought he knew it.'" The General smiled, reminiscently, and had another drink. "*That's* how I stand with Lincoln," he said proudly.

The soft thudding sound of horses' hooves came through the open window. Shultz hurriedly walked over and looked out.

"Hoof steps," said Grant, with a curious chortle.

"It is General Lee and his staff," said Shultz.

"Show him in," said the General, taking another drink. "And see what the boys in the back room will have."

Shultz walked smartly over to the door, opened it, saluted, and stood aside. General Lee, dignified against the blue of the April sky, magnificent in his dress uniform, stood for a moment framed in the doorway. He walked in, followed by his staff. They bowed, and stood silent. General Grant stared at them. He only had one boot on and his jacket was unbuttoned.

"I know who you are," said Grant. "You're Robert Browning, the poet."

"This is General Robert E. Lee," said one of his staff, coldly.

"Oh," said Grant. "I thought he was Robert Browning. He certainly looks like Robert Browning. There was a poet for you, Lee: Browning. Did ja ever read 'How They Brought the Good News from Ghent to Aix'? 'Up Derek, to saddle, up Derek, away; up Dunder, up Blitzen, up Prancer, up Dancer, up Bouncer, up Vixen, up—'"

"Shall we proceed at once to the matter in hand?" asked General Lee, his eyes disdainfully taking in the disordered room.

"Some of the boys was wrassling here last night," explained Grant. "I threw Sherman, or some general a whole lot like Sherman. It was pretty dark." He handed a bottle of Scotch to the commanding officer of the Southern armies, who stood holding it, in amazement and discomfiture. "Get a glass, somebody," said Grant, looking straight at General Longstreet. "Didn't I meet you at Cold Harbor?" he asked. General Longstreet did not answer.

"I should like to have this over with as soon as possible," said Lee. Grant looked vaguely at Shultz, who walked up close to him, frowning.

"The surrender, sir, the surrender," said Corporal Shultz in a whisper.

"Oh sure, sure," said Grant. He took another drink. "All right," he said. "Here we go." Slowly, sadly, he unbuckled his sword. Then he handed it to the astonished Lee. "There you are, General," said Grant. "We dam' near licked you. If I'd been feeling better we *would* of licked you."

LAWRENCE DURRELL

La Valise

"IF THERE IS ANYTHING worse than a soprano," said Antrobus judicially as we walked down the Mall towards his club, "it is a mezzo-soprano. One shriek lower in the scale, perhaps, but with higher candle-power. I'm not just being small-minded, old chap. I bear the scars of spiritual experience. Seriously." And indeed he did look serious; but then he always does. The aura of the Foreign Office clings to him. He waved his umbrella, changed step, and continued in a lower, more confidential register. "And I can tell you another thing. If there is anything really questionable about the French character it must be its passion for *culture*. I might not dare to say this in the F.O., old man, but I know you will respect my confidence. You see, we are all supposed to be pro rather than anti in the Old Firm—but as for me, frankly I hate the stuff. It rattles me. It gives me the plain untitivated pip, I don't mind confessing."

He drew a deep breath and after a pause went on, more pensively, drawing upon his memories of Foreign Service life: "All my worst moments have been cultural rather than political. Like that awful business of *La Valise,* known privately to the members of the Corps as The Diplomatic Bag Extraordinary. Did I ever mention it? She was French Ambassadress in Vulgaria."

"No."

"Shall I? It will make you wince."

"Do."

"Well it happened while I was serving in Vulgaria some years ago; an unspeakable place full of unspeakable people. It was the usual Iron Curtain post to which the F.O. had exposed its soft white underbelly in the person of Smith-Cromwell. Not that he was a bad chap. He was in fact quite intelligent and had played darts for Cambridge. But he was easily led. As you know in a Communist country the Corps finds itself cut off from every human contact. It has to provide its own amusements, fall back on its own resources. And this is where the trouble usually begins. It is a strange thing but in a post like that it is never long before some dastardly Frenchman (always French) reaches for the safety-catch of his revolver and starts to introduce *culture* into our lives. Invariably.

"So it fell out with us in Sczbog. Sure enough, during my second winter the French appointed a Cultural Attaché, straight from Montmartre—the place with the big church. Fellow like a greyhound. Burning eyes. Dirty hair. A moist and Fahrenheit handshake. You know the type. Wasn't even married to his own wife. Most Questionable fellow. Up till now everything had been quiet and reasonable—just the usual round of diplomatic-social engagements among colleagues. Now this beastly fellow started the ball rolling with a public lecture—an undisguised public lecture—on a French writer called, if I understood him correctly, Flowbear. Of course we all had to go to support the French. Cultural reciprocity and all that. But as if this wasn't enough the little blackhead followed it up with another about another blasted French writer called, unless my memory is at fault, Goaty-eh. I ask you, my dear fellow, what was one to do. Flowbear! Goaty-eh! It was more than flesh and blood could stand. I myself feared the worst as I sat listening to him. The whole thing cried out for the chloroform-pad. I had of course wound up and set my features at Refined Rapture like everyone else, but inside me I was in a turmoil of apprehension. Culture spreads like mumps, you know, like measles. A thing like this could get everyone acting unnaturally in no time. All culture corrupts, old boy, but French culture corrupts absolutely. I was not wrong.

"The echoes had hardly died away when I noticed That Awful Look coming over peoples' faces. Everyone began to think up little tortures of their own. A whole winter stretched before us with practically no engagements except a national day or so. It was clear that unless Smith-Cromwell took a strong line the rot would set in. He did not. Instead of snorting when *La Valise* embarked on a cultural season he weakly encouraged her; he was even heard to remark that culture was a Good Thing—for the Military Attaché.

"At this time of course we also had our cultural man. Name of Gool. And he looked it. It was a clear case of Harrow and a bad third in History. But up to now we had kept Gool strictly under control and afraid to move. It could not last. He was bound to come adrift. Within a month he was making common cause with his French colleague. They began to lecture, separately and together. They gave readings with writhings. They spared us nothing, Eliot, Sartre, Emmanuel Kant —and who is that other fellow? The name escapes me. In short they gave us everything short of Mrs. Beeton. I did my best to get an armlock on Gool and to a certain extent succeeded by threatening to recommend him for an O.B.E. He knew this would ruin his career and that he would be posted to Java. But by the time I had got him pressed to the mat it was too late. The whole Corps had taken fire and was burning with the old hard gem-like flame. Culture was spreading like wildfire.

"A series of unforgettable evenings now began, old boy. Each mission thought up some particularly horrible contribution of its own to this feast. The nights became a torture of pure poesy and song. An evening of hellish amateur opera by the Italians would be followed without intermission by an ear-splitting evening of yodelling from the Swiss, all dressed as edelweiss. Then the Japanese mission went berserk and gave a Noh-play of ghoulish obscurity lasting seven hours. The sight of all those little yellowish, inscrutable diplomats all dressed as Mickey Mouse, old boy, was enough to turn milk. And their voices simply ate into one. Then in characteristic fashion the Dutch, not to be outdone, decided to gnaw their way to the forefront of things with a recital of national poetry by the Dutch Ambassadress herself. This was when I began to draft my resignation in my own mind. O God! how can I ever forget Madame Vanderpipf (usually the most kind and normal of wives and mothers) taking up a stance like a grenadier at Fontenoy, and after a pause declaiming in a slow, deep—O unspeakably slow and deep—voice, the opening verses of whatever it was? Old Boy, the cultural heritage of the Dutch is not my affair. Let them have it, I say. Let them enjoy it peacefully as they may. But spare me from poems of five hundred lines beginning, 'Oom kroop der poop'. You smile, as well indeed you may, never having heard Mrs. Vanderpipf declaiming those memorable stanzes with all the sullen fire of her race. Listen!

> Oom kroop der poop
> Zoom kroon der soup
> Soon droon der oopersnoop.

"And so on. Have you got the idea? Perhaps there is something behind it all—who am I to say? All I know is that it is no joke to be on the receiving end. Specially as she would pause from time to time to give a rough translation in pidgin for Smith-Cromwell's benefit. Something like this: 'Our national poet Snugerpouf, he says eef Holland lives forever, only, how you would say?, heroes from ze soil oopspringing, yes?' It was pulse-stopping, old man. Then she would take a deep breath and begin afresh.

> Oom kroop der poop
> Zoom kroon der soup.

"In after years the very memory of this recitation used to make the sweat start out of my forehead. You must try it for yourself sometime. Just try repeating 'oom kroop der poop' five hundred times in a low voice. After a time it's like Yoga. Everything goes dark. You feel you are falling backwards into illimitable black space.

"By this time Smith-Cromwell himself had begun to suffer. He leaned across to me once on this particular evening to whisper a message. I could tell from his popping eye and the knot of throbbing veins at his temple that he was under strain. He had at last discovered what culture means. 'If this goes on much longer,' he hissed, 'I shall confess everything.'

"But this did go on; unremittingly for a whole winter. I spare you a description of the cultural offerings brought to us by the remoter tribes. The Argentines! The Liberians! Dear God! When I think of the Chinese all dressed in lamp-shades, the Australians doing sheep-opera, the Egyptians undulating and ululating all in the same breath. . . . Old boy, I am at a loss.

"But the real evil demon of the peace was La Valise. Whenever culture flagged she was there, quick to rekindle the flame. Long after

the Corps was milked dry, so to speak, and had nothing left in its
collective memory except nursery rhymes or perhaps a bluish limerick
or two, *La Valise* was still at it. She fancied herself as a singer. She
was never without a wad of music. A mezzo-soprano never gives in,
old boy. She dies standing up, with swelling port curved to the stars.
. . . And here came this beastly attaché again. He had turned out to be
a pianist, and she took him everywhere to accompany her. While he
clawed the piano she clawed the air and remorselessly sang. How she
sang! Always a bit flat, I gather, but with a sickening lucid resonance
that penetrated the middle ear. Those who had hearing-aids filled them
with a kapok mixture for her recitals. When she hit a top note I could
hear the studs vibrating in my dinner-shirt. Cowed, we sat and watched
her, as she started to climb a row of notes towards the veil of the
temple—that shattering top E, F or G: I never know which. We had
the sinking feeling you get on the giant racer just as it nears the top
of the slope. To this day I don't know how we kept our heads.

"Smith-Cromwell was by this time deeply penitent about his earlier
encouragement of *La Valise* and at his wits' end to see her stopped.
Everyone in the Chancery was in a bad state of nerves. The Naval
Attaché had taken to bursting into tears at meals if one so much as
mentioned a forthcoming cultural engagement. But what was to be
done? We clutched at every straw; and De Mandeville, always resource-
ful, suggested inviting the Corps to a live reading by himself and
chauffeur from the works of the Marquis De Sade. But after delibera-
tion Smith-Cromwell thought this might, though Effective, seem Questionable, so we dropped it.

"I had begun to feel like Titus Andronicus, old man, when the
miracle happened. Out of a cloudless sky. Nemesis intervened just as
he does in Gilbert Murray. Now *La Valise* had always been somewhat
hirsute, indeed quite distinctly moustached in the Neapolitan manner,
though none of us for a moment suspected the truth. But one day after
Christmas M. De Panier, her husband, came round to the Embassy
in full *tenue* and threw himself into Cromwell-Smith's arms, bathed
in tears as the French always say. 'My dear Britannic Colleague,' he
said, 'I have come to take my leave of you. My career is completely
ruined. I am leaving diplomacy for good. I have resigned. I shall return
to my father-in-law's carpet-factory near Lyons and start a new life.
All is over.'

"Smith-Cromwell was of course delighted to see the back of *La
Valise*; but we all had a soft corner for De Panier. He was a gentle-
man. Never scamped his *frais* and always gave us real champagne on

Bastille Day. Also his dinners were dinners—not like the Swedes; but I am straying from my point. In answer to Smith-Cromwell's tactful inquiries De Panier unbosomed.

"You will never credit it, old man. You will think I am romancing. But it's as true as I am standing here. There are times in life when the heart spires upward like the lark on the wing; when through the consciousness runs, like an unearthly melody, the thought that God *really* exists, really *cares;* more, that he turns aside to lend a helping hand to poor dips *in extremis*. This was such a moment, old boy.

"*La Valise* had gone into hospital for some minor complaints which defied diagnosis. And in the course of a minor operation the doctors discovered that she was *turning into a man!* Nowadays of course it is becoming a commonplace of medicine; but at the time of which I speak it sounded like a miracle. A *man,* upon my soul! We could hardly believe it. The old caterpillar was really one of *us*. It was too enchanting! We were saved!

"And so it turned out. Within a matter of months her voice—that instrument of stark doom—sank to a bass; she sprouted a beard. Poor old De Panier hastened to leave but was held up until his replacement came. Poor fellow! Our hearts went out to him with This Whiskered Wonder on his hands. But he took it all very gallantly. They left at last, in a closed car, at dead of night. He would be happier in Lyons, I reflected, where nobody minds that sort of thing.

"But if he was gallant about this misfortune so was *La Valise elle-même*. She went on the halls, old boy, as a bass-baritone and made quite a name for herself. Smith-Cromwell says he once heard her sing 'The London Derrière' in Paris with full orchestra and that she brought the house down. Some of the lower notes still made the ash-trays vibrate a bit but it was no longer like being trapped in a wind-tunnel. She wore a beard now and a corkscrew moustache and was very self-possessed. One can afford to be Over There. He also noticed she was wearing a smartish pair of elastic-sided boots. O, and her trade name now was Tito Torez. She and De Panier were divorced by then, and she had started out on a new career which was less of a reign of terror, if we can trust Smith-Cromwell. Merciful are the ways of Providence!

"As for poor De Panier himself, I gather that he re-entered the service after the scandal had died down. He is at present Consul-General in Blue Springs, Colorado. I'm told that there isn't much culture there, so he ought to be a very happy man indeed."

A Visit to America

ACROSS THE United States of America, from New York to California and back, glazed, again, for many months of the year, there streams and sings for its heady supper a dazed and prejudiced procession of European lecturers, scholars, sociologists, economists, writers, authorities on this and that and even, in theory, on the United States of America. And, breathlessly between addresses and receptions, in 'planes and trains and boiling hotel bedroom ovens, many of these attempt to keep journals and diaries.

At first, confused and shocked by shameless profusion and almost shamed by generosity, unaccustomed to such importance as they are assumed, by their hosts, to possess, and up against the barrier of a common language, they write in their notebooks like demons, generalising away, on character and culture and the American political scene. But, towards the middle of their middle-aged whisk through middle-western clubs and universities, the fury of the writing flags; their spirits are lowered by the spirit with which they are everywhere strongly greeted and which, in ever-increasing doses, they themselves lower; and they begin to mistrust themselves, and their reputations—for they have found, too often, that an audience will receive a lantern-lecture on, say, Ceramics, with the same uninhibited enthusiasm that it accorded the very week before to a paper on the Modern Turkish Novel. And, in their diaries, more and more do such entries appear as, 'No way of escape!' or 'Buffalo!' or 'I am beaten,' until at last they cannot write a word. And, twittering all over, old before their time, with eyes like rissoles in the sand, they are helped up the gangway of the homebound liner by kind bosom friends (of all kinds and bosoms) who boister them on the back, pick them up again, thrust bottles, sonnets, cigars, addresses, into their pockets, have a farewell party in their cabin, pick them up again, and, snickering and yelping, are gone: to wait at the dockside for another boat from Europe and another batch of fresh, green lecturers.

There they go, every spring, from New York to Los Angeles: exhibitionists, polemicists, histrionic publicists, theological rhetoricians, historical hoddy-doddies, balletomanes, ulterior decorators, windbags and bigwigs and humbugs, men in love with stamps, men in love with

11

steaks, men after millionaires' widows, men with elephantiasis of the reputation (huge trunks and teeny minds), authorities on gas, bishops, best-sellers, editors looking for writers, writers looking for publishers, publishers looking for dollars, existentialists, serious physicists with nuclear missions, men from the B.B.C. who speak as though they had the Elgin marbles in their mouths, potboiling philosophers, professional Irishmen (very lepri-corny), and, I am afraid, fat poets with slim volumes.

And see, too, in that linguaceous stream, the tall monocled men, smelling of saddle soap and club armchairs, their breath a nice blending of whisky and fox's blood, with big protruding upper-class tusks and county moustaches, presumably invented in England and sent abroad to advertise *Punch,* who lecture to women's clubs on such unlikely subjects as 'The History of Etching in the Shetland Islands'; and the brassy-bossy men-women, with corrugated-iron perms, and hippo hides, who come, self-announced, as 'ordinary British housewives', to talk to rich minked chunks of American matronhood about the iniquity of the Health Services, the criminal sloth of the miners, the *visible* tail and horns of Mr. Aneurin Bevan, and the fear of everyone in England to go out alone at night because of the organised legions of coshboys against whom the police are powerless owing to the refusal of those in power to equip them with revolvers and to flog to ribbons every adolescent offender on any charge at all.

And there shiver and teeter also, meek and driven, those British authors unfortunate enough to have written, after years of unadventurous forgotten work, one bad novel which became enormously popular on both sides of the Atlantic. At home, when success first hit them, they were mildly delighted; a couple of literary luncheons went sugar-tipsy to their heads, like the washing sherry served before those luncheons; and perhaps, as the lovely money rolled lushly in, they began to dream, in their moony writers' way, of being able to retire to the country, keep wasps (or was it bees?) and never write another lousy word. But in come the literary agent's triggermen and the publisher's armed narks: 'You must go to the States and make a Personal Appearance. Your novel is *killing* them over there, and we're not surprised either. You must go round the States lecturing to women'. And the inoffensive writers, who have never dared lecture anyone, let alone women—they are frightened of women, they do not understand them women, they write about women as creatures that never existed, and the women lap it up—these sensitive plants cry out, 'But what shall we lecture about?' 'The English Novel'. 'I don't read novels'. 'Great Women in Fiction'. 'I don't like fiction *or* women'. But off they are wafted, first-class, in the plush bowels of the *Queen Victoria,* with a list of engagements long as a New York menu or a half-hour with a book by Charles Morgan, and soon they are losing their little cold-as-goldfish paw in the great general glutinous handshake of a clutch of enveloping hostesses.

I think, by the way, that it was Ernest Raymond, the author of *Tell England,* who once made a journey round the American women's clubs, being housed and entertained at each small town he stopped at, by the richest and largest and furriest lady available. On one occasion he stopped at some little station and was met, as usual, by an enormous motor-car full of a large horn-rimmed business-man—looking exactly like a large horn-rimmed business-man on the films—and his roly-poly pearly wife. Mr. Raymond sat with her in the back of the car, and off they went, the husband driving. At once, she began to say how utterly delighted she and her husband and the committee were to have him at their Women's Literary and Social Guild, and to compliment him on his books. 'I don't think I've ever, in all my life, enjoyed a book so much as *Sorrel and Son'*, she said. 'What you don't know about human nature! I think Sorrel is one of the most beautiful characters ever portrayed'.

Ernest Raymond let her talk on, while he stared, embarrassed, in front of him. All he could see were the three double chins that her husband wore at the back of his neck. On and on she gushed in praise of *Sorrel and Son* until he could stand it no longer. 'I quite agree with you', he said. 'A beautiful book indeed. But I'm afraid I didn't write *Sorrel and Son.* It was written by an old friend of mine, Mr. Warwick Deeping'. And the large horn-rimmed doubled-chinned husband at the wheel said without turning: 'Caught again, Emily'.

See the garrulous others, also, gabbing and garlanded from one nest of culture-vultures to another: people selling the English way of life and condemning the American way as they swig and guzzle through it; people resurrecting the theories of surrealism for the benefit of remote parochial female audiences who did not know it was dead, not having ever known it had been alive; people talking about Etruscan pots and pans to a bunch of dead pans and wealthy pots in Boston. And there, too, in the sticky thick of lecturers moving across the continent black with clubs, go the foreign poets, catarrhal troubadours, lyrical one-night-standers, dollar-mad nightingales, remittance-bards from at home, myself among them booming with the worst.

Did we pass one another, *en route,* all unknowing, I wonder; one of us spry-eyed, with clean, white lectures and a soul he could call his own, going bouyantly west to his remunerative doom in the great State University factories; another returning dog-eared as his clutch of

poems and his carefully-typed impromptu asides? I ache for us both.
There one goes, unsullied as yet, in his pullman pride, toying—oh boy!
—with a blunderbuss bourbon, being smoked by a large cigar, riding
out to the wide open spaces of the faces of his waiting audience. He
carries, besides his literary baggage, a new, dynamic razor, just on the
market, bought in New York, which operates at the flick of a thumb
but cuts the thumb to the bone; a tin of new shaving-lather which is
worked with the other, unbleeding, thumb, and covers not only the
face but the whole bathroom and, instantly freezing, makes an arctic,
icicled cave from which it takes two sneering bellboys to extract him;
and, of course, a nylon shirt. This, he dearly believes from the advertisements, he can himself wash in his hotel, hang to dry overnight,
and put on, without ironing, in the morning. (In my case, no ironing
was needed, for, as someone cruelly pointed out in print, I looked anyway like an unmade bed.)

He is vigorously welcomed at the station by an earnest crew-cut
platoon of giant collegiates, all chasing the butterfly culture with net,
notebook, poison-bottle, pin and label, each with at least thirty-six terribly white teeth, and nursed away, as heavily gently as though he
were an imbecile rich aunt with a short prospect of life, into a motor-
car in which, for a mere fifty miles or so travelled at poet-breaking
speed, he assures them of the correctness of their assumption that he is
half-witted by stammering inconsequential answers in an over-British
accent to their genial questions about what international conference
Stephen Spender might be attending at the moment, or the reactions
of British poets to the work of a famous American whose name he did
not know or catch. He is then taken to a small party of only a few
hundred people all of whom hold the belief that what a visiting lecturer
needs before he trips on to the platform is just enough martinis so that
he can trip off the platform as well. And, clutching his explosive glass,
he is soon contemptuously dismissing, in a flush of ignorance and fluency, the poetry of those androgynous literary ladies with three names
who produce a kind of verbal ectoplasm to order as a waiter dishes up
spaghetti—only to find that the fiercest of these, a wealthy huntress
of small, seedy lions (such as himself), who stalks the middle-western
bush with ears and rifle cocked, is his hostess for the evening. Of the
lecture, he remembers little but the applause and maybe two questions:
'Is it true that the young English intellectuals are *really* pyscho-
logical?' or, 'I always carry Kierkegaard in my pocket. What do you
carry?'

Late at night, in his room, he fills a page of his journal with a
confused, but scathing, account of his first engagement, summarises

American advanced education in a paragraph that will be meaningless tomorrow, and falls to sleep where he is immediately chased through long, dark thickets by a Mrs. Mabel Frankincense Mehaffey, with a tray of martinis and lyrics.

And there goes the other happy poet bedraggledly back to New York which struck him all of a sheepish never-sleeping heap at first but which seems to him now, after the ulcerous rigours of a lecturer's spring, a haven cosy as toast, cool as an icebox, and safe as skyscrapers.

Essays of Our Time I ● *Part* 2

ELMO ROPER, *after twelve years of experience in the jewelry business, became convinced that it was fundamental to learn what the public wanted. He became a pioneer in public-opinion research and now has an organization with a staff of more than three hundred field interviewers and research coordinators. His book* You and Your Leaders *is a study of recent American political history.*

DAVID RIESMAN *took a Harvard degree in biochemistry and then went on to law school. Before he settled into his career in social science he worked as an executive for Sperry Rand. His provocative and perceptive studies of American culture,* The Lonely Crowd *and* Faces in the Crowd, *have gained him prominence as one of the keenest observers of our society. He is currently teaching at Harvard.*

ARTHUR KOESTLER, *novelist and journalist, was almost executed by the Franco forces during the Spanish Civil War* (Spanish Testament) *and barely survived a notorious French detention camp in 1939* (Scum of the Earth). Darkness at Noon, *based upon his understanding of the Moscow Trials, is a gripping novel that later became a Pulitzer Prize–winning play. He prides himself on being the only writer who has twice changed the language in which he writes: from Hungarian to German at the age of seventeen and from German to English at the age of thirty-five.*

STEPHEN ULLMAN, *professor of romance philology at the University of Leeds, was educated at the University of Budapest and the University of Glasgow, where he later taught for six years. His books include* Words and Their Use, Principles of Semantics, *and* Style in the French Novel.

ELMO ROPER

Roadblocks to Bookbuying

FIRST, I WANT to suggest some reasons why, in my opinion, more books are not sold. Second, I want to tell you why *I* think it not only is desirable, but imperative for the American public, that more books be sold. And finally, I will offer a few suggestions on how the sale of books might be increased—but I warn you in advance that the main suggestion is one on which you will need a lot of help if it is to be effective.

Because our company does marketing and opinion research, I usually am able to base my observations on research findings, but there seems to be comparatively little marketing research in the bookselling field. Whether you deplore that fact or not, I'm sure it will come as no surprise to you that *I* do. Nevertheless, by drawing on personal experiences, secondary resources and inferences from other areas of business and marketing, I hope that the suggestions I have will not be wholly meaningless.

I suppose that most of you in the book trade assume that the product you sell is associated with pleasure. You would say that reading a book is a pleasure whereas, in contrast, a pharmacist's product is associated with displeasure: taking medicine is not a pleasure. I use this sharp contrast to emphasize a point that is easy to forget, namely that reading books is not a pleasure to a great many people. There is little doubt that reading books is hard intellectual labor for the majority of people, and that the pleasure component only outweighs the hard work component by a little bit for a large additional group of the population. Reading a book is sheer pleasure alone for a very small minority of people.

You and I, and most of the people we spend time with from day to day, belong to the FSM's. The FSM's are a small, select group of the population. The initials, FSM, of course, stand for Facile Symbol Manipulators. In order to see yourself in perspective, as an FSM, let me remind you of the Easterner who got stranded in the hinterlands of Wyoming. He walked into a ranch and asked the rancher for help in getting to town. The rancher said, "Sure, go out to the south corral

---

This essay was originally a speech delivered to a convention of book publishers.

and get a horse. You can leave it in the livery stable in town." Our Easterner was no ignoramus; he was an ordinary, fairly competent citizen. But by the time he found the corral, located a saddle and bridle, caught a horse, got the saddle and bridle on, and rode to town, he felt he deserved no less than a ceremonial dinner—preferably a buffet dinner.

When we FSM's say: "Read books; it's fun," we sound to a lot of people like the rancher when he said, "Get a horse."

Spoken words are symbols that substitute for things and ideas. *Printed* words are symbols that substitute for spoken words. Reading is therefore the process of understanding symbols of symbols of things and ideas. Reading is hard work. We FSM's tend to forget that fact. And if you think I have been setting up a straw man, reflect for a moment on the size of the book-reading public in comparison with the publics for radio, television, motion pictures, comic books and picture magazines—media that do not require the facile manipulation of printed symbols. Harold Guinzburg, president of the American Book Publishers Council, recently reported that "Americans currently spend more money on *repairs* to their radio and television sets than they do on all kinds of books."

I hope I have convinced you that if you want to expand materially the book-reading public, you should think of reading a book as an undertaking—as something of a project—not as an impulse activity or as a comforting bit of self-indulgence. Let's face it: Reading books is hard intellectual labor for most people.

Now, how about *buying* a book? For present purposes let's think in terms of a four-dollar book. A book costs enough so that people think about it before they buy. Four or five or six dollars is well above the range of impulse expenditures—for most people. People want to make a good purchase—they want to get their money's worth when they spend four or five dollars. I don't claim to understand it, but it seems to me that it is especially important that a book be worth its price precisely because it *doesn't* wear out or get used up. A man will pay four or five dollars for a steak that turns out to be mediocre, or for a brand of whiskey that doesn't quite suit his taste, and beyond a momentary complaint, he probably says no more about it. But if he buys a book that turns out to be stupid or superficial or boring, I have an idea that his dissatisfaction lasts much longer. Maybe it is because he expects a reward more commensurate with the effort he puts into reading it than with the price of it. Maybe it is because the book on his shelf is a perpetual reproach to him for having made a bad purchase.

And in addition to any other reasons, buying a book is a risky invest-ment because you are always conscious of the alternative of getting it free from the library.

The role of the free public library and of rental libraries brings us face to face with the obvious fact that it is not necessary to buy books in order to read them. Why then, should a person buy them? We FSM's consider even the question to be vulgar. Obviously, there should be books in a home. A person who is intellectually alive wants access to the great ideas, the high points of thought and feeling, the record of the past, the epic achievements of knowledge, the best in wit, fun and adventure—this cultural treasure lives through good books, and we FSM's want books as part of our environment and are quite willing to pay for them. But apparently a lot of people don't feel that way. I suppose that most people read more books during their school years than during any comparable span of years, and probably the books read during school years that either bored or baffled them outnumber the ones that excited or stimulated them by a ratio of at least 2 to 1. The impetus to buy books is not very strong for Joe Doakes. His major experience in buying books was in school where he was required to buy them and then to fight his way through them. Recommendations by people of authority would appear to get off to a rather bad start. How then does he know if a book is worth his money? He doesn't until he's read it, and then it's too late. Book buying must seem like a risky business to many people.

Having ventured the opinion that book reading is hard work, and book buying is a risky way to spend money, how about book owning? A real estate man called on a friend of mine who was admiring an end-wall of book shelves that he had just had built at a cost of some hun-dreds of dollars. The real estate man said, "Well, they look nice, but of course they depreciate the market value of your house by a thousand dollars or so. Nobody else will want them!" This, I want to add, took place a few months ago in a wealthy community that is known as a choice place for leisure, "culture," and retirement.

An incident that took place about four years ago in a New York suburb tends to confirm that real estate man's opinion. In this case a young couple bought a beautiful old house that had been owned by an FSM. He was one of our well-known foreign correspondents. This man had had bookshelves built on one wall of the living room and had taken special pride in his private library. The new people—college graduates, good citizens, income around $15,000, two bright children in school—were enthusiastic about the house except for the bookshelves.

After long and careful consideration, they solved the problem by simply boarding them up. Tearing them out would have cracked too much plaster.

Owning books is a sometime thing. A fine, private library is the purest of wealth to a few, but to most people it is simply unthought of, and to many the owners of private libraries probably seem odd and a little pretentious. I don't know whether it is true or not, but I have heard it said that many people regard books as a cloudy window through which the timid view a life they are incapable of experiencing directly. For such people, books are not the symbol of enriched experience and broadened horizons. Quite the opposite. Books are a sign of pinched and second-hand living.

I'll end this dreary part of my remarks by summarizing three road-blocks that I suspect you face: Book reading is intellectually taxing. Book buying is regarded by many as economically risky. Book owning is socially deviant.

Now I want to tell you why I consider it not only desirable but imperative that more books be sold. In order to make my point, I want to talk for a moment about baseball. We all marvel at the consummate skill of big league baseball players. As you watch them, fantastic feats of speed and coordination blend into the graceful sort of motion that combines the ruggedness of sports with the beauty of the arts. Fierce competitiveness blends with observance of a complex code of rules in a way that releases aggressiveness within the boundaries of discipline. Creative ingenuity blends with custom and deeply engrained habit in a way that allows intuition to rise from a platform of habits. The end performance is without parallel in its field. It excites the population at large, it is admired without envy, it is spurred on by true connoisseurs and it becomes a national rallying point. Share croppers, factory workers, housewives, merchants, politicians, school teachers, financiers, presidents, *everybody* gets into the act regarding baseball.

Now, how does this sort of thing come about? I suspect that an important part of the answer is what has been referred to as the *folk status* of baseball in our society. Through the length and breadth of the land, and up and down the social and economic brackets, it is considered a good thing for a father to play catch with his son. It is a good thing for a boy to get outside and play ball with the other kids. Churches, volunteer firemen, trade unions, and country clubs all sponsor little leagues. A home run is a thing of value whether it is hit with a broomstick and soars over the barn or is hit with a regulation bat and clears the bleachers. There is a folk tradition about baseball that touches our whole population, that seeks out talent, that nurtures it toward its potential, that prods and praises and disciplines exceptional ability, that recognizes achievement at various levels between the sand lot and the World Series, and that selects and honors and rewards according to the outcome of uncompromising competition. A few hundred big league players are the apex of a seething social pyramid with a base composed literally of millions of hopefuls who do their best, progress according to their ability, and then move on to continue their interest as fans who pay the freight for the pros.

Baseball has folk status in our society. So does show business, and so also does business management. But what about intellectual achievement? Does it have comparable folk status in our society? I think that you will agree with me that it does not.

It is true that nearly all parents want their children to be able to read and write and do a bit of arithmetic. It is desirable, throughout our society, to get enough education to get a good job. There is a growing segment of the population that recognizes college as required training for the good jobs, or that sees college as a useful device for gaining social status or business connections or an appropriate spouse. But intellectual achievement, beyond the point where it yields an immediate, practical return, is rather generally viewed with reserve and sometimes even with a bit of alarm.

There is no widespread folk tradition that seeks out and trains and sponsors and takes pride in exceptional intellectual talent. There are no "little leagues" of the mind. It is good if a child gets high grades on his report card; but beyond that, a love of abstract ideas, a thirst for knowledge, a gnawing intellectual curiosity—these are more likely to be regarded as worrisome symptoms than as promising abilities. We cling to the old wives' tale that the highly intelligent are especially prone to neurosis or insanity. We chuckle at the observation regarding college professors that "them that can does and them that can't teaches." And note that we seem to like especially the bad grammar in this canard.

We can hardly blame the students if they think that if they can just get that "sheepskin," their education will be complete—done. They pick up that illusion from adults.

And adults, at least the intelligent adults, should know better. Harold Guinzburg conducted a little survey of his own; his findings very strongly suggest that most college communities *don't even have* a trade book store. If this is true, or even *close* to true, it is a glaring symptom of failure by the business community to provide young people with an intellectual challenge within our capitalistic economy. Maybe it's even a reflection on our universities and colleges.

Where does a potentially great chemist or mathematician or novelist or historian or composer get the kind of stimulation, nourishment, motivation, deference from his community that the bush league pitcher or the high school quarterback gets? The question itself seems ludicrous. Our grass roots society simply does not recognize or promote or value or respond to intellectual achievement as it properly does to athletic achievement.

Let's face it: Intellectual achievement and the intellectual elite are alien to the main stream of American society. They are off to the side in a sub-section of esoteric isolation labeled "odd-ball," "high brow," "egghead," "doubledome."

Our ribbing of intellectual preoccupation is a well-established American tradition. It has been considered deplorable or good clean fun, depending on your point of view—until about a year ago. But there has been a change. Let me repeat a question that I characterized as ludicrous a moment ago: Where does a potentially great chemist or mathematician or novelist or historian or composer get the kind of stimulation, nourishment, motivation, deference from his community that the bush league pitcher or the high school quarterback gets? You know the answer, and that answer is stark and practical and dangerous and, I think, more than a little humiliating. The intellectually talented are nurtured and recognized in this way in Communist Russia—in, of all places, one of the worst police states in the history of mankind! And I hardly need to add that it is paying off—for them!

What has all of this to do with selling books? It seems to me that it has a very direct connection. And as I turn to this third and final section of my remarks, I can't help observe that when a man talks about mixing profits and patriotism, he gets on very thin ice. But I am going to do just that because I believe that as a matter of simple fact the expansion of bookselling and the promotion of the general welfare lie parallel to each other today. In fact, I believe that the booksellers stand so directly in the line of fire in this battle for intellectual leadership that they will either contribute handsomely to the victory or they will be guilty of gross negligence.

The United States must experience an intellectual renaissance or it will experience defeat. For the most unpleasant of reasons, the nurturing of intellectual excellence is no longer optional. The search for wisdom and the love of knowledge for its own sake can no longer be left to a gifted and stubborn few of our own people together with the great intellects that foreign dictators have hounded out of their own countries and to our shores.

It is not enough to pluck a few bright adolescents out of their home communities and to plunge them into a frantic few years of intellectual forced feeding in a restricted area of specialization. The intellectual renaissance must begin in the homes of our country. It must become part and parcel of our whole way of life if our full potential is to be realized. A task of this size obviously cannot be accomplished by any one group. It calls for cooperative endeavor by the schools, the churches, the service clubs and fraternal groups, by trade associations, by individual leaders in government and in business, certainly by all of the media. But with all due regard for the many sources of strength in our society, the greatest single repository of our intellectual heritage and the fullest record of our current achievements lies in good books. Our society needs more learned men and a *sine qua non* for learned men is the reading of books.

Good books are to pore over, to be discussed, criticized and debated, to be read with one's children, to be re-read and cherished and owned. Bookshelves are a symbol of the inquiring mind. We must move beyond the stage where the major controversies about books revolve around whether or not specific ones ought to be allowed.

Now I want to review the inhibitions to book buying with which I began. But this time I hope that my remarks may be on the constructive side.

Book reading is intellectually taxing. What might be done about it? Well, booksellers and publishers, too, might join with the schools in an all-out attack on the educational psychology of reading. A deplorable number of students never learn to read with ease even among those who are well endowed to do so. If you should join with the school people in grappling with the confusions and inadequacies in the teaching of reading—not just with a passing gesture, but from the point of view of expanding your market, while rendering a basic public service —I venture that you could make a very substantial contribution toward increasing the skill with which reading is taught.

Working for you is a well-known fact: Intellectually difficult tasks, like many other hard jobs, become challenging and rewarding when doing them wins social *approval*. The intrinsic rewards of reading apparently have not been enough. The approval of parents, participation by parents, discussion of books by youngsters with their peers, in congenial social situations, a wide variety of recognition and of social rewards would lighten the effort and enrich the yield of serious reading.

I would avoid conveying the bland and blanket impression that reading is easy, that reading is fun, and that everybody who is anybody reads books. In the first place, it isn't true, but more important is the fact that young people who find reading difficult are put into the position of thinking that if most people find it easy, they must be stupid. Rather than redoubling their efforts in such cases, they are likely to feel defensive and to avoid books in an effort to sustain self-respect. Reading is not easy. It is—for most—hard. I would suggest that you recognize the *achievement* represented by reading skill, and feature the status and the rewards that are reserved for those who acquire this skill—a skill which leads to a higher goal—The Learned Man.

The second inhibition that I mentioned is that book buying is economically risky. The central question is this: How are you going to get on speaking terms with the general public? How are you going to gain their attention? If that question seems a little blunt, let me remind you of some marketing research findings. Some ten years ago, we asked a nationwide cross section of people how long it had been since they read any book at all that they were not required to read for school or for their work. Only 18% were currently reading a book and less than a third even claimed to have done any voluntary book reading during the preceding month. Some 18% (as many as reported current reading) didn't claim *ever* to have read a book that they weren't required to read. At about that same time, George Gallup asked a cross-section sample this question: "Do you happen to be reading any books or novels at present?" This question includes any books at all—and only 21% claimed to be currently reading a book. Gallup repeated this question in 1957. He found the percentage of adults claiming to be reading any book at all to be—not 21% but 17%. He reports figures from four foreign countries to compare with our 17%. They are: Canada, 31%; Australia, 33%; West Germany, 34%; and England, 55%.

Perhaps then, it is not too brash to ask how you are going to get on speaking terms with the general public. I wonder whether the time has come for a hard look at criticism, commentary, and the reviewing of books. I wonder whether you detect, as I think I do, the groundswell of interest and enthusiasm for the candor, the profuseness and variety of criticism in a competing field. I refer, of course, to the phonograph record industry. A friend of mine recently shocked a book publisher by saying that he had *almost* stopped buying books: that practically all the household budget money that used to go into books he now put into hi-fi records.

The book publisher wanted to know why, and my friend gave three reasons: the gamble of being stuck with a turkey was less; the criticism of records was more honest and dependable; and the inherent value received per dollar spent was greater. Now you may argue with this, since subjective judgments are heavily involved, but my friend made a great point of the honesty, the candor, the profuseness, and the variety of disc *criticism*. Certainly, critics always air their prejudices and play their favorites—but with hi-fi records there are not just dozens and dozens, but hundreds and hundreds of items of *capsule* criticism going the rounds: in new magazines devoted exclusively to recorded music, or in old magazines that have set up new departments—or even in newspapers. Contrast this with the one-book-per-day pace of only a few of our best newspapers, or the weekly book review sections in still fewer papers, in which the criticism is too often vague, or pompous, or overliterary, or an essay about how much more the reviewer knows than the author of the book he is supposed to be discussing. Might something be done to put book reviewing on the same hard, sharp plane that has grown up for records? It seems to me that book reviewing is being done the same old way it was fifty years ago, except that there is even less of it. If reporting and commentary on books should become just one-tenth as large, and should be just one-tenth as important to the American public as commentary on sports is, the book business would boom.

I come now to the third inhibition, namely that book owning is socially deviant. Too few people know the pleasures and rewards available only to book owners: their beauty as decoration, the satisfaction of book plates, the additional meaning that comes with underlining and making marginal notes, the stimulation of looking things up when the questions arise instead of planning to do so *sometime,* the comfortable sureness of re-reading a treasured passage, the companionship of introducing a child to just the right book at just the right time, the pleasure of documenting an argument during a hammer and tong discussion—these are a few points that come to my mind. I suppose that others who love books could greatly extend this list.

The point that I am suggesting is that book owning is deviant because so many people can't see why any sensible person would *want* to own books. They don't know that owning books does something that is good and satisfying. And this points straight at one of the biggest discoveries of all time in the field of advertising, namely that one of the best ways to sell any product is to sell the satisfaction and the service that the purchaser will derive from using the product. The book advertising that I see is almost exclusively devoted to selling the content of the book. Now advertising with product orientation is, of course, of major importance. I wouldn't for a moment discount its basic role. But it isn't the *only* kind of good advertising. Automobile companies advertise the mechanical characteristics of their cars, and clothing stores advertise the quality of their fabrics and the calibre of their tailoring. But you also see a lot of stress on what cars and clothing will *do for you* if you buy them. Could we find a way to sell people on the satisfaction and rewards of owning and reading books?

I have purposely compared books with automobiles and clothing, and book reading with playing baseball, and book criticism with hi-fi commentary because I want to challenge you to get books out of the idyllic backwaters of American society, and into the turbulent main stream. If this intellectual renaissance that I'm talking about is going to take place, it won't be a matter of the American people giving up the competitive, time driven, slightly anxious hurly-burly that has always characterized our society and moving into a new and placid life of contemplation. It will be the other way around. Books and ideas, scientific thinking and honest intellectual controversy will have to muscle in on the turbulent main stream of our great and free society. And if this happens, the oddness of book-owning and of book-reading will simply go out of fashion.

Now to summarize: I have suggested that the business interests of booksellers lie parallel with an important facet of the general public interest in our society. There is an urgent need—in fact a national survival need—for invigorating intellectual life, for upgrading the general regard for intellectual excellence, for broadening the base of intellectual interests—for a renaissance that establishes a genuine folk status for things of the mind—respect for the Learned Man. Booksellers can and should play a significant leadership role in this enterprise. But your efforts may have to be only as a catalytic agent—the force that arouses a half hundred other groups into action. It's a job that's bigger than even your great force.

I hope that in some small way I have conveyed my enthusiasm for the business you are in, and my sense of its importance. Your merchandise is the prime repository of our intellectual heritage. And we have come to the time when we must cultivate wisdom in freedom, or bow to the intellectual product of coercion.

DAVID RIESMAN

Books: Gunpowder of the Mind

INVENTIONS ARE AS MUCH the mother of necessity as the reverse, and the Western world as we know it now is inconceivable without print— just as World War II could hardly have been fought without the telephone and the IBM machine. This is one reason why it is hard for the print-raised generations to contemplate the decline of reading relative to the rise of other media, for each medium of communication not only brings in its wake an elite attuned to its potentialities but alters the forms of perception, the bonds of sympathy, and the channels of conflict that hold a society together.

I should like to present here certain suggestions, highly tentative and exploratory, concerning three questions: first, what are the differences between cultures which depend entirely on the spoken word and those which depend on print; second, what will be the significance of the written word now that newer mass media, less demanding psychologically and yet perhaps more potent politically, have developed; third, what is likely to happen in those countries where the tradition of books is not fully established and where the new media are already having a decisive impact.

In Ruth Underhill's transcript of the autobiography of a Papago Indian woman are some passages which convey a sense of the impact of the spoken word in a culture where no other modes of communication compete with it. One passage goes as follows:

> The men from all the villages met at Basket Cap Mountain, and there my father made them speeches, sitting with his arms folded and talking low as all great men do. Then they sang war songs. . . . Many, many songs they sang but I, a woman, cannot tell you all. I know that they made the enemy blind and dizzy with their singing and that they told the gopher to gnaw their arrows. And I know that they called on our dead warriors who have turned into owls and live in the Apache country to come and tell them where the enemy were.

In the many passages of this sort that one can find in ethnographic accounts, we become aware of the immense emotional force that can be harnessed by the spoken word in such a group—so powerful here that at least in fancy it can shatter the morale of a distant enemy. Implicit here is the fact that a society dependent on oral traditions and oral communications is, by our standard, a slow-paced one: there is time enough, for grownups as well as children, to roll back the carpet of memories; nobody has to miss the ceremonies in order to catch the 8:05 the next morning from Scarsdale—or to run the train itself. To be sure, the teen-age girls today who learn by heart the lyrics of popular songs do seem to have time enough on their hands to memorize verses, but even they must learn a new repertory every year and will surely not, as parents, sing these songs of their dating years to their own children.

What I have said needs to be qualified in several respects familiar to those of you who have done group singing informally. I do have the impression, strengthened by assiduous reading of juke-box labels, that there is a kind of sediment of tunes and ballads—"Stormy Weather," for example—which binds at least the jazz generations into an occasional songfest, more or less barber-shop-quartet style. Then there are the folk songs and madrigals sung by the college-educated, such as the highbrow variants of "Boola Boola" and "10,000 Men of Harvard." But for none of these songs is it terribly important to know the right words—the lyrics are not altogether meaningless even, I suppose, in the so-called "nonsense" songs, but neither do they encapsulate the history of the tribe or the patterns of heroic behavior.

What I am getting at is that the spoken or sung word is particularly impressive when it monopolizes the symbolic environment; but once books have entered that environment the social organization can never be the same again. Books bring with them detachment and a critical attitude that is not possible in a society dependent on the spoken word. We can occasionally have second thoughts about a speech, but we cannot hear it, as we can read a book, backwards as well as forwards —that is, the writer can be checked up on in a way that the speaker cannot be.

People tend to remember best the things they have felt most deeply. The memorable words in a culture wholly dependent on the spoken word will often be those most charged with group feeling; and we would expect communication to keep alive in an individual the childhood sense of dependence, childhood's terrors and elations, and something of its awe for the old.

The shift to a literate culture, historically decisive as it is, does not of course occur all at once; only a tiny minority could read prior to the age of print, and the reading of manuscripts altered styles of communication rather less than one might today think. For one thing, manuscripts, having to be slowly deciphered, promoted memorization, which in turn promoted arguments by quotation and commentary. Manuscripts were often read aloud and, with their beautiful illuminations, were regarded not simply as rationalistic vehicles of knowledge but also as shared artifacts. By exteriorizing, by making palpable, the processes of thinking and discussion, they promoted individuation only partially, while also promoting adherence to tradition.

The book, like an invisible monitor, helps liberate the reader from his group and its emotions and allows the contemplation of alternative responses and the trying on of new emotions. Max Weber has stressed the importance of the merchant's account book in rationalizing the merchant and his commerce; and other historians have made familiar the role of the printed Bible in encouraging dissident sects to challenge the authority of the Roman Church—indeed, to challenge the given forms of social life itself. At the same time, while the printed book helped people to break away from their family circle and parish, it helped link them into noncontiguous associations of true believers.

Arthur E. Morgan, speaking in *Search for Purpose* of his child-hood among small-town folk of limited horizons, remarks, "This library [in the town] was like foster parents to me." Thomas and Znaniecki describe an analogous process in their book on *The Polish Peasant in Europe and America;* the Polish peasant who learned to read and write became identified with the urban world of progress and enlightenment, of ideology and utopia, even while physically still in the peasant world. This identification had many of the elements of a conversion, print itself and the world it opened up being a kind of gospel. Today, in this country of near-universal literacy, we have forgotten the enthusiasm for print which can burst on people newly literate: the "each one teach one" movements of Mexico, the Philippines, and elsewhere; the voracity for books in the Soviet Union and other recently industrialized lands.

Among the highly educated, and in the countries of long-established literacy, there is little comparable enthusiasm. We have become less excited about books as such, or even about "good books," and instead are more discriminating in terms of fields, of tastes, of literary fashions. Our world, as we know all too well, is full of many other things which compete with books, so that some of that minority who were avid readers as children, shutting out parents and peers with faces (as the latter would charge) buried in a book, are now buried as adults in activities that exclude books or push them to the periphery of attention.

In any case, our experience in recent years with mass literacy and mass communications has generally been disillusioning—much as with universal suffrage. Thus, we no longer believe, as numerous thoughtful people did in the 1920s, that radio offers a second chance for stimulat-ing adult education and civic literacy. Likewise, despite a few shining hours, few observers today regard educational TV as anything like an adequate counterweight to the endlessly smiling, relaxed informalities and (for many in the audience) lack of challenge of low-pressure uneducational TV. Paradoxically, however, the coming of TV has given new possibilities back to the radio in the bedroom, for the TV audience is now the mass audience, and the radio can appeal to the wish for privacy, and to specialized tastes and minority audiences. With rare exceptions, it is now the massness of the mass media, rather than their mediating and individuating power, which frightens and depresses many educated people—so much so that we frequently lose faith in enlightenment itself as a goal, let alone in the three easy lessons with which our predecessors sought to reach it. Sometimes, in fact, despair goes to such lengths that the writers of bombast on behalf of books, as if in answer to the spreaders of bombast on behalf of TV, are apt to urge that if only people would read books once more, long and serious books that require close attention, the evils of the modern world would be undone and we would be saved.

The fact is, however, that books, whatever their liberating power in society as a whole, can be used, of course, in nonliberating ways. For instance, a child can be forced into slavery to print through the fanaticism of parents or pedagogues. Indeed, we tend to consider the education of John Stuart Mill by his high-pressure father, in which he learned to read at three and studied the classics before he was ten, as monstrous as it is amazing. We think the French and the Orthodox Jews are cruel to make small children mind their lessons with no time out for sports, let alone for cultivating the "whole child."

But few are the American homes today, or the schools and colleges (even those run by Catholic orders), where these patterns still prevail; on the contrary, both home and school seek to come to terms with life at its most unbookish (just as many books for children—and TV shows, too—are not in search of fantasy but in search of documentary detail).

While the classics are having a small revival at a few colleges and schools, the more general situation is that Americans, with increasing world power, will insist that everyone learn to speak American while not compelling our children to learn any other language—and in many schools not even our own in any full measure. Yet languages, like systems of musical notation, must be carried in the bones and bodies of the living if the accomplishments and experiences of the dead are not to be lost to us. It may be that some residual feeling of this sort— some fear that children may be growing up as barbarians and away from us of the older generations—may be one element behind the ominous success of Rudolf Flesch's demagogic best seller, *Why Johnny Can't Read,* a book that would lose the exaggerated edge of its power if *its* readers could read, or were not too frightened to keep their wits about them. Flesch and his followers never ask the crucial question I am asking here: namely, what distribution of not only reading skills but reading enthusiasms, for what systems of notation (including music, languages, and mathematics), is desirable if we are not only to pass on the heritage—the world's library of art and imagination—but also to contribute to it? They take it for granted that Johnny should read just because John Alden or John Adams did read; in the case of most of the reactionary critics of our public schools who are riding so high today, such terms as "heritage" are merely snob tags, status labels, which they can use to pull rank on schoolteachers, educationists, psychological counselors, and other relatively defenseless people. I suspect that many such critics would like to restore drill and to make reading more of a chore than it needs to be as a sublimated form of hazing the young, though some chore and bore elements will certainly be part of any educational program which aims to reach all who can possibly be reached by books or by any other media which connect people with a noncontiguous world, the world of yesterday and tomorrow as well as of the here and now.

Certainly, in an era of abundance we can afford to read books for pleasure, and it may on the whole be a good thing that a boy in school or a soldier in camp can unself-consciously pull out a pocketbook without feeling that there is anything esoteric or status-labeled in the act. Even so, casual pleasures in our society, hard as they often are to come by, will not suffice to absorb young people's energies and aspirations. On the contrary, young people need at some time in their lives to extend themselves, to work at the height of their as yet untapped powers (indeed, lacking better ways, some seek to do this in forms the society defines as delinquency). Since the world's work no longer offers this opportunity for exertion for most nonfarm Americans, we may think it fortunate—though in some respects arbitrary—that the world's storehouse of culture unfailingly does. While we can perhaps imagine a post-literature culture in which people are challenged primarily by other media than print and musical scores, and no doubt we have already a culture in which even in the most bookish strata many media cooperate, yet at the moment I think it is not just prejudice and snobbery which lead us to rely heavily on books as our traditional badge of enlightenment and on libraries as the great storehouse of our culture.

These problems I have been discussing—and I cannot emphasize too strongly the tentativeness of what I have said—would be less important and less apparently insoluble if the book, and other printed matter, stood at the end of the road of social development, as was true from the fifteenth century to the end of the nineteenth. The rule of black print on white paper may be said to mark the epoch of the rise and increasing influence of the middle class, the class of clerks and bookkeepers, merchants and engineers, instruction-givers and instruction-readers, the class of the time-attentive, the future-oriented, the mobile. Reading and education were the highroads this class made use of to rise in the world and to move about in it during the great periods of colonization.

Even the novel, denounced as frivolous and sensuous by the Puritans, had an important function in the changing society. I think not so much of its use as a device for reform and civic adult education, like *Oliver Twist* or *Uncle Tom's Cabin,* as of its less obvious use as a device by which people might prepare themselves for novel contacts and novel life-situations, a form of what psychologists term "anticipatory socialization"—that is, a preparation in imagination for playing roles that might emerge in one's later career. In fact, the very conception of life implicit in the notion of a career is facilitated by the dramatic structure of the novel, especially the *Bildungsroman,* with its protagonist, its interest in motive, its demand on the reader that he project himself into the experiences portrayed.

The rise of the newer media of communication has coincided with a certain loss of power by the older, print-oriented middle class. Yellow journalism, coming on top of universal suffrage, did begin to shake that hegemony. Indeed, the very term "yellow journalism" is significant as marking a change from the monotone of black on white (just as the fact that only 10 per cent of the cars turned out this year are black and all the rest are technicolor says a good deal about our loss of Puritan inhibitions). The comic book, also, is part of this same revolution. And of course the movies and broadcasting, while not displacing the book, shake its monopoly and with it the monopoly of the middle class.

But the consequences of these shifts in the focus of attention and in the emotional impact of the media differ very much depending on whether one speaks of a country where print has long been institutionalized or of a country which had previously been largely illiterate. In the former, the shifts of power tend to be subtle and unclimactic. Thus, it is not a major revolution in America that TV has made preadolescent children even more hep than they were before, more apt to be one up on their parents even about politics, more ready psychologically to empathize with other conditions of man than their own. But in the less industrially advanced countries the shift can be explosive. A study (done by Daniel Lerner at Columbia University) of foreign radio listeners in seven Middle East countries is illuminating. In many villages such people as the grocer who has a radio, or the young bus driver who has seen movies in the capital and can bring news of the great world, are displacing the village elders in positions of leadership. To rise in such a way, these upstarts do not need to acquire the stern discipline typical for the print-oriented person; rather, they need the same equipment American children have who go about in Davy Crockett suits—a willingness, often quite passive and unstrenuous, to let fancy roam at the dictates of the mass media. The political parties of the Middle East are now beginning to make use of this willingness, and as we all know, programs can be fanatically pursued which promise to supply Cadillacs and cinemas to peasants who are told they can have these things without working, just as Americans do, if only they will vote and believe. Thus, in the illiterate masses there tends to be created a new kind of literacy, an often terrifying emotional and political fluency, with all the emancipations of print and hardly any of its restrictions and disciplines.

The movies, of course, are a boundary-annihilating form, easily transmissible past linguistic and cultural barriers (as well as barriers of literacy). They may also be, as Arnold Hauser suggests in *The Social History of Art,* a democratizing form because of their mobility, the absence of traditional stage conventions and proprieties. Art historians have recently noted that when Renaissance painters shifted the Virgin Mary from frontface to profile it marked a decline of Catholic religiosity and a less devout approach to the Trinity. The camera can be even more impudent, and can put aesthetic laws to use in all kinds of ways, leading the audience, as Hauser says, to the events, rather than leading and presenting the events to them, with the voyeuristic intimacy which we can see in such a film as Hitchcock's *Rear Window.* A movie can tell its story as though we are telling it to ourselves, or as though we are actually dreaming it; it can force us to identify with its chosen moods and people. The camera, by moving around, subtly invites us to embrace one character and exclude another; to look up and feel awe of a hero or fear of a villain; to look down and feel contempt or pity. A sidelong glance of the camera alerts us for trouble; a right-to-left pan, reversing the righthandedness Hermann Weill discusses in his book on symmetry, invests people and places with a spooky feeling. I need not labor the catalogue of the director's powers, aided as they are by the near-hypnotic effect of the concentrated brightness of the screen while other sights and sounds are at a low ebb. The movie is the novel in motion; it is potentially the least rationalistic, the most subjectivized medium. And like the broadcast, the rally, or the fireside council of the tribal chief, it demands attention now, this minute, in this time and at that place; unlike a book, it cannot wait for your mood.

Where the movies and the book are both in circulation, the written word and the screen image compete in making our sensibility mobile and empathic, though for many of us even now the movies have pretty well replaced the novel as the powerful medium for anticipatory socialization. Conceivably, when every man has his own movie camera and home projector, and his own movie library as we now have our record collections, he will become more critical and less vulnerable—this being the usual effect of do-it-yourself. Likewise, study of the movies, as it is

encouraged by some of the documentary film societies, can help put
movie-goers in the director's place, permitting them to be more critical
of him.

But all this betokens a society like ours in which radio and film
are cumulative media for the better-educated strata—a society in which
a certain uneasy balance of powers exists among the media, a society
in which the librarians have been vigilant of freedom, while the movie
magnates have generally failed to fight down their fears of the Legion
of Decency and the other censoring groups who to some degree have
tempted the films in the direction of sadism in exchange for the often
circumvented pieties surrounding sex. In the Middle East, where the
movies and radio arrived ahead of the book, there is no such balance—
though I suppose Turkey comes paradoxically closest, where Kemal
Ataturk detached the young from even the literate old by imposing the
Roman script; here the print-oriented are not simply the students of
the Koran but are up-to-date and Westernized.

Oral communication keeps people together, binds people to each
other, while print in our day loosens these bonds, creates space around
people, even isolates them in some ways. People who would simply
have been deviants in a preliterate tribe, misunderstanding and misunderstood, can through books establish a wider identity—can understand and even undermine the enemies of home and hearth and herd.
While the geographic migrations of preliterate peoples have something
in common with the incomprehending movement of flocks of deer, the
readers of the Age of Discovery were prepared mentally for some of
the experiences of their geographic mobility—they had at any rate left
home in imagination even if they had not roamed as far or among as
strange people as they were actually to meet. The bookish education
of these inner-directed men helped harden them for voyages; they
wanted to convert the heathen, civilize them, trade with them. If anyone changed in the encounter, it would be the heathen, while they, as
they moved about the globe or up the social ladder, remained very
much the same men. The epitome of this was the Englishman in the
tropics who, all alone, dressed for dinner with home-guard ceremonial,
toasted the Queen, and, six months late, read with a proper sense of
outrage the leader in the London *Times*. His ties with the world of
print helped steady him in his course far from home.

Today, the successors of these men are men molded as much by
the mass media outside their formal education as by their schooling;
men who are more public-relations-minded than ambitious; men soft-
ened for encounters rather than hardened for voyages. If they move
about the globe it is often to win the love of the natives or to try to

understand their mores, rather than to exploit them for gain or the glory of God. Meanwhile, as we have seen, the natives (as they used to be called) are themselves in many cases on the move, and the sharp differences between societies dependent on the oral tradition and those dependent on print are tending to be less important with the coming of radio and film. Often the decisive difference is among the peasants themselves within a country now moving out of the stage of oral tradition—the difference between those who listen to the radio and go to movies and those who shut these things out as the voice of the Devil or as simply irrelevant for them. In the Middle East studies it was found that those peasants who listened to Radio Moscow or the BBC or the VOA already had, or perhaps acquired, a different sensibility from those who did not.

It is too soon, however, to say whether the epoch of print will be utterly elided in the underdeveloped countries, just as, with the coming of electrical and atomic energy, they may skip the stage of coal and water power. Conceivably, the movies and broadcasting will eventually help to awaken a hunger for print, when their own novelty is worn off and when they come to be used as tie-ins with print—as in Lyman Bryson's *Invitation to Learning.* Just as the barbarians of Europe in the Middle Ages pulled themselves up by Greek bootstraps, so the nonindustrial countries can for a long time draw on the storehouse of Western science and technology, including the science of social organization; and there are still enough inner-directed men in our society who are willing to go out and help build the armies of Iran and the factories of Istanbul.

In this connection, it is striking that the Soviet Union, paying at least nominal heed to the scriptures of Marx and Lenin, has created what is in some ways a replica of the Victorian industrial world rather than the modern consumer world. As a result, treatises on Marxism and Hollywood movies may be seen as alternative lures to the preindustrial nations, with national pride voting for steel plants and Karl Marx, and personal taste for cars, Coca-Cola, and the stereotype of America. To be sure, Communism may seem the quickest way to the consumers' utopia, with its apparent power to mow down all vested interests, including one's own. I should parenthetically add that the appeal to the consumer mentality in the East, the glamour of America's image, is almost never the result of our official propaganda concerning the alleged "American Way of Life," but is rather a by-product of the characteristic American virtuosity in the newer media and the products of American enterprise they bespeak.

It is apparent that the mass media, like other forms of technological

innovation, bring about new polarizations in society and between societies. The readers and the nonreaders, the listeners and the nonlisteners,
may belong to the same castes, the same economic and social groupings,
and yet may slowly diverge as they form different values and tastes and
turns of mind. In this way, feudal and other hierarchical forms are
upset, with the spread of literacy beyond a small group of clerks; and
it is perhaps no accident that self-taught and self-made men like Ben
Franklin and Andrew Carnegie should have put such emphasis on
libraries: in their day, books were the gunpowder of the mind, the way
of nonmilitary glory and social and intellectual mobility.

Today, in contrast, there are many thoughtful Americans who
despair of the role of the book as a vehicle either of social enlightenment or of personal mobility. They point to the low percentage of
Americans (compared with Danes or Japanese, Britishers or Germans)
who ever read a book when through with school; they point to the
rarity of book stores (even when we include those that sell mainly
greeting cards) and to the financial crisis of the libraries (not to speak
of the frequent pressure on them to censor their shelves). The newer
media seem in tune with the times in a number of ways; they often
require less close attention than a book, and they are "social" in two
senses: they are usually viewed in company, and they present celebrities or "just folks" in a kind of pseudo intimacy with the viewer—so
much so that for TV performers "sincerity" has become the symbol both
of what they admire and of what they are cynical about. Discussion,
as in this article, of historical developments sometimes engenders a
feeling of inevitability, and a cause, such as that of books, is declared
lost because not everyone votes for it and because research brings us
the latest returns from the worldwide competitive election campaigns
of the several media.

Yet one's own pleasure in books does not rest, beyond a certain
break-even point, on the numbers who share such pleasures, but rather
on the whole quality of life in a culture. What books can do for that
quality, in broadening horizons, in encouraging fantasy, in promoting
individuation, can in some measure be done by other media—witness
the Third Programme in England, the great post-war Italian films, and
some television drama in this country. The newer media can be used
to promote empathy and vicariousness in terms of emotional depth, and
not simply in terms of political nationalism and consumer-goods sophistication. Even so, what the newer media can seldom do is to promote
privacy. As I have just remarked, the people on the TV screen are
"company" for the viewer, even if they don't seek to make him a pseudo
participant along with the rubberneck studio audience. The people in

a book are "company" for the reader in a different sense: to "see" them the reader must make an effort, and he must do so—whatever guidance he gets from critics, teachers, and friends—in relative isolation (in a recent cartoon, one person at a cocktail party asks another if he's read a certain book, and the latter answers "not personally"). In a world which threatens us with a surfeit of people, this role of the book becomes again as important as in the preliterate tribes where, also, there was no escape from others; and, as America becomes one vast continental pueblo, the book—whatever its residual trajectory as a revolutionary social force—comes into its own as a guarantor of that occasional apartness which makes togetherness viable.

ARTHUR KOESTLER

The Boredom of Fantasy

ONCE UPON A TIME, more precisely on the 17th June, A.D. 4784, Captain Kayle Clark stepped into a public telescreen box to call up his fiancée, secret agent Lucy Rall. He was told that Lucy was not available as she had got married a week before. "To whom?" cried the exasperated Captain. "To me," said the man to whom he was talking. Taking a closer look at the telescreen, the Captain discovered with a mild surprise that the man he was talking to was himself.

The startling mystery was solved by Mr. Robert Headrock, the first immortal man on earth. Headrock, using his electronic super-brain computer, discovered that Captain Clark had taken a trip in a time-machine; that he had made a loop into the past, and married Lucy Rall without his unlooped present self knowing about it. Through this little frolic, he also became the richest man on earth as he knew the movements of the Stock Exchange in advance. When the point in time was reached where Clark had looped off in the time-machine, the past Clark and the present Clark became again one, and lived happily ever after. Meanwhile, Robert Headrock, the immortal man, sent a journalist called MacAllister several million trillion years back into the past and made him cause a cosmic explosion, which gave rise to our planetary system as we know it.

The book from which I was quoting is called *The Weapon Shops of Isher* by A. E. van Vogt. Mr. van Vogt is probably the most popular of contemporary American science-fiction writers. The book was recently published in England in a science-fiction series which signals, together with the founding of the British Science-Fiction Club, that the new craze, a kind of cosmic jitterbug, has crossed the Atlantic.

I had better confess at this point that while I lived in the United States I was a science-fiction addict myself and am still liable to occasional relapses. Reading about space travel, time travel, Martian maidens, robot civilisations and extra-galactic supermen is habit-forming like opium, murder thrillers and yoghurt diets. Few people in this country realise the extent and virulence of this addiction in the United States. According to a recent survey, the average sale of a detective story or a Western thriller in America is four thousand copies; the average sale of a science-fiction novel is six thousand copies, or fifty per cent higher. Every month, six new novels of this type are published in the U.S.A. and three large publishing firms specialise exclusively in science-fiction. There is a flood of science-fiction magazines, science-fiction clubs, science-fiction films, television programmes and so on. The addicts are called "fen", which is the plural of fan. Fen gather in clubhouses called slanshacks, "slan" meaning a biologically mutated superman, and hold conferences, called fenferences. The characters in science-fiction speak a kind of cosmic R.A.F. slang (it ought to be called, evidently, "cosmilingo"). Young space cadets, for instance, dislike meeting Bems— for bug-eyed Monsters—in alien galaxies unless armed with paraguns— paralysis-causing rayguns. They swear "By space", "By the seven rings of Saturn", or "By the gas-pits of Venus".

If grown-ups betray these strange symptoms, one can imagine how the kiddies react. Your friends' children no longer plug you with six-shooters; they atomise you with nuclear blasters. They wear plastic bubbles around their heads which look like divers' helmets and enable them to breathe while floating in gravity-free interstellar space. These are sold by the thousand in department stores together with other cosmic paraphernalia, and are steadily replacing cowboy equipment, just as on the television screen Tom Corbett, Space Cadet, is in the process of replacing Hopalong Cassidy as the children's national hero. Even the housewife, listening in to the radio while on her domestic chores, is becoming cosmic-minded. The soap opera has branched out into the space opera. Imagine the opposite number of Mrs. Dale in Texas or Minnesota: "I am so worried about Richard not being back from his luncheon date on Jupiter. Maybe he's got space-happy and gone on to Venus. Or one of those nasty meteors may have deflected him from his orbit."

So much for the grotesque side of science-fiction. But a craze of such vast dimensions is never entirely crazy. It always expresses, in a distorted way, some unconscious need of the time. Science-fiction is a typical product of the atomic age. The discoveries of that age weigh like an undigested lump on the stomach of mankind. Electronic brains which predict election results, lie-detectors which make you confess the truth, new drugs which make you testify to lies, radiations which produce biological monsters—all these developments of the last fifty years have created new vistas and new nightmares, which art and literature have not yet assimilated. In a crude and fumbling fashion, science-fiction is trying to fill this gap. But there is perhaps another and more hidden reason for this sudden hunger for other ages and other worlds. Perhaps, when they read about the latest hydrogen bomb tests, people are more aware than they admit to themselves, of the possibility that human civilisation may be approaching its end. And together with this may go a dim, inarticulate suspicion that the cause lies deeper than Communism or Fascism, that it may lie in the nature itself of *homo sapiens;* in other words, that the human race may be a biological misfit doomed to extinction like the giant reptiles of an earlier age. I believe that some apocalyptic intuition of this kind may be one of the reasons for the sudden interest in life on other stars.

As a branch of literature, science-fiction is, of course, not new. As early as the second century Lucian, a Greek writer, wrote a story of a journey to the moon. Swift wrote science fiction; so did Samuel Butler, Jules Verne, H. G. Wells, Aldous Huxley, George Orwell. But while in the past such exercises were isolated literary extravaganzas, they are now mass-produced for a mass audience. Moreover, modern science-fiction takes itself very seriously. There are certain rules of the game which every practitioner must observe, otherwise he will be torn to shreds by the critics. The basic rule is that the author may only operate with future inventions, gadgets and machines which are extrapolations (that is, logical extensions) of present discoveries, and do not go against the laws of nature. A number of physicists, doctors and biologists are employed by the film and television industries to make sure that, even in the children's science-fiction show, every detail is correct. Some of the best-known science-fiction authors in America are actually scientists, several of international repute, who write under pen-names. The most recent and distinguished recruit to their ranks is Lord Russell. All this is a guarantee of scientific accuracy, but unfortunately not of artistic quality.

Mr. Gerald Heard has recently expressed the opinion that science-fiction is "the mark of the dawn of a new vision, and the rise of a new art", and simply *the* future form of the novel. Other well-known critics overseas also believe, in all seriousness, that science-fiction, now in its infancy, will grow up and one day become the literature of the future.

I do not share their opinion. I believe that science-fiction is good entertainment, and that it will never become good art. It is reasonably certain that within the next hundred years we shall have space-travel, but at that stage the description of a trip to the moon will no longer be science-fiction but simple reportage. It will be fact, not fantasy, and the science-fiction of that time will have to go even further to startle the reader. What Mr. Heard's claim really amounts to is the replacement of the artist's disciplined imagination by the schoolboy's unbridled fantasy. But day-dreaming is not poetry, and fantasy is not art.

At first sight one would of course expect that imaginative descriptions of non-human societies on alien planets would open new vistas for the somewhat stagnant novel of our time. But most disappointingly this is not the case, and for a simple reason. Our imagination is limited; we cannot project ourselves into the distant future any more than into the distant past. This is the reason why the historical novel is practically dead to-day. The life of an Egyptian civil servant under the Eighteenth Dynasty, or even of a soldier in Cromwell's army, is only imaginable to us in dim outline; we are unable to identify ourselves with the strange figure moving through such a strange world. Few Englishmen can really understand the feelings and habits of Frenchmen, much less of Russians, much less of Martians. And without this act of identification, of intimate understanding, there is no art, only a thrill of curiosity which soon yields to boredom. The Martian heroes of science-fiction may have four eyes, a green skin and an accent stranger than mine—we just couldn't care less. We are tickled by them for a few pages; but because they are too strange to be true, we soon get bored.

For every culture is an island. It communicates with other islands but it is only familiar with itself. And art means seeing the familiar in a new light, seeing tragedy in the trivial event; it means in the last resort broadening and deepening our understanding of ourselves. Swift's *Gulliver*, Huxley's *Brave New World*, Orwell's *Nineteen-Eighty-Four*, are great works of literature because in them the gadgets of the future and the oddities of alien worlds serve merely as a background or pretext for a social message. In other words, they are literature precisely to the extent to which they are not science-fiction, to which they are works of disciplined imagination and not of unlimited fantasy. A similar rule holds for the detective story. Georges Simenon is probably the greatest master in that field, yet his novels become works of art precisely at the point where character and atmosphere become more important than the plot, where imagination triumphs over invention.

Thus the paradoxical lesson of science-fiction is to teach us modesty. When we reach out for the stars, our limitations become grotesquely apparent. The heroes of science-fiction have unlimited power and fantastic possibilities, but their feelings and thoughts are limited within the narrow human range. Tom Corbett, Space Cadet, behaves on the third planet of Orion exactly in the same way as he does in a drugstore in Minnesota, and one is tempted to ask him: "Was your journey really necessary?" The Milky Way has become simply an extension of Main Street.

Travel is no cure for melancholia; space-ships and time-machines are no escape from the human condition. Let Othello subject Desdemona to a lie-detector test; his jealousy will still blind him to the evidence. Let Oedipus triumph over gravity; he won't triumph over his fate.

Some twenty years ago the German writer, Alfred Döblin, wrote a novel in which humanity discovers the secret of biological self-transformation: by a click of their fingers people can change themselves into giants, tigers, demons, or fish—much like Flook in the *Daily Mail* cartoon. At the end of the book the last specimens of this happy race sit, each on a solitary rock, in the shape of black ravens, in eternal silence. They have tried, experienced, seen and said everything under the sun, and all that is left for them to do is to die of boredom—the boredom of fantasy.

STEPHEN ULLMAN

The Prism of Language

LANGUAGE IS SO MUCH part of our lives that we seldom stop to think about it. We take it for granted that our words are mere passive tools, means of self-expression and of communication. But there is another way of looking at language. Words certainly are the vehicles of our thoughts, but they may be far more than that: they may acquire an influence of their own, shaping and pre-determining our processes of thinking and our whole outlook.

At first sight, this picture of language as an active force may seem strange and far-fetched. For most people, words are something purely external, the mere 'dress of thought', as Dr. Johnson put it; how could they influence the working of our minds? And yet some of our everyday experiences should warn us that language can play a more active part. When we translate from one idiom to another, our thoughts are apt to suffer a subtle transformation, a kind of sea-change; and if one tries to re-translate the text into the original, one is surprised to see how far it has moved from its starting point. The translator's task is even more complicated if the two languages belong to different civilisations; there can be no exact correspondence between the vocabulary of an Englishman and a Chinese.

The problem becomes almost insoluble when one has to translate from a civilised into an uncivilised language. We come up at once against a fundamental discrepancy between our own speech-habits and those of primitive races. Missionaries and others have noted, time and again, that these races have a multiplicity of concrete, specialised terms but are remarkably poor in generic ones. They would have, for example, separate names for each variety of tree, but no general word for 'tree' itself. Their verbs show the same pattern: there is no single term for the act of 'cutting' but a number of expressions for cutting various objects. In some cases the missionaries may have failed to elicit the right word, but the general tendency stands out clearly, and it also fits in with what we know about the history of our own languages.

How far does this affect the mental development of the individual native speaker? It means that he is born with a language which has no provision for general ideas, which does not help him in classifying his impressions and experiences. He could, no doubt, develop higher concepts of his own if the need arose, but this would cost him an effort which more fortunate speakers, born with a more differentiated linguistic equipment, need not make: the work has been done for them by their mother tongue, or rather by previous generations whose accumulated experience is deposited in the language.

It could be argued that the predominance of particular terms may be due not to faulty powers of abstraction but to biological necessity. The Lapps of the arctic regions have no general term for 'snow', only a number of special names for each state and form of it: snow is so important a factor in their lives that they have to specify its various aspects. The fact remains that they have failed to take the next step, that of subordinating these aspects to the higher concept of snow; and this failure has been perpetuated by their language. There is a curious form of reciprocity between language and thought: language reflects our thoughts but it also reacts upon them, by crystallising and preserving the picture of the world which they build up.

The savage with his over-concrete vocabulary has a strange parallel in the civilised speaker who has lost the full power of speech. Experiments on patients suffering from head wounds during and after the first world war have revealed some significant facts about the interaction of words and thought. Such injuries may affect any element of speech: elocution, grammar, comprehension, and even the very basis of language, the connection between words and their meanings. One of these patients was suffering from a rare condition: he had forgotten the names of colours. In some ways he behaved as if he were colour blind; yet his physical sense of colour was unimpaired. In one experiment he was faced with a number of coloured threads, all different in shade, and was asked to pick out those belonging to the same colour. But he found this task meaningless: to him, the various shades of green and blue were totally different as he had no term for, and therefore no concept of, 'greenness' or 'blueness' to which they could be subordinated. Language had classified the endless variety of colours into a few cardinal types; now that this key had been lost, the man-made order relapsed into chaos.

But we need not go to the Australian bushmen or to the nerve specialist to study the impact of language on thought. Our own languages contain ample evidence of the same influence. In each of them, the raw material of experience is analysed, docketed, and arranged in a unique way; every vocabulary embodies a scale of values and a philosophy of life. The concepts which it comprises have been elaborated and organised by preceding generations; the child assimilates them with the mother tongue and accepts them as the natural way of viewing the world, though he may later on modify some detail in the light of his own experience. Even the impressions reaching us through our senses have to be sifted and organised by language; and each language will organise them in its own way. Take the problem of colours. To us, our own system of distinctions seems the only natural one; but in the spectrum itself there are no boundaries: each language can divide it into as many, or as few, sections as it chooses. When it was first realised that some of our shades of colour were absent from the Homeric epics, it was suggested that Homer must have been colour blind. Later on, the whole of classical antiquity was included in the same diagnosis. And, indeed, the Greeks and the Romans had a simpler system than ours. But neither the ancient nor the modern scheme can be held up as the only valid one: they are merely two of the many possible attempts at organising what nature had left unorganised.

Our intellectual and moral concepts are even more language-bound than our vision of the physical world. Every community will single out and label those qualities which it considers important, whereas other features will remain unnamed and therefore undifferentiated. In medieval society, cleverness as such was not recognised as an independent quality; at the same time, courtly and non-courtly, chivalric and non-chivalric skill were systematically distinguished and provided with separate names. Once again, we see the reciprocity of relations between language and thought. The vocabulary reflects a certain hierarchy of values, but it also hardens it and hands it down to successive generations. Its action is essentially conservative; it is one of the most powerful factors building up traditions and ensuring continuity.

In some cases, even the presence or absence of a single word may be significant, though here we should beware of hasty and biased interpretation. Take the case of the German word *Schadenfreude,* 'malicious joy', which has no exact equivalent in English or French. Should one infer from this, as has been done, that Germans suffer more from this vice than do other nations? One could maintain with equal justification that they are more likely to be immune from it, as the very existence of the word puts them on their guard. Be that as it may, it is a fact that the young German is born with a linguistic medium where malicious joy is identified and given a name of its own, whereas elsewhere it remains in the limbo of anonymity.

Various analogies have been suggested to bring out the essential features of the influence of language on thought. Some thinkers are obsessed by a kind of linguistic claustrophobia: they conjure up a dramatic picture of man trapped between the walls of his mother tongue. It is perhaps more appropriate to visualise each language as a prism, unique in structure, through which we view the world and which refracts and analyses our experiences in its own particular way. This is seen most clearly in the vocabulary, but grammatical structure tells a similar story. The impact of grammatical conventions on the human mind is even more far-reaching than that of single words. Pronouns of address are an example in point. Most languages have two or more such pronouns, which will be used according to degree of intimacy, social status, and other factors. English, however, differs from the rest: since the elimination of 'thou' in the late Middle Ages, there is no possibility of choice. This may lead occasionally to awkward ambiguities, but the risk is more than offset by the amount of snobbery and arrogance, of inhibitions and inferiority complexes, which the English-speaking world has been spared thanks to this simple device.

Other grammatical features reach down to deeper layers of our consciousness. Even the experience of time has a linguistic dimension. Modern physics has taught us that time is relative, and this applies also to its grammatical expression. The number and nature of tense distinctions differs from one language to another; some idioms, especially the

Slavonic ones, are actually less interested in time proper than in the complete or incomplete nature of a given action. The late Professor Entwistle has given an interesting analysis of this peculiarity:

> We are concerned with an attitude of mind in which the continuance or completion of some action is of more importance than its reference to past, present, or future time. This emphasis may be connected with the agricultural occupation of most Slavs as contrasted with the urban precision imposed on westerners. . . . The preference we westerners have for tense is probably due partly to the influence of European modes of life, which depend on the clock, and not, like the agricultural, on the completion of operations.

One may wonder whether recent industrial progress in the Slav world will result in some modification of their time scale. Meanwhile, the time-perspective of the mother tongue is bound to have an influence on the individual speaker's conception of time.

The characteristic features of a language may thus tell us a great deal about national psychology. Particularly instructive in this respect are the habitual patterns of word-order which determine the channels along which our thoughts will flow. The vast majority of English and French sentences are built on a rigid pattern: the sequence subject— verb—object, as in 'Peter sees Paul'. This sequence may be regarded as inherently logical: first, we state the subject of the utterance, that which we are talking about; then we say something about it; finally, we may add any further details required. There is little possibility of departing from this arrangement, as English and French words are uninflected and their position alone marks their role in the sentence. In inflected languages, such as German, there will be a wider margin, and the logical scheme may be superseded by emphasis and other considerations. There is also another significant difference. While English and French sentences proceed in a straight line, German syntax prefers elaborate constructions which have been described as 'incapsulating'; they are like boxes fitted into one another. A prefix, for example, will be detached from its verb and relegated to the very end of the sentence; it is as if we said in English: 'An epidemic broke last year in England out'. This requires a certain amount of planning in which some people may detect a characteristic trait of the German mind. It would be idle to speculate as to which system is preferable: both involve some effort and discipline, though each in its own way.

Some modern thinkers are haunted by the fear that many philosophical problems are pseudo-problems generated by the structure of our languages. One often hears statements of this type: 'If Aristotle had spoken Chinese or Dacotan, he would have had to adopt an entirely different logic'. But it still has to be shown in detail how linguistic structure can influence philosophical structure. Other philosophers are more concerned with those features of language which may distort or confuse our thoughts. Abstractions have been singled out for special attention, and we are constantly warned against the habit of setting up our 'isms' and other abstract formations as real entities, and of assuming that where there is a label there must necessarily be some reality behind it. The very ease with which some languages, in particular German, are able to coin an unlimited number of abstract terms may thus become a potential danger to clear thinking.

Ambiguities are also denounced by the philosopher, though they may be deliberately contrived by the poet. Words with two or more meanings may not only give rise to misunderstandings; they may even create confusion in our thoughts. Proust once drew attention to the effects ·which the ambiguity of the French adjective *grand* may have on an unsophisticated mind. *Grand* can mean both physical and moral greatness: the Frenchman has only one word where the Englishman can choose between *big* and *great*. One of Proust's most entertaining characters, the maid Françoise, falls into the trap laid by language: she imagines that physical and moral greatness are somehow inseparable. The author likens her vocabulary to a stone which had here and there a flaw casting darkness into her very thoughts. In much the same way, a Swedish verb which may mean either 'to read' or 'to learn' has been held responsible for the widespread misconception that having read a passage means having learned it.

Does everything I have been saying come down to this, that language is an inadequate medium of expression? Many writers and thinkers believe that it is, though few would agree with Plato's defeatist verdict: 'No intelligent man will ever be so bold as to put in language those things which his reason has contemplated'. Yet even the most intransigent critic of language will have to admit that it has some redeeming features. Our speech is not confined to the communication of facts and thoughts; we also talk to express our feelings, to arouse feelings in others, and to influence their behaviour. Clarity and precision are essential on the rational plane, but the emotive side of language will benefit by the suggestiveness of vague words with blurred outlines and rich overtones. At the same time, the very limitations of language are a challenge and a means of self-discipline: our thoughts become more articulate and more elegant by being forced into the moulds of a plastic and yet resistant medium.

Essays of Our Time I ● *Part* 3

ROBERT LOWRY *started writing at nine and has continued ever since as book reviewer, novelist, and short-story writer. Among his books are* The Big Cage *and* Find Me in Fire. *About his work he has written:* "You write a book in three big jumps: you write it to explain it to yourself, you write it again to explain it to somebody else, then you take out all the explanation and let it stand for what it is."

BRUCE CATTON *has many interests other than baseball. He is the author of a multivolume study of the Civil War, from which* A Stillness at Appomatox *was chosen for the Pulitzer Prize and the National Book Award in 1954. He worked many years as a newspaperman and now serves as editor of* The American Heritage.

JOHN KEATS *turned from a reporter's job to free-lance writing to produce several popular books about phases of American culture. He wrote on education in* Schools without Scholars, *suburbia in* The Crack in the Picture Window, *and automobiles in* The Insolent Chariot. *The titles of his books reveal his attitudes toward his subjects.*

Blood Wedding in Chicago

"HUNH! HUNH!" Bang Bang breathed. "Hunh! Hunh! Hunh!"

Bang Bang hit the heavy bag. Hard. Flashing much enthusiasm with both hands, hooking that heavy bag, straightening it out, dancing around it. And lashing out flirtatiously with big bright attractive eyes at whoever was looking on.

At George Gainford, that is, who stood with casual arrogance off to one side and caught the performance on the bias. Before Bang Bang might decide to raise his right hand in triumph as Heavy-Bag Champion of the World, George Gainford said "What you tryin to do there, Bang Bang? You ain't got no knockout punch *yet.*"

A door closed and Soldier Jones came in out of the cold, his shoulders wet with New Jersey snowflakes, his big flat feet, a little pigeon-toed, moving sure and direct not toward an opponent, the way they had moved across a hundred rings fifteen years ago, but toward the spaceheater. He felt the spaceheater and was satisfied.

"Cold out there," Soldier Jones said, shuffling over and picking up a rag and putting it on the shelf behind the spaceheater. More softly, like an echo, he repeated, "Cold out there," and at that moment noticed us.

"What you boys standing up for? They's chairs."

On the other side of the ring, by the window that looked out on the road that came winding up the cold mountain, Bang Bang was tapping the light bag with the persistence of a hungry woodpecker, but George Gainford wasn't watching now. He was leaning over, using a handkerchief to improve the shine on his shoes.

"We've been driving for about an hour," Yogi said to Soldier Jones. "So we've just *been* sitting down."

I sat down because somebody I didn't know had invited me to. Soldier Jones sat down too, planting those big feet far apart in front of him. Soldier Jones knew how to be comfortable.

"From New York?" he asked.

"Yeah."

"Where 'bouts you live?"

Yogi, my impassioned boxing guide, told him where he lived: midtown, Sixth Avenue near Fifty-sixth Street, but Soldier Jones had

51

trouble getting it straight. He frowned slightly and couldn't quite place it. "That's below Central Park," Yogi said. "West Side."

"Oh . . . yeah," Soldier Jones said. "That must be *down*town. . . . You boys fighters, ain't you?"

It was a piece of straight-faced flattery that Soldier Jones knew how to hand out; he had us cornered while we admitted we weren't fighters, and Yogi broke clean with a question: "Is this his first day for sparring?"

"First day," Soldier Jones said. "He'll be along soon."

"What's his weight?" Yogi asked, still standing; a slender twist of charged wire, unable to relax, his eyes in that small neat head the kind of bright, glittering eyes that hunting birds have.

"Weighs about '56," said Soldier Jones, who knew how to relax. "That's his *good* weight. Have no trouble makin' weight. He'll leave that to the other man to worry about."

He got up, eased his bulk through the ropes, and walked, bending slightly, across the sparring ring. "Leave the *other* man worry about that," he said to nobody in particular as he climbed through the other side and began straightening up a few things on the rubdown table.

Now a bigger boy than Bang Bang, and lighter-complexioned—a middleweight with a neckless head buried between the broadest shoulders on the Eastern Seaboard—came in, changed into trunks, and began shadow-boxing around the ring. "Hunh! Hunh!" breathed this big boy, hitting shadows. Bang Bang came into the ring with him. "Hunh! Hunh!" breathed Bang Bang. They danced parallel to each other, from side to side of the ring, the big boy uninterested in everything except the terrible shadow he was beating back, but Bang Bang shooting glances at us, his pleasant young face pleased with whatever audience was around. (Could be the sports writers up from New York, looking him over, finding out he looked almost as good as the champ, putting it in the paper that way.)

June the trainer ambled in wearing a sweater—a slender Negro neither young nor old whose deep-furrowed face had been molded through thirty or forty years by the play of a tough and ironic intelligence. Like Soldier Jones, he said, "Make yourselves comfortable. He'll be along soon."

"Who'll he spar with today?" Yogi asked.

June rolled with the question, out of an old racial habit. "He don't have any *regular* sparring partners—he don't *hire* people to box with him. You go round hiring people and then they turn out to be the wrong ones, like you go in a store and buy something and then get it home and it's not what you want at all. So he spars with whoever is around the camp, like Bang Bang over there. Or maybe some fellow comes up for a visit and he looks kind of good to us, we'd say—" and he pointed right at me—"we'd say, 'Hey—you—you put on the gloves and go in there with him.'"

"I'd be glad to do it," I said, "except I'm paralyzed on both sides and my head hurts."

"All I mean is," June went on without losing his thought, "there ain't any *official* way we got for sparring partners."

Yogi said there was certainly a lot of difference between this place and Pompton Lakes—the size, and so on.

"Well, the camp at Pompton Lakes is for the public, kind of for show. This here's just *his*. We ain't training for the public here. We're training for the man in the ring."

We watched him slip through the ropes on his way over to the gym part of the cabin, and now, though all the bustle of Bang Bang and the wide boy and Soldier Jones and June continued, there was above everything a quiet expectancy, as if all this was only a little incidental activity to fill up time until the main event started.

Then he came in, from the cabin he used as living quarters next door, without a sound—looking to anyone who had ever seen him in newsreel shots or on television or in photographs very small, unmuscular, maybe because he wore clothes (a yachting cap on the back of his round head, a small tight-fitting windbreaker) and in his official appearances he wore almost nothing at all. He was twenty-nine years old, weight 156 pounds, stood five feet eleven, had a reach of 72½ inches, an unexpanded chest of 36½ inches, an expanded chest of 38 inches, a waist 28½ inches around, thighs 19¾ inches, calves 13½ inches, biceps 11¾ inches, forearms 10¾ inches, neck 15 inches. He wore all these measurements, which added up to a very graceful, very fast and very powerful man, with an easy, unalerted modesty. His heavy mouth, turned up faintly at the corners, gave his oval face a slightly sardonic look. But his dark eyes, made long and narrow by high cheekbones, were set in dead-focus on whatever was in front of him. They were the kind of eyes that some men gain in moments of vision or in the grip of a powerful but passing emotion or through the use of drugs, but that this man had all the time, probably as a result of a tempered, street-corner shrewdness and a super-normal latent energy that he could call on when he had to. His face was smooth and unscarred. He stood there, sway-backed, nonchalant, unattached—like some passer-by who had heard all the boxing going on in here and had come in out of the cold to see who was doing it. Actually he was the camp's owner, the camp's star, and the only reason the camp had for its existence. His name was Ray Robinson, called Sugar by the people who don't know him and Ray by those who do. He was the welterweight boxing champion of the world.

"Hey, Yogi! Where you been, man? I ain't seen you for a long time," he said with just a flick of his eyes.

Yogi told him we'd come up from New York to see him train.

"Ain't you a little thinner than when I saw you last time, Yogi?"

Yogi thought not.

"Yes you are—you're getting thin, Yogi."

"No, as a matter of fact, I'm probably heavier."

"Heavier—yeah, well, that's what I mean. Did I say thinner? I guess I really meant heavier."

A faint, fast smile lit his face—this was his own special brand of kidding in the style of his boxing.

"Guess I'll go over and change clothes."

He climbed through the ropes of the ring that was empty now, and when he got to the other side he turned and, smiling, said, "Come on over."

We went over, two men too many in the small space of the gym. He took off his clothes and Soldier Jones got out the sweating cream and began rubbing it on Ray's belly, near his groin.

"What are you doing there, man? I don't want to lose weight down there. Here, gimme that stuff." He took the salve away from Soldier Jones and began apply it himself.

"How'd you like Paris, Ray?" asked Yogi.

"I could take some more of that Paris," Ray said. "I can't wait to get over there again. You'd be crazy about it."

"Did you get around to the nightclubs?"

"Man, I didn't go to the nightclubs, the nightclubs came to me."

"My brother's in Paris," Yogi said. "I told him to look you up, but he had a little trouble getting in touch with you."

"Don't send any men around to see me when I'm in Paris," Ray said, watching June tape his right hand. "When I'm in Paris I'm not interested in *men*."

He moved out, in bag-gloves and jockstrop and trunks and socks and gymshoes, to the heavy bag. He worked on ring time, hitting the bag three minutes, resting when George Gainford rang the bell, hitting the bag again three minutes, resting, moving on to the light bag, resting, hitting, resting, stooping into the ring to shadow-box—Bang Bang and the wide boy with him. Now the three of them moved on parallel lines across the ring ("Hunh! Hunh! Hunh!") and back again ("Hunh! Hunh! Hunh!") in a fantastic ritual dance that removed these three naked men from the drab, scuffed surroundings and placed them in some new dimension of space and experience where the reach in inches of a left plus the cubic displacement of air of a right became the official currency, the means of survival, the moral law.

The bell halted them in their tracks, but they did not talk or look at one another; they continued to move their heads and shoulders and arms restlessly, each man completely separate and alone in his battle with a phantom that any day or week now would turn into hard flesh and angry blood and come jabbing, hooking, weaving in.

The bell started them forward again as a shine of sweat highlighted their three faces. Only Bang Bang found time to roll his eyes outward beyond the ropes that bound their world. The wide boy crouched and plunged and reached with sweeping punches that bruised the air. Ray boxed upright, his right held almost perpendicularly in front of his chin, his left singing out like a long cruel whip. In their very separateness and determination they seemed laced together into a single unit that hardly brushed the canvas as it worked its way from one set of ropes to the other and back again and back again—a unit that extended by a long throbbing artery down through several million years of history to the first man's first fear.

Outfitted with headgear, Ray sparred with the wide boy now. The wide boy never jabbed but, crouched low, came at him with hopeful barrelhouse rights and left hooks. Ray moved delicately from side to side and backward, blocking the blows and feeding in the sharp straight left—a toedancer with flesh that melted to nothing under a punch and resolidified immediately a few inches away. Toward the end of the session he stopped evading and moved in on his man, chattering with his left and bringing the right down savagely and then hooking not once but twice with his left before his man could get away.

Later, tossing the medicine ball hard against George Gainford's mild paunch and taking it from Gainford very hard against his own flat belly, he said, "I was a little glove-shy today."

The wide boy was wiping himself with a towel, his eyes blurry. "Man, what did you say you were? My head don't feel like you were glove-shy."

Everybody laughed and the wide boy, his face bruised, laughed too. Still stopping and starting with the bell, which rang insistently at three-minute intervals, Ray began to skip, holding the two ends of the skipping rope in his right hand and then transferring it to his left without missing a beat and then to his right and to his left again; then holding an end of the rope in each hand and skipping in perfect reflex to the fast tapping of the rope on the floor—June looking on with absolute concentrated interest.

We said so long to him as he lay on the rubdown table, breathing easily, his face once more composed in a look that was at the same time dead-certain and half-amused at its own certainty.

"You come up next week, then," Ray said.

Stepping outside into the whirling snow, we bumped into Soldier Jones. "You come up again," Soldier Jones echoed. "You'll see more if you come up in a week or so, when he's further along in the training."

By the door of the other cabin, where Ray and Bang Bang and the wide boy and June and George Gainford and Soldier Jones all lived during these months of isolation before Ray's big fight, two men were struggling with a huge television aerial. Soon it would be perched on top of the living quarters, a tall reminder of all the long, dedicated days and nights there were still to get through here on this mountainside before Ray finally went out to Chicago.

"Nobody mentioned LaMotta," I said, turning the Ford around, and heading down the drive past a little marker that named the place Cabin in the Sky.

"But his ears are probably burning," Yogi said. "Everybody there was thinking about him all the time. Did you notice how Ray's sparring partner was imitating LaMotta's style?"

"LaMotta had better be better than that," I said. "Maybe we ought to look in on him."

"It's not much fun," Yogi said. "It's grim. I don't like white training camps."

But I talked him around, and four days later we took a cab uptown to a sooty Bronx street-corner bounded on one side by the El and on the other by a newspaper kiosk and a lot of traffic. A door said GLEASON'S GYM—COME IN & LEARN HOW TO BOX. We climbed the stairs. At the top a bored-looking man wearing a brown felt hat relieved us of fifteen cents apiece.

There was already a crowd, sitting on undertaker's chairs rowed up on two sides of an elevated ring where nobody was boxing. They were high-school hoods and closed-down bookies and old men with fifteen cents to spend and ex-pugs and admirers of a certain glum, plodding brand of East Side, Jewish-Italian-American minority courage. Everybody looked very glum and very plodding. Jacob LaMotta, middleweight boxing champion of the entire world, was nowhere to be seen, but a man who should have been able to beat him, a poker-faced, light-heavyweight gorilla with deep corrugations at the nape of his neck and no back to his head, was working out on the heavy bag in front of us. Maybe not, though—his punch looked good, with a big body and big arms behind it, but he moved very slowly and his reflexes, as he circled the bag, looked sluggish.

When a nose has been broken and spread and rebroken and re-spread, and when the brows have been flattened by a thousand blows and pasted over with a thick layer of scar tissue, and the cheekbones and mouth and ears and jaw have all been slightly distorted from having been available to too many punches through a dozen years of prize-fighting—a man's face is apt to take on a sad, rather sincere look that it would never have taken on if it had been allowed to grow old in a less brutal way. This melancholy face, which was the face that Jake LaMotta carried with him in the ring or in training or merely when sitting across the breakfast table from his spectacular blond wife, was actually a handsome prideful monument to what the middleweight champion could do best: take a punch, take a lot of punches, and keep plowing in; and often win because he kept plowing in strong, and ordinary punches could not stop him. He was exceptionally proud of the fact that in ninety-five professional fights since 1941 he had never been knocked off his feet. He had been beaten, of course—thirteen times on points and once by technical knockout—but never floored. And since a man must pride himself on what he can do and not on what he cannot do, this was Jake LaMotta's pride, this vertical position which he managed to assume at all times in the ring. It could not be Ray Robinson's pride because he had been knocked off his feet on a few occasions, once during the five bouts he had fought with LaMotta between 1942 and 1945, before either had become a champion. But even so, Ray had won four of those five fights by decision, and lost one by decision, and, out of 127 pro fights in a career which in time-span almost exactly paralleled LaMotta's, had been beaten only once—that one time by LaMotta. All this is important to know to be able to judge the precise value, in terms of pride and in terms of winning boxing bouts, of a face like Jake LaMotta's.

Wearing this sad, flat face above a short, hairy, powerful, olive-skinned body, the middleweight champion came out of the dressing room on the far side of Gleason's Gym and climbed up into the ring. He shadow-boxed—a hard, compact rock of a man, the muscles in his barrel chest and wide shoulders and short, bulging arms covered over with a thick layer of tissue that was the padding with which he absorbed blows and withstood them. His footwork was elemental, a mere hopping from foot to foot; he stayed close to the ground, his head and chest turtled in, and moved forward with short, mean bodyblows, ten at a time in rapid succession, snorting furiously through that big bent nose of his as he grimly murdered nobody against the ropes.

Now the boy he was going to spar with climbed into the ring after him and began to shadow-box too. This boy, a pale colored boy, was tall, limber and a little gawky. He towered above LaMotta, not only because he was three or four inches taller than LaMotta's five feet seven, but also because he fought upright. When a bell rang they began to spar, the colored boy imitating Ray's style. Everything that LaMotta hoped would come true when he went to Chicago to defend his title was acted out before our eyes. LaMotta bored grimly in, torpedoing his tall opponent, who wanted to box, and blasting him to pieces before he could even get set to throw a punch. Working in close on the body, he continually threw sharp, stunning uppercuts—most of them here only phonies which by intention fell inches short of the tall boy's chin, as if LaMotta understood completely that these blows from his gloves were more than any man should be expected to take unless he were getting twenty or thirty grand for doing it.

As we climbed the El steps on our way to neutralize that three-buck cabfare with a cheap trip back downtown, Yogi, white and tense and bored as he always was after he had been in the presence of something or someone he disliked or disapproved of, asked, "What do you think?"

"He looks like a strong, mean man," I said. "The pleasure is all Ray's."

"You mind if I stop and get my wife a box of candy?" the cab driver asked me when he pulled up for a light. "It's curtains if I don't come home with something tonight. Valentine's Day."

"We'll never make it," I said. "It's eight twenty-five and look at this traffic. Why don't you get it coming back?"

He got away on the yellow. "Okay," he said. "You're the boss. I've been trying to get it for the last hour but nobody'll let me."

"You ought to knock off anyhow after you get me there and watch the fight in a bar," I told him. "This one will be something to see."

"I got enough fights at home," the cab driver said. "I don't need to watch nobody else's fights."

What I saw out the windshield was a double line of cars that extended farther than you could see down the long avenue that ran from Chicago's Loop to the Stadium. A promised piece of high-priced violence in a roped-off twenty-by-twenty-foot area of canvas was paying off tonight.

The cars honked and brayed and the beefy Windy City cops were everywhere. Chicago was a good spot to stage the kind of organized violence we all were out for. Walking around this afternoon after getting off the train and checking into a Loop hotel, I'd seen that, for all that had happened to the rest of the world in the last ten or fifteen years, Chicago really hadn't changed much. There was still a raw, drab depression squalor about the dingy bars and four-bit burlesque houses and vacant stores and boarded-up buildings along South State and South Wabash. It was true that the stagger-bums hit you for a quarter now instead of a dime; but the breath smelled the same and the eyes were no more in focus and the big dirty hand held on as tightly as ever. In the mammoth-columned granite architecture of the banks and commercial buildings around the Board of Trade, there was an overpowering, gold-lettered arrogance that you seldom saw in Eastern buildings; an arrogance stemming from the same small seed of inferiority before the older East that sent shoots into every area of Chicago's social and intellectual life. Any newspaper obit-writer who had never been east of Lake Shore Drive could tell you what a bunch of gold-plated phonies they were back there in New York or Boston; any housewife had a civic pride that swelled like a bull's hump at mere mention of Chicago's housing projects or Chicago parks. Beneath this tough crust of arrogance, the same restless urge toward violence that marks most of America's big inland cities bubbled and boiled. So it was a good place to stage a fight. It was a good place for Ray Robinson to fight Jake LaMotta for the Middleweight Championship of the World.

"I'd better get out," I said. "It's eight-thirty and we're not moving."

"You got a big walk ahead of you, buddy."

I put some money in his hand. "I wouldn't want to miss this," I said, and hit out down the avenue past block after block of creeping cars; past one scalper after another begging to buy fight tickets; past program hawkers, newspaper boys, and hundreds of people who were not selling anything or going anywhere but had been drawn here to the streets around the Stadium by the attractive thought of the battle that would take place inside. Something that looked like a full-scale riot was swarming around the Stadium's doors. But I elbowed my way through, had my twenty-buck ticket torn by the doorman, and high-tailed it toward my entrance.

No dice. Thirty or forty of us heard from the usher blocking the steps that the single prelim that preceded the main bout had already started and nobody could be seated until it was over. I edged my way up the steps and got to the top just in time to hear the drawn-out *awwwwwwwwww* from the crowd that means pain to someone, and to see Bang Bang hit the canvas flat on his face, his big bright eyes rolled up into his head, his fight over and done with.

Now, while his seconds helped Bang Bang to his corner, and the announcer crooned: ". . . in twooooo minutes and fiiiii seconds of the fifth rooooouuuuund . . . " and Bang Bang's conqueror stood by the announcer's elbow, waiting to have his hand raised, I scrambled for my seat and sat down on it. An organ was playing a tune that echoed back and forth into a mash of sounds in the mammoth, noisy, smoky cavern of the Stadium.

All the people you always see at fights were here, except that tonight there were more of them. Instead of two or three platinum and peroxide blondes in seven-and-a-half-inch heels, I counted eighteen—all with chins held high and lashes lowered to half-mast. Gorgeous Negro women all around me offset the blondes with a beauty that most white people have no idea exists, since in their isolation they deal only with Negro girls not pretty enough to do something better than vacuum rugs and scrub pots in a white woman's house. This sweep of faces in the great bowl of the Stadium made a black-and-white checkerboard pattern, a pattern that added a colorful border of latent violence to the square patch of brilliantly lit canvas which it surrounded.

The ring was empty now, and empty it had the same meager look of over-inflated importance that a battlefield has after one battle has ended and before another has begun. On the canvas near the center of the ring was a faint, fresh smear of Bang Bang's blood.

The lights across the Stadium went out. The organ stopped. Only the ring, small and deserted over there, still gleamed. Fifteen thousand people cannot be completely silent, but when they try to be it is an awesome thing. They tried to be now, as two long poles of light, spotted from somewhere near the ceiling, suddenly sprang down, felt their way hesitantly back and forth across the audience a few times, then crossed, in gigantic, accidental symbol of the suffering that was about to take place here, and came to rest on the doors at opposite ends of the Stadium.

The doors opened, almost simultaneously. From each emerged a champion.

Preceded and followed by a long train of manager and trainer and doctor and handlers and friends. As the two groups moved with painful slowness toward the ring and toward each other, a low, thrilled rumble of passion greeted them. The white hood covering each fighter's head somehow suggested that these two grave processions were the components of a strange wedding soon to be solemnized. And perhaps a wedding would have the same powerful attraction if the audience were allowed to witness, beyond the altar ritual, the consummation as well. This wedding tonight would be in the grand style of those marriages of other centuries, in which an unwilling, frightened bride sometimes battled her groom for a dozen nights before, bloody and scratched and weary, he finally took her.

Three quarters of that long distance to the ring, the champion in the leopard-skin robe, Jake LaMotta, halted, and the crowd applauded him . . . while Ray Robinson, challenger, continued on. There is as much ritual in a championship boxing bout as there is in the battling of walruses on an Arctic island. One ritual is the appearance in the ring of the challenger first, and as Ray Robinson slipped between the ropes and faced his handlers with no shadow-boxing, no overhead handshake, no gesture toward the crowd, he got a mild round of applause that was nothing like the roar that went up when LaMotta entered and turned his thick, rugged body slowly around with one mighty right arm upraised for all the world to gaze at.

It was apparent from the beginning who the crowd wanted to see win; and they wanted it for a complex of reasons, some of them the best reasons, some the worst. There were people here who were cheering for LaMotta because he was the underdog (even in the defense of his own title against a lighter man), and underdogs, which all audiences are, should win even when they are inferior. There were people here who wanted to see as brutal a contest as possible, and so did what they could to persuade LaMotta to put up the fight of his life against a man who had already beaten him four times. There were also people here curiously sensitive to human coloring, who wanted to see any white man beat up any Negro under any circumstances. On either side of me and behind me was a group of Italian-Americans who knew one another and who had brought their patriotism along with them. As a defense against their partisanship, I pulled out a black cigar, lit it, and laid down a dense blue smoke screen, as the announcer spoke of things to come ("Next week, in this arena . . ."), the ringside celebrities were alerted ("Please come up quickly when you hear your name") and "The Star-Spangled Banner" was played.

The classic contest, whether in mythology, in history, in a bullring, or in a boxing ring, is always the same: a fragile, keen, and handsome man battles an ugly beast larger and stronger than himself and defeats it. The beast is brave and charges with no regard for its own safety. The man is also brave, but he has to find weapons other than his own blind strength to win. The knight uses his sword to slay the dragon; David uses a slingshot to vanquish Goliath; the matador befuddles and tires the bull with a cape; the real boxer uses his brain, and blocks out his fight round by round, pacing himself. It was Ray Robinson's plan to tire his bull right down to its toes before he dedicated and sacrificed it. Since this would take seven or ten or twelve rounds of hitting and eluding a powerful, determined animal, the plan was filled with danger. It was this special kind of danger that would give the fight the special interest it had beyond other great fights.

But in the very first round, as Jake LaMotta, no leopard but only a man after he had shed his robe, came crouched and eager across the ring after Robinson, with his left up-pointed at a 45-degree angle straight at Robinson's face, something else became apparent: the bull was inspired by the magnitude of the occasion to an effort greater than anyone had counted on, and it is such inspiration—beauty and brains and plans and agility notwithstanding—that sometimes comes through to win.

Ray Robinson, his own man giving his own performance, jabbed that left in hard and got away and jabbed again and got away and missed and missed again but got away. And LaMotta, willing to take punishment in return for the privilege of dealing it out, kept after him, his face exposed to that cutting left hand but his own hands busy at Ray's face and his body. A crowd interested not in plans but only in aggressiveness and courage cheered LaMotta till their ears rang and their own blood blinded them. Cheered him through the second and third and fourth and fifth and sixth and seventh and eighth and ninth rounds.

They did not see that the man moving in is not always the man who is winning; that a fighter of Robinson's exceptional skill can hit harder going away than most fighters can hit going forward; that Ray's plan was to bleed his bull, and lead him on and tire him until those iron hands drooped of their own weight and those slow feet stopped coming in. The crowd preferred not to notice that in each succeeding round LaMotta wore one more red badge for his courage: a bright crimson patch, like a birthmark, around his nose; tiny, painful cuts on both cheeks; a swollen left eye.

But in the ninth round Ray indicated in what direction the fight was going by aggressively hooking, jabbing, punishing his man, instead of backing up and countering. The bull still kept coming in, but it was a wearier bull and it was growing soft. It was trying now not to outpoint its tormentor and win rounds, but merely to keep coming in and somehow, by some wild miracle, to throw that lucky punch that would win the fight.

But it was later for LaMotta than anyone knew. What Ray Robinson had merely indicated in the ninth, he now chose to demonstrate in the tenth; and continuing the demonstration in the eleventh, he ran into the death throes of a champion—that rousing, tragic moment when Jake LaMotta came back from the dead and cornered him and hit him with everything he didn't have. Hit a man all closed up, all elbows and gloves and forearms and moving parts, who bled the bull of its last ounce of aggressive energy and then maneuvered by it and began the final phase.

Through the twelfth and part of the thirteenth rounds, LaMotta's pride in being able to stand on his own two feet in anybody's prize ring remained intact, while the face that went with that pride underwent terrible changes. A crowd that had come for blood was seeing blood; seeing a man beat up; seeing, too, a plan emerge from what had seemed at first merely a round-by-round contest in punching strength and evasiveness between two men. The crowd, standing up and screaming as one hoarse, super-human animal, was a fickle crowd; for it had forgotten LaMotta and now it was screaming for what it had really come to see: the blood, the pain, the violence, and a new champion himself hurt and bleeding, emerging in momentary, blood-smeared glory.

Pity can sometimes squeeze itself even between the ropes of a prize ring, and Robinson in the thirteenth round, with his man wide open, bent double and stumbling backwards, at moments stopped his assault and seemed almost reluctant to hit him again. Nobody would notice this in the newspapers the next day, for most sports writers were watching for other things. But it was those moments of hesitation in the thirteenth round, before the referee stopped the fight and led the new champion back to his corner, that gave Ray Robinson a stripe of greatness.

Later, as LaMotta, a semiconscious mass of beaten flesh and an ex-champion now, huddled on his stool in the corner, Ray stood alone facing the crowd, his gloves removed but his hands still taped, his right hand raised and his fingers greeting the people he knew out there. Across the taped palm was a long stain of blood, his own or LaMotta's. Smiling slightly, his mouth bleeding and his eye bruised, he looked very small and very human and very much alone.

BRUCE CATTON

The Great American Game

BY THE CAREFULLY repeated definition of men who stand to make money out of its acceptance, baseball is the Great American Game. The expression was invented long ago and it has been rammed home by talented press agents ever since, even in times when most Americans seemed to be interested very largely in something else. But what has given the phrase its sticking power is not the fact that a big industry has kept plugging it, or the allied fact that unceasing repetition has dinned it into an unreflecting public's ear for generations, but simply the fact that in its underlying essence it is perfectly true.

Baseball is the American game, great or otherwise, because it reflects so perfectly certain aspects of the American character that no other sport quite portrays.

It has few of the elements of pure sportsmanship, as that dubious word is commonly accepted, and it is not notably a game for gentlemen. But it does embody certain native-born fundamentals, including above all others the notion that the big thing about any contest is to win it. It also is built upon the idea that anything you can get away with is permissible, and it is the only sport (at least the only one since the Roman populace sat in the thumbs-down section at the gladiatorial games) that puts an invitation to homicide in one of its enduring sayings: "Kill the umpire!" (The thing has actually been attempted, too, more than once.) It is pre-eminently the sport for the professional rather than for the amateur, the sport in which the well-intentioned duffer neither is given nor especially wants a part.

Almost everyone in the country has played it at one time or another, but almost nobody except the professional dreams of going on playing it once full manhood has come. It is a spectator sport in which each spectator has had just enough personal experience to count himself an expert, and it is the only pastime on earth that leans heavily on the accumulation of page upon page of inherently dry statistics. It is also an unchanging pageant and a ritualized drama, as completely formalized as the Spanish bullfight, and although it is wholly urbanized it still speaks of the small town and the simple, rural era that lived before the automobile came in to blight the landscape. One reason for this is that in a land of unending change, baseball changes very little. There has been no important modification of its rules for well over half a century. The ball in use now will go farther when properly hit, and the gloves worn on defense are designed to do automatically what personal skill once had to do, but aside from these things the game is as it was in the early 1900's. Even the advent of night baseball, which seemed like pure sacrilege when it was introduced two decades ago, has made little difference; the pictorial aspect of the game—which is one of its most important features—has perhaps even gained thereby. The neat green field looks greener and cleaner under the lights, the moving players are silhouetted more sharply, and the enduring visual fascination of the game—the immobile pattern of nine men, grouped according to ancient formula and then, suddenly, to the sound of a wooden bat whacking a round ball, breaking into swift ritualized movement, movement so standardized that even the tyro in the bleachers can tell when someone goes off in the wrong direction—this is as it was in the old days. A gaffer from the era of William McKinley, abruptly brought back to the second half of the twentieth century, would find very little in modern life that would not seem new, strange, and rather bewildering, but put in a good grandstand seat back of first base he would see nothing that was not completely familiar.

But that is only the surface part of it. Baseball, highly organized, professionalized within an inch of its life, and conducted by men who like dollars better than they like sport, still speaks for the old days when nine young men in an open park somehow expressed the hot competitive instincts of everybody and spoke for home-town pride.

And perhaps the central part of all of this is the fact that in its essence baseball is still faintly disreputable and rowdy. Its players chew tobacco, or at least look as if they were chewing it; many of them do not shave every day; and they argue bitterly with each other, with their opponents, and with the umpires just as they did when John McGraw and Ed Delehanty were popular idols. They have borrowed nothing from the "sportsmanship" of more sedate countries; they believe that when you get into a fight you had better win, and the method by which you win does not matter very much. Anything goes; victory is what counts.

This John McGraw, for example. When he was playing third base and there was a runner there, and someone hit a fly to the outfield, McGraw would unobtrusively hook his fingers in the player's belt so that the take-off for the plate, once the ball was caught, would be delayed by half a second or so. He got away with it, too, and no one thought the worse of him, until one day a base runner unbuckled his belt in this situation and, legging it for home, left the belt dangling in McGraw's hand, tangible evidence of crime. Note, also, that baseball knows about the bean ball—the ball thrown at the batter's head to drive him away from the plate and hamper his hitting process. A big leaguer was once killed by such a pitch; it has been condemned by everybody since then, and it is still a regular feature of the game.

In its essentials, then, baseball is plebeian, down-to-earth, and robustious. Even half a century ago it was dwindling to the rank of secondary sport in the colleges. Professors who have adjusted themselves to the presence on the campus of *soi-disant* students who are paid to attend college so that they may play football have a way of considering the football player one cut above the baseball player. The former may be a hulking behemoth of pure muscle, wholly incapable of differentiating between Virgil's *Eclogues* and Boyle's law, but he does not seem quite as uncouth as the baseball player—who, in his own turn, may also be on the campus as a paid hand, the difference being that he is being paid by some major-league team that wants to see his athletic skills developed, while the football player gets his from ardent alumni who want to see the college team beat State on Homecoming Day next fall. There has never been any social cachet attached to skill on the diamond.

The reason, obviously, is that baseball came up from the sand lots —the small town, the city slum, and the like. It had a rowdy air because rowdies played it. One of the stock tableaux in American sports history is the aggrieved baseball player jawing with the umpire. In all our games, this tableau is unique; it belongs to baseball, from the earliest days it has been an integral part of the game, and even in the carefully policed major leagues today it remains unchanged. Baseball never developed any of the social niceties.

In the old days, when (as we suppose, anyway) most of us lived in small towns, or at least in fairly small cities, the local baseball team represented civic pride, to say nothing of representing at the same time the dreams of a great many young men who wished to be much more athletic than they actually were. In very small towns, its games were usually held in Farmer Jones's pasture, where the difficulty, in a hot moment of split-second play, of distinguishing between third base and some natural cow-pasture obstacle sometimes led to odd happenings; and in slightly larger places the county fairground or a recreational park at the end of the streetcar line provided the arena. In any case, muscular young men, wearing the singularly unbecoming uniforms that were standardized 75 years ago, presently took their positions on the grass, and the game was on.

It was, and still is, hotly competitive, and within reasonable limits anything goes. If the umpire (there was just one, in the old days) could be suborned to give all vital judgments in favor of the home side, all well and good; no one ever blushed to accept a victory that derived from an umpire's bias. If he could be intimidated, so that close decisions would go as the spectators wanted them to go, that also was good. This often happened; an umpire who decided a crucial play against the home team was quite likely to be mobbed, and few pictures from the old-time sports album are more authentic or more enduring than the vision of an umpire frantically legging it for the train, pursued by irate citizens who wished to do him great bodily harm. It took physical courage to render impartial judgments in old-time small-town baseball, and not all umpires were quite up to it.

If the umpire could be deceived while the game was on, that also was good. A man running from first to third on a base hit would cut twenty feet short of second base if he thought he could get away with it, and no one dreamed of censuring him for it. If an opposing player could be intimidated, so that he shirked his task, that was good, too. Not for nothing was the greatest baseball player who ever lived, Ty Cobb, famous for sitting on the bench just before the game sharpening his spikes with a file. An infielder, witnessing this, and knowing that Cobb was practically certain to ram those spikes into his calf or thigh in a close play, was apt to flinch just a little at the moment of contact, and out of that split second of withdrawal Cobb would gain the hair's edge of advantage that he needed. It was considered fair, too, to denounce an opponent verbally, with any sort of profane, personal objurgation that came to mind, on the off-chance that he might become unsettled and do less than his best. (This still goes on, like practically all of the other traditional things in baseball, and the "bench jockey"—the man who will say anything at all if he thinks it will upset an enemy's poise—can be a prized member of a big-league team even now.)

Baseball is conservative. What was good enough in Cap Anson's day is good enough now, and a populace that could stand unmoved while the federal Constitution was amended would protest with vehemence at any tampering with the formalities of baseball. It looks as it used to look; the batter still grabs a handful of dust between swings, the catcher still slams the ball over to third base after a strike-out, and the umpire still jerks thumb over right shoulder to indicate a put-out. (Dismayingly enough, some umpires now grossly exaggerate this gesture, using an elaborate full-arm swing, but possibly the point is a minor one.)

An inning begins; the pitcher takes his warm-up tosses, now as in the days half a century ago, and after three, four, or five of these he steps aside and the catcher whips the ball down to second base. The second baseman tosses it to the shortstop, two yards away, and the shortstop throws it to the third baseman, who is standing halfway between his own base and the pitcher's box; the third baseman, in turn, tosses it over to the pitcher, and the inning can get started. To vary from this formula is unthinkable; from the little leaguers up to Yankee Stadium, it is as one with the laws of the Medes and the Persians.

Then action: players shifting about, pounding their gloves, uttering cries of encouragement (which, like all the rest, are verbatim out of the script of 1900); and the batter approaches the plate, swinging two bats (another ironclad requirement), tossing one aside, planting his feet in the batter's box, and then swinging his single bat in determined menace. The fielders slowly freeze into fixed positions; for a moment no one anywhere moves, except that the pitcher goes into his stretch, takes a last look around, and then delivers—and then the frozen pattern breaks, the ball streaks off, men move deftly from here to there, and the quick moments of action are on.

In all of this there is unending fascination, coupled with the knowledge that wholly fantastic athletic feats may at any moment be displayed by any one of the players. Even an easy fly ball to the outfield or a simple grounder to short can call forth a nonchalant, effortless expertness that a man from another land would find quite incredible. (I once took an Englishman to see his first baseball game, and he was dumfounded by the simplest plays, marveling at what all the rest of us took for automatic outs.) In no contest can the split second be so important. A routine double play can make both outs with no more than half a second to spare, and if the half second is lost anywhere, the player who lost it will be derided for a clumsy oaf.

Primarily a team game, baseball is also the game for the individualist. The team play is essential, and when you watch closely you can see it, but the focus is usually on one man. A base runner streaks for second with the pitch, falls away while in full stride, and slides in in a cloud of dust, baseman stabbing at him with gloved hand, umpire bending to peer through the murk and call the play; an outfielder runs deep and far, arching ball coming down—apparently—just out of his reach, trajectories of fielder and baseball coming miraculously together at the last, gloved hand going out incredibly to pick the ball out of the air; a pitcher who has been getting his lumps looks about at filled bases, glowers at the batter, and then sends one in that is struck at and missed . . . always, some individual is trying for an astounding feat of athletic prowess and, now and then, actually accomplishing it.

Hence baseball celebrates the vicarious triumph. The spectator can identify himself completely with the player, and the epochal feat becomes, somehow, an achievement of his own. Babe Ruth, mocking the Chicago Cubs, pointing to the distant bleachers and then calmly hitting the ball into those bleachers, took a host of Walter Mittys with him when he jogged around the bases. (There is some dispute about this, to be sure; he was jawing with the Cubs, but purists say he did not actually call his shot. This makes no difference whatever.) It was the same when old Grover Cleveland Alexander, the all-but-washed-up veteran of many baseball wars, came into the seventh inning of a decisive World Series game, found the bases filled with Yankees, and struck out Tony Lazzeri, going on to win game and Series; and this was after a wearing night on the tiles, Alexander having supposed that his work was over until next spring. Many an aging fan shared in Old Alex's triumph.

These things are part of baseball's legend for the game never for-

gets its gallery of immortals. That it actually has a tangible Hall of
Fame, with bronze plaques to commemorate the greatest, is only part of
the story; the noble deeds of the super-players are handed down in bar-
side stories, year after year, losing nothing in the telling. Some of the
heroes have been supermen, in a way, at that. There was, for instance,
Shoeless Joe Jackson, barred from baseball in mid-career because he let
himself be bribed to help lose a World Series. (He did not do very well
at losing; even under a bribe, he batted .375 in that Series—a natural
hitter who just couldn't make himself miss even when paid to do so.)
A sand-lot pitcher tells of a day, a whole generation later, when, pitching
for a textile-mill team in the Carolinas, he found on the opposing team
none other than Jackson—a pathetic, fat, doddering wreck in his late
fifties, with a monstrous belly like some disreputable Santa Claus, still
picking up a few odd bucks playing semi-pro ball under an assumed
name. The young pitcher figured Jackson would be easy; a low inside
curve, coming in close to the overhang of that prodigious paunch, was
obviously the thing to throw. He threw, Jackson swung, and swung
as he used to thirty years earlier, and the ball went far out of the park,
one of the most authoritative home runs the young pitcher ever witnessed. Old Jackson lumbered heavily around the bases, and halfway
between third and home he turned to accost the young pitcher. "Son,"
he said, "I always could hit them low inside curves."

There were others cast in similar molds. . . . Rube Waddell, the
wholly legendary character who, when cold sober, which was not often,
may have been the greatest pitcher of them all: the man who now and
then, on a whim, would gesture the entire outfield off the premises
and then retire the side without visible means of support; Walter Johnson, who once pitched fifty-odd consecutive scoreless innings, and who
to the end of his days had nothing much in his repertoire except an
unhittable fast ball; Tris Speaker, who played such a short center field
that he often threw a batter out at first on what ought to have been a
legitimate down-the-middle base hit; and lean Satchel Paige, who in
his great days in the Negro leagues had a way of pointing to the shortstop and then throwing something which the batter must hit to short,
and who then would go on around the infield in the same way, compelling the opposition to hit precisely where he wanted it to hit. The
legends are, in some ways, the most enduring part of the game. Baseball
has even more of them than the Civil War, and its fans prize them
highly.

Under the surface, baseball is always played to a subdued but
inescapable tension, because at any second one of these utterly fabu-
lous events may take place. The game may be distressingly one-sided,

and the home team may come up in the ninth inning five runs behind, and in a clock game like football or basketball the margin would be physically unbeatable; but in baseball anything can happen, and the tiniest fluke can change everything. (Remember the World Series game the Yankees won when a Brooklyn catcher dropped a third strike with two men out in the ninth?) A commonplace game can turn into a hair-raiser at any moment, and things do not actually need to happen to create the suspense. A free-hitting, high-scoring game may be most eventful, but few strains are greater than the strain of watching a pitcher protect a 1–0 lead in the late innings of a routine game. Nothing, perhaps, actually happens—but every time the ball is thrown the game may turn upside down, and nobody ever forgets it.

All of this is built in, for the spectator. Built in, as well, is the close attention to records and statistics. Batting averages and pitchers' records are all-important; to know that a Rogers Hornsby, for instance, could bat more than .400 in three different years—that is, could average getting two hits for every five times he came to the plate, 154 games a year, for three years—is important. It has been suggested, now and then, that big league playing schedules be reduced from 154 games to some smaller figure, and the suggestion has always been howled down: it would upset all the averages. Unthinkable; how do you compare today's pitcher with Walter Johnson or Lefty Grove if today's pitcher plays in fewer games every year?

The circumstances under which baseball is played nowadays have changed greatly, to be sure. Less than half a century ago, every town that amounted to anything at all was represented in some league of professional players, and these leagues—the minor leagues, of hallowed memory—have been dissolving and vanishing, as more and more spectators get their games by television or by radio and ignore the local ball park. The Little Leagues have come up, and semi-subsidized sand-lot leagues, and even college baseball is here and there enjoying a new lease on life—after all, the new players in the big leagues have to come from somewhere, and besides, young Americans still like to play baseball; but the old pattern is gone, and even the major leagues themselves have undergone profound changes and, to a purist from the old days, are all but unrecognizable. Where are the St. Louis Browns, or the Philadelphia Athletics, or the Boston Braves—or, for the matter of that, even the magnificent New York Giants, and the Brooklyn Dodgers? Gone forever, to be sure, with new cities taking over, and with a few old-timers muttering that the last days are at hand.

Actually, the last days are probably a long, long way off, for baseball even in its modern guise has not changed in its essentials. It is a rough, tough game, encased by rules that were made to be broken if the breaking can be accomplished smoothly enough, a game that never quite became entirely respectable, a game in which nobody wants to do anything but win. It will undoubtedly be around for a good time to come, and it will continue, in spite of its own press agents, to be in truth the great American game.

Or so, at least, believes one old-time fan.

JOHN KEATS

The Call of the Open Road

ALL ADVERTISEMENTS show automobiles in unusual circumstances. They depict smiling, handsome people in evening clothes arriving in glittering hardtops beneath the porte-cocheres of expensive tropical saloons. A polished convertible, top down, filled with laughing young people in yachting costumes, whispers along an idealized shoreline. A ruggedly healthy Mom, Pop, Sis and Buzz smile the miles away as their strangely dustless station wagon whisks over the Rockies. Sometimes, automobiles strangely shine on pedestals; sometimes they slip through astral voids like comets. None of the advertisements show you and me in the automobile as most of us know it—that is, wedged in a fuming line of commuter traffic at 8:30 A.M., or locked in an even worse outbound line at 6 P.M.

A manufacturer, of course, would commit economic hara-kiri if he were to try to sell us a car on truthful grounds, for how could he ask anyone to pay $4,500 for a three-hundred-horsepower contraption on grounds that it would be used only two hours a day for 240 working days a year, and would at all other times—except briefly, on vacations —be parked in an expensive parking lot or sit depreciating at a curb? Would you buy such a car if it were truthfully put to you that the thing would cost you more than $9 an hour to use? No manufacturer in his right mind would plead with you to buy a luggage compartment only slightly smaller than Delaware in order that you could use part of this space just twice a year. Manufacturers know very well that the American automobile is not primarily a means of transportation and that it cannot be sold as such. Therefore, their advertisements invariably portray the automobile as A Flying Carpet—as a thing to sweep us off to ineffable lotus lands—and this, we discover, is the greatest lie of all. Yet, we cannot plead surprise, because—as a friend remarked—if we now suspect that our automobiles are overblown, overpriced monstrosities built by oafs for thieves to sell to mental defectives, it is only logical to expect that there is not much point in driving them, and that any place an automobile can go is probably not worth visiting. Nevertheless, the advertisements have a certain appeal, because the dream they represent once had substance. There was a time in man's memory when travel was exciting.

It is difficult to say just when the last shred of fun disappeared from the American highway. Some people think it was in 1927, when Henry Ford stopped making the Model T, but other authorities put the date in the late 1930s when the first national restaurant chains spread like plague. Speculation is idle, because we must accept things as they are, and there is no question today but that family travel in America is apt to be one of life's more crashing bores. Let me wipe off the lens a bit for a quick look at two generations of the Foresight family:

Early in the 19th century, Abel Foresight, his wife, Hope, and their children, Prudence, Faith and Jonah, set out from Morgantown, Pennsylvania, in a wagon. They chopped through forests, crept over mountains, forded floods, shot their suppers, struggled with savages, and trusted in God and in their strength to cross an unknown continent. They were more than a year en route, but the Foresight family arrived in California with the look of eagles in their eyes. Theirs was the age of travel adventure.

In the summer of 1958, Roger Foresight followed the path of his longfathers across his native land.

"We take the car it's cheaper," he told his wife June, in the curious English of his day. "You don't see the country you take the train or fly."

Whereupon, Roger gripped the Deep-Dish Command Wheel of his twenty-foot-long Flite-Flo Hacienda Wagon, stirred the Jet-Boom Eight's Power-Plus into life, pressed a master button that wound up all the Saf-T-Tint windows, adjusted the Koolaire to a desired temperature, pushed another button to bring the Flote-Fome seat to its proper level and distance, pressed yet another to cut in the Glyde-Ryde Dynamatic Turbo-mission, and swung away from his Cape Cod Tri-Level's Kar Porte to begin three thousand miles of driving pleasure.

A week later, the Foresights arrived on the opposite coast a little tired from sitting so long on foam rubber, but otherwise they were quite the same people who had left home. There was still that look of vague disappointment in their eyes, because Roger and June Foresight dwell in the tasteless, or Pablum, stage of family travel.

Several springs feed Roger Foresight's sense of disappointment. Even after the West was subdued and the automobile devised, there was a time when motoring was not dull and tasteless, and together with many Americans, Roger Foresight can remember it. Therefore, we can say that today's realities disappoint Foresight's memories. Next, we can say his disappointment was inevitable because Foresight was dead wrong in three major assumptions. He was wrong in imagining there might be some significant difference between New York and San Francisco, or indeed, that there might be any fundamental differences among any American cities. Oh, there are plenty of superficial differences, to be sure. San Francisco has hills and a lovely harbor and New York does not. Denver has a magnificent public park system and Chicago is simply a blot on the landscape. The point, however, is that the cultural anthropology of our cities is much the same; the life of the average citizen of City A is very like the life of the citizen of City B because the ecology of one big town is quite like that of any other, particularly in a nation of standard brands, chain stores and national fads. Neither you, nor I, nor Roger Foresight would be able to tell whether we were in Philadelphia or New York if we joined a crowd of shoppers in Gimbels, because the shoppers in Gimbels Philadelphia store look exactly like the shoppers in Gimbels New York store and come from the same economic classes, have the same kind of jobs and entertain much the same hopes of Eternity. No doubt there are many reasons for this situation, but one of the more massive seems to be the automobile, as we'll see in a moment. Meanwhile, allow me to suggest that Roger Foresight was also wrong in thinking he'd see more of the American continent if he drove. He was also hopelessly wrong in assuming that driving across the nation would be cheaper than flying or taking a train. Here are matters that merit investigation, so let's dispose of the easiest of them first, giving Roger Foresight the benefit of every doubt, even if he might not deserve it. Consider the matter of cost:

We remember the current national average operating cost of a $2,300 automobile is $.1042 per mile; thus the cost of driving the 3,030 miles between New York and San Francisco would be $315.72. (Roger's Flite-Flo Hacienda Wagon is a dreamboat in the $4,500 class, and it costs a good deal more than this to run, but we're going to give Roger all the breaks and use the low average figure.) He will have to drive 473 miles a day to make the trip in a week. If we can possibly imagine that he and June together can spend only $9 a day for food and only $5 a night for lodgings, it will cost them a rock-bottom $413.73 to make the trip—one way.*

The cost of two Pullman berths—lower berths—for the same trip is $374.62, and the Foresights would be only three days in transit. Even when we consider the outrageous prices of railroad dining car meals, and the necessary tips to porters, it would be cheaper for the Foresights to take the train.

An airline will sell Roger two one-way tickets from New York to San Francisco for $317.70, one meal included, and the trip takes half a day.

If we further presume the Foresights will return, we must note that there is no round-trip saving if they drive, but that there is a sub-stantial round-trip saving on air or rail transportation. Purely for argu-ment's sake, let's say that driving is no strain on the Foresights, and that time is no object. They are as insensate as two bags of wool. Even if we grant this preposterous assumption, the economics of the thing indicate the Foresights are silly to drive unless, perhaps, they like to throw their money away. Some people do. In fact, we find them buying Flite-Flo Hacienda Wagons. Nevertheless, we might imagine Roger Foresight to be a little disappointed to find that his trip cost him more than he had thought it would.

The major reason for the lackluster look in the Foresights' eyes, however, was their discovery that it is now possible to drive across the face of the nation without feeling you've been anywhere or that you've done anything. The Foresights remembered the first days of the twen-tieth century, when most Americans lived out their modest lives within five miles of the rumpsprung hamlets of their births. In those days, there was difference and variety in the land. Tennessee's troubadors were mercifully pent within Tennessee's forgotten hills, and did not wail and whine from every jukebox. A visible, palpable cultural dis-tinction then existed between Philadelphia and Chicago. In 1900, a man could cross the nation and smell different smells, taste different

---

* Obviously, few people would—yet some do—drive across the country in a week. I use seven days here to indicate this is the shortest possible time it would take you to drive if you traveled approximately 500 miles a day instead of setting a killing pace. The point to be made is that transcontinental driving is neither saving of time nor money.

To simplify the arithmetic in both regards, I've presumed the Foresights have no children. If you want to give them three kids, please reduce the driving time to include tinkle stops, imagine the traumatic experience of being cooped up in a car with three babies all howling at once, and add what you will for food and lodging.

foods, hear different accents and be cheated by different methods. Driving anywhere was almost as much of a demanding adventure as was waddling along in Abel's wagon. The hardy motorists took joy in being his own mechanic, and he was ever watchful for signs of trouble among the natives, for in those days rustics buried rakes tines-up in the dust of country lanes to puncture the tires of the devil-cart that frightened the horses.

As the automobile became more general, the various tumult of our native land subsided, and now that nearly everyone has at least one car, scarcely one American in fifteen lives anywhere near his birthplace, and Americans drift about their continent as easily as tumbleweeds, and with as much sense of direction or purpose. No matter. Like tumbleweeds, they may expect to find a congenial ecology wherever they go; one Howard Johnson restaurant is exactly like all the others.

If you fly across the nation, it is still possible to observe some variety, because you look down on a geological exhibit. The bones of the land are still apparent from ten thousand feet up. You can see rivers eating through the plains; see the mountains thrusting up from the dead shores of unknown epiric seas. At a convenient altitude, it is still possible to sense the majesty of old Abel Foresight's accomplishment; you are overwhelmed by America's space.

If you take the train, you have not the same Olympian perspective, but you can see more of the country than if you drive, because you rattle along miles of open landscape and you have some opportunity to look at it, for your view is not blocked by billboards and your attention is not commanded by the demands of the road.

The road. Ah yes, the road. Let us think of *this* together, you and I.

For centuries, "road" was a word of magic. Armies, gypsies, beggars, tinkers, peasants, merchants, highwaymen, scholars, minstrels and runaway apprentice boys were once found upon the road. As recently as fifty years ago, you could still build your house beside the road and be a friend to man, because mankind passed your doors. Today, this is not so. The road belongs entirely to the automobile, and he who builds his house beside it can only watch the Fords go by, because there is no human life on the road itself. Indeed, so mechanical, so abstract, so inhuman have our roads become that American drivers never think of passing the people ahead; they think of passing the car ahead.

If this point seems somewhat frivolous to us, it is by no means frivolous to occasional visitors from less peppy lands where horsepower is still a word relating to the power of a horse, and where the word "road" still has connotations of Pilgrim's Progress, or of the royal road to romance. Last year, America was host to one Dan Jacobson, a South African, who expressed his sense of bewilderment to the editors of *The Reporter* magazine.

"The six and eight lanes of traffic are flung into swathes of tar and concrete that fill the sky in loops and curves dwarfing even the city beneath them," Mr. Jacobson wrote. "There the roofs of the cars, curved like the wing cases of beetles, flash above the concrete parapets in a hundred different colors; there are no shops there, no billboards, there are no people and nowhere for people to walk but a kind of narrow catwalk along the side of the parapet where a man can clamber to the emergency telephones if his car breaks down. There, where there is no place for a man outside his moving car, the road reaches its purest, most abstracted state—it can be used for nothing but to carry cars from one end of its giant structures to the other. The colors are black and gray; from afar it is desolate and beautiful, but unlike a natural desert, it has no peace. . . ."

Significantly enough, Mr. Jacobson at no point suggests that man has anything to do with the road—not even with its creation. He reflects the road's sole concession to animal life is a catwalk—but this leads only to the telephone that summons help for the broken car. Mr. Jacobson was talking about the superhighway, or Autobahn, which is the road's ultimate abstraction, serving cars, not men. As the automobile evolved from Tin Lizzie to the overblown Cleopatra's barge we see today, she demanded wider, smoother, straighter roads, and every human juice was distilled from road building in order to accommodate the desires of the automobiles. The automobiles' demands constantly multiply faster than we can build Autobahns, however, and thus traffic engineers say that the U.S. Government's plans for new superhighways to be completed by the end of 1975 are already hopelessly inadequate in terms of the number and kind of automobile Detroit expects to spew forth in the next *twelve* years. Therefore, if our automania persists, we shall ever need ever wider roads and the townless superhighway, desolate as the desert Mr. Jacobson says it is, is clearly the shape of our future. A part of Roger Foresight's transcontinental journey was undertaken on such a road, and this is how it was for him:

His left leg kept falling to sleep because there was nothing for his left foot to do in the pushbutton Flite-Flo Hacienda Wagon. His neck grew stiff from having to hold his head fixed straight ahead as he stared down the endlessly unrolling straight strip of black tarmac. Traveling at speed, he dared not take his eyes from it. The banked, graded, militarily landscaped road was identical for all its fantastic length, and thus there was no new thing to entrance June Foresight's idle eyes. On this road, a thing as monotonous as an indoor track built for six-day bicycle races, the Foresights had no idea of miles because the scenery never changed. Thus, they kept track of time. It was so many hours from one town to another; from one service area to the next. All the service areas, with their uniform gas pumps and their identical restaurants and their identical jittery travelers, served to illustrate the proposition that America has achieved a peculiarly high degree of standardization in our time. Modern Americans that they were, it did not occur to June and Roger Foresight that there was anything odd in classifying food as a service.

The Foresights passed each Autobahn night in a neon-lit AAA-approved motel that was exactly like the motel of the night before and like the motel of the night to come, and thanks to television in every room, the Foresights never missed an instant of Mark Sade's coast-to-coast quiz show, *Can You Take It?* All along the everlasting monotony of the Autobahn, the same national voices beat into the Foresights' ears during the day, thanks to the miracle of the Flite-Flo's radio. Thus, Roger and June were spared the burden of having to think of something to say to each other as they hurtled across the continent, but even for souls more lost than they, a ride on the Autobahn is apt to be a journey in Limbo. No one can say it is in any way a pleasure to sit like a lump for endless hours while one speeds along in a vacuum, and no one does. Instead, the Foresights—and every other American user of Autobahns—say that *where* they want to go is far more important than the act of *going there*. This statement not only strips travel of at least half its pleasure, but it is as ironical as it is pitiful, as we will very shortly see.

Meanwhile, it is clear that not all American roads are Autobahns, but our secondary highways are just as devoted to the needs of the automobile. They are distinguished from Autobahns by a hardy species of anthropoid life that clings to their edges, just as weeds curiously flourish among the cindery desolation of railroad yards. Here, along the berms, are to be found the proprietors of cut-rate filling stations, the sellers of fried foods, the owners of ice-cream palaces shaped liked bulldogs, the concierges of the motels that Mr. J. Edgar Hoover regards as "camps of crime . . . little more than camouflaged brothels," the juke joints that sell knickknacks and balsam-stuffed pillows that say For Mother on one side and Souvenir of Lake On-Wee on the other. Here are the small businessmen who have put away their masks and riding boots to set up roadside garages. Here are the stands that sell hooked rugs, cut bait and plaster garden sculpture all at once. Here are the proprietors of junkyards and the businesses of those who tow broken cars out of the way of the cars that still work. Here are the birds that pick the crocodile's teeth; the pilot fish that flit ahead of the shark;

here are the practitioners of twentieth century symbiosis. Here, along the edges of America's highways, is the detritus of our century—the fields of burnt and rusting automobile carapaces; the billboards that suggest the only thing keeping you out of the voluptuous arms of a hot woman is your dreadful stench. Here are the broken beer bottles and the signs that ask you to help keep America green and the signs that strangely hope that Jesus saves. Here, in a word, is U.S. 1—perhaps from Philadelphia to Washington; from the old capital to the new.

The Foresights moved over these roads, too, and discovered that travel along them is merely an endless passage down an indefinitely extended, unplanned Main Street. It is disheartening to admit that America generally accepted the billboards and the brothels, the ice cream and the junk, long before it came to the conclusion that such a street with its innumerable entrances, exits, crossings, pull-offs, winking neon signs and varying speed limits was unsafe for the automobile and should therefore be abandoned. Yet, the fact that the cluttered two-way highway is unsafe is solely responsible for the present transition to the sterile Autobahn, and so we may say that even the last vestige of adventure—physical danger—may disappear from American motoring as our Pablum stage of travel wears on.

When Roger and June Foresight drove across the country, they ever felt time's winged chariot hurrying near, and thus they did not explore the only American roads that are neither boring nor blatant. In short, they did not travel our rural lanes, and it is a pity they did not, for they may never have a chance to see one again. Parochial politicians have already covered most of them with asphalt in a naked bid for the peasant vote, but until quite recently the little roads have been the quiet routes of reapers and wains, and the few automobiles to use them merely carried unsuccessful agriculturalists to the village post offices on the first of the month when the government checks arrive. Today, all this is rapidly changing. The back country roads have been discovered by the rich, who go wistfully popping and bouncing over them in their little foreign cars, still trying to discover the automobile's once-hinted promise of fun.

Unfortunately, the handwriting is on the wall. Within the next ten years, there won't be a lane in the land that lacks its Jaguar agency, its French restaurant and branch of Abercrombie & Fitch. Next will come the middle classes, aping their betters as is their wont, but demanding wider, straighter roads for their less agile Buicks, and the French restaurants will print menus in English and serve Parker House rolls. The country-day schools will appear, and the rich will be forced once again to search for private amusement in yet another corner of the world. By this time, the lower middle classes will be pushing in, as they do, and the former country lane will be well on the way to becoming the four-lane highway, lined with filling stations and leering with used car lots, connecting the housing development to the shopping center that offers plenty of everything and the best of nothing.

Thus we see that the smaller road, built more to the human scale, is inevitably de-humanized as the volume of traffic increases; the country lane of today is the cluttered highway of tomorrow and the abstract Autobahn of the day after. At this point, the triumph of the automobile is complete and the full attention of driver and passenger is directed to the automobile itself. From this point on, the only possible emotions available to the passengers are boredom or terror.

We note the Autobahn is somewhat safer for the automobile than the cluttered highway, but safety is always a relative term. It should be remembered that our automobiles are not built with safety in mind; quite the contrary; and you put your life in the automobile's trust the moment you leave your driveway, because the car was born accident-prone if not downright bloody-minded. In 1905, for instance, there were only two automobiles in the whole of the sprawling Kansas City area. Somehow, they managed to find one another and collide. Since then, a national folk saying has grown up, used whenever anyone wishes to cajole anyone else into a dangerous undertaking. The hazard, we say, is no greater "than crossing the street," and everyone knows what we mean. We mean to say the street is damned risky, and you have to have your wits about you to negotiate it in good health, but if you take every precaution and obey all the rules, you might just make it. Indeed, when Roger Foresight drove across America, he ran a much higher risk of disembowelment en route than did his ancestor Abel, who had to contend with the hostiles. It is possible to come to a sticky end at any moment through no fault of your own on the safest of our Autobahns, but as if determined that better roads will not reduce unduly the quality of danger, and so denude happy motoring of its one last thrill, Detroit keeps on producing faster, more powerful cars and shows an equal genius in making them progressively more collapsible. I beg you to recall the not-so-hard tops.

Curiously enough, the increasing power and speed of the automobile contains a contradiction. On the one hand, speed adds a quality of danger, but at the same time, speed helps to make auto travel even more bland, because whatever scenery there might have been between City A and City B passes faster than the passenger's eye can comprehend it, and speed requires the driver's eye to be fixed on the unrelenting road. This is why Keats' Law of Autobahn Travel says the only possible emotions are terror or boredom, depending on the individual phlegm quotient of the traveler, as influenced by speed. We state this mathematically in two formulae:

Let T stand for terror and IPQ for individual phlegm quotient. R stands for rate, or speed, and B for boredom. The formulae will now read: T equals IPQ times R; B equals IPQ divided by R. It will be seen that speed is the crucial factor, no matter what the IPQ.

These formulae most usually apply to visiting Europeans, however, because the IPQ of most Americans is 0. Most Americans, like the Foresights, are content to work out the more familiar formula, Distance equals Rate times Time. Like the Foresights, they never think of, much less try to solve the equation in terms of Distance. They always seek Rate in order to find Time. International marriages often demonstrate conflicts of attitudes, and fortunately we have an example close at hand.

Muriel, an English girl, was only a few days arrived in America when her Yankee bridegroom told her they would have supper the following day with friends who lived thirty miles away. Early the following morning, Muriel began packing for the trip, selecting clothes and putting up a picnic lunch. She envisioned a pleasant outing along placid lanes. She looked forward to savoring new sights; to see something of the natives and of their curious customs and dress. Muriel dreamed of a picnic beside a stream at midday; of a little post-prandial nap with her love in the shade of the trees; then to taking high tea at an American inn, and ultimately arriving at their hostess' house in time to dress for a champagne supper—staying the night and returning the following day. Now, Muriel is as good at arithmetic as anyone, but it never occurred to her to think of a supper invitation in terms of D = RT. She had anticipated a civilized little holiday on the continental order, where the distance to be traveled is something to be explored and enjoyed. Therefore, she was somewhat startled when her bridegroom, used to dividing America's Distance by the automobile's Rate, slipped her the word in terms of Time. He solved the formula in his head, automatically.

"Say, honey," he said, "I got noos for you. It on'y takes fordy minnits to get there."

Now, wiser in the ways of Ammedica, Muriel understands. One does not sup in Ammedica; one eats. One does not cover distance; one travels through time, and the sooner the better, because the distance is such a bore with nothing much to see if the billboards let you see it. Her husband always puts it thus:

"You wanna get there, don't you?"

A new veteran of America's roads, Muriel sometimes agrees with him, but most often she says, "Why don't we just stay home?"

We must admit Muriel has a point, the point being that there isn't much point in going to, or being in any place in America other than where you happen to find yourself at the moment, and we have the automobile to thank for this. We have seen what the automobile has done to the road, but now let's look at what it has done to our cities and to our vacation resorts. Perhaps then we will better understand Muriel's resignation and that dull look of disappointment in the Foresights' eyes.

On their way between New York and San Francisco, Roger and June Foresight passed through Cleveland, Chicago, Hannibal, St. Joseph, Denver, Salt Lake City, Reno and Sacramento. They could tell when they were leaving a town because little pennants began to appear on the gasoline stations at the city limits, and when the Foresights next saw pennants on gas stations, they realized they were approaching another city—not a new city, mind you, but just another one.

Had the Foresights wished, they might have reflected that a curious kind of national square dance goes on night and day in downtown Cleveland, in downtown Denver, in downtown Anywhere, U.S.A. Stop! the lights say, and twenty million automobiles jerk to a halt. Walk! the lights say, and seventy million pedestrians obey. Go! the lights say, and twenty million automobiles lurch ahead. Necks snap, eyes pop, legs flex, lights blink, whistles blow, horns honk, fumes choke, and we call this civilization. From time to time we are asked to defend it.

Obviously, this civilization is exclusively designed to meet the demands of our automobiles, and since all automobiles have the same demands, all our cities are built alike. All of them tend to become as inhuman and as abstract as the Autobahn that struck poor Mr. Jacobson all of a heap.

It remained for *Yank*—a soldier-edited, Army-sponsored magazine —to drive the point home during World War II. Thinking to remind the brave soldier boys of Mom, Sis, and the Girl Next Door, *Yank* decided to run pictures of sundry American Main Streets. Several hundred photographs were selected, whereupon one sly editor suggested running a number of uncaptioned photographs on the same page, challenging the readers correctly to identify their home towns. The venture was a morbid success, for devil a soldier could find devil a bit of difference among the pictures, and the nasty suspicion grew that *Yank* had merely taken several snapshots of the same street full of automobiles from several minutely different angles. Few believed *Yank's* answer to its puzzle was on the up-and-up.

If all our downtowns are somewhat surrealistic landscapes populated by automobile-dominated automatons, what can we say of the suburban housing developments which fester around the edges of these civic wounds? Here are mantraps as devoid of originality as anything that ever rolled off a Detroit assembly line. Here, too, are robot populations that are slaves to the automobiles that make the developments possible in the first place. A housing development anywhere is—in two dirty words—a car pool.

If in traveling from coast to coast, the Foresights had merely seen more mechanical roads, more mechanical Main Streets, more mass-produced suburbs and more mechanical people riding in machines to their mechanical tasks, we might reasonably expect them to be entitled to a little routine disappointment on discovering that New York is just a larger version of San Francisco, except for superficial, or detailed differences, particularly if they had misty memories that some kind of real difference once existed. They might have wondered, privately, if their trip had really been necessary. All this is as easy for us to see as it is discouraging, but wait—a more massive disappointment clamors for attention. Suppose the Foresights had more than seven days to spend on themselves. Let's say they floated free as disembodied spirits, seeking out those lotus lands the automobile advertisements seem to guarantee as part of the purchase price. Let us imagine the Foresights at Cape Cod.

On Cape Cod, the Foresights found the natives much the same as natives anywhere else in America—the Cape Codders' beady little eyes glittered through their glasses as they smiled the empty smile of commerce and made change at their cash registers. The tourists were gaudy blotches of color moving on crowded sidewalks; there was a honk of horns in the street; there was a frenzy of fat ladies in shorts and thin ladies in dirndls; a coming and going of paunchy, knock-kneed men in Bermuda shorts and polo shirts. There were up-tilted sun-glasses everywhere, and shops where you could buy souvenir postcards of places you had never seen and would never visit, and other postcards that built little jests around the presence of wasps in the outhouse. Cape Cod was a flow of hot children, an ebb of exhausted mothers, a drift of people walking in between people who were taking pictures of each other. Cape Cod was waves of juke boxes, Coca-Cola, suntan lotion, high prices, sand in the shoes, twenty-three flavors of ice cream and there was one peculiar odor which, from time to time, ate through the grease smoke of the restaurants and the exhaust fumes of the automobiles. A child asked, "What's 'at funny smell?"

"It's the sea," his mother explained.

At Ausable Chasm, there was not the disquieting smell of the sea, but a fungus-scent of damp growths in the narrow gorge, and girls seeking immortality added their names in lipstick to the thousand other names on the rocky walls. Otherwise, the Foresights found Ausable Chasm to be like Cape Cod in all significant respects, and when they drove to the top of Mount Washington, they found the same tourists, the same natives, the same indigestibles, and the same souvenir post-cards a few thousand feet above sea level.

Of course, the Foresights could have gone to the Catskills where the planned entertainment is so well planned that nobody has a chance to be alone or to do anything but follow the leader through a round of merriment that includes wearing funny hats and blowing tinsel horns. Or, they could have gone to the Golden West, to join the fantastic line of automobiles slowly inching along the precipice of Yellowstone Canyon. Or, perhaps, they could have sought out some sylvan retreat in Minnesota, to join the hundreds of other people who were either water-skiing on the lake or throwing beer cans into it.

It would not matter where the Foresights drove to their vacation. The scenes everywhere are much the same, because where one auto-mobile can go, all other automobiles *do* go, and wherever the auto-mobile goes, the automobile's version of civilization surely follows. To be sure, there are still some vacation resorts not yet in a stage of full development, but there are none in a stage of *arrested* development.

Twenty years ago, the slogan, See America First, still had some point. Nowadays, the fact is that if you've seen one part of America, you've seen it all. The automobile did not put the adventure of travel within reach of the common man. Instead, *it first gave him the oppor-tunity to make himself more and more common,* so that when he reached the point in his development where he could find leisure for travel, the lotus lands had disappeared *because he was already there.*

Still, it cannot be said that the common man knows this. We find him constantly trying to pretend otherwise. Who, for instance, do you think really is in that advertised hardtop that swirls to a stop beneath the porte-cochere of the expensive tropical saloon?

Queen Marie of Roumania?

No.

It is merely Roger and June Foresight, or perhaps even Tom and Mae Wretch, listlessly fetching up at one more deadfall—this one in Miami—there to try to escape for a few numbing hours from the fan-tastic boredom of aimless wandering in the automobile age. They seek surcease in the familiar national joys of tough steaks, cigarette smoke, watered drinks, insolent service, padded bills and a noisy band.

Man, they say, is really living it up these days.

Essays of Our Time I ● *Part* 4

RUSSELL LYNES *is the managing editor of* Harper's Magazine. *A shrewd and witty observer of the American scene, he popularized the terms "high-brow," "middle-brow," and "low-brow" in a book that has become a classic commentary on American social classes,* The Tastemakers. *His most recent volume is* A Surfeit of Honey.

GEOFFREY GORER, *a social anthropologist, studied at Cambridge, the Sorbonne, and at the Universities of Berlin and Florence before he published his* African Dancers. *He also studied at Columbia University before he joined its staff. In 1950 he returned to England, bought a farm in Sussex, and devoted himself to writing, gardening, and farming. His best-known work is the informed and perceptive* The American People.

E. E. CUMMINGS *(who never uses capitals in his name) has, like Jean Cocteau, been interested throughout his life in a variety of artforms, ranging from drawing to drama. His reputation, however, is based mainly upon his poetry. Among his prose writings is the excellent war novel* The Enormous Room. *He was educated at Harvard and is a long-time resident of Greenwich Village in New York.*

ALDOUS HUXLEY, *novelist, journalist, and essayist, is the grandson of the great Victorian scientist Thomas Huxley. He abandoned his plans for a medical career when his eyesight became weak, and turned to writing witty, biting satires on the disillusioned and decadent intellectuals and society of England in the 1920s. Later he became interested in pacificism and Indian mysticism. In the late 1930s he took up residence in California and has written scenarios for Hollywood. His most popular book in the United States remains* Brave New World.

RUSSELL LYNES

Teen-agers in the Looking Glass

THE NUMBER OF 13-year-olds is increasing at a rate twenty times faster than the rest of the population. "Between 1958 and 1960," a recent report of the David L. Babson Company of Boston says, "the number of children crossing the 13-year-old threshold will rise by nearly 40 per cent. By 1965 there will be a 35 per cent increase in the 14-17 age group." The total population grows by a comparatively sluggish 2 per cent a year. We are obviously reaping the whirlwind of post-World War II romance.

One of the specters that haunt our time is the sprawling expansion of the population, and it is more and more difficult not to picture the future as though it were going to be life in a sardine can. If the figures on the teen-age population are correct (and they must be), it's going to be a boisterous, noisy, squirming can indeed.

There are those who view this prospect with alarm for they fear that civilization, as we know it, will be swept away by juveniles—if not entirely delinquent, then at least objectionable. Others, who have a hand in the teen-ager's pocket, consider the explosion the best sort of news. It seems to me unlikely that civilization is doomed, at least not by teen-agers, and I would like to suggest that if we want to know what the teen-agers will do to us, we should look at ourselves.

In all the brouhaha about teen-agers we are inclined to forget, it seems to me, that they are primarily reflections of us, our foibles and fumblings and aspirations, our fears and frustrations, our hopes and our beliefs. They are, in effect, a magnifying mirror of their elders—like a shaving mirror in which our eyes seem to bulge, our pores to be extinct volcanoes, and our eyebrows thickets of thistles.

Consider their rebellious natures. Of a New York Times Youth Forum last year it was reported: "A group of high school students said * * * that teen-agers were increasingly rebellious toward authority—especially parental authority. And the tension behind teen-agers' attitudes comes from a lack of close understanding with their parents." The students also blamed this rebelliousness on "the terrible age we live in" and the "looseness of family ties."

This is where we come in. These are not things the teen-agers thought up for themselves; they are ideas that have been impressed on them by the rest of us. We have drummed into their heads their "need to be understood," and they would be less than human not to use this ready-made excuse as an escape hatch for their natural high spirits.

A few years ago two revealing studies of teen-agers appeared, one of them something of a shocker, the other reassuring. They both throw some light on ourselves. The first was a book called "The American Teen-ager," a summary for the general reader of the findings of a fifteen-year investigation of teen-agers made at Purdue University under the direction of Dr. H. H. Remmers. The second was called "Adolescent Girls" and was a study made for the Girl Scouts by the Survey Research Center at the University of Michigan.

From "The American Teen-ager" one gets the superficial impression that our youngsters are monsters. (One also gets this impression from the newspapers, of course.) Teen-agers believe, the book says, in wire-tapping, in search without warrant, in "censorship of books, newspapers, magazines and other media as protection of the public against improper ideas." Furthermore, they believe that "most people aren't capable of deciding what's best for themselves," and they "see no harm in the third degree." Not all of them, to be sure, but a good many more than half of them.

I find this rather chilling, less because of what it says about the teen-agers than what it says about their parents. But the Girl Scouts' report takes a somewhat more optimistic view.

Their study found that by and large the youngsters of this era are "conservative." Far from being rebellious, the study exposed them as idealistic and practical, more eager than their mothers had been for advanced education, but not, in general, wanting to be high-powered executives or movie stars. Fewer than a fifth of them had a good thing to say for "going steady." In many respects they are more independent than their mothers were at the same age. They have weekly allowances that give them more freedom to choose their fun; they have part-time jobs, and they play a larger role in making family plans. The attitude of the family has come a long way since the "children should be seen and not heard" era. No one would now say, as my wife's grandmother used to, that there was nothing to do with children but "put them in a barrel and feed them through the bunghole until they're 21."

Somewhere along the line we stopped thinking of teen-agers as just young people in transition between childhood and the state of being "grown up," and we began to regard them as a minority pressure group in our society. We now look on them not as just "kids," as we used to, but as a sub-culture with a powerful effect on the culture as a whole.

You will look in vain (or at least I have looked in vain) for refer-

ences to "teen-agers" in the literature of my parents' day. You will find
"youngsters" and "schoolboys" and "schoolgirls," but you will not find
teen-agers as a group, treated as thought they were something between
menaces and the hope of the world, a class by themselves, a threat to
adult sanity.

The change came during and after the second World War, the
result of the dislocation of families both physically and spiritually. Children were asked to adjust to change rather than to continuity, to pulling
up stakes rather than to putting down roots. They began to look more
than ever to their contemporaries for security, and they began to look
for their own set of rules to live by. The practice of "going steady," for
example, was an attempt to establish formal relationships that promised
some sort of continuity and sense of belonging to some one person.

The songs popular with youth, you may have noticed, belie the
old Tin Pan Alley cliché that a hit can't be made on the theme of
married love. As Arnold Shaw has pointed out, "Honeycomb" and
"Kisses Sweeter than Wine," both songs of marriage, have been taken
to the hearts of teen-agers whose popular hits are "a growing literature
of * * * protest." "Born Too Late," they sing, and "Why Won't They
Understand?"

At the same time they want to be a self-sufficient and rebellious
group, they reach out for a hand to guide them. Their accusation that
adults "fail to understand" them is a reflection of our "wanting to understand," and their "rebelliousness" is, in part at least, a reflection of our
fairly new belief in "permissiveness" and in our encouraging them to
make up their own minds. They seem to be in a terrible hurry to be
grown-up, to have grown-up respect paid to them, at the same time
that they resent the group they most want to be part of—a not uncommon human condition.

They have reason to resent us, and if the reflection of ourselves
that we see in them is not a pretty one, we should not be surprised.
Let's look a little deeper into the mirror of our society and see theirs.

There was a time not long ago when parents not only preached
the virtues of work but practiced them. The work week was ten or fifteen hours longer than it is now for father, and his day off each week
was a restorative to enable him to do a better job on the other six days.
Now leisure has become a kind of job in its own right, and it is going
to become still more of a job. When the work week shrinks, as economists say it will, to twenty hours, it is going to be difficult indeed for
father to preach to his children the old gospel that "the devil finds work
for idle hands." There is plenty of evidence around us now of what
happens to young people deprived of the opportunity to work and with-

out the resources, either cultural or social, to put their time to good use. But time on parental hands has still further effects. At its worst it is corrosive and it is stultifying. It passively accepts what is put before it. It wallows in ways to make time pass—hours of sitting before the television or in aimless puttering. Or it can be dangerously aggressive against society, or against self, as in dope addiction or alcoholism.

Less spectacular, but also corrosive, undirected leisure takes itself out in consumption for consumption's sake, in buying gadgets that save time, when time is the thing that least needs saving for the already time-ladened. It shows itself in ostentation and in competition with one's neighbors. Everyone wants to be the biggest Jones in the block. These are the lessons that the young learn when leisure is not constructive and does not enrich the spirit. It can, of course, be otherwise, but it is the parents who show the direction.

There is another direction they show. A good deal of journalistic space is occupied these days by articles about the number of young people who cheat on exams. Is this, after all, very different from padding an expense account or, more important, shading the truth on an income-tax return? If colleges and universities promote gifts in such a way that it is sometimes possible for a donor to make money by giving gifts to them, doesn't the line of academic honesty become a little blurred?

Or take another matter that is related to schools. It is not uncommon today to find youngsters who, when they have graduated from high school, wished they had been made to work harder. Why? Suddenly adults have been spurred into believing that only education will save us from lagging behind the Russians; suddenly bright students have a new status which a few years ago they sadly lacked—often to the point of being ostracized by their contemporaries. The "grind" and the "brightie" were looked down upon, a reflection of intellectual distrust on the part of parents. Now the winds blow in a different direction.

Or take the shibboleth of "conformity" with which the critics of our society plague us. (In my opinion this is a convenient tag that has been greatly overused to describe one aspect of a highly industrialized nation.) How is the teen-age custom of "going steady" a reflection of our own insecurity? To what extent is it, as I have suggested, an attempt to inject a kind of formality into relationships among young people that they miss in this age of informality?

The Girl Scouts may say that they are against it, but it has become a tribal custom of the young that they observe with almost universal respect all the same.

We are inclined to be indulgent about the hero-worship of the teen-ager for the movie glamour boys, for the Presleys and the James Deans and Eddie Fishers and Ricky Nelsons. We should be. We are hero-worshipers ourselves. It is evident in our political attitudes, in the numbers of us who don't even bother to vote, presumably because we are willing to "leave it to the boss." It is evident in our reverence toward leaders of business and industry, toward scientists, toward anybody who we think can lead us by the hand through the maze of complications that beset us.

To what extent is our fear of the Russians, for example, responsible for the teen-ager's belief in censorship, in wire-tapping, in search without warrant? If we are worried, as we should be, about their attitudes toward personal liberties, hadn't we better look to our own?

It is easy to take this subculture, this minority group, the teen-agers, and read our characters and future in them as though they were tea leaves. We can see adumbrated in them our attitudes toward religion, toward the arts and toward education more clearly than we can by looking at ourselves. We are likely to be more indulgent in looking at ourselves than at them; we smooth over our own exaggerations while we view theirs with alarm.

But I can see no reason why the simple statistical fact that there are going to be a great many more teen-agers in the next few years should be cause for anything more than the usual alarm. Unquestionably they will cause problems, just as we caused problems when we were teen-agers. But they will also give delight. There will be more noisy households than we are accustomed to, more telephones endlessly tied up, more records strewn around the living-room floor, more starry-eyed young lovers, more hard questions to answer, more nonsensical fads to throw up the hands about.

There will be something that will take the place of rock 'n' roll, bobby socks, and hot rods, something that will seem ludicrous to those who will have recently grown out of their teens into adulthood, and alarming to the parents who have to put up with it.

Possibly I am lucky. I have just lived through the teen-ages of a son and a daughter. There were moments when I thought murder was too good for them; there were moments when they thought murder was much too good for me. Sometimes their anguish was my anguish; sometimes their cussedness was my fury; occasionally their pleasure was my despair. But I saw myself sometimes distorted, sometimes all too clearly, in them as a mirror. I suspect I learned from them as much as I taught them, and I wouldn't have missed it for anything.

GEOFFREY GORER

Success and the Dollar

FOR EVERY RIGHT-THINKING American the object of life—indeed almost the justification for living—is to be a success, to "make good." To make good things, and more of them, is the best and most concrete way of making good, and is the reason for the very high prestige and respect accorded to the successful businessman, manufacturer, and engineer. But not all people can make things, and everyone should make good. When there are no things, how can one be sure that a person is a success?

This could be a very great problem in America because of the enormous diversity of pursuits inherent in a complex society, and because there is no accepted hierarchy of social values. Compared with the situation in Europe, the contrast between the prestige inherent in different professions and occupations is relatively slight. A few vocations have relatively low social prestige, especially when their esteem is compared with European countries—politics, the civil service, peacetime soldiering, teaching for men (it is essentially a somewhat feminine pursuit)— but this is because they are thought to be safe and easy, demanding too little initiative and tainted with the suspicion of authority, rather than from any absolute standards. Other things being equal, clean work is preferable to dirty work, a white-collar job to a shirt-sleeves job. But what makes other things equal? With the increasing lack of emotional involvement in most work, there is only one lowest common denominator by which jobs can be compared, by which success in one pursuit can be compared with success in quite a different one, and that is the social value accorded to each; and in a relatively unstructured commercial society this can only be measured in one way: in dollars.

From one aspect, dollars can be considered an adult equivalent of the marks and grades which signified the school child's relative position in regard to his fellows. An adult's income shows his rating in relation to his fellows, and a relatively good income is as much a matter for legitimate pride and boasting as getting A's in all subjects on one's report card. It is an outward and visible sign that one has striven successfully.

It should be emphasized that incomes are normally judged from a relative and not from an absolute standpoint. Grades are relative within the class: to get all A's in the first grade is as meritorious as to get all A's in the twelfth, but absolutely this does not mean that the work of the first grader is equal in value to the work of the twelfth grader; so, in the same way, the young doctor or typist is not measured against John D. Rockefeller, Jr., or Doris Duke (or whoever today has the highest income in the United States) but against other doctors starting in practice at the same time, other typists who have been in the office about the same time. Competition is still primarily among near equals.

The analogy with school life can be carried further. Just as in school, success in one grade qualifies one for entry into the tougher competition of the next grade, and so on indefinitely, so success in one area of adult life qualifies one for competition in the next "income bracket" or professional group. Success is always relative, never absolute. There are practically no positions in American life where it will be generally conceded that a person has achieved final success and need make no further effort. There is always a higher grade.

In childhood and youth good grades in school were rewarded by the love and praise of the parents, especially the mother; and consequently good grades quickly came to symbolize a promise of love. Dollars in adult life would seem to have something of the same function, signs that one is worthy of love and should receive it. And just as most Americans are insatiable for the personal signs of friendship and love, so do many appear insatiable for the dollars which are also the promissory notes of love. In the biographies of many of the conspicuously successful, a recurring theme is the stern upbringing or harsh childhood which forced them early to seek success.

In adult life there is one important modification in relative rating which is not easily paralleled from school: the past is an important factor in assessing present performance. Where incomes and positions are equal, greater respect is usually accorded to the man who has started with fewer advantages in parental wealth, education, and opportunity; outside the South and, to a much lesser extent, New England, Mr. Bounderby is more worthy of respect than Mr. Gradgrind.

This "rating" aspect of money is for Americans, at least for the two-thirds who are not "ill-fed, ill-clothed, ill-housed," at least as important as any of the uses to which it can be put. Of course the purchasing power of the dollar is important for securing the basic necessities of life (and these are variously defined); but once these have been secured, its social value is at least as great as its purchasing power.

It is this doubly symbolic value of the dollar which makes the American attitude toward money so paradoxical to the European. To phrase it briefly, Americans talk far more about money than Europeans and generally value it far less. Incomes and prices are of great social importance for rating people and goods in relation to one another; until you know the income bracket of a stranger, and he knows yours, your mutual relationship is unsatisfactory and incomplete; and the easiest method of evaluating a strange article and putting it into relationship with other articles is to know what it cost. As a result, money and prices figure greatly and consistently in American writing and conversation; the income bracket of an individual or the cost of an article is a necessary and useful piece of social information; to inform a stranger on such points, when he is likely to be ignorant, is an act of neighborliness.

It is a great mistake, however, to deduce from the fact that Americans pay so much verbal attention to money the supposition that they give corresponding importance to the possession of money, as such. The contrary is more nearly true; compared with most Europeans, Americans rate the possession, and above all the retention, of money very low. Income—the money that comes in to you—fixes your relative position in regard to your fellows; but once it has done that, it has fulfilled its chief purpose, and there is no deep emotional reason for retaining it. Saving, except for the purpose of putting money back in one's business and thereby increasing one's future income, is not laudable; a prudent man will have some cushion against unexpected illness or misfortune; but saving, as an aim in itself, is not regarded as praiseworthy today, a marked change from earlier attitudes. The contrast with the attitude of such peoples as the Scots or the French, for whom saving has or had an almost automatic virtue, is very marked.

The financial duties expected of an American whose income exceeds his necessary expenditures are defined and limited. He should "carry" enough life insurance to make certain that, should he die suddenly, his wife and children should not be in want; he should, either by insurance, or by saving, provide for his children the best possible education, preferably better than he had enjoyed himself; he should not let his parents, or his spouse's, suffer actual want; and he may buy an annuity against his retirement. That is all. There is no demand or expectation that an American, whatever his fortune, should leave substantial sums to his children; provided he has brought them to adulthood with every advantage he can give them, he has done the whole of his duty toward them. Indeed, inherited money can in some respects be regarded as a handicap; with such a head start, a man has to make correspondingly much more before he can be considered to have made good, to be a success. With the partial exception of New York and its satellite resorts, there is no place or position anywhere in American life for the young man of inherited means who is not gainfully employed. Before the war a small number used to emigrate to Europe, where there was still a cosmopolitan leisure class; but these were exceptions, and the general practice was and is for millionaires' and multimillionaires' sons to go into business (preferably one with which the father has no connection, to avoid the suspicion of favoritism, of having things easy) and make their own money, prove their own worth in the competition of life.

It can be said that, as a general rule, the acquisition of money is very important to Americans, but its retention relatively unimportant. One's worth is confirmed by every extra dollar one brings in, and therefore, in the way of business, the harder the bargain one strikes the more one is worthy of respect, and so of love; but once the money has been brought in, it loses much of its emotional importance; it can be spent, or given away or, figuratively, thrown into the gutter without deep involvement or regret; it only becomes important again if it is used in another business transaction, for then it again becomes a test of one's shrewdness, one's acumen, one's success.

This attitude is almost certainly an important component in American gambling. American gambling differs from European not in its diffusion—there is probably a greater proportion of small gamblers in most European countries—but in its intensity. Probably because of the relative unimportance of retaining money, Americans at nearly all income levels will risk a far greater proportion of the money they hold in wagers and gambling games than most of their European equivalents. The term of opprobrium for a timid gambler—"piker"—has no common equivalent in any Western European language. In gambling "for fun" most Americans will risk proportionately far more than most Europeans. To determine that one's "luck is in" is as good a use for money as another.

Gambling is also a respected and important component in many business ventures. Conspicuous improvement in a man's financial position is generally attributed to a lucky combination of industry, skill, and gambling, though the successful gambler prefers to refer to his gambling as "vision." Like the gambler "for fun" the American businessman is generally prepared to take proportionately far greater risks than his European equivalent.

Gambling apart, few people in the world are less involved in the destination of their money than the Americans, provided there is no suggestion of a business transaction, in which one's ego is necessarily implicated; and no people in the world give their money away with greater ease.

American generosity and hospitality are rightly famous. In no other country does the majority of the citizens give so easily and freely, almost without counting the cost. In the summer of 1940, when there were plans for sending to America large numbers of English children from the threatened invasion, a quite astonishing number of American families from every region and every income level were ready to accept, as it seemed then for the rest of their lives, responsibility for threatened children whom they had never seen and of whom they knew nothing except that they were threatened. Similarly, when Tokyo was partially destroyed by the 1923 earthquake, it was in great part rebuilt by money given by millions of Americans, the vast majority of whom had never seen a Japanese. These instances are conspicuous, but they could be reduplicated very many times. For any cause that can be considered worthy, Americans will give their money with the greatest generosity, and not merely out of their superfluity; in many cases such gifts are made at the expense of considerable personal sacrifice.*

This great and ungrudging generosity is limited by one fear: the suspicion that one may be being exploited, "made a sucker." Maybe the claimant on one's charity is feckless rather than in want, wishing to live lazily on the money one has worked so hard to get, refusing to make the efforts and undergo the privations one has had to make and undergo oneself.

This suspicion is very general, especially among American men (it would seem to be much less strongly developed among women). The reason for the general prevalence of this fear is obscure to me; I would suggest tentatively that it is linked with the already discussed obsessive American fear of lapsing into passivity; of being exploited physically in the one case, financially in the other. Among the American men of my acquaintance, those who were most prone to such suspicions in the financial sphere showed clear indications of having such unconscious fears also; and the metaphors so frequently used in such contexts (America being sexually exploited) bear out the supposition.

When this suspicion is not aroused, American money is given freely and without afterthought, and American hospitality is without self-consciousness and with a certain pride. In those houses—the vast majority—where people normally eat in the kitchen (or a dining nook

---

* Incidentally, Americans give their money with very much greater ease than they give their food. Whereas money, once it has been acquired, loses much of its importance, the quasi-magical values of good American food remain constant; money, in most cases, can be replaced with relative ease; but if there were a shortage of food one would not only be depriving oneself, one would be threatening the future of one's children.

just off the kitchen) the stranger is warmly welcomed, without ostentation and without shame. In the dining-room class pretension and the maneuvering for social advantage are more likely to be evident; after a certain financial status has been obtained and demonstrated, other methods of scoring relative success may be called into play: ancestry, creed, length of residence of oneself or one's ancestors in the town, in the state, in the country can all be used as scoring points in the fight for success once the financial status is, or has been, established.

The chief emotional value of one's money income is as a sign of one's relative success; but though in theory a certified pay check would be adequate, in practice one can only demonstrate the fact that one has made good by conspicuous expenditure. Consequently every possession becomes doubly important, not only for its own use or beauty, but as a palpable symbol of its owner's or purchaser's relative position in the competition of life. A new car is not desirable and enviable merely because it is better (few Americans would question that "new" and "better" were synonyms) but also because it is an outward and visible sign of an inward and spiritual grace; the man who can afford to acquire a new car demonstrates to the world that he is making good—and "good" has a moral as well as a material significance.

The pattern of competitive conspicuous expenditure is summed up in one current, almost proverbial, phrase: "Keeping up with the Joneses." One significant implication of this phrase is that competition could not easily be less clearly defined. The Joneses are undefined regionally, socially, locally, ethnically (Anglo-Saxon surnames were often provided by the immigration officers to new arrivals with unpronounceable names; it would be rash to suppose that an American Jones had Welsh ancestors); they are the people one has to keep up with, and only inspection can demonstrate in a given instance who they are.

As a general rule it can be said that in the smaller towns (up to, say, fifty thousand inhabitants) and in the suburbs the Joneses are one's neighbors, in the larger towns, people engaged in similar pursuits and holding similar positions. Each family has its own "Joneses" and is itself a "Jones" for others. Just as in the childhood world of the play group, the parents of one's children's playmates set a standard with which it was difficult not to conform, so, in the adult world of conspicuous expenditure, the Joneses influence, not only how much one will spend, but what one will spend it on.

This is true at almost every level of income and social aspiration. At the lowest level of subsistence the possibility of choice is obviously extremely limited; and among the very rich, or those whose ancestors were very rich, the pattern takes an idiosyncratic form. Between these two extremes, the proper expenditure at any level of income in any given area is defined with remarkable exactness and precision.

In any city the price and the social value (which may not completely correspond) of any house on any street is well known to the greater number of the inhabitants, and this information will be freely passed on to any stranger. As a consequence the neighborhood and the house in which a person lives are an immediate and patent sign of his income, and income, far more than taste, will in most cases under normal circumstances indicate where a person's residence shall be. Except among the very rich or the descendants of rich ancestors (and with the partial exception of anomalous intellectuals and artists) the place where one lives is valued as a symbol of one's current economic and social position, and not (at least in the first instance) for any amenities inherent in it or associations attached to it. The majority of Americans, at least until they near the retirement age, regard themselves as transient inhabitants of their house or apartment, ready to move to the bigger and better dwelling which will be appropriate to the greater success hoped for in the future. The vast majority of urban Americans are transient; before the current housing difficulties, it was an exceptional person who had lived in the same place for five years. This mobility accounts for the peculiar significance given by Americans to the word "home"; "home" is a place where one would like to live, at least as much as it is the place where one is living at present; the term is applied consistently to the more desirable houses in a neighborhood. A neighborhood may be described as consisting of "lovely homes" by a person who has never been inside one of the houses so commended.

To a great extent, the residence dictates a great number of other conspicuous expenditures. Few Americans, without elaborate explanations and excuses, would dare have only one car in a house which has a two-car garage. In the normal American house (as opposed to the apartment) nearly everything is open to the inspection of the world; no hedges, walls, or gates separate the building from the road; and though the shades are generally halfway down during the day, even though there be no glare, they are also halfway up at night, and some of the furnishings of most lighted rooms can be detailed from the street. Incidentally, this proper position of the shades has an almost fetishist importance; cases have been recorded of people with an excessive desire for light being asked to surrender their lease because the furled shades in one house lowered the appearance of the whole neighborhood. Even in apartments the conformity is generally great; there is an often repeated story of the tenant in 13/B visiting the tenant in 2/B and telling her her furniture was in the wrong place.

Not only the cost but also the style of furniture and domestic appliances are controlled by the Joneses. American women—for decoration is by general consensus an exclusively feminine interest—take good taste very seriously; they attend lectures on the subject and read magazine articles about it (and many of the women's magazines have circulations running into the millions); in the more prosperous groups, a woman's taste is almost a complement to her husband's earning capacity as an index of comparative social success. These standards, needless to say, are abetted and enhanced by the manufacturers and advertisers. The result is twofold. The average standard of taste in the furnishings of nearly all American homes at almost any income level is remarkably high, and the similarities between the furnishings of homes of the same income level is equally remarkable. It is rare in American homes to come across that crowded absence of taste which distinguishes so many European interiors; and it is almost equally rare to come across a house with decorations distinctive enough to be remembered apart from its peers for more than a few days. The decorations of a house are meant to "express the woman's personality"; but these personal expressions are normally limited to relatively slight variations in the color scheme and the choice of the smaller ornaments; any major variation is either an affront to the Joneses, by rejecting the accepted standards, or else a challenge to rivals; in which case the innovator becomes the "Jones" whom the rivals will attempt to equal and surpass as soon as their means allow.

Among those who are building their position, the most modern is the most desirable, though a woman may "express her personality" by collecting small antique objects; but at the top of the social or economic hierarchy these values are reversed, and furniture and domestic appliances become esteemed to the extent that they are not modern, not labor saving. Since trained domestic servants are (outside the Negroes of the South) rare and highly paid, the demonstration that one has no need to rely on labor-saving devices is one of the most impressive methods of advertising one's income, one's success. Moreover, when incomes are relatively large and relatively equal, additional scoring points can be made on the grounds of ancestry; and articles of furniture which can be ascribed to grandparents or greataunts advance a permanent claim for respect from those less well-ancestored or with fewer generations of American-born forebears. It is worth noting in this connection that an interest in genealogy, like an interest in decoration or in flowers, is considered essentially feminine, and unworthy of a proper man, who should be judged on his achievements alone.

As with decoration, so with clothes and personal adornment. A man is known by his wife's fur coat. American methods of mass production have been as successfully applied to clothes as to more durable articles; and women, save for those at the very top and very bottom of the social scale, who do not dress in the current fashion can be regarded as lowering the tone of the neighborhood. The store patronized, the material used, and innumerable more subtle touches will indicate clearly enough to other women the level of expenditure; but the current fashion is attainable at a great range of income levels and can be safely ignored only by the poorest and the richest.

The face and figure should approximate as closely as possible to that of the Joneses. Individual variations there cannot help but be, but they should be minimized as much as possible. Diet, exercises, massage, girdles and other "foundation garments," false breasts, can modify irregularities of the figure; permanent waves (or, in the case of Negroes, straightening), variations in the hair; the excellent American dentists make discolored or uneven teeth a sign of poverty or of unsocial behavior; make-up, hand creams, nail polish take care of the uniformity of the skin, deodorants and perfumes of any individual exhalation. Here again, the necessary commodities are within the reach of nearly every income. All the necessary ingredients and appliances can be bought at the five-and-ten (and, according to *Consumer's Union,* often the best); inspection of the advertisement pages of the *New Yorker* or such luxury magazines as *Vogue* or *Harper's Bazaar* shows how much can be paid for similar articles and appliances. One brand of scent advances as the only reason why anybody should buy it the fact that it is "the costliest perfume in the world."

Until the last fifteen years, such detailed physical conformity was more demanded from women than from men; but today there is increasing stress on male beauty treatments. Padded shoulders and shoes with hidden elevators can alter some of the unnecessary variations of nature, and masculine cosmetics (delicately referred to as "toiletries") are a great and growing industry.

Even children can be molded nearer to the proper pattern. It is not uncommon for girls to get their first permanent wave at the age of four, and even younger tots can occasionally be seen with tinted finger nails. This latter adornment may be more in the nature of playing at being grown up than serious make-up, but the other beautifications are in earnest.

Because of the relative uniform structure of American society, and because success is only defined in relative, and not absolute, terms, everything that a man has, or is responsible for, becomes important as an index of his status and position. And because there are few absolute standards of value, of desirability, or of beauty, the way most likely to win the envy and approval of one's neighbors and rivals—the goal and object of life—is to approximate as closely as possible to the standards they have adopted, but to attempt to be a little bit bigger, a little bit better.

E. E. CUMMINGS

i & selfdiscovery

AS IT WAS MY miraculous fortune to have a true father and a true mother, and a home which the truth of their love made joyous, so—in reaching outward from this love and this joy—I was marvellously lucky to touch and seize a rising and striving world; a reckless world, filled with the curiosity of life herself; a vivid and violent world welcoming every challenge; a world worth hating and adoring and fighting and forgiving; in brief, a world which was a world. This inwardly immortal world of my adolescence recoils to its very roots whenever, nowadays, I see people who've been endowed with legs crawling on their chins after quote security unquote. "Security?" I marvel to myself "what is that? Something negative, undead, suspicious and suspecting; an avarice and an avoidance; a self-surrendering meanness of withdrawal; a numerable complacency and an innumerable cowardice. Who would be 'secure'? Every and any slave. No free spirit ever dreamed of 'security'—or, if he did, he laughed; and lived to shame his dream. No whole sinless sinful sleeping waking breathing human creature ever was (or could be) bought by, and sold for, 'security.' How monstrous and how feeble seems some unworld which would rather have its too than eat its cake!"

> *Jehova buried, Satan dead,*
> *do fearers worship Much & Quick;*
> *badness not being felt as bad,*
> *itself thinks goodness what is meek;*
> *obey says toc, submit says tic,*
> *Eternity's a Five Year Plan:*
> *if Joy with Pain shall hang in hock*
> *who dares to call himself a man?*

For the benefit of any heretical members of my audience who do not regard manhood as a barbarous myth propagated by sinister powers envisaging the subjugation of womankind, let me (at this point) cheerfully risk a pair of perhaps not boring anecdotes.

Back in the days of dog-eat-dog—my first anecdote begins—there lived a playboy; whose father could easily have owned the original superskyscraper-de-luxe: a selfstyled Cathedral Of Commerce, endowed with every impetus to relaxation; not excluding ultraelevators which (on the laudable assumption that even machinery occasionally makes mistakes) were regularly tested. Testing an ultraelevator meant that its car was brought clean up, deprived of safety devices, and dropped. As the car hurtled downward, a column of air confined by the elevator shaft became more and more compressed; until (assuming that nothing untoward happened) it broke the car's fall completely—or so I was told by somebody who should know. At any rate, young Mr X was in the habit not only of attending these salubrious ceremonies, but of entering each about-to-be-dropped car, and of dropping with it as far and as long as the laws of a preEinsteinian universe permitted. Eventually, of course, somebody who shouldn't know telephoned a newspaper; which sent a reporter: who (after scarcely believing his senses) asked the transcender of Adam point-blank why he fell so often. Our playful protagonist shrugged his well-tailored shoulders—"for fun" he said simply; adding (in a strictly confidential undertone) "and it's wonderful for a hangover."

Here, I feel, we have the male American stance of my adolescence; or (if you prefer) the adolescent American male stance of what some wit once nicknamed a "lost generation": whereof—let me hastily append—the present speaker considers himself no worthy specimen. My point, however, isn't that many of us were even slightly heroic; and is that few of us declined a gamble. I don't think we enjoyed courting disaster. I do feel we liked being born.

And now let me give you my second anecdote: which concerns (appropriately enough) not a single human being whose name I forget, but a millionary mishmash termed The Public.

Rather recently—in New York City—an old college chum, whom I hadn't beheld for decades, appeared out of nowhere to tell me he was through with civilization. It seems that ever since Harvard he'd been making (despite all sorts of panics and panaceas) big money as an advertising writer; and this remarkable feat unutterably depressed him. After profound meditation, he concluded that America, and the world which she increasingly dominated, couldn't really be as bad as she and it looked through an advertising writer's eyes; and he promptly determined to seek another view—a larger view; in fact, the largest view obtainable. Bent on obtaining this largest obtainable view of America and America's world, my logical expal wangled an appointment with a subsubeditor of a magazine (if magazine it may be called) possessing the largest circulation on earth: a periodical whose each emanation appears simultaneously in almost every existing human language. Our intrepid explorer then straightened his tie, took six deep breaths, cleared his throat, swam right up, presented his credentials, and was politely requested to sit down. He sat down. "Now listen" the subsubeditor suggested "if you're thinking of working with us, you'd better know The Three Rules." "And what" my friend cheerfully inquired "are The Three Rules?" "The Three Rules" explained his mentor "are: first, eight to eighty; second, anybody can do it; and third, makes you feel better." "I don't quite understand" my friend confessed. "Perfectly simple" his interlocutor assured him. "Our first Rule means that every article we publish must appeal to anybody, man woman or child, between the ages of eight and eighty years—is that clear?" My friend said it was indeed clear. "Second" his enlightener continued "every article we publish must convince any reader of the article that he or she could do whatever was done by the person about whom the article was written. Suppose (for instance) you were writing about Lindbergh, who had just flown the Atlantic ocean for the first time in history, with nothing but unlimited nerve and a couple of chicken (or ham was it?) sandwiches—do you follow me?" "I'm ahead of you" my friend murmured. "Remembering Rule number two" the subsub went on "you'd impress upon your readers' minds, over and over again, the fact that (after all) there wouldn't have been anything extraordinary about Lindbergh if he hadn't been just a human being like every single one of them. See?" "I see" said my friend grimly. "Third" the subsub intoned "we'll imagine you're describing a record-breaking Chinese flood—millions of poor unfortunate men and women and little children and helpless babies drowning and drowned; millions more perishing of slow starvation: suffering inconceivable, untold agonies, and so forth—well, any reader of this article must feel definitely and distinctly better, when she or he finishes the article, than when he or she began it." "Sounds a trifle difficult" my friend hazarded. "Don't be silly" the oracle admonished. "All you've got to do, when you're through with your horrors, is to close by saying: but (thanks to an all-merciful Providence) we Americans, with our high standard of living and our Christian ideas, will never be subjected to such inhuman conditions; as long as the Stars and Stripes triumphantly float over one nation indivisible, with liberty and justice for all—get me?" "I get you" said my disillusioned friend. "Good bye."

So ends the second anecdote. You may believe it or not, as you wish. As far as I'm concerned, it's the unbelievable—but also unquestionable—selfportrait of a one hundred and one percent pseudoworld: in which truth has become televisionary, in which goodness means not hurting people, and in which beauty is shoppe. Just (or unjust) how any species of authentic individualism could stem from such a collective quagmire, I don't—as always—know; but here are four lines of a poem which didn't:

> (While you and i have lips and voices which
> are for kissing and to sing with
> who cares if some oneeyed son of a bitch
> invents an instrument to measure Spring with?

As regards my own self-finding, I have to thank first of all that institution whose initial I flaunted unknowingly during my very earliest days. Officially, Harvard presented me with a smattering of languages and sciences; with a glimpse of Homer, a more than glimpse of Aeschylus Sophocles Euripides and Aristophanes, and a deep glance at Dante and Shakespeare. Unofficially, she gave me my first taste of independence: and the truest friends any man will ever enjoy. The taste of independence came during my senior year, when I was so lucky as to receive a room by myself in the Yard—for living in the Yard was then an honour, not a compulsion; and this honour very properly reserved itself for seniors, who might conceivably appreciate it. Hitherto I had ostensibly lived at home; which meant that intimate contacts with the surrounding world were somewhat periculous. Now I could roam that surrounding world sans peur, if not sans reproche: and I lost no time in doing so. A town called Boston, thus observed, impressed my unsophisticated spirit as the mecca of all human endeavors—and be it added that, in this remote era, Boston had her points. Well do I recall how our far from hero (backed by the most physically imposing of his acquaintances) dared a stifling dump near Howard Street, denominated Mother Shannon's; and how we stopped short, to avoid treading on several spreadeagled sailors; and how my backer, with irreproachable nonchalance, exchanged a brace of dollar bills for two tumblers of something even viler than honest Jack Delaney served during soi-disant prohibition; and finally how, having merely sampled our nonbeverages, we successfully attained Scollay Square—to be greeted by the dispassionate drone of a pintsize pimp, conspicuously stationed on the populous sidewalk under a blaze of movie bulbs and openly advertising two kinds of love for twenty-five cents each. Moreover that distant Boston comprised such authentic incarnations of genius as Bernhardt, whose each intonation propitiated demons and angels; Pavlova, who danced a ditty called Nix On The Glowworm into the most absolute piece of aristocracy since Ming; and a lady of parts (around whose waist any man's hand immediately dreamed it could go three times) named Polaire. Those where the days (and nights) of The Turkey Trot and The Bunny Hug; of Everybody's Doing It, Alexander's Ragtime Band, Has Anybody Here Seen Kelly, There's A Little Bit Of Bad In Every Good Little Girl, On The Banks Of The Saskatchewan, and Here Comes My Daddy Now (O Pop, O Pop, O Pop, O Pop). Nothing could exceed the artistry of Washington Street bartenders, who positively enjoyed constructing impeccable Pousse-Cafés in the midst of Ward Eights and Hop Toads; nor could anything approach the courtesy of Woodcock waiters, who never obeyed any ring but your own and always knocked twice before entering. I am further indebted to Boston town for making me acquainted (and in no uncertain manner) with the sinister splendors of censorship. One evening, The Old Howard would be As Is; the next, you guessed you were embracing a funeral.

When Miss Gertrude Hoffman brought her lissome self and her willowy girls to Boston, they and she were violently immersed in wrist- and ankle-length underwear. A local tobacconist drew jail for selling a box of cigars adorned with the usual gauzily apparelled but unmistakably symbolic females—and vainly did an outraged lawyer object that his client was happily married. Meanwhile, watching-and-warding Mr Sumner's matchless collection of indecent items constituted a favorite topic of conversation with high and low alike. But if the predations of puritanism astonished me nearly forty years ago, I was recently more than amazed to learn that you cannot now show a woman's entire breast in any American moviehouse unless she isn't (to coin a plagiarism) white. Verily, democracy unquote is a strange disease: nor (I submit) can any human being help sympathizing, in his or her heart of hearts, with the bad bald poet who sings

> come (all you mischief-
> hatchers hatch
> mischief) all you
>
> guilty
>   scamper (you bastards throw dynamite)
>   let knowings magic
>   with bright credos each divisible fool
>
>   (life imitate gossip fear unlife
> mean
>   -ness, and

to succeed in not
   dying)
   Is will still occur; birds disappear
   becomingly: a thunderbolt compose poems
not because harm symmetry
   earthquakes starfish (but
      because nobody
         can sell the Moon to The) moon

ALDOUS HUXLEY

Mother

HEAT AND GRAVITY, molecular motion and atomic disintegration—these
are the physical prime movers of our economy. But there are also energies of thought, energies of feeling, instinct and desire—energies which,
if canalized and directed, can be made to do useful work and ring up
handsome profits. Some of these invisible energies were harnessed at
the very dawn of civilization and have been turning the wheels of
industry ever since. Personal vanity, for example, has powered half the
looms and supported all the jewelers. The horror of death and the wish
for some kind of survival have raised pyramids, have carved innumerable statues and inscriptions, have given employment to whole armies
of painters, masons, embalmers and clergymen. And what of fear, what
of aggressiveness and the lust for power, what of pride, envy and greed?
These are the energies which, from the time of chipped flints to the
time of split atoms, have powered the armament industry. In recent
years manufacturers and retailers have been turning their attention to
other, hitherto unexploited sources of psycho-industrial power. Directed
by the advertisers into commercially profitable channels, snobbery and
the urge to conformity have now been made to yield the equivalent of
millions of horsepower of energy. The longing for sexual success and
the dread of being repulsive have become the principal motive force in
the ever growing cosmetics and deodorant industries. And how brilliantly our psychological engineers have tackled the problem of turning
religious tradition, children's phantasies and family affection to commercial use! Read Dickens's account of an old-fashioned Christmas in

The Pickwick Papers and compare what happened at Dingley Dell to what the victims of the modern American Christmas are expected to do now. In Dickens's time the Saviour's birthday was celebrated merely by overeating and drunkenness. Except for the servants, nobody received a present. Today Christmas is a major factor in our capitalist economy. A season of mere good cheer has been converted, by the steady application of propaganda, into a long-drawn buying spree, in the course of which everyone is under compulsion to exchange gifts with everyone else—to the immense enrichment of merchants and manufacturers.

And now compare the activities of the children described in *Little Women*, in *Puck of Pook's Hill*, in *Winnie the Pooh*, with the activities of children growing up in the age of electronics. Before the invention of television, the phantasies of childhood were private, random and gratuitous. Today they are public, highly organized and cannot be indulged in except at considerable expense to the parents, who must pay for a second TV set, buy the brands of breakfast food advertised by the purveyors of phantasy, and supply the young viewers with revolvers and coonskin caps.

The same process of publicizing the private, standardizing the random and taxing the gratuitous may be observed in the field of personal relationships. The family is an institution which permits and indeed encourages the generation of immense quantities of psychological energy. But until very recent times, this energy was allowed to run to waste without doing any good to industry or commerce. This was a situation which, in a civilization dependent for its very existence on mass production and mass consumption, could not be tolerated. The psychological engineers got to work and soon the private, random and gratuitous sentiments of filial devotion were standardized and turned to economic advantage. Mother's Day and, despite the growing absurdity of poor Poppa, Father's Day were instituted, and it began to be mandatory for children to celebrate these festivals by buying presents for their parents, or at least by sending them a greeting card. Not a letter, mind you; letters are private, random and bring money only to the Post Office. Besides, in these days of telephones and Progressive Methods of teaching orthography, few people are willing to write or able to spell. For the good of all concerned (except perhaps the recipients, who might have liked an occasional hand-written note), the greeting card was invented and marketed.

A few weeks ago I found myself, half an hour too early for an appointment, in the World's Largest Drug Store. How was the time to be passed? I had all the pills and toothpaste I needed, all the typing paper, electric light bulbs, alarm clocks, whisky, cameras, folding card tables. I had no use for toys or nylon hosiery, for skin food or chewing gum or fashion magazines. Nothing remained but the greeting cards. They were displayed, hundreds upon hundreds of them, in a many-tiered rack not less (for I made a rough measurement) than fifty-four feet long. There were cards for birthdays, cards for funerals, cards for weddings and for the consequences of weddings in all numbers from singles to quadruplets. There were cards for the sick, for the convalescent, for the bereaved. There were cards addressed to brothers, to sisters, to aunts, to nephews, to uncles, to cousins, to everyone up and down the family tree to the third and fourth generation. There were serious cards for Father, tender cards for Dad, humorous cards for Pop. And finally there was an immense assortment of cards for Mother. Each of these cards, I discovered, had its poem, printed in imitation handwriting, so that, if Mom were in her second childhood, she might be duped into believing that the sentiment was not a reach-me-down, but custom-made, a lyrical outpouring from the sender's overflowing heart.

> Mother dear, you're wonderful
> In everything you do!
> The happiness of fam'ly life
> Depends so much on YOU.

Or, more subtly,

> You put the sweet in Home Sweet Home
> By loving things you do.
> You make the days much happier
> By being so sweet, too.

And so on, card after card. In the paradise of commercialized maternity no Freudian reptile, it is evident, has ever reared its ugly head. The Mother of the greeting cards inhabits a delicious Disneyland, where everything is syrup and Technicolor, cuteness and Schmalz. And this, I reflected, as I worked my way along the fifty-four-foot rack, is all that remains of the cult of the Great Mother, the oldest and, in many ways, the profoundest, of all religions.

For paleolithic man, every day was Mother's Day. Far more sincerely than any modern purchaser of a greeting card, he believed that "Mother dear, you're wonderful." Just how wonderful is attested by the carvings of Mother unearthed in the caves which, twenty thousand years ago, served our ancestors as cathedrals. In limestone, in soapstone, in mammoth ivory—there they stand, the Mother images of man's earliest worship. Their bowed heads are very small and their faces are perfectly featureless. They have next to no arms and their dwindling legs taper off, with no hint of feet, into nothing. Mother is all body, and that body, with its enormously heavy breasts, its prodigal wealth of belly, thigh and buttock is the portrait of no individual mother, but a tremendous symbol of fertility, an incarnation of the divine mystery of life in defiance of death, of perpetual renewal in the midst of perpetual perishing. Mother was felt to be analogous to the fruitful earth and, for centuries, her images were apt to exhibit all the massiveness of her cosmic counterpart. In Egypt, for example, Mother sometimes modulated imperceptibly into a hippopotamus. In Peru she often appeared as an enormous female Toby-jug, and everywhere she manifested herself as pot, jar, sacred vessel, grail.

The facts which we only think about (if we think about them at all) scientifically, in terms of biology and ecology, of embryology and genetics, our ancestors evidently thought about all the time. They did not understand them analytically, of course, but directly experienced them with their whole being, physiologically, emotionally and intellectually, whenever they were confronted by one of their Mother symbols.

How is it that we have permitted ourselves to become so unrealistic, so flippantly superficial in all our everyday thinking and feeling about man and the world he lives in? "The happiness of fam'ly life Depends so much on you." This, apparently, is as deep as the popular mind is now prepared to go into the subject of Mother. And the minority opinion of those who have graduated from greeting cards to Dr. Freud is hardly more adequate. They know that Mother dear can be wonderful in more ways than one—that there are wonderful, possessive mothers of only sons, whom they baby into chronic infantility, that there are wonderful, sweet old vampires who go on feeding, into their eighties, on the blood of an enslaved daughter. These are uncomfortable facts, which we must recognize in order to cope with. But this sort of thing is still a very long way from being the whole story of Mother. To those who would like to read something like the whole story I recommend a book which, as it happened, I had finished on the very morning of my encounter with the greeting cards at the World's Largest Drug Store. This book is *The Great Mother* by Erich Neumann, recently published as Number 47 of the Bollingen Series. It is not an easy book to read: for the author is a psychologist of the school of C. G. Jung and he writes, as most of Jung's followers write, with all of the old master's turgid copiousness. Jungian literature is like a vast quaking bog. At every painful step the reader sinks to the hip in jargon and generalizations, with never a patch of firm intellectual ground to rest on and only rarely, in that endless expanse of jelly, the blessed relief of a hard, concrete, particular fact. And yet, in spite of everything, the Jungian system is probably a better description of psychological reality than is the Freudian. It is not the best possible description—far from it; but it does at least lend itself to being incorporated into such a description. If you were to combine Jung with F. W. H. Myers, and if you were then to enrich the product with the theories of Tantrik Buddhism and the practices of Zen, you would have a working hypothesis capable of explaining most, perhaps indeed all, the unutterably odd facts of human experience and, along with the hypothesis, a set of operational procedures by means of which its unlikelier elements might be verified.

And now let us return to Mother. For our ancestors, as we have seen, Mother was not only the particular person who made or marred the happiness of fam'ly life; she was also the visible embodiment of a cosmic mystery. Mother manifested Life on all its levels—on the biological and physiological levels and also on the psychological level. Psychologically speaking, Mother was that oceanic Unconscious, out of which personal self-consciousness (the masculine element in subjective experience) is crystallized and in which, so to speak, it bathes. More obviously, Mother was the source of physical life, the principle of fecundity. But the principle of fecundity is also, in the very nature of things, the principle of mortality; for the giver of physical life is also, of necessity, the giver of death. Ours is a world in which death is the inevitable consequence of life, in which life requires death in order to renew itself. Wherever she has been worshiped—and there is no part of the world in which, at one time or another, she has not been worshiped—the Great Mother is simultaneously the Creator and the Destroyer. Mother gives and Mother takes away; she builds up and then tears down that she may build again—and yet again tear down, forever. For us, as self-conscious individuals, as social beings governed by law and trying to live up to ethical ideals, this divine impartiality can only seem appalling. Theologians have always found it exceedingly difficult to "justify the ways of God to man." They have, indeed, found it impossible; for the ways of God cannot be justified in merely human terms. In that profoundest and most splendid product of Hebrew thought, the Book of Job, God refuses to justify Himself; he is content to ask ironical questions and to point to the vast, incomprehensible fact of a world which, whatever else it may be, is most certainly not a world created according to human specifications.

The Book of Job was written in the fifth or perhaps even the fourth century B.C., when the ancient matriarchal system of thought and social organization had been replaced by the patriarchal, and the supreme God was worshiped, not as Mother, but as Father. The originality of the book consists in its demonstration that this masculine God had a great deal in common with the Great Mother of earlier religions. Jehovah is, by definition, the God of righteousness, of willed morality and self-conscious idealism; but He is also, insists the author of Job, the God of the fathomless Unconscious, the Lord of the irrational Datum, the First Principle of the incomprehensible Fact. A God of righteousness, Jehovah is at the same time the impartial creator, not only of all good things, but also of all that we regard as evil—the impartial destroyer, in His cosmic play, not only of evil, but of all that we regard as good. Long before the God of Job—the God who ironically makes nonsense of all the moralistic notions of Job's comforters—the Great Mother had her negative as well as her positive aspects. She was the Terrible Mother as well as the Beneficent Mother, the Goddess of Destruction as well as the Creator and Preserver. Terrible Mothers are to be found in every religious tradition. In Mexico, for example, Mother often appears with a grinning skull for a head and a skirt of woven rattlesnakes. Among the ancient Greeks she is, in one of her numerous aspects, the snaky-haired Gorgon, whose glance has power to turn all living things to stone. In India, Kali, the Great Mother, is sometimes beneficent, sometimes terrible. She nourishes and she devours; she is serenely beautiful and she is a cannibalistic monster. In her positive aspect, she is simultaneously Nature and Intuition, the creator of spiritual no less than of physical life. She is the Eternal Feminine that leads us up and on, and she is the Eternal Feminine that leads us down and back. She puts the sweet in "Home Sweet Home," after which she drinks our blood.

Life giving birth to death, destruction preparing the way for new creation, self-consciousness emerging from the unconscious and finding itself torn between the urge to return to the impersonal darkness of nescience and the urge to go forward into the impersonal light of the total awareness—these are the cosmic and subjective mysteries, for which our ancestors found expression in their countless symbols of the Great Mother. Nothing of all this was made clear, nothing was analyzed or conceptualized. It was a non-logical system of potential science, of latent metaphysics. From their contemplation of these symbols men could derive no definite knowledge, only a kind of obscure understanding of the great scheme of things and their own place within it.

To cope with the mysteries of experience, modern man has no such cosmic symbol as the Great Mother; he has only science and technical philosophy. As a scientist, he observes the facts of generation, growth and death, he classifies his observations in terms of biological concepts, he tests his hypotheses by means of experiment. As a philosopher, he uses the methods of Logical Positivism to prove to his own satisfaction (or rather to his own deepest dissatisfaction) that all the theories of the metaphysicians, all the pregnant hints and suggestions of the symbol-makers have no assignable meaning—in a word, are sheer nonsense. And of course the Logical Positivists are perfectly right—provided always that we accept as self-evident the postulate that no proposition has meaning unless it can be verified by direct perception, or unless we can derive from it other "perceptive propositions," which can be so verified. But if we admit—and in practice we all behave as if we did admit it—that "the heart has its reasons" and that there are modes of understanding which do not depend upon perception or logical inferences from perception, then we shall have to take the metaphysicians and especially the metaphysical symbol-makers a little more seriously. I say "especially the symbol-makers"; for whenever we are dealing with a cosmic or subjective mystery, the verbalized concept is less satisfactory as a means of presentation than the pictorial or diagrammatic symbol. Symbols can express the given, experienced paradoxes of our life without analyzing them, as words (at any rate Indo-European words) must necessarily do, into their self-contradictory elements. Modern man still creates non-verbal symbols, still makes use of them, in many of the most important junctures of life, as a substitute for analytical thinking. Such symbols as flags, swastikas, hammers and sickles have had an enormous and, in the main, disastrous influence on the life of our time. All these, it should be noted, are social and political symbols. When it comes to symbolizing cosmic, rather than all too human, matters, we find ourselves very poorly equipped. Our religious symbols, such as the Cross, refer only to the realms of ethics and of what may be called pure spirituality. We have no religious symbols covering the other aspects of the cosmic mystery. The Hindu religion knows how to symbolize Nature and its processes of unceasing creation and unceasing destruction. The Christian, Jewish and Mohammedan religions do not. In the West, Nature has been completely isolated from the religious context, in which our ancestors used to view it. Our non-human environment and our own physical existence have now become domains exclusively reserved for science. Such exclusiveness is wholly to the bad. What we have to learn is some way of making the best of both worlds, of all the worlds—the world of clear conceptual knowledge and the world of obscure understanding, the world of verbal analysis and the world of comprehensive symbols, the world of science and the world of religion and metaphysics. Will it ever be possible to revive the Great Mother, or create some equivalent symbol of the cosmic mysteries of life and death? Or are we doomed to remain indefinitely, or until the masses lose their minds and run amuck, on the level of the greeting card? Triviality and make-believe are much more easily turned to economic advantage than realistic profundity. Much more than the schoolteachers and the professors, the philosophers and the theologians, our commercial propagandists are the real educators of the masses. If triviality and make-believe are to the advantage of their employers, triviality and make-believe are the attitudes these molders of modern thought will inculcate.

Essays of Our Time I ● *Part* 5

JEROME ELLISON *has had a distinguished career as journalist, writer, and teacher. He served as an editor of* Life *when it was in its infancy, of* Reader's Digest, *and of the now defunct magazines* Liberty *and* Colliers'. *He began teaching at New York University, and at present is a professor of Journalism at Indiana University. His fiction and nonfiction have appeared in leading American magazines.*

LOUIS FINKELSTEIN, *the son of a Lithuanian immigrant, is chancellor and Solomon Schecter Professor of Theology at the Jewish Theological Seminary in New York. A student of the civil and ritual law of the Talmud, he was the pastor of a congregation in the Bronx before he began to teach at the Seminary.*

BERTRAND RUSSELL, *one of the best-known contemporary philosophers and mathematicians, is an English nobleman. His has been a provocative critical voice in the United States and England throughout the twentieth century. Though his major works are philosophical—*Why I Am Not a Christian, The Conquest of Happiness, The History of Western Philosophy—*Lord Russell was awarded the Nobel Prize for literature in 1950.*

SHUNZO SAKAMKI *is professor of history and dean of the summer sessions at the University of Hawaii. He has contributed to American periodicals, and one of his special interests is the relationship of oriental and occidental thought.*

VANCE PACKARD *describes his now famous* The Hidden Persuaders *as an exposé of Madison Avenue's attempt "to channel our unthinkable habits, our purchasing decisions, our thought processes by use of insights gleaned from psychiatry and the social sciences." Recently, his book* The Status Seekers *stirred up as much controversy as his earlier success. When not lecturing at New York University, he writes at his Connecticut home. He recently completed another best seller,* The Waste Makers.

JEROME ELLISON

Are We Making a Playground
out of College?

DURING A SUNNY day one autumn a colleague of mine was counseling a freshman girl at the University of Georgia. He explained that a certain course could not be taken without prerequisites amounting to about two years' work. "But I won't be here that long," the lass protested. "At the end of this school year I'm getting married."

Just to be nice my friend asked who the lucky man was. "Oh, I've just got here," said the miss, "and haven't met him yet." Out of curiosity, the professor kept tabs. The wedding took place in a burst of orange blossoms just after the close of the next semester, as planned.

This sort of thing is so common in the large, tax-supported coeducational plants that turn out more than half of all our college graduates, that most people assume it's probably all right.

After four years on the inside, as a member of a university faculty, I, for one, am not at all sure it's all right. It's part of a growing national inclination to push education aside whenever it interferes with love or comfort, money or fun.

In today's world I question whether we can afford it. Communists and free men agree on at least one thing—the abler, better-informed side in this contest is more likely to prevail. Higher education will play an increasingly vital role in the struggle. We water it down, it seems to me, at our own great peril. And watering it down we certainly are.

The boys, I have noticed, go along in the business as readily as the girls. In one of my own courses at Indiana University there enrolled, not long ago, a male predentistry student. He was a sophomore, personable, fairly intelligent, had a car, and was going steady with a girl in his home town, a hundred miles away.

"Man, this is wearing—driving back and forth to Kokomo twice a week!" he said one time when on the carpet about a late assignment. Later, on a like occasion, "Man, this is killing—all these science courses!"

He shortly solved all his problems by marrying the girl, moving into a university-subsidized apartment on campus, and switching from dentistry to recreation—a curriculum which allows one to become a bachelor of science without ever having to study mathematics, language, chemistry, physics, history or science, but only things like volley ball, archery, lacrosse, deep breathing and refereeing.

My quarrel here is not with the change in career, but with the reasons. Our crowded, roaring slums testify to our need for trained recreation people. But this young oaf switched, not because he had discovered a national need, but because he thought recreation would be easier. One has a feeling that when the sun beats hot on the city pavements and the slum kids really need him, he'll be at home in front of the air conditioner.

Frequently, when counseling a bright student, I point out that we live in an age of science, that one of the bases of science is mathematics, and that the educated man of our day should have a little math. The point that math matters is never questioned. "But," I am almost always told, "it's hard!" The student paws through the catalogue again, seeking a course which is easier but probably irrelevant to his total plan.

Similarly, we often cite the need—in a nation that has a mere 6 per cent of earth's people, and must for its survival learn to get on with the other 94 per cent—for language training. Here again, the cry goes up, "Too hard!"

Some students go to extremes to avoid a language. I worked with one lad who planned from the first to be a journalist, and who has now, at last, become one. But the course in journalism required eighteen hours of a foreign tongue. He enrolled in a teacher-training course, which did not require a language for a degree, and took his journalism in electives—"on the side"!

The prevalence of this sort of thing, and the extent to which school authorities play along with it, is something, I here assert, really to be exercised about.

I have seen too much of the power of higher education to widen and ennoble human life to stand by without protest while this vital power is vitiated. It was through a land-grant university that my father worked his way from the rudest of back-country farms into the vastly expanded horizons of a respected profession. A similar school helped me to spend my own life in the kind of work I love. And if I have learned anything from that work—twenty-five years of editing, writing, teaching and publishing—it is that the fate of man depends now more than ever before upon an educated citizenry. Half-educated won't do. Man's survival hangs now upon his wisdom.

In the light of this conclusion, some things about our mass higher education seem basically immoral. I am not here referring to the sexual aspect of morality. An informal consensus of deans seems to be that the standard in this particular is possibly a shade higher than that of the parents of today's students. Of course, young people in and out of college, today as always, get into scrapes through mismanagement of their sex lives. But for sheer bawdy brazenness I have seen nothing to vie with the letter to the Wisconsin student paper which opened: "We who are not virgins smile at the notion that we have lost our self-respect," and went on to expound the "fuller" life. This was written in the 1930's by a girl who may now be a staid grandmother.

The thing that concerns me is an intellectual immorality—the encroachment upon the main business of college of an accumulation of irrelevancies which together make up a "Second Curriculum" that often takes precedence over the first.

The Second Curriculum is that odd mixture of status hunger, voodoo, tradition, lust, stereotyped dissipation, love, solid achievement, and plain good fun sometimes called "college life." It drives a high proportion of our students through college chronically short of sleep, behind in their work, and uncertain of the exact score in any department of life.

To gain some notion of the extent to which the Second Curriculum has taken over, we'll whisk through, in a moment, an ordinary year's calendar at a Big Ten school. First let us set the scene. You start with a broad expanse of tree-studded lawn, perhaps half a mile square, dotted with buildings rendered in several versions of collegiate architecture.

One of these structures is the student union, a rallying point for snacking, dalliance and amusement. From morning until night it resounds to the blare of the jukebox, the clink of coffee cups, the clatter of bowling pins, the click of billiard balls, the slap of playing cards, the gentle creak of lounge chairs and, in the plushier ones, the splash of languid bodies in tepid swimming pools. There's likely to be an informal dance here every Friday and Saturday night. They have a ball— banquet or name-band dance—about every weekend in the ballroom.

Fringing the main campus and sprawling for a mile in every direction are student living quarters—fraternities and rooming houses both stately and squat, trailer camps, huge residence units resembling, according to the architectural mood, medieval castles or modern luxury hotels.

The whole panorama—so well has Joe College sold his old man on the principle that a car is needed for study—is overrun with automobiles. Our big campuses are churning in a traffic turmoil that almost has to be seen to be believed. Some schools—Indiana is one—issue stickers, dubbed "hunting licenses," which permit the student to park on campus if he can find a space. Others, following a method used at Wisconsin, provide parking at some distance from the university and charge a fee, which covers shuttle-bus service to school.

In some of the better-motorized universities, more than half the students have cars. Duke, Fairleigh Dickinson, Johns Hopkins, Houston, Louisiana, Maryland, Nebraska, Oregon State, Syracuse, Texas and Iowa all average—according to a study made at the University of Houston—over half a car, and up to one car, per student. Ohio State's 19,000 students operate 11,640 motor vehicles. The student-to-car ratio at Wisconsin, 15,000–5800; at Purdue, 13,000–5100; at Northwestern, 15,000–2500; at Illinois, 23,000–5000; at Indiana, 11,000–4500; at Michigan State 19,000–6400. These cars support enterprises—drive-in restaurants, drive-in theaters (known in college jargon as "passion pits"), miniature golf courses, roller-skating rinks, gin mills—many miles from the campus.

More than a fifth of the students are married. This statistic has profoundly affected university life at all levels. For one thing, the housing people have been caught short. The Indiana campus, which is typical, was several hundred units short in married-student housing last fall, while newly completed quarters for single students stood vacant. The big coed plants are building married housing pell-mell, trying to catch up with a growing trend. In eleven state universities with a total enrollment of 160,000, more than 21 per cent of last autumn's students were married. The expected figure for four years hence is one in four.

The large married minority strongly influences the single majority. Most of the girls are striving, sometimes with unladylike eagerness, to get married—the Georgia coed mentioned earlier has her counterparts in every state. The steps to success are going steady, "pinning"—exchange of fraternity badges or other club symbols—formal engagement and marriage. Monthly box scores of pinnings, published by some college papers, are read with sports-page avidity.

Since even the bottom rung of the coed success ladder cannot be mounted unless one is dated, the pressure to date is enormous. The emotional backlash of failure to date is profound, particularly among women students. A Wisconsin coed, writing in the student daily, reports that half the sorority pillows are "wet with tears" of a Saturday night— no dates. I know of one attempted suicide over the business.

The male reacts to the same pressures in a variety of ways. He may affect a cynical Don Juanism or a guarded wariness. Or his own pillow may be wet with tears, or he may simply yield to community pressure and start populating the nursery school the university maintains for married students' children. In any event, both male and female live in daily tension, varying from mild to acute, over some aspect of dating or mating.

It is in this over-all atmosphere that the Second Curriculum is pursued. An important part of it is, of course, the standard, souped-up program of professionalized athletics. Since this phenomenon has been ably dealt with in a number of recent articles, it is enough to note here that a normal season may include eight major basketball games and four football games. Each has its influx of alumni and visitors, its bands and cheering sections, its squads of bench warmers, its round of dances and fights, its frenzy of warm-ups, post-mortems, hospitality and decorations.

For the Homecoming Game, each housing unit prepares elaborate lawn statuary, built of papier-mâché and crepe paper on the colossal scale. These devices, illuminated and sometimes animated by intricate machinery, consume vast ingenuity and time. The control panel for one of the displays at Indiana was hardly less complex than the switchboard of a fair-sized telephone exchange. A recent prize winner was an enormous red bull (Indiana) towing a corn cutter which mowed down cornstalks (Iowa men) and delivered them in bags. There were fifty-one entries in Wisconsin's Homecoming decoration contest. The winner was a gigantic prostrate Indian whose eyes lighted up and moved from side to side, whose head moved on a swivel and whose chest heaved.

Each spring has its special big weekend. Indiana has a fifty-mile bicycle relay race in May. Work on it begins the preceding November, with the appointment of a student committee of 192 persons. The bike teams practice all year. One rider makes weekend trips to Indianapolis, fifty miles away, on his bike, just to keep in shape. The big weekend itself offers a tricycle relay race featuring costumed sorority girls, a golf tournament, social activities at each of the university's fifty fraternities and sororities, two all-campus dances and a home-talent vaudeville show, in addition to the main race.

Every weekend is special for something. Illinois has a Dad's Day Revue, a stunt show, a Hawaiian-hoop contest, the John Street Pajama Race, the burning of a twenty-five-foot statue called Winter's Gloom, and Men's Economic Recovery Campaign Week, during which coeds make dates and pay for them. Ohio State has a Circus Party with real elephants, a Greek Week, a May Week Carnival, a Rose Formal and and a Pumpkin Prom.

All-campus dances at Indiana include the Freshman Frolic, the First Fling, the Sophomore Cotillion, the Junior Prom, the Dames Ball, the Military Ball, the Mardi Gras Ball, the Blanket Hop, the Bicycle Bump, the Opening of Formal, the Street Dance, the Wellhouse Waltz and a jitterbug contest. Wisconsin fraternities specialize in costume dances inviting the nearest tolerable approach to nudity—a Mammoth Brawl, simulating caveman days, a Roman Party in togas, the Cherokee Chugalug in loincloths and the Pajama Party.

Each week has its list of home-talent entertainments and stunts. Our calendar brings us the Jordan River Tug of War, The Watermelon Mess, the Fall Carnival (coeds dressed as underworld characters, running wheels of chance and performing skits for charity), the all-university competitive sing, numerous pep rallies, including the burning in effigy of John Purdue; the Gridiron Banquet, the Football Banquet, the Athletic Banquet, the Turtle Derby, the Greek Week Chariot Race, the Fun Frolic (rides, concessions and a Ferris wheel), a fashion show, a Panhellenic Circus, a Barbecue, a Round-up and a Sports-Car Rally. Wisconsin has all this plus a Man-with-the-Most-Beautiful-Legs Contest, a Yell-like-Hell Contest and the Haresfoot musical show, in which the boys dress up as girls.

In the big coeducational schools an immense amount of time and energy goes into the election of "queens"—a reflection, perhaps, of the statistic that 35 per cent of all college students are females. At Indiana the queen season opens in September with the nomination of two queens from each women's dormitory or sorority to appear at a pep rally, where one of them is designated football queen. Later in the same month, after an all-campus sweepstakes, including preliminaries, semi-finals and finals, somebody is crowned sweater queen.

In October and November various queens and sweethearts—a sweetheart of, say, Beta Theta Pi, Sigma Chi or Dodds House, is about the same as a queen—are elevated. With sandwich men, posters, torch-light and sports-car parades, students elect a homecoming queen, a military-ball queen, a queen of the autumn formal, a yearbook queen, a queen of the athletic lettermen, a junior-prom queen, and some others. This year some publications students, seeking a device to promote the sale of the college annual, came up with the idea of electing a *queen* queen. Nobody was eligible who had not previously been a queen of something. Forty-three young women qualified.

Our queen program, my research has revealed, lags somewhat behind Big Ten standards. Ohio State has everything we have plus a pumpkin-prom queen, a rose queen, a Greek Week queen, a May queen, and a boat-race queen. Illinois has a men's-residence-hall queen, a sno-ball queen, a dolphin queen, a Miss Photoflash, a star-and-scroll queen, a Sheequon queen and a plowboy-prom queen.

As with the goose, so with the gander—bachelors and kings are selected from among the male students. The Indiana campus elects a bachelor of the year, Illinois elevates a most-eligible bachelor, Ohio State elects a Greek Week king, Wisconsin honors a campus clown, a dorm duke, a KD king and a Kat's Meow.

Once a year at Indiana there's a protest against the whole silly business in the form of a "most-useless-man" contest. Typical campaign ad: "He's so useless the state has paid his tuition for ten years to keep him out of industry."

One time a few years ago some pranksters, fed up with queens, ran a nanny goat for prom queen. Horrified campus politicians protested that she was not female and therefore not eligible. When her backers produced a veterinarian to attest her femininity, her foes finally got her disqualified on the ground that she had not been in residence on campus the preceding year. Nevertheless, she ran a strong third in the voting.

These diversions are, of course, over and above those amusements which are considered by school authorities to have cultural, educational or recreational value. Every university schedules a dazzling string of road shows for its auditorium. A typical year will bring two Broadway musical comedies, two celebrated violinists, two world-famous symphony orchestras, a renowned opera company, two first-rate ballet companies and an assortment of nationally advertised jazz musicians, pianists, sopranos, bands and lecturers. Besides this, university academic departments, particularly those of music, theater and dance, offer several entertainments and lectures weekly for the diversion of the student.

But come, does not all work and no play make Jack a dull boy? Lest ennui overtake Jack, the typical student union offers a bridge club, an arts-and-crafts club, a chess club, a photo club, a sailing club and a golf club besides bowling, billiards and record concerts. We shall have sound minds in sound bodies—as long as both can stand the strain. The year-round program of intramural sports is open to all students— touch football, softball, badminton, golf, table tennis.

In schools which offer what is considered an adequate Second Curriculum, each college generation is expected to produce its quota of pranks, "outbreaks" and illegal highjinks. Last year, five Ohio State freshmen got drunk in Kentucky, stole a corpse from an undertaking parlor, transported it a hundred miles and placed it in front of the union building on the Columbus campus.

The same year, Athens, Ohio, police had to use tear gas to break up a riot, over nothing in particular, of 3000 students who invaded the city's business district. The riot started with a few students pelting each other with oranges, and wound up with twenty-eight of them in jail on charges of disorderly conduct, assault and battery, throwing firecrackers, resisting arrest, blocking traffic, and unsafe operation of motor vehicles.

Illinois' contribution to this lore is the celebrated water fight of April, 1958, in which 6000 berserk students opened fire hydrants, routed the local fire department and drenched the dean of students. I am impressed by the fact that the year in which college students in Hungary started an immortal revolution to free their country from tyranny, the big thing on the Indiana campus was a panty raid. On the day in which a local school was bombed and the countdown began for one of our major satellite attempts, a Big Ten student paper carried the headline, LIZ HAMILTON ELECTED HOMECOMING QUEEN.

Fun, yes; love, certainly; marriage in good time, of course. But shall these things be gained out of season, at too dear a price? Some of us are beginning to ask what very little work and an awful lot of play makes Jack.

What should be done? Half a dozen useful suggestions are in circulation and receiving minority support among the faculties of our colleges and universities. All that is needed to place them on the action agenda is a little public outcry.

The first step would be to prohibit automobiles. There would be a pitiable bleating, but all, I am sure, would pronounce the action a benefit. Princeton men do not appear unhappier than most, and their scholarship ranks with the world's best. Yet they are not allowed to operate motor vehicles while attending college.

The next step would be to disband fraternities and sororities. Here, I must confess, my heart skips a beat as I turn in my old badge. I have even shed a quiet tear, for the associations of my college fraternity are deep and dear. But the plain fact is that the system has outlived its usefulness. This fact must be faced, even by sentimental fraternity men like myself. Glenn H. Goodman, of the Ohio State faculty, has let fly at fraternities for "picking top men and isolating them in an atmosphere of football, adolescent discussions, dating and drinking."

I could add other serious charges. Besides providing the prime breeding grounds of the "minimum effort" attitude, fraternities too often breed a tawdry Don Juanism, a callow and provincial snobbishness, the habit of getting drunk and a world view no broader than a dollar bill. Worst of all, they consume quantities of time, effort, money and emotional stress—with their chronic financial troubles, panicked rushing season, and social-alcoholic-political monkeyshines—out of all proportion to the good they offer in terms of fellowship.

My apologies are tendered to chapters which do not deserve such harsh words. But enough of them do, and have deserved them for so long a time that they doom the whole system.

The same apology goes to those students—and I have known quite a number—with the integrity and plain nerve to resist the pressures of the conforming mob, place the Second Curriculum firmly in second place and do a job in college. The fact that a few unusual individuals

can win through to an education does not, however, weaken my case—
which is that universities have no right to make it almost impossible
for students to study.

Several other things might be done to cut down ill-formed attitudes toward scholarship, toward marriage, and toward the relationship
between them. Plush university housing should not be offered until the
head of the house is at least a senior, usually achieved at the age of
twenty-one. This would remove cheap, pleasant, subsidized living—an
abnormal condition which the young couple cannot expect to find later
on—as a temptation to impulsive teen-age marriage. At the same time
it would not obstruct love so deep and true, though young, that it is
determined to find a way.

Standards of scholarship are responsive to public expectation. Our
state universities face a rising—and, in my thinking, justified—public
opinion that education beyond high school is every child's right. Let us,
then, offer a two-year university curriculum, crowned with an associate-
in-arts degree for those who pass it successfully. Our many junior colleges have set the precedent. Let it be tough, and let it be the same for
everybody. Those who wish to go on for the full four years would
return to college in a frame of mind to get down to business. A re-
entrance examination at the beginning of the junior year should be
tough enough to weed out those who are in college mainly for the
Second Curriculum.

These are some of the suggestions currently in the air, and there
are others—the problem is nationwide. Citing popular pressure for easy,
fun-packed college degrees, Richard B. Hovey of Western Maryland
College, addressing the College English Association, has come down
smartly on the head of the nail.

Hovey has pointed out that a shocking number of college graduates
can't even write grammatically or spell correctly, and has asked the
reasons. He finds that standards are shot, and that there's not much a
teacher can do about it. "An individual teacher cannot suddenly decide
to have standards; let him fail half or more of a class, and he will soon
be in trouble with his administrators." He finds, moreover, that students
understand this and take advantage of it: "Our student knows that
unless he is . . . unforgivably negligent, he will get by."

The burden of the Second Curriculum is wryly acknowledged
everywhere. To him who may question its baleful effect, I extend the
invitation to take my place some morning. Let him face an early class
he's knocked his brains out to prepare for. Let him address the blank
stares and vacant faces of a roomful of students who knocked their
brains out the night before at the Sophomore Twitch, the Winter

Willies, the Monumental Maul, the Greek Tweak or, in short, at goofing off.

Now that we're over on the teaching side, what about the teachers? The faculty, as certain current novels suggest, is far from perfect. Entering the academic life from the "outside world," one is disappointed by the banality of conversation at social gatherings, and by attitudes of old-fashioned trade-unionism centering on "tenure," a word which means that after they've kept you on for seven years it's almost impossible for them to fire you. This concern for tenure bends many teachers toward cautious utterance, often blunting the kind of searching, outspoken discourse that might explode into exciting teaching and learning.

Here, though, I'd like to say a word in defense of the kind of repetitious teaching called "time serving." There are certain foundation subjects, often humdrum, that the student simply has to "get." These are the barren places in the terrain of learning which must be crossed to reach the thrilling peaks beyond. The work is a rut, and here the patient Mr. Chips serves well.

For inspiration one looks to the faculty "stars," and every faculty has some bright ones. When my own resolve flags, I can look to men like H. J. Muller, our Nobel Prize winner in genetics; Bob Byrnes in history; Bill Wilson in English; Schuyler Otteson in economics and Bill Moore in physiology, and I become refreshed. These men have broken the confines of their own specialties to look at the universe and have found courage to state their views regardless of what special interest may be offended.

In intellectual daring of this order we may hope to find, through education, the glory of the future. And what a future beckons! The purely mechanical side already has been pretty well publicized—the two-day work week, the trips through space, world tours as a standard part of grade-school education, the time when the deserts will bloom and the jungles will be made into gardens.

The new day of the human soul has, however, scarcely been mentioned. Some think the long-sought substitute for war is close to being found—that peaceful means actually exist for converting an enemy into a co-operative and willing friend. In the resulting leisure and plenty, man might begin to develop his potential in art and philosophy. The artist and poet in each of us would find expression. We would stand before the goal of goals for all men—the penetration into the deepest meaning of life itself.

These wonders will not drop into our laps without our effort. Indeed, to avoid a quick catastrophe, we'll have to work as never before. And the kind of work most urgently demanded is work of the mind.

We'll have to *think* our way out of this one. We need tough, seasoned, disciplined thinkers, incorruptible, enormously well informed, skilled in their chosen specialties, but with an appreciation of all specialties—thinkers who cannot be diverted to limited or shoddy goals—and we need a lot of them.

For these reasons, the Second Curriculum must be trimmed. This must be done, not in spite or through outraged morality, but to make room for something wonderfully better.

We who are concerned about Jack and Jacqueline would like to see more, not less, love on the campus. Besides the inevitable and proper love of comfort and fun, of boy for girl, of status and position, of exercise and sport, of family and children, we'd like to see some love of truth and intellectual achievement, of discovery and high adventure, of beauty, harmony, design and great precision, of mankind and its farthest destiny. We would like, in short, to see the First Curriculum come first.

LOUIS FINKELSTEIN

The Businessman's Moral Failure

IF AMERICAN BUSINESSMEN are right in the way most of them now live, then all the wise men of the ages, all the prophets and the saints were fools. If the saints were not fools, the businessmen must be.

Too many businessmen never stop to ponder what they are doing; they reject the need for self-discipline; they are satisfied to be clever, when they need to be wise. They worry about their place on the economic ladder, but are not concerned sufficiently with whether the civilization in which they work is likely to collapse. They can defeat a local competitor, but may well be defeated by the competitor of us all, which is moral decay.

Now the American executive is very often a man of some vision, motivated by a spirit that generates great energy. Underlying the efficiency of our business community there is the principle of teamwork, cooperation, a reasonable degree of pleasure in the success of co-workers, a comparatively broad welcome to talent, and freedom in human relationships. Granted, these are virtues of no mean order. But the American businessman is losing his insight into the moral sources of American economic strength.

Our country could not have reached its present heights without the blessing of natural resources; but the U.S. would have failed at the outset without a philosophy developed by men more concerned with the betterment of the human spirit than the comforts of the body. These men were inspired by the writings of immortal philosophers and religious thinkers. The modern business leader is more often than not bewildered at the suggestion that the future of the Republic is in some way related to the ideals and ideas of John Locke, not to mention Spinoza, the medieval Scholastics, the Rabbinic sages, and the ancient Greek philosophers.

Ask the U.S. businessman why he is successful today, and he may explain to you the advantages of capitalism, the profit motive, and the "American system." He may, with due modesty, point out the superiority of his own products and marketing. But he will largely ignore the philosophic foundations of the American system. He tends to ignore the great ethical laws as they apply immediately to his work. The truth is that he is preoccupied chiefly with gain, coasting on the spiritual momentum of the past, divorced from our sources of inspiration. He is the leading citizen of a largely hedonistic nation propelled by meaningless drives toward materialistic and frequently meaningless goals.

Clearly no institution will survive if it is dedicated *only* to self-preservation. A business has a goal beyond simple success. It is not a biological organism whose survival is a virtue in itself. Rather, it is a man-created institution, an integral part of our culture, and as such must make a contribution of service to society (as well as a profit for itself) if it hopes to survive. It cannot do this out of a focus on self-gain or pride.

Why do I single out the American businessman for indictment, when he is probably no more materialistic than any of the rest of us? I do so because of the responsibility he bears, because his role in American society is so great. Ours is an industrial society, and the customs and morals and attitudes of businessmen pervade our whole life. Virtually all of us in America have adopted in some degree the pragmatic ethical standards of our business society; and to that degree we have abandoned our ethical and religious traditions.

Our American tragedy is that we fail to see the signs of our decay. But the signs are apparent in the vulgar ostentation all around us, in the sexual laxity revealed by the Kinsey studies, in the demoralization of American captives in the Korean war, in the widespread defiance of law. The signs are apparent in our general toleration of wrongdoing, which is itself an evil and corrupting force.

Curiously, this breakdown of moral discipline has occurred when institutionalized religion is flourishing as never before. But even religion in America now tends to be superficial. For many laymen it consists of writing an occasional check and sporadic attendance at church or synagogue, rather than in personal commitment. There is a dearth of saints, and many ministers themselves are unduly concerned with security in this world. While the percentage of truly dedicated pastors may be no smaller than in previous generations, today they suffer a special disability—a failure to communicate with the members of their flocks.

Human history is studded with the ruins of empires that came to a similar pass. Nations have been wrecked because they lacked an overriding moral goal to which individuals could commit themselves. History shows us that when we become success-dominated, we lose sight of our real reasons for living.

In its youth, America *was* ideal-dominated. Both individual citizens and the country as a whole had an impelling motive in life that was not limited to industrial, political, or economic growth. The men who gathered in 1787 could muster all their intellectual energies to formulate the national charter, overcome differences of background and interest—all because these men were laboring for a larger goal.

An equally vital role awaiting the American businessman today will be suggested at the end of this article. Time and again in American history the businessman has transcended his industrial role and become the buttress not only of government but of the public welfare. Today's crisis demands of him leadership in still another dimension—one where he has thus far conspicuously failed.

A young executive rapidly moving up the financial ladder unequivocally stated in private conversation with me, *"It is impossible to conduct business in the U.S. today without breaking the law."*

If the statement is exaggerated, it nevertheless retains distressing validity for one like myself who was educated in New York City and has resided there over half a century. A considerable portion of my time has been spent with men engaged in a great variety of businesses, who keep an equal variety of balance sheets.

The most casual observer is aware of the transgressions that go on daily in the American business community. He hears of tax returns that are outright perjury; he hears of purchasing agents who are taking bribes from suppliers, of businessmen offering bribes for false testimony or for police protection of some dubious enterprise. He reads of industries attempting to suborn state legislators for favorable legislation. He reads of businessmen bestowing favors on government officials to win special privileges. Even in my ivory tower on Morningside Heights, I have been urged by businessmen to accept a gift for the Theological

Seminary in return for admitting a student—and have been threatened by withdrawal of contributions to the school if I failed to do so.

We hear of businessmen using wire taps to obtain information about their competitors, of management acting in collusion with racketeers, of men using prostitution to promote the sale of their goods. We hear of businessmen violating the most elementary requirements of city building codes and profiting from rat-infested tenements. We hear of financiers deliberately lying about their operations and the financial condition of their companies to mislead investors so that insiders can make killings in stock.

There are less overt practices in the business community that may appear to be only on the borderline of unethical behavior: for example, concealing the true price of goods behind time-payment schemes that are actually usurious; employing advertising that is actually a flagrant misrepresentation of a product's worth. These and other clever dodges are accepted by many as normal phases of competition.

I would not deny that competition is the basis of our free enterprise and of our industrial success. Competition surely induces better efforts and greater production. But to compete in ways that are designed to destroy someone else is very different from competing in terms of doing better than your rival. Years ago in Lithuania, Rabbi Israel Salanter found two boys quarreling over which was the taller. One forced the other to stand in a ditch to settle the argument. Seeing this, Rabbi Israel sadly commented, "Isn't this characteristic of the world where to prove his superiority man must prove others inferior? After all, the same purpose could have been achieved by standing on a chair!"

When two companies are each trying to produce superior values, one may well be more successful than the other, and deservedly earn greater profits. But to seek a crippling advantage over another company is hardly fair competition and is certainly miserable ethics.

It seems to me that a management which is worthy of success is very different from a management which just wants success. One management conducts its affairs in the spirit of contribution, the other in the spirit of selfishness. Contributions to the general good have of course been made by men seeking only their own advantage, but selfishness cannot be made a principle of life and in our time might easily be fatal. Management worthy of success remembers that the true justification for profit is an incentive to serve the community. Success is paid to business by the community for the services it renders. In this sense, profits must clearly be an earned increment.

This reasoning can certainly be understood if stated in terms of the individual. We understand the meaning and value to the individual of "a good reputation." Every businessman knows that his reputation for integrity is one of his major assets. Certainly, a man's progress in a corporation depends in large measure on the reputation he earns through his daily behavior. It is immensely difficult to falsify such a reputation over any extended period of time. We are soon known by those around us for who we *are* rather than what we would like others to think about us. This is a man's "character" in the profoundest sense of the word.

I was interested to hear a major executive point out that the criteria he uses for selecting employees run in this order: character, intelligence, experience. "A really bright executive picks up experience very quickly," he told me. "But the man we need and want most, in important places, is a man with character sufficient to resist many kinds of pressures when the going gets rough. We find, then, that character is the most important ingredient of all, particularly if the man is to be responsible for policy making. An executive can buy brains and can buy experience, but character is something he must supply himself."

And what *is* a man's character but his personal moral dimension, the goals he sets for himself, his sense of honesty and of responsibility, his relations with others? This does not mean, however, that the value of character derives from its contribution to success.

Unquestionably, ethics have a practical value, inseparable from their ultimate one: the creation of better men and women. Rivalry for goodness should, in the long run, make for pragmatic gain. But it is not enough for the individual or the corporation merely to mean well. Men as individuals and as corporations must make an effort to understand what they are doing, and why they are doing it.

The first step in the ethical life is self-criticism. As the Talmud puts it, "Cleanse yourselves, and then cleanse others." Ethics is a branch of thought starting with self-discipline. Discipline, whether among children or adults, whether self-imposed or external, is not popular in America today. And a welter of codes—in companies, in industries, in combines of industries, in labor—do not meet the situation.

Before anyone can think creatively about the moral life, he must feel in his bones a few principles that are part of any civilized ethic, without which civilization would be meaningless. I wish I could say with hope of being understood that of these the most important is awareness of God and love for Him. But as those words tend to become clichés, I say instead that we have to feel the wonder and significance of life and its unique opportunity for achievement. Each of us has only one life on earth. When that life is used unwisely, the loss is irreparable for oneself and for one's fellows.

A businessman who understands these truths will develop an almost automatic pattern of behavior. Certain ancient rules apply with equal force to Jew and Christian, atheist and agnostic, to all men in all situations. These immutable laws are expressed in various ways. The Pentateuch reveals the Decalogue and the Golden Rule of Leviticus 19:18: "Thou shalt love thy neighbor as thyself," which the Gospels restate in Matthew 7:12: "All things whatsoever ye would that men should do to you, do ye even so to them." Similar commandments are promulgated in the literature of the other great traditions of East and West.

Yet these and other binding commandments are often violated in the American business community. A man fears he may be risking his business if he obeys them, forgetting, however, that if he violates them he risks the world.

Business leaders who generously advised me in the preparation of this article said, "The majority of the American business community are not evil men, and want to do right. Let us say we admit the indictment and accept our responsibility—what can we do?"

To begin with, a businessman can develop an awareness that *every* decision of his life involves moral considerations. He can help develop this sensitivity in employees and associates, through example, through discussing with them the moral implications of company actions, through constant reminders that he has values in life above profit or economic security.

There are some corporations which insist that their executives assume responsibility for civic and community improvement. But the businessman can go further. In his training school for management he can introduce students of ethics, as well as management experts and psychologists, to consider the responsibilities of the business executive. He can overcome his anti-intellectualism. He can try to gain knowledge that will clarify the problems of wise decision making.

The businessman must realize that the inculcation of moral sensitivity starts in early childhood and continues throughout life. American society has achieved this kind of indoctrination in other fields. To take two familiar examples: virtually every American child is brought up with a concern for personal hygiene; virtually every female child is indoctrinated with the need to be as physically attractive as possible. Our culture is probably unique in the emphasis it places on these two patterns of education.

The businessman can, without "moralizing" (which would be deadening and self-defeating), transform his home into a school for moral responsibility. Avoiding precept, the businessman can make even his conversation at table serve the vital end of character education for himself, his wife, his children, and his guests. The stories he tells, the gestures he makes, the conversation he chooses and avoids, can all show that he has at least some notion of what life, America, and freedom are about. Without being in the slightest degree priggish, and eventually without self-consciousness, he may help his family and friends obtain insight into the ethical life.

The American businessman, then, should literally *place ethics on the agenda*—for himself at home and in the office, for his company and trade association:

1. His calendar should include regular meetings of management to discuss the moral dimensions in his specific business. One firm that instituted such meetings finds it continually gains valuable insights into new relationships with the many other organizations with which it does business.

2. He should seek expert advice on ethics. Existing resources in the field will gladly be made available to him.

3. He should put moral health on the same level as mental and physical health, indeed above them. This means he should read literature dealing with ethics; devote time to the study of ethics, alone and with colleagues and scholars; work for the establishment of research in ethics, as he has worked magnificently for the development of research in science and technology.

Whatever else may or may not be involved in the application of such principles, it will demand direction of effort—not merely doing what one happens to like at a given moment and following the easy path of self-indulgence. Wisdom begins with sacrifice of immediate pleasures for long-range purposes. There is a widespread view that belief in God and personal immortality leads to this discipline. The fact, however, is that the discipline itself is also indispensable to real belief in God and human immortality. That is why the role of the businessman in American ethics is no less crucial than that of the religious leader or scholar.

Today's crisis demands the businessman's leadership in the area of human behavior. The kind of criticism with which enlightened businessmen could confront philosophers and theologians could be a challenge. Then superficiality in religion would cease to be fashionable, and laymen would soon detect its shallowness. Morally sensitive and informed businessmen can compel American philosophy and religion to focus on the basic problems troubling mankind.

We Americans will then no longer warrant William James's description of us as worshippers of "the bitch-goddess, Success." Our best young minds would strive for genuine, rather than apparent, achievement. If we can overcome the tendency to measure intellectual productivity by quantity rather than quality, America might produce works and insights into the ethical realm comparable to the eternal creations that have emerged from other civilizations. Without such creations, rallying the spiritual energies of all men, America and the Free World will not endure.

Civilization needs men and women whose every act and decision will bear the stamp of responsibility. The world cannot long survive, at least in freedom, if decisions are made irresponsibly—that is, without disciplined consideration of individual and general consequences. At the present moment, this may seem almost impossible to achieve. Yet without many dedicated men and women exercising disciplined consideration of each of their actions, none of the great philosophic or religious traditions could have survived.

Modest steps to focus different types of experience on the complex issues of our day have been taken in various ways, one of which is the work of a group of scholars who drew together in 1939 in New York. The group includes physical scientists, social scientists, philosophers, and theologians of different faiths, who were stirred by the apparition of Nazism but recognized it as a symptom of a chronic disease of our time rather than the disease itself. They hoped they could clarify today's moral problems. Once a year, sometimes once in two years, these scholars have met. Some participants are frankly agnostic, some atheistic, others devout. For a long time their discussions were at cross-purposes. There were frequent outbursts when varied types of mind and experience confronted one another. Gradually, they arrived at an astoundingly simple conclusion: the problem of their concern may be summed up in a single word—"responsibility."

This conference of scholars is hopeful of establishing nothing less than a World Academy of Ethics and an Institute for Practical Ethics for Everyday Living, drawing on the wisdom not only of Christianity and Judaism but of Islam, Buddhism, Confucianism, and other traditions. The scholars need the help and participation of businessmen.

Does all of this sound as though the American businessman had to take on new burdens, and rush even more prematurely to his grave? On the contrary, one of man's primary duties to himself, his family, the community, and to God is preservation of his life on earth, so that he can realize his potentialities for good. The businessman who will take time to contemplate and to ponder the ethical dimension of life will discover new realms in which he can develop his talents, freeing himself from the bondage to private gain that menaces the maturing business executive. Clearly understanding the principles of a meaningful life, he will share them with his family, especially with his wife. He will accept philosophically the occasional defeats and frustrations of his business career. He will carry his burdens serenely and thus preserve his own life, as well as that of the community.

Before he decides that the moral discipline required to build a better society is too arduous for him and that he is too busy to master a new dialect of thought, before he flees his responsibility, he might do well to ponder the story of Moses in the third chapter of Exodus.

The father of Prophecy was heavy of tongue. He, too, preferred the ease of Midian and the pleasures of shepherd life to the burdens imposed by the leadership of men. He could not believe that the task presented to him could not be done by another. For a moment he doubted that it could ever be accomplished. But sometimes, because of unique combinations of circumstances surrounding him, an individual is indispensable for a specific role in history. Whether or not he wished it, Moses was one of the great spiritual leaders of mankind. He could neglect his duty, but he could not assign it to anyone else.

To rise to his full stature, the American businessman—who at his best embodies many of the Prophetic virtues—must also shoulder a unique burden of responsibility. The fate of the world hangs on his decisions, for above all, the world needs ethical leadership from those it respects as supremely practical.

The words spoken by Moses to his contemporaries more than three thousand years ago apply literally to us in this latter day: "See, I have set before thee this day life and good, and death and evil." If the American businessman can bring himself to choose life and good, he can save not only our own but future generations. Surely he will heed the ancient Prophet's plea: "Therefore, choose life, that thou mayest live, thou and thy seed."

BERTRAND RUSSELL

The Good Life

THERE HAVE BEEN at different times and among different people many varying conceptions of the good life. To some extent the differences were amenable to argument; this was when men differed as to the means to achieve a given end. Some think that prison is a good way of preventing crime; others hold that education would be better. A difference of this sort can be decided by sufficient evidence. But some differences cannot be tested in this way. Tolstoy condemned all war; others have held the life of a soldier doing battle for the right to be very noble. Here there was probably involved a real difference as to ends. Those who praised the soldier usually consider the punishment of sinners a good thing in itself; Tolstoy did not think so. On such a matter no argument is possible. I cannot, therefore, prove that my view of the good life is right; I can only state my view and hope that as many as possible will agree. My view is this: *The good life is one inspired by love and guided by knowledge.*

Knowledge and love are both indefinitely extensible; therefore, however good a life may be, a better life can be imagined. Neither love without knowledge nor knowledge without love can produce a good life. In the Middle Ages, when pestilence appeared in a country, holy men advised the population to assemble in churches and pray for deliverance; the result was that the infection spread with extraordinary rapidity among the crowded masses of supplicants. This was an example of love without knowledge. The late war afforded an example of knowledge without love. In each case, the result was death on a large scale.

Although both love and knowledge are necessary, love is in a sense more fundamental, since it will lead intelligent people to seek knowledge, in order to find out how to benefit those whom they love. But if people are not intelligent, they will be content to believe what they have been told and may do harm in spite of the most genuine benevolence. Medicine affords, perhaps, the best example of what I mean. An able physician is more useful to a patient than the most devoted friend, and progress in medical knowledge does more for the health of the community than ill-informed philanthropy. Nevertheless, an element of benevolence is essential even here if any but the rich are to profit by scientific discoveries.

136

Love is a word which covers a variety of feelings; I have used it purposely, as I wish to include them all. Love as an emotion—which is what I am speaking about, for love "on principle" does not seem to me genuine—moves between two poles: on one side, pure delight in contemplation; on the other, pure benevolence. Where inanimate objects are concerned, delight alone enters in; we cannot feel benevolence toward a landscape or a sonata. This type of enjoyment is presumably the source of art. It is stronger, as a rule, in very young children than in adults, who are apt to view objects in a utilitarian spirit. It plays a large part in our feelings toward human beings, some of whom have charm and some the reverse, when considered simply as objects of aesthetic contemplation.

The opposite pole of love is pure benevolence. Men have sacrificed their lives to helping lepers; in such a case the love they felt cannot have had any element of aesthetic delight. Parental affection, as a rule, is accompanied by pleasure in the child's appearance but remains strong when this element is wholly absent. It would seem odd to call a mother's interest in a sick child "benevolence," because we are in the habit of using this word to describe a pale emotion nine parts humbug. But it is difficult to find any other word to describe the desire for another person's welfare. It is a fact that a desire of this sort may reach any degree of strength in the case of parental feeling. In other cases it is far less intense; indeed it would seem likely that all altruistic emotion is a sort of overflow of parental feeling, or sometimes a sublimation of it. For want of a better word, I shall call this emotion "benevolence." But I want to make it clear that I am speaking of an emotion, not a principle, and that I do not include in it any feeling of superiority such as is sometimes associated with the word. The word *sympathy* expresses part of what I mean but leaves out the element of activity that I wish to include.

Love at its fullest is an indissoluble combination of the two elements, delight and well-wishing. The pleasure of a parent in a beautiful and successful child combines both elements; so does sex love at its best. But in sex love, benevolence will only exist where there is secure possession, since otherwise jealousy will destroy it, while perhaps actually increasing the delight in contemplation. Delight without well-wishing may be cruel; well-wishing without delight easily tends to become cold and a little superior. A person who wishes to be loved wishes to be the object of a love containing both elements, except in cases of extreme weakness, such as infancy and severe illness. In these cases benevolence may be all that is desired. Conversely, in cases of extreme strength, admiration is more desired than benevolence: this is the state of mind of potentates and famous beauties. We only desire other people's good wishes in proportion as we feel ourselves in need of help or in danger of harm from them. At least, that would seem to be the biological logic of the situation, but it is not quite true to life. We desire affection in order to escape from the feeling of loneliness, in order to be, as we say, "understood." This is a matter of sympathy, not merely of benevolence; the person whose affection is satisfactory to us must not merely wish us well but must know in what our happiness consists. But this belongs to the other element of the good life—namely, knowledge.

In a perfect world, every sentient being would be to every other the object of the fullest love, compounded of delight, benevolence, and understanding inextricably blended. It does not follow that, in this actual world, we ought to attempt to have such feelings toward all the sentient beings whom we encounter. There are many in whom we cannot feel delight, because they are disgusting; if we were to do violence to our nature by trying to see beauties in them, we should merely blunt our susceptibilities to what we naturally find beautiful. Not to mention human beings, there are fleas and bugs and lice. We should have to be as hard pressed as the Ancient Mariner before we could feel delight in contemplating these creatures. Some saints, it is true, have called them "pearls of God," but what these men delighted in was the opportunity of displaying their own sanctity.

Benevolence is easier to extend widely, but even benevolence has its limits. If a man wished to marry a lady, we should not think the better of him for withdrawing if he found that someone else also wished to marry her: we should regard this as a fair field for competition. Yet his feelings toward a rival cannot be *wholly* benevolent. I think that in all descriptions of the good life here on earth we must assume a certain basis of animal vitality and animal instinct; without this, life becomes tame and uninteresting. Civilization should be something added to this, not substituted for it; the ascetic saint and the detached sage fail in this respect to be complete human beings. A small number of them may enrich a community; but a world composed of them would die of boredom.

These considerations lead to a certain emphasis on the element of delight as an ingredient in the best love. Delight, in this actual world, is unavoidably selective and prevents us from having the same feelings toward all mankind. When conflicts arise between delight and benevolence, they must, as a rule, be decided by a compromise, not by a complete surrender of either. Instinct has its rights, and if we do violence to it beyond a point it takes vengeance in subtle ways. Therefore in aiming at a good life the limits of human possibility must be borne in mind. Here again, however, we are brought back to the necessity of knowledge.

When I speak of knowledge as an ingredient of the good life, I am not thinking of ethical knowledge but of scientific knowledge and knowledge of particular facts. I do not think there is, strictly speaking, such a thing as ethical knowledge. If we desire to achieve some end, knowledge may show us the means, and this knowledge may loosely pass as ethical. But I do not believe that we can decide what sort of conduct is right or wrong except by reference to its probable consequences. Given an end to be achieved, it is a question for science to discover how to achieve it. All moral rules must be tested by examining whether they tend to realize ends that we desire. I say ends that we desire, not ends that we *ought* to desire. What we "ought" to desire is merely what someone else wishes us to desire. Usually it is what the authorities wish us to desire—parents, schoolmasters, policemen, and judges. If you say to me, "You ought to do so-and-so," the motive power of your remark lies in my desire for your approval—together, possibly, with rewards or punishments attached to your approval or disapproval. Since all behavior springs from desire, it is clear that ethical notions can have no importance except as they influence desire. They do this through the desire for approval and the fear of disapproval. These are powerful social forces, and we shall naturally endeavor to win them to our side if we wish to realize any social purpose. When I say that the morality of conduct is to be judged by its probable consequences, I mean that I desire to see approval given to behavior likely to realize social purposes which we desire, and disapproval to opposite behavior. At present this is not done; there are certain traditional rules according to which approval and disapproval are meted out quite regardless of consequences. But this is a topic with which we shall deal at some other time.

The superfluity of theoretical ethics is obvious in simple cases. Suppose, for instance, your child is ill. Love makes you wish to cure it, and science tells you how to do so. There is not an intermediate stage of ethical theory, where it is demonstrated that your child had better be cured. Your act springs directly from desire for an end, together with knowledge of means. This is equally true of all acts, whether good or bad. The ends differ, and the knowledge is more adequate in some cases than in others. But there is no conceivable way of making people do things they do not wish to do. What is possible is to alter their desires by a system of rewards and penalties, among which social approval and disapproval are not the least potent. The question for the legislative moralist is, therefore: How shall this system of rewards and punishments be arranged so as to secure the maximum of what is desired by the legislative authority? If I say that the legislative authority has bad desires, I mean merely that its desires conflict with those of some section of the community to which I belong. Outside human desires there is no moral standard.

Thus, what distinguishes ethics from science is not any special kind of knowledge but merely desire. The knowledge required in ethics is exactly like the knowledge elsewhere; what is peculiar is that certain ends are desired, and that right conduct is what conduces to them. Of course, if the definition of right conduct is to make a wide appeal, the ends must be such as large sections of mankind desire. If I defined right conduct as that which increases my own income, readers would disagree. The whole effectiveness of any ethical argument lies in its scientific part, i.e., in the proof that one kind of conduct, rather than some other, is a means to an end which is widely desired. I distinguish, however, between ethical argument and ethical education. The latter consists in strengthening certain desires and weakening others. This is quite a different process.

We can now explain more exactly the purport of the definition of the good life with which this essay began. When I said that the good life consists of love guided by knowledge, the desire which prompted me was the desire to live such a life as far as possible, and to see others living it; and the logical content of the statement is that, in a community where men live in this way, more desires will be satisfied than in one where there is less love or less knowledge. I do not mean that such a life is "virtuous" or that its opposite is "sinful," for these are conceptions which seem to me to have no scientific justification.

SHUNZO SAKAMAKI

Zen and Intuited Knowledge

FROM EARLY TIMES men have sought to apprehend reality through logic, theology or metaphysics. In general such an effort is conceived of as that of a "thinking reed," a divine child or a seer surveying and interpreting the nature and meaning of life and the world, on the presupposition that such apparent dichotomies as self and other, subject and object, good and evil, spirit and matter are valid universal assumptions.

We also have efforts to apprehend reality through unmediated contact, such as, for instance, in Zen. The term "Zen" is generally translated into English as "meditation," for lack of a more suitable equivalent. This is indeed a semantic shame, for Zen seeks knowledge of reality derived not from meditation or contemplative cogitation but from intuitive cognition. In this context, intuition does not mean a hunch, a clever guess, a shrewd shot in the dark, but rather a direct contact with a realm that transcends categorization.

Most people operate on the level of non-intuition or of common sense—the touchstone *sine qua non* of their thoughts and actions. At this level of understanding they are prone to be cocksure that black is black, white is white, truth is truth, error is error. Their judgments are based on knowledge by description or on ordinary perceptions which evoke subjective responses or emotions reflecting the perceiver's preconceptions, feelings and notions about the world external to the self.

Reality is assumed to be the co-ordinate of the names and symbols that are devised to differentiate its multifarious components. Increasing awareness of the size and complexity of the physical universe is accompanied by a corresponding growth of the mass of postulations and verbalizations seeking to describe and explain it all. But trying to comprehend the universe has become an increasingly awesome undertaking, for the outer fringes of our perceptions are being inexorably thrust farther and farther away. The universe that once was a relatively comprehensible one, when depicted as an orderly world created and watched over by a paternal divinity, has begun to look more and more like the Great Void of Buddhism or the Great Tao of Taoism.

It is not strange, then, that increasing attention is being paid by Western scholars to Zen, which is a product of both Mahayana Buddhism and Taoism. However, a word of caution is in order, for most accounts of Zen experience become preoccupied with the seemingly bizarre behavior of Zen practitioners. In this preoccupation, these accounts often fail to show that the enigmatic utterances and actions of Zen masters are intended to wean their pupils away from proclivity for conceptual verbalization and toward intuited, non-postulational cognition of reality.

What is emphatically not desired in Zen is intellection or any form of studied or contrived mental or physical action that is predicated on the conception of a world composed of an infinite multiplicity of objects and events. Rather, the world is to be approached as an undifferentiated whole, "just as it is," unencumbered by notions of time, space, cause and effect, value, purpose. When freed from the fetters of symbolization, man would blend imperceptibly into the reality of the indeterminate continuum. There would then be no abstractions or postulates to direct or to block the intuitive flow of thoughts and feelings and actions, so that these would become spontaneous, unhesitating, and unaffected, like ordinary breathing or seeing or hearing, or like a ball bouncing and drifting on a mountain stream, or like birds soaring and gliding on invisible currents of air, with no conscious effort or design.

The practice of Zazen, or Seated Zen, does not seek to obliterate sensory perceptions or to become oblivious to them through some form of mental black-out or complete vacuity of mind. Nor does it seek, on the other hand, to concentrate attention on and formulate categorizations about some specific mundane thing or problem. Any seeking or grasping, as of the mind to know itself, or self to control itself, or "this" to do "that," is like reaching the hand into a pool of water and clutching at the water. The water eludes the grasping hand. But what if the hand were to be lowered gently into the pool and kept there for a time to experience directly, without thought or comment, the reality of the water that is there?

Zazen seeks to apprehend the "eternal now" and the "suchness" or "thusness" of the world, the world "just as it is." This it does by having the perceptive facilities in a state of serene tranquillity and utter receptivity, alert and watchful, but unpurposive, like a muddy pond quietly but without thought waiting for the water to clear. This mood is aptly expressed in a famous Zen verse that reads: "Seated serene (and) tranquil; Spring comes (and) grass grows of itself"; or the well-known Taoist observation: "Nature does nothing, and yet nothing remains undone." The placid, unruffled "mind" or "self" would reflect or mirror whatever it perceives as spontaneously and naturally as a quiet pool of water would reflect the moon—without hesitation or thought or purpose. The moon is a Zen favorite because of its soft, diffused, limpid luminosity in which everything appears or is revealed in its "thusness," "just as it is," natural and undistorted.

Another Zen favorite is the sky—the limitless expanse of the heavens that is both immutable and perpetually in flux. After a time moving objects no longer distract the viewer's attention and the sky begins to assume the qualities of pure sensation as the viewer starts to sense or experience its innate unity and purity and boundless pervasiveness. All consciousness is presently lost of the very act of viewing, of distinction between prehender and prehended, of self and other.

When we consciously think of viewing the sky, we are verbalizing a perceptual situation in which the prehending self makes inferences about a prehended object located in time and space. In unpurposive viewing of the sky, however, discursive postulations about the observer and the observed fade away and the sky is apprehended "of itself," or "just as it is." There is not even a pantheistic identification of self and sky, such as might result from empathy or other forms of self-conscious reflection. Indeed, the realm of concepts has been left behind, and knowledge "about" has given way to direct knowledge.

When conceptualizations have been left behind, a mystic intuitive vision seems to open the doors directly to the very nature of primordial knowledge—knowledge which can be apprehended only through acquaintance, not description. This non-vicarious contact with reality is ineffable. Any attempt at description would perforce seek out its determinate, differentiated, sensed qualities, while futility would mark any effort to conceptualize the experience of an all-embracing, undifferentiated continuum or manifold.

Enlightenment, or the Seeing of Reality, may occur in a sudden flash of insight or an instantaneous awakening that resolves all doubts and uncertainties. Whether or not we find ourselves some day traversing the Zen path to reality will depend on how successful we are in delivering ourselves from the binding imperatives of the non-intuitive commonsense world and moving into the realm of intuited non-conceptual knowledge.

The Packaged Soul?

*Truly here is the "custom-made" man
of today—ready to help build a new
and greater era in the annals of
diesel engineering.*

                                    Diesel Power

THE DISTURBING Orwellian configurations of the world toward which
the persuaders seem to be nudging us—even if unwittingly—can be
seen most clearly in some of their bolder, more imaginative efforts. . . .

In early 1956 a retired advertising man named John G. Schneider
(formerly with Fuller, Smith and Ross, Kenyon and Eckhardt, and
other ad agencies) wrote a satirical novel called *The Golden Kazoo*,
which projected to the 1960 Presidential election the trends in political
merchandising that had already become clear. By 1960 the ad men
from Madison Avenue had taken over completely. Schneider explained
this was the culmination of the trend started in 1952 when ad men
entered the very top policy-making councils of both parties, when "for
the first time" candidates became "merchandise," political campaigns
became "sales-promotion jobs," and the electorate was a "market."

By 1960 the Presidency is just another product to peddle through
tried-and-true mechandising strategies. Speeches are banned as too dull
for citizens accustomed to TV to take. (Even the five-minute quickies
of 1956 had become unendurable.) Instead the candidate is given a
walk-on or centerpiece type of treatment in "spectaculars" carefully designed to drive home a big point. (Remember the election-eve pageant
of 1956 where "little people" reported to President Eisenhower on why
they liked him?)

The 1960 contest, as projected by Schneider, boiled down to a
gigantic struggle between two giant ad agencies, one called Reade and
Bratton for the Republicans and one simply called B.S.&J. for the
Democrats. When one of the two candidates, Henry Clay Adams, timidly suggests he ought to make a foreign-policy speech on the crisis in
the atomic age his account executive Blade Reade gives him a real lecture. "Look," he said, "if you want to impress the longhairs, intellectuals, and Columbia students, do it on your own time, not on my TV
time. Consider your market, man! . . . Your market is forty, fifty million
slobs sitting at home catching your stuff on TV and radio. Are those

144

slobs worried about the atomic age! Nuts. They're worried about next Friday's grocery bill." Several of the merchandising journals gave Mr. Schneider's book a careful review, and none that I saw expressed shock or pain at his implications.

So much for fictional projections into the future. Some of the real-life situations that are being heralded as trends are perhaps more astonishing or disconcerting, as you choose.

A vast development of homes going up at Miramar, Florida, is being called the world's most perfect community by its backers. *Tide,* the merchandisers' journal, admonished America's merchandisers to pay attention to this trail-blazing development as it might be "tomorrow's marketing target." The journal said of Miramar: "Its immediate success . . . has a particular significance for marketers, for the trend to 'packaged' homes in 'packaged' communities may indicate where and how tomorrow's consumer will live. . . ." Its founder, youthful Robert W. Gordon, advises me Miramar has become "a bustling little community" and is well on its way to offering a "completely integrated community" for four thousand families.

What does it mean to buy a "packaged" home in a "packaged" community? For many (but apparently not all) of the Miramar families it means they simply had to bring their suitcases, nothing more. No fuss with moving vans, or shopping for food, or waiting for your new neighbors to make friendly overtures. The homes are completely furnished, even down to linens, china, silver, and a refrigerator full of food. And you pay for it all, even the refrigerator full of food, on the installment plan.

Perhaps the most novel and portentous service available at Miramar—and all for the one packaged price—is that it may also package your social life for you. As Mr. Gordon put it: "Anyone can move into one of the homes with nothing but their personal possessions, and start living as a part of the community five minutes later." Where else could you be playing bridge with your new neighbors the same night you move in! In short, friendship is being merchandised along with real estate, all in one glossy package. *Tide* described this aspect of its town of tomorrow in these words: "To make Miramar as homey and congenial as possible, the builders have established what might be called 'regimented recreation.' As soon as a family moves in the lady of the house will get an invitation to join any number of activities ranging from bridge games to literary teas. Her husband will be introduced, by Miramar, to local groups interested in anything from fish breeding to water skiing."

In the trends toward other-mindedness, group living, and consumption-mindedness as spelled out by Dr. Riesman [in *The Lonely Crowd*], Miramar may represent something of an ultimate for modern man.

Another sort of projection, a projection of the trend toward the "social engineering" of our lives in industry, can be seen perhaps in a remarkable trade school in Los Angeles. It has been turning out students according to a blueprint and in effect certifies its graduates to be co-operative candidates for industry. This institution, National Schools, which is on South Figueroa Street, trains diesel mechanics, electricians, electrical technologists, machinists, auto repairmen and mechanics, radio and TV mechanics, etc. (Established 1905.)

I first came across this breeding ground for the man of tomorrow in an article admiringly titled "Custom-made Men" in *Diesel Power*. The article faced another on "lubrication elements" and appeared in the early days of the depth approach to personnel training. The diesel journal was plainly awed by the exciting potentialities of social engineering, and said that while miraculous advances had been made in the technical field "one vital branch of engineering has been, until recently, woefully neglected—the science of human engineering." It went on to be explicit: "Human engineering, as we refer to it here, is the science of molding and adjusting the attitude of industrial personnel. By this process a worker's mechanical ability and know how will be balanced by equal skill in the art of demonstrating a co-operative attitude toward his job, employer, and fellow employees."

The newest trend, it went on to explain, is to develop in the worker this co-operative outlook prior to his actual employment, while he is receiving his training, when "he is most receptive to this new approach." National Schools in Los Angeles, it said, has been a unique laboratory in developing many phases of human engineering. It followed the progress of the graduate as he went out into industry and checked not only on the technical skills he showed but on "his attitude toward his work and associates." These findings were compared with a transcript of his school work. By such analysis plus surveying employers on the traits they desire in employees National Schools, it said, has been able "to develop the ideal blue print for determining the type of personnel industry needs." National students, it stated, were taught basic concepts of human behavior, and "special emphasis is placed on the clear-cut discussion and study of every subject that will tend to give the student a better understanding of capital-labor co-operation. To this end . . . representative authorities in the diesel industry have been made associate faculty members at National Schools—where they lecture." Truly, it exulted, here was the "custom-made" man ready to help build a greater tomorrow for diesel engineering!

The kind of tomorrow we may be tending toward in the merchandising of products may be exemplified by the use of depth probing on little girls to discover their vulnerability to advertising messages. No one, literally no one, evidently is to be spared from the all-seeing, Big Brotherish eye of the motivational analyst if a merchandising opportunity seems to beckon. The case I am about to relate may seem extreme today—but will it tomorrow?

This case in point, involving a Chicago ad agency's depth probing on behalf of a leading home-permanent preparation, was proudly described by the agency's president in a speech to an advertising conference at the University of Michigan. He cited it in detail, with slides, to illustrate his theme: "How Motivation Studies May Be Used by Creative People to Improve Advertising."

The problem was how to break through women's resistance to giving home permanents to their little girls. Many felt the home permanents ought to wait until high-school age, "along with lipstick and dating." (Some mothers, I've found in my own probing, also suspect home permanents are bad for the hair of little girls and have some moral pangs about it.) At any rate, the agency found, by depth interviewing mothers, that they needed "reassurance" before most of them would feel easy about giving home permanents to their little ones. The agency set out, by depth probing little girls, to find a basis for offering such reassurance. It hoped to find that little girls actually "need" curly hair, and to that end devised a series of projective tests, with the advice of "leading child psychologists and psychiatrists," which were presented to the little girls as "games." When the little girls were shown a carefully devised projective picture of a little girl at a window they reportedly read into the picture the fact that she was "lonely because her straight hair made her unattractive and unwanted." When they were given projective sentence-completion tests they allegedly equated pretty hair with being happy and straight hair with "bad, unloved things."

The agency president summed up the findings of the probing of both mothers (their own early childhood yearnings) and daughters by stating: "We could see, despite the mothers' superficial doubts about home permanents for children, the mothers had a very strong underlying wish for curly-haired little girls." (This is not too hard to believe in view of the fact that hair-preparation merchandisers have been hammering away to condition American females to the wavy-hair-makes-you-lovely theme for decades.)

A seven-and-a-half-pound volume of data detailing all the probings was turned over to the agency's "creative" people and a series of "creative workshops" was held with "a leading authority in the field of child psychology" conducting the discussions. This authority apparently needed to reassure some of the creative people themselves about the project because the authority stated: "Some of you may react, as many older women do, and say, 'How awful to give a child a permanent,' and never stop to think that what they are really saying is, 'How awful to make a girl attractive and make her have respect for herself.'"

The child psychologist analyzed each piece of copy, layout, and TV story board for its psychological validity to make sure it would "ring true to parents." One upshot of all this consulting was a TV commercial designed to help a mother subconsciously recognize "her child's questions, 'Will I be beautiful or ugly, loved or unloved?' because they are her own childhood wishes, too."

Another possible view of tomorrow may be seen in the search to find ways to make us less troublesome and complaining while staying in hospitals. Dr. Dichter undertook this exploration, and his findings were reported in detail in a series of articles in *The Modern Hospital*. The study was undertaken because of the constant complaints of patients about food, bills, routine, boredom, nurses. They were generally irritable, and hospitals that tried to remove the complaints by changing routines, diets, etc., seemed to get nowhere.

So the depth probing of patients began. One fifty-year-old woman recalled her shame at being chided by a hospital aide for calling out for her mother several times during the night. Probers found that patients in hospitals were often filled with infantile insecurities. They weren't just scared of dying but scared because they were helpless like a child. And they began acting like children. Dr. Dichter reported that his most significant finding "deals with the regression of the patient to a child's irrationality. . . . Over and over in each of the interviews, in one form or another, there echoed the basic cry, 'I'm frightened. . . .'" He said the grownup's regression to a child's helplessness and dependence and his search for symbolic assurance were clear. In searching for this symbolic assurance the patient begins seeing the doctor as father and the nurse as mother.

What should the hospitals do with all these adult-children? The answer was obvious. Treat them like children, apply to grownups the same techniques they had been applying in the children's wards to make the children feel loved and secure. For one thing there mustn't be any signs of dissension between doctor and nurse because it would remind the patients of their childhood fears when mother and father quarreled.

Eventually—say by A.D. 2000—perhaps all this depth manipulation of the psychological variety will seem amusingly old-fashioned. By then perhaps the biophysicists will take over with "biocontrol," which is depth persuasion carried to its ultimate. Biocontrol is the new science of controlling mental processes, emotional reactions, and sense perceptions by bioelectrical signals.

The National Electronics Conference meeting in Chicago in 1956 heard electrical engineer Curtiss R. Schafer, of the Norden-Ketay Corporation, explore the startling possibilities of biocontrol. As he envisioned it, electronics could take over the control of unruly humans. This could save the indoctrinators and thought controllers a lot of fuss and bother. He made it sound relatively simple.

Planes, missiles, and machine tools already are guided by electronics, and the human brain—being essentially a digital computer—can be, too. Already, through biocontrol, scientists have changed people's sense of balance. And they have made animals with full bellies feel hunger, and made them feel fearful when they have nothing to fear. *Time* magazine quoted him as explaining:

> The ultimate achievement of biocontrol may be the control of man himself. . . . The controlled subjects would never be permitted to think as individuals. A few months after birth, a surgeon would equip each child with a socket mounted under the scalp and electrodes reaching selected areas of brain tissue. . . . The child's sensory perceptions and muscular activity could be either modified or completely controlled by bioelectric signals radiating from state-controlled transmitters.

He added the reassuring thought that the electrodes "cause no discomfort."

I am sure that the psycho-persuaders of today would be appalled at the prospect of such indignity being committed on man. They are mostly decent, likable people, products of our relentlessly progressive era. Most of them want to control us just a little bit, in order to sell us some product we may find useful or disseminate with us a viewpoint that may be entirely worthy.

But when you are manipulating, where do you stop? Who is to fix the point at which manipulative attempts become socially undesirable?

Essays of Our Time I ● *Part* 6

IAN STEVENSON is *professor and chairman of the department of psychiatry at the University of Virginia's Medical School. No follower of established concepts, he has written such ground-breaking articles as "Why Medicine Is Not a Science" and has become the articulate defender of researchers in extrasensory perception.*

BRUNO BETTELHEIM *received his Ph.D. from the University of Vienna in 1938 and then spent a year in the Dachau and Buchenwald concentration camps. His study based upon this experience, "Individual and Mass Behavior in Extreme Situations," became required reading for United States military-government personnel. Another volume, "The Informed Heart," has recently been published, based upon his studies. Since 1944 Bettelheim has been principal of the Sonia Shankman Orthogenic School at the University of Chicago.*

RONALD MELZACK, *a psychologist, teaches at the University College of London University. There, at McGill University, and at the Pain Clinic of the University of Oregon, he studied the psychology and physiology of pain. Frequently he reports the results of his study on the British broadcasting system.*

IAN STEVENSON

The Uncomfortable Facts
about Extrasensory Perception

FOR CENTURIES some persons have believed they could perceive or influence events at a distance without known physical means of communication or action.

Scientific investigation of such claims began about seventy-five years ago. The branch of science born then, known variously as psychical research and parapsychology, has slowly developed in method and productivity. Two veteran parapsychologists, Dr. J. B. Rhine and Dr. J. G. Pratt, recently published the first avowed textbook on the subject. The publication last year of this book and of another, *ESP and Personality Patterns*, by G. R. Schmeidler and R. A. McConnell, indicate the increasing maturity of the subject and also a shift in emphasis on the part of parapsychologists.

For both these books depart from tests and proofs of whether extrasensory perception occurs, and chiefly report studies of when and how it occurs. I do not mean that the mere occurrence of extrasensory perception has lost its novelty or its interest for parapsychologists. Striking demonstrations are still too rare to be taken for granted—indeed they may always be so. But parapsychologists believe the case for the occurrence of extrasensory perception is so solidly established that they see no reason to engage in further combat with die-hard skeptics who remain obdurate not—as the proponents see it—from lack of evidence, but rather from failure to examine or accept the evidence already abundantly available. Today parapsychologists insist that the fact of extrasensory perception is beyond debate, and they are therefore working more and more toward *understanding* extrasensory perception (and kindred phenomena) with regard to its processes and its relations to other parts of scientific knowledge. At this turning point, then, interested laymen may find useful a review of present knowledge of the subject.

This knowledge derives from a great many sources, but we can divide these conveniently into two large groups: (1) naturally occurring events and (2) planned experimental observations. As in other branches of science, the experimental aspects developed as men tried to understand better their observations of spontaneous occurrences.

Unfortunately, most of the vast literature of the past about spontaneous occurrences of extrasensory perception has no value today, because the reporters did not adopt what we would now consider proper scientific precautions in recording their observations. Most witnesses of strange, ghostly events did not write down their accounts until considerably after the events. Many such events have had only one witness. Such conditions would permit both a free play to the imagination and also the kind of inaccurate recollection which frequently obscures even the records or ordinary happenings which originally occurred under controlled circumstances.

Many modern experiments, moreover, have shown that nearly everyone will hallucinate when his expectation of seeing something becomes sufficiently heightened. For example, one experimenter arranged for a group of persons to bring pressure on one of their number (left out of the conspiracy) to say that he had seen what they pretended to see. Almost invariably the victim yielded and denied his own senses.

This kind of influence can work both ways. We know, for example, that the Middle Ages venerated and encouraged visions. Subsequently, the churches—both Catholic and Protestant—turned against persons who claimed to have visions and accused them of witchcraft. Many burned to death in the fires of the Inquisition. A reaction to this cruelty set in, and also some enlightenment developed, so that from the eighteenth century to the present persons who have had visions have generally been thought not wicked but sick. This attitude had led to more humane treatment but not necessarily to greater understanding of their experiences. The power of such cultural influences—either to stimulate perceptions or to force their concealment—has made many students conclude that we should believe nothing of what has come down to us on this subject from its pre-scientific period.

Yet even before the modern period of scientific inquiry, some instances of extrasensory perception were witnessed and recorded by able observers. For example, we have a number of accounts attested to by reliable witnesses, of exhibitions of clairvoyant powers by the Swedish mystic and scientist, Emanuel Swedenborg. In 1759, for instance, he returned from a trip to England and dined with friends in Göteborg.

About six o'clock, Swedenborg went out, and returned to the company quite pale and alarmed. He said that a dangerous fire had just broken out in Stockholm, on Sodermalm (where his house was), and that it was spreading very fast. He was restless and went out often. He said that the house of one of his friends, whom he named, was already in ashes, and that his own was in danger. At eight o'clock after he had been out again, he joyfully exclaimed, "Thank God! The fire is extinguished, the third door from my house." On Tuesday morning (three days later) the royal courier arrived at the Governor's with the melancholy intelligence of the fire, of the loss which it had occasioned, and of the houses it had damaged and ruined, not in the least differing from that which Swedenborg had given at the very time when it happened, for the fire was extinguished at eight o'clock.

I have quoted the description of this incident by the philosopher Kant, who although not himself a witness, took great pains to inquire through an agent of those who had witnessed the episode.

Until the late nineteenth century, no one had ever studied in a systematic way the numerous incidents of apparitions and clairvoyant powers which seemed to call for scientific scrutiny. Then a group of men, mostly scholars of Cambridge University, organized the Society for Psychical Research in England. Its declared purpose, from which it has not since departed, was to study all such phenomena without officially formulating any opinion as to their nature. Individual members have naturally formed and independently published their own opinions—but the Society (and the similar American Society for Psychical Research) has remained a scientific agency and a forum for discussion and review; it does not promulgate a settled opinion on any issue which might come to its attention. This attitude has earned the Society the contempt of many who believe the evidence, for example, of human survival of physical death already beyond dispute. On the other hand, it has won the praise of those who believe that only the most rigorous scientific method will advance the subject. William James said of the Society for Psychical Research:

> According to the newspaper and drawing-room myth, soft-headedness and idiotic credulity are the bond of sympathy in this Society, and general wonder-sickness its dynamic principle. A glance at the membership fails, however, to corroborate this view. [James then lists some of the distinguished scientists and philosophers who were active in the early days of the Society.] . . . In fact, were I asked to point to a scientific journal where hard-headedness and never-sleeping suspicion of sources of error might be seen in their full bloom, I think I should have to fall back on the Proceedings of the Society for Psychical Research.

Shortly after the founding of the Society, the members undertook what was called a census of hallucinations. This began with the questioning of about 17,000 people regarding any quasi-sensory experiences (without any apparent physical cause) which they had while awake. About 10 per cent said that they had had some such experience. Similar questionnaires since then have produced approximately the same percentage of affirmative replies. For this reason and because the inquirers adopted certain precautions in sampling, the census of hallucinations probably studied an adequately representative group of people.

The investigators made further detailed inquiries concerning the experiences of those who had reported seeing apparitions or having other hallucinations. They rapidly eliminated a great many cases where the testimony might be fallacious. The inquirers believed that the remaining experiences could not reasonably be explained as having occurred through normal physical channels of communication. The societies in England and the United States have continued to study such cases.

Emotional crises seem to promote extrasensory communications. Many, although by no means all, instances of apparitions relate to persons who are dying or dead. In a large number of the cases collected by the Society for Psychical Research, a person is "seen" in an entirely different place, perhaps hundreds of miles away, just before or after his death. I have already mentioned that expectation can certainly promote hallucinations. But in the best cases, the person seeing the apparition has no knowledge whatever that the person seen is dying or even ill. Indeed, often the person of the apparition has not even been known to the percipient and is only subsequently recognized from details in a photograph or description.

Some of the most interesting cases collected by the Society describe experiences in which a person believes himself out of his physical body and able to look at it, as if from the point of view of another person. Some of these experiences we can attribute to a simple dream. In others, however, the person having the experience becomes aware of objects or events of which he could have had no normal knowledge and which could be later verified. These cases are by no means restricted to those collected by the Society for Psychical Research. Recently, for example, a clergyman who underwent an operation afterwards reported in detail what had happened while he was clearly anesthetized and ostensibly unconscious. He accurately described the surgeon's having left the operating room to get another instrument, and the details of the conversations of those in the operating room.

Sometimes such "out-of-the-body" experiences, as they are called, occur when several persons simultaneously observe another person whose physical body is actually elsewhere. An example involving three persons occurred in the nineteenth century. A Mr. Wilmot was cross-ing the Atlantic from Britain to rejoin his wife in the United States. He shared a cabin with another man. The cabin had a sloping side so that the upper berth was set back from the lower one. One night during a storm, Mr. Wilmot thought he dreamed that his wife came to the cabin, hesitated at the entrance, then entered and kissed him. When he awoke, his cabin-mate reproached him for having a female visitor and then described the appearance of his wife exactly as Mr. Wilmot had seen her in his dream.

When Mr. Wilmot landed and met his wife, to continue the story in his own words, ". . . almost her first question when we were alone was, 'Did you receive a visit from me a week ago Tuesday?' 'A visit from you?' said I. 'We were more than a thousand miles at sea.' 'I know it,' she replied, 'but it seemed to me that I visited you.' 'It would be impossible,' said I. 'Tell me what makes you think so.' My wife then told me that on account of the severity of the weather and the reported loss of the 'Africa' . . . she had been extremely anxious about me. On the night . . . when the storm had just begun to abate, she had lain awake for a long time thinking of me, and about four o'clock in the morning it seemed to her that she went out to seek me. Crossing the wide and stormy sea, she came at length to a low, black steamship, whose side she went up, and then descending into the cabin, passed through it to the stern until she came to my stateroom. 'Tell me,' she said, 'do they ever have staterooms like the one I saw where the upper berth extends further back than the under one? A man was in the upper berth looking right at me, and for a moment I was afraid to go in, but soon I went up to the side of your berth, bent down and kissed you and embraced you and then went away.'"

It seems that the circumstances of dying not only favor the appear-ance of the dying person as an apparition, but also sometimes give the dying heightened powers of extrasensory perception. Usually, deathbed visions comprise only ramblings of delirium like Falstaff's "babbling of green fields." But occasionally they seem to include communications of a paranormal kind.

An elderly woman in this country became seriously ill. When the doctors said that she did not have long to live, the family gathered around her bed. Suddenly she seemed much more alert and the expres-sion on her face changed to one of great pleasure and excitement. She raised herself slightly and said: "Oh, Will, are you there?"—and fell back dead.

Of the many members of the family who were present, no one was named Will. After her death, the family questioned who Will might be and found that the only Will in the family was a great-uncle who lived in England. Not long after the grandmother's death, word was received from England that her brother Will had died about two days before her death.

This little story strongly suggests the occurrence of extrasensory awareness in the dying woman of the recent death on the other side of the Atlantic of her brother. However, it also illustrates some of the difficulties in the investigation of spontaneous cases of extrasensory perception. Although more than one witness heard the dying woman, none of them made a written record of the event before word came from England of the brother's death. Thus the whole story might be explained as a retrospective falsification of memory.

Many instances of such retrospective distortion have occurred. I am not suggesting that this is always a satisfactory explanation. On the contrary, the evidence in many cases quite clearly supports their interpretation as instances of paranormal communication. Yet the difficulties of obtaining reliable testimony—and the small returns—have dissuaded many investigators from investing the extraordinary effort, time, and patience required to sift the evidence carefully.

This discouragement was itself helpful, however, in turning the investigators in another direction, that of experimental testing. Some of the early research workers of the nineteenth century studied extrasensory perception by quantitative methods, which included attempts at card-guessing. However, serious quantitative studies began with the work of Dr. J. B. Rhine in 1930 at Duke University. For almost thirty years now, Dr. Rhine and his colleagues have conducted an extensive series of experiments exploring many aspects of the subject. The scientific scope and discipline of these experiments have slowly won respect from many other scientists.

Dr. Rhine's experiments have mostly used the technique of having the percipient guess cards which an experimenter has shuffled into a random order. The percipient may call his guesses while someone else—an "agent"—looks at the cards one after the other (telepathy); or he may guess the order without anyone else's looking at the cards while he does so (clairvoyance). In either case, the order of the cards and of the guesses are independently recorded before being compared. Some of Dr. Rhine's earlier experiments used procedures which critics objected could not absolutely exclude sensory cues, errors, or other factors which would permit attributing the positive results to normal perceptions.

By separating constructive criticism from mere invective, Dr. Rhine and others working in this research have slowly tightened the conditions of the experiments until they seem to have eliminated alternative explanations of the results. Some of the adopted precautions may seem unnecessary to those unfamiliar with the range of normal perceptions, the possibilities of self-deception, and the temptations for fraud to be found in this work. To give one example only, it might be thought sufficient—and was at first—to keep the cards to be guessed by the subject face down on a table even if their backs remained visible to him. But printing can emboss a pattern on cards which can show through, so that some persons have read cards through their backs. Now screens separate the subject and the cards if they are in the same room.

In addition, the experimenters have further excluded the possibility of sensory cues by conducting a number of successful experiments with percipient and agent separated by distances of from several hundred yards to several hundred miles. By using additional witnesses they have controlled errors in recording the guesses and comparing them to the "target" cards. They have also given much attention to the statistical problems involved in estimating the likelihood that a percipient might come up with seemingly high scores on the basis of chance alone. Some subjects show such slight capacities for extrasensory perception that it is hard to refute this possibility in their cases. However, certain unusual subjects have shown such extraordinary ability at card-guessing that the odds against their having done so without some extrasensory knowledge of the cards are astronomically high.

A number of able mathematicians beginning as far back as the 1930s have acknowledged publicly the soundness of the statistical procedures used in parapsychology. However, the interpretation of the results with regard to probability remains controversial for some scientists. Critics have sometimes alleged that parapsychologists say the results of the experiments they cite as evidence of extrasensory perception could not have occurred by chance. In fact they say no such thing, because one can never say *anything* could not have occurred by chance. Obviously a great many unusual events—such as drawing a hand of thirteen spades at bridge—do occur by chance. Accordingly, parapsychologists simply calculate the probability that the scores in their experiments would occur by chance alone. In experiment after experiment the probability has been exceedingly small.

Recently Mr. Spencer Brown in England has challenged the use of current concepts of chance and its statistical evaluation in parapsychology. In this he has received attention but little support from other scientists—not that a majority vote should decide such a matter. The reluctance of other scientists to discard the statistical methods used in parapsychology derives from the support which many other branches of science obtain from these methods. Only a Samson of theory could bring down the temple erected on this foundation.

Dr. Rhine's experiments, as I have mentioned, showed that extrasensory perception does not depend upon space. Those of Dr. S. G. Soal in London showed that it apparently does not depend on time. Dr. Soal is an experimenter of extraordinary tenacity who worked to duplicate Dr. Rhine's results for five years without success. He had almost abandoned the attempt when another investigator, Mr. Whately Carington, persuaded him reluctantly to review his data for the possibility that percipients might have guessed not the "target" card up for guessing at that moment, but one or several cards before or later. Carington had already found evidence of this effect in experiments of his own.

The task of rechecking Dr. Soal's data for this "displacement" effect proved a tedious chore, but resulted in the discovery of two remarkably gifted subjects. These showed unusually high scores in the guessing of the cards immediately ahead of the target cards.

Following this discovery, Dr. Soal recalled one of these subjects and in a further and most carefully controlled series of experiments repeated the observations of the displacement effect, thus demonstrating that it was not due to a *post hoc* interpretation of the data in the first series of experiments. These experiments of Dr. Soal provide an experimental confirmation of precognition, of which a number of spontaneous cases had already given some evidence. Since the work of Dr. Rhine and Dr. Soal, other independent investigators have provided further confirmation of the occurrence under controlled conditions of extrasensory perception.

Dr. Rhine's group seems to have demonstrated also that some persons have a capacity to influence physical objects without physical means—a process called psychokinesis. The usual experiments call for attempts to influence the fall of dice in particular ways. These experiments have included the standard precautions against error and have also received confirmation from other investigators, notably Mrs. Laura Dale in New York City and Dr. R. A. McConnell of the University of Pittsburgh. However, the evidence for psychokinesis is generally considered less substantial than that for ESP.

Much of the recent work on extrasensory perception has studied not its occurrence as such, but its processes—what facilitates it and what inhibits it. The newness of this work forbids more than tentative conclusions. It appears that some ability in extrasensory perception is widespread and indeed all people may have it at some time or other in their lives. However, marked degrees of it occur only rarely. Also, the capacity fluctuates rather widely and may vanish altogether. The novelty of tests of extrasensory perception stimulates many beginning subjects to performances which are well above chance but which they do not sustain after the initial enthusiasm wears off.

Dr. Gertrude Schmeidler has just summarized, in the book mentioned earlier, an extensive series of experiments on the relationship between the capacity for extrasensory perception and certain features of personality, especially the attitude which the subject has toward extrasensory perception itself. In experiments conducted over more than ten years, she has found significant differences between those who accept the possibility of their having an ability to demonstrate extrasensory perception (sheep) and those who deny this possibility (goats). "Sheep" score on the average significantly above chance, "goats" below chance. The scoring below chance of many of the goats seems to indicate—paradoxically—that they use some extrasensory communication in order to do this. They must know what *not* to guess in order not to guess at a chance level.

The processes of extrasensory perception apparently are unconscious and can rarely be modified by conscious efforts or training. In altered states of consciousness—induced by barbiturates or by hypnosis —some subjects score better but the changes are rarely spectacular.

Of special importance is the relationship between the percipient and the sender (or "agent"), and often also that between either of these and the experimenter. Investigators have known for many years that some subjects reached high scores with one sender but not with another. Recently, a Dutch investigator who is also an inspector of schools in Amsterdam, Mr. J. G. van Buschbach, made extensive studies of extrasensory perception in children of elementary and junior high schools when their teachers acted as agents. He found highly significant above-chance scores among the elementary school children—but not among the older children. These differences he attributed to the greater emotional closeness of the pupils and teachers in the younger group.

Two American experimenters, Miss Margaret Anderson and Miss Rhea White, have sharpened this a little by studying extrasensory capacity in relation to the expressed liking or disliking of the pupils and teachers for each other. They found that when pupils liked teachers the scores with the teachers as co-experimenters were higher than when the pupils disliked the teachers. Even better results occurred when the teachers also liked the pupils.

This kind of relationship psychiatrists have called rapport. They would like to know much more about it, because they believe that successful psychotherapy requires the attainment of rapport between the psychotherapist and his patient. But to name a relationship does not explain its processes. In studying relationships between persons who have a higher-than-average degree of communication by extrasensory perception, psychiatrists can perhaps help the parapsychologists as well as learn from them. A number of psychiatrists have reported instances of extrasensory perception in their patients under circumstances which permitted rather close study of the current personal relationships of the patient. These few studies have illustrated also the occurrence of transient extrasensory perceptions during periods of strong emotional involvement with another person, often the psychotherapist.

The foregoing absurdly condensed survey of parapsychology shows that its work is little more than started. But at least it seems to have arrived as a respectable branch of science. Professor Henry Sidgwick of Cambridge, one of the founders and the first president of the Society for Psychical Research, said at the time of its founding that he aimed at finding evidence about psychical matters of such strength that his critics would accuse him of fraud. This exalted, if perhaps masochistic, wish has often come true.

The most recent instance occurred in an article in the professional journal of American scientists, *Science,* in 1955. The author, Dr. G. R. Price, said that the apparent evidence for extrasensory perception, if accepted, will require a drastic revision of our current concepts of physics. He found this impossible to contemplate, and therefore proposed that the apparent evidence for extrasensory perception derived from the deliberate practice of fraud. He could not specify any particular fraud, but believed this the only sensible explanation. The wrath of parapsychologists found expression in subsequent correspondence about this article, but was not unmixed with some satisfaction that the matter had been put by Dr. Price with such clear alternatives.

For indeed, it seems that scientists must soon accept and incorporate in their concepts the data of parapsychology. Many continue intransigent but necessarily uncomfortable. Professor C. D. Broad, of Cambridge University—one of a handful of philosophers who have recognized the importance of these phenomena—has described their position as follows:

> It compels one either to ignore all the phenomena in question, or to be continually occupied in explaining them away. The former course is not scientifically respectable; for it is quite certain that many people quite as sensible as oneself and far more expert, have personally investigated these matters and have persuaded themselves of the genuineness of these phenomena and of the impossibility of explaining them completely by fraud or mistake. And the latter course may at any moment be barred by some fact which we simply cannot explain away.

I do not mean to suggest that the opposition to the data of parapsychology derives exclusively from the ignorance or prejudice of other scientists. I hope I have made sufficiently clear that the investigators of the last seventy-five years have only made a modest beginning. Data are still scant and so are successful repetitions of the same experiments. Critics often complain about the lack of repeatability of the parapsychological experiments. But as I have tried to make clear, many experiments have been repeated both by the same experimenter and by different experimenters. Yet it remains true that the capacity for extrasensory perception frequently fades even in high-scoring subjects and parapsychologists are far from being able to turn it on at will. We know much more about what interferes with the capacity than about what facilitates it.

And we know even less about the nature of the capacity for extrasensory perception. Some students of the subject have theorized that current human capacities for extrasensory perception are a faint residue of a once much stronger power which has gradually diminished with evolution—being displaced by the known sensory capacities which can locate the origin of stimuli and thus may serve man better in his adaptation to his current environment. But this is pure speculation. Parapsychologists have no really satisfactory theory of extrasensory perception to market even to available buyers.

It is unfortunate for the progress of the subject that parapsychologists remain few in number and short of funds. We can still count on the fingers of one hand the number of laboratories engaged in parapsychology across the world. And even these sustain a precarious life through the generosity of a few ardent supporters. Fortunately, the subject has happened to interest a number of remarkable people whose energy has compensated partly for their lack of numbers and money. The work continues and slowly expands, in the discovery of fundamental data and in making ties with other branches of science for which it may become increasingly relevant.

Both enthusiasts and skeptics sometimes state that the acceptance of parapsychology implies an overthrow of the present scientific view of the universe. This opinion seems to have impelled Dr. Price to his accusations of fraud since for him the alternative seemed so improbable and appalling. Such delights or alarms may prove unjustified.

The facts of extrasensory perception and kindred phenomena may not alter greatly our view of the physical world. They will, I believe, revolutionize our view of man. It is perhaps not more surprising that a man should influence the fall of dice thrown by a machine than that he should activate his own hand to throw the dice. In either case, a man's mind acts on a physical object whether dice or his own hand.

But we do not know how mind acts on matter—whether part of the same organism or outside it.

Many persons have thought that mind is merely a name for certain kinds of experiences; that minds have no real existence; and that mental activity cannot occur apart from the brain. A number of evidences interfere with the acceptance of this view. Parapsychological studies provide one group of such evidences. For they show that the mind can function without its physical senses. Thus they open—or re-open as religious believers would say—the possibility that the mind can also function without the brain or body to which those senses are attached.

BRUNO BETTELHEIM

Joey: A "Mechanical Boy"

JOEY, WHEN WE began our work with him, was a mechanical boy. He functioned as if by remote control, run by machines of his own powerfully creative fantasy. Not only did he himself believe that he was a machine but, more remarkably, he created this impression in others. Even while he performed actions that are intrinsically human, they never appeared to be other than machine-started and executed. On the other hand, when the machine was not working we had to concentrate on recollecting his presence, for he seemed not to exist. A human body that functions as if it were a machine and a machine that duplicates human functions are equally fascinating and frightening. Perhaps they are so uncanny because they remind us that the human body can operate without a human spirit, that body can exist without soul. And Joey was a child who had been robbed of his humanity.

Not every child who possesses a fantasy world is possessed by it. Normal children may retreat into realms of imaginary glory or magic powers, but they are easily recalled from these excursions. Disturbed children are not always able to make the return trip; they remain withdrawn, prisoners of the inner world of delusion and fantasy. In many ways Joey presented a classic example of this state of infantile autism. In any age, when the individual has escaped into a delusional world, he has usually fashioned it from bits and pieces of the world at hand.

Joey, in his time and world, chose the machine and froze himself in its image. His story has a general relevance to the understanding of emotional development in a machine age.

Joey's delusion is not uncommon among schizophrenic children today. He wanted to be rid of his unbearable humanity, to become completely automatic. He so nearly succeeded in attaining this goal that he could almost convince others, as well as himself, of his mechanical character. The descriptions of autistic children in the literature take for their point of departure and comparison the normal or abnormal human being. To do justice to Joey I would have to compare him simultaneously to a most inept infant and a highly complex piece of machinery. Often we had to force ourselves by a conscious act of will to realize that Joey was a child. Again and again his acting-out of his delusions froze our own ability to respond as human beings.

During Joey's first weeks with us we would watch absorbedly as this at once fragile-looking and imperious nine-year-old went about his mechanical existence. Entering the dining room, for example, he would string an imaginary wire from his "energy source"—an imaginary electric outlet—to the table. There he "insulated" himself with paper napkins and finally plugged himself in. Only then could Joey eat, for he firmly believed that the "current" ran his ingestive apparatus. So skillful was the pantomime that one had to look twice to be sure there was neither wire nor outlet nor plug. Children and members of our staff spontaneously avoided stepping on the "wires" for fear of interrupting what seemed the source of his very life.

For long periods of time, when his "machinery" was idle, he would sit so quietly that he would disappear from the focus of the most conscientious observation. Yet in the next moment he might be "working" and the center of our captivated attention. Many times a day he would turn himself on and shift noisily through a sequence of higher and higher gears until he "exploded," screaming "Crash, crash!" and hurling items from his ever present apparatus—radio tubes, light bulbs, even motors or, lacking these, any handy breakable object. (Joey had an astonishing knack for snatching bulbs and tubes unobserved.) As soon as the object thrown had shattered, he would cease his screaming and wild jumping and retire to mute, motionless nonexistence.

Our maids, inured to difficult children, were exceptionally attentive to Joey; they were apparently moved by his extreme infantile fragility, so strangely coupled with megalomaniacal superiority. Occasionally some of the apparatus he fixed to his bed to "live him" during his sleep would fall down in disarray. This machinery he contrived from masking tape, cardboard, wire and other paraphernalia. Usually the maids would pick up such things and leave them on a table for the children to find, or disregard them entirely. But Joey's machine they carefully restored: "Joey must have the carburetor so he can breathe." Similarly they were on the alert to pick up and preserve the motors that ran him during the day and the exhaust pipes through which he exhaled.

How had Joey become a human machine? From intensive interviews with his parents we learned that the process had begun even before birth. Schizophrenia often results from parental rejection, sometimes combined ambivalently with love. Joey, on the other hand, had been completely ignored.

"I never knew I was pregnant," his mother said, meaning that she had already excluded Joey from her consciousness. His birth, she said, "did not make any difference." Joey's father, a rootless draftee in the wartime civilian army, was equally unready for parenthood. So, of course, are many young couples. Fortunately most such parents lose their indifference upon the baby's birth. But not Joey's parents. "I did not want to see or nurse him," his mother declared. "I had no feeling of actual dislike—I simply didn't want to take care of him." For the first three months of his life Joey "cried most of the time." A colicky baby, he was kept on a rigid four-hour feeding schedule, was not touched unless necessary and was never cuddled or played with. The mother, preoccupied with herself, usually left Joey alone in the crib or playpen during the day. The father discharged his frustrations by punishing Joey when the child cried at night.

Soon the father left for overseas duty, and the mother took Joey, now a year and a half old, to live with her at her parents' home. On his arrival the grandparents noticed that ominous changes had occurred in the child. Strong and healthy at birth, he had become frail and irritable; a responsive baby, he had become remote and inaccessible. When he began to master speech, he talked only to himself. At an early date he became preoccupied with machinery, including an old electric fan which he could take apart and put together again with surprising deftness.

Joey's mother impressed us with a fey quality that expressed her insecurity, her detachment from the world and her low physical vitality. We were struck especially by her total indifference as she talked about Joey. This seemed much more remarkable than the actual mistakes she made in handling him. Certainly he was left to cry for hours when hungry, because she fed him on a rigid schedule; he was toilet-trained with great rigidity so that he would give no trouble. These things happen to many children. But Joey's existence never registered with his mother. In her recollections he was fused at one moment with one event or person; at another, with something or somebody else. When she told us about his birth and infancy, it was as if she were talking about some vague acquaintance, and soon her thoughts would wander off to another person or to herself.

When Joey was not yet four, his nursery school suggested that he enter a special school for disturbed children. At the new school his autism was immediately recognized. During his three years there he experienced a slow improvement. Unfortunately a subsequent two years in a parochial school destroyed this progress. He began to develop compulsive defenses, which he called his "preventions." He could not drink, for example, except through elaborate piping systems built of straws. Liquids had to be "pumped" into him, in his fantasy, or he could not suck. Eventually his behavior became so upsetting that he could not be kept in the parochial school. At home things did not improve. Three months before entering the Orthogenic School be made a serious attempt at suicide.

To us Joey's pathological behavior seemed the external expression of an overwhelming effort to remain almost nonexistent as a person. For weeks Joey's only reply when addressed was "Bam." Unless he thus neutralized whatever we said, there would be an explosion, for Joey plainly wished to close off every form of contact not mediated by machinery. Even when he was bathed he rocked back and forth with mute, engine-like regularity, flooding the bathroom. If he stopped rocking, he did this like a machine too; suddenly he went completely rigid. Only once, after months of being lifted from his bath and carried to bed, did a small expression of puzzled pleasure appear on his face as he said very softly: "They even carry you to your bed here."

For a long time after he began to talk he would never refer to anyone by name, but only as "that person" or "the little person" or "the big person." He was unable to designate by its true name anything to which he attached feelings. Nor could he name his anxieties except through neologisms or word contaminations. For a long time he spoke about "master paintings" and "a master painting room" (*i.e.*, masturbating and masturbating room). One of his machines, the "criticizer," prevented him from "saying words which have unpleasant feelings." Yet he gave personal names to the tubes and motors in his collection of machinery. Moreover, these dead things had feelings; the tubes bled when hurt and sometimes got sick. He consistently maintained this reversal between animate and inanimate objects.

In Joey's machine world everything, on pain of instant destruction, obeyed inhibitory laws much more stringent than those of physics. When we came to know him better, it was plain that in his moments of silent withdrawal, with his machine switched off, Joey was absorbed in pondering the compulsive laws of his private universe. His preoccupation with machinery made it difficult to establish even practical contacts with him. If he wanted to do something with a counselor, such as play with a toy that had caught his vague attention, he could not do so: "I'd like this very much, but first I have to turn off the machine." But by the time he had fulfilled all the requirements of his preventions, he had lost interest. When a toy was offered to him, he could not touch it because his motors and his tubes did not leave him a hand free. Even certain colors were dangerous and had to be strictly avoided in toys and clothing, because "some colors turn off the current, and I can't touch them because I can't live without the current."

Joey was convinced that machines were better than people. Once when he bumped into one of the pipes on our jungle gym he kicked it so violently that his teacher had to restrain him to keep him from injuring himself. When she explained that the pipe was much harder than his foot, Joey replied: "That proves it. Machines are better than the body. They don't break; they're much harder and stronger." If he lost or forgot something, it merely proved that his brain ought to be thrown away and replaced by machinery. If he spilled something his arm should be broken and twisted off because it did not work properly. When his head or arm failed to work as it should, he tried to punish it by hitting it. Even Joey's feelings were mechanical. Much later in his therapy, when he had formed a timid attachment to another child and had been rebuffed, Joey cried: "He broke my feelings."

Gradually we began to understand what had seemed to be contradictory in Joey's behavior—why he held on to the motors and tubes, then suddenly destroyed them in a fury, then set out immediately and urgently to equip himself with new and larger tubes. Joey had created these machines to run his body and mind because it was too painful to be human. But again and again he became dissatisfied with their failure to meet his need and rebellious at the way they frustrated his will. In a recurrent frenzy he "exploded" his light bulbs and tubes, and for a moment became a human being—for one crowning instant he came alive. But as soon as he had asserted his dominance through the self-created explosion, he felt his life ebbing away. To keep on existing he had immediately to restore his machines and replenish the electricity that supplied his life energy.

What deep-seated fears and needs underlay Joey's delusional system? We were long in finding out, for Joey's preventions effectively concealed the secret of his autistic behavior. In the meantime we dealt with his peripheral problems one by one.

During his first year with us Joey's most trying problem was toilet behavior. This surprised us, for Joey's personality was not "anal" in the Freudian sense; his original personality damage had antedated the period of his toilet-training. Rigid and early toilet-training, however, had certainly contributed to his anxieties. It was our effort to help Joey with this problem that led to his first recognition of us as human beings.

Going to the toilet, like everything else in Joey's life, was surrounded by elaborate preventions. We had to accompany him; he had to take off all his clothes; he could only squat, not sit, on the toilet seat; he had to touch the wall with one hand, in which he also clutched frantically the vacuum tubes that powered his elimination. He was terrified lest his whole body be sucked down.

To counteract this fear we gave him a metal wastebasket in lieu of a toilet. Eventually, when eliminating into the wastebasket, he no longer needed to take off all his clothes, nor to hold on to the wall. He still needed the tubes and motors which, he believed, moved his bowels for him. But here again the all-important machinery was itself a source of new terrors. In Joey's world the gadgets had to move their bowels, too. He was terribly concerned that they should, but since they were so much more powerful than men, he was also terrified that if his tubes moved their bowels, their feces would fill all of space and leave him no room to live. He was thus always caught in some fearful contradiction.

Our readiness to accept his toilet habits, which obviously entailed some hardship for his counselors, gave Joey the confidence to express his obsessions in drawings. Drawing these fantasies was a first step toward letting us in, however distantly, to what concerned him most deeply. It was the first step in a year-long process of externalizing his anal preoccupations. As a result he began seeing feces everywhere; the whole world became to him a mire of excrement. At the same time he began to eliminate freely wherever he happened to be. But with this release from his infantile imprisonment in compulsive rules, the toilet and the whole process of elimination became less dangerous. Thus far it had been beyond Joey's comprehension that anybody could possibly move his bowels without mechanical aid. Now Joey took a further step forward; defecation became the first physiological process he could perform without the help of vacuum tubes. It must not be thought that he was proud of this ability. Taking pride in an achievement presupposes that one accomplishes it of one's own free will. He still did not feel himself an autonomous person who could do things on his own. To Joey defecation still seemed enslaved to some incomprehensible but utterly binding cosmic law, perhaps the law his parents had imposed on him when he was being toilet-trained.

It was not simply that his parents had subjected him to rigid, early training. Many children are so trained. But in most cases the parents have a deep emotional investment in the child's performance. The child's response in turn makes training an occasion for interaction between them and for the building of genuine relationships. Joey's parents had no emotional investment in him. His obedience gave them no satisfaction and won him no affection or approval. As a toilet-trained child he saved his mother labor, just as household machines saved her labor. As a machine he was not loved for his performance, nor could he love himself.

So it had been with all other aspects of Joey's existence with his parents. Their reactions to his eating or noneating, sleeping or wakening, urinating or defecating, being dressed or undressed, washed or bathed did not flow from any unitary interest in him, deeply embedded in their personalities. By treating him mechanically his parents made him a machine. The various functions of life—even the parts of his body—bore no integrating relationship to one another or to any sense of self that was acknowledged and confirmed by others. Though he had acquired mastery over some functions, such as toilet-training and speech, he had acquired them separately and kept them isolated from each other. Toilet-training had thus not gained him a pleasant feeling of body mastery; speech had not led to communication of thought or feeling. On the contrary, each achievement only steered him away from self-mastery and integration. Toilet-training had enslaved him. Speech left him talking in neologisms that obstructed his and our ability to relate to each other. In Joey's development the normal process of growth had been made to run backward. Whatever he had learned put him not at the end of his infantile development toward integration but, on the contrary, farther behind than he was at its very beginning. Had we understood this sooner, his first years with us would have been less baffling.

It is unlikely that Joey's calamity could befall a child in any time and culture but our own. He suffered no physical deprivation; he starved for human contact. Just to be taken care of is not enough for relating. It is a necessary but not a sufficient condition. At the extreme where utter scarcity reigns, the forming of relationships is certainly hampered. But our society of mechanized plenty often makes for equal difficulties in a child's learning to relate. Where parents can provide the simple creature-comforts for their children only at the cost of significant effort, it is likely that they will feel pleasure in being able to provide for them; it is this, the parents' pleasure, that gives children a sense of personal worth and sets the process of relating in motion. But if comfort is so readily available that the parents feel no particular pleasure in winning it for their children, then the children cannot develop the feeling of being worthwhile around the satisfaction of their basic needs. Of course parents and children can and do develop relationships around other situations. But matters are then no longer so simple and direct. The child must be on the receiving end of care and concern given with pleasure and without the exaction of return if he is to feel loved and worthy of respect and consideration. This feeling gives him the ability to trust; he can entrust his well-being to persons to whom he is so important. Out of such trust the child learns to form close and stable relationships.

For Joey relationship with his parents was empty of pleasure in comfort-giving as in all other situations. His was an extreme instance of a plight that sends many schizophrenic children to our clinics and hospitals. Many months passed before he could relate to us; his despair that anybody could like him made contact impossible.

When Joey could finally trust us enough to let himself become more infantile, he began to play at being a papoose. There was a corresponding change in his fantasies. He drew endless pictures of himself as an electrical papoose. Totally enclosed, suspended in empty space, he is run by unknown, unseen powers through wireless electricity.

As we eventually came to understand, the heart of Joey's delusional system was the artificial, mechanical womb he had created and into which he had locked himself. In his papoose fantasies lay the wish to be entirely reborn in a womb. His new experiences in the school suggested that life, after all, might be worth living. Now he was searching for a way to be reborn in a better way. Since machines were better than men, what was more natural than to try rebirth through them? This was the deeper meaning of his electrical papoose.

As Joey made progress, his pictures of himself became more dominant in his drawings. Though still machine-operated, he has grown in self-importance. Another great step forward is represented in a picture in which he has acquired hands that do something, and he has had the courage to make a picture of the machine that runs him. Later still the papoose became a person, rather than a robot encased in glass.

Eventually Joey began to create an imaginary family at the school: the "Carr" family. Why the Carr family? In the car he was enclosed as he had been in his papoose, but at least the car was not stationary; it could move. More important, in a car one was not only driven but also could drive. The Carr family was Joey's way of exploring the possibility of leaving the school, of living with a good family in a safe, protecting car.

Joey at last broke through his prison. In this brief account it has not been possible to trace the painfully slow process of his first true relations with other human beings. Suffice it to say that he ceased to be a mechanical boy and became a human child. This newborn child was, however, nearly 12 years old. To recover the lost time is a tremendous task. That work has occupied Joey and us ever since. Sometimes he sets to it with a will; at other times the difficulty of real life makes him regret that he ever came out of his shell. But he has never wanted to return to his mechanical life.

One last detail and this fragment of Joey's story has been told. When Joey was 12, he made a float for our Memorial Day parade. It carried the slogan: "Feelings are more important than anything under the sun." Feelings, Joey had learned, are what make for humanity; their absence, for a mechanical existence. With this knowledge Joey entered the human condition.

RONALD MELZACK

The Personal Pain

IN AN ESSAY 'On Being Ill', Virginia Woolf touches on one of the difficulties of the subject of pain. 'English', she writes, 'which can express the thoughts of Hamlet and the tragedy of Lear, has no words for the shiver and the headache . . . The merest schoolgirl, when she falls in love, has Shakespeare or Keats to speak her mind for her; but let a sufferer try to describe a pain in his head to a doctor and language at once runs dry'.

Most of us, I am sure, have had similar experiences. A lengthy description of our pains may help to convey an idea of what we feel to others, yet it remains a poor approximation. Our aches and pains are intensely personal, and the great varieties and subtleties of pain are virtually impossible to describe. But this is only part of what I mean by 'the personal pain'.

Even though pain is a private, personal experience, most of us know what we mean by the word. When we cut a finger, or drop a heavy weight on our foot, or get a cramp in our leg, we say that we have pain. We may agree, then, when we use the word 'pain' in normal conversation. But if I were asked to define the word rigorously in order to let you know exactly what I mean by it, I would not be able to do so. In fact, no one who has worked on the problem of pain has yet defined it to his satisfaction. It is a complex psychological experience, and there are many facets to the problems it presents.

Most of us tend to think that pain is a 'bad' thing, that it is harmful in its own right. Indeed, it sometimes is: severe chronic pain can become a strain on people, and by itself make them gloomy and miserable, and sometimes can even bring about physical and mental deterioration. But, on the other hand, there is a positive aspect to pain. Its presence usually means that something biologically abnormal is happening to us, that damage is being done to our bodies, and by warning us in this way, it plays an important role in our lives. It helps us to avoid objects and situations that will cause us harm.

Clearly, then, pain has value for the survival of the individual. And most of us would therefore expect it to occur invariably after injury. Also, we would expect the intensity of pain we feel to be directly related to the amount and extent of the damage. But this is not always the case, because in recent years it has been shown that psychological factors also play a major role in our perception of pain. There is a considerable body of evidence that, in higher species at least, pain is not simply a function of the amount of biological damage alone; but rather that the amount and quality of pain we feel is also determined by our past experiences and how well we remember them, by our ability to understand the cause of the pain and to grasp its consequences. But it goes much further than that—in fact the significance pain has in the culture in which we have been brought up, as well as our previous experiences with it and the meaning of the situation in which we receive it, all play an enormous role in how we feel and respond to it.

In some cultures, damage to the body does not evoke the kind of perceptions we expect in our Western culture. Instead, it may evoke some perception entirely devoid of unpleasantness. There are many reports of major surgery being carried out on people belonging to some of the African tribes without eliciting a wince or any other sign that pain is being felt. In our culture, childbirth is considered to be one of the worst pains a human being can undergo. Yet anthropologists have described a number of cultures in which the women have virtually no distress during childbirth.

In some of these cultures, a woman who is going to have a child continues to work in the fields and attend the crops until the baby is just about to be born. Her husband then gets into bed and moans and groans as though he is in great pain, while she bears the child. The husband stays in bed, with the child, to recover from the terrible ordeal he has just gone through, while the mother almost immediately returns to attend the crops and bring home the supper for her poor, sick husband. What does this mean? That all women in our culture are making up their pain? Certainly not. Simply, it would seem it is part of our culture to recognise childbirth as dangerous to the life of the mother. Young girls learn to fear childbirth in our culture, and the fear induced is so strong that it is dispelled only with great difficulty.

Some recent experiments carried out with animals have shown the same sort of thing. The animals were raised from infancy to maturity in such a way that they had little or no opportunity to receive painful stimulation. That is, they were protected from the bodily damage that most young animals get in the course of growing up, like being pinched, bitten, hit, and so on. When these animals were observed at maturity, they were found to show very little response to injury. A young chimpanzee, for example, who was reared in this way, responded to pin pricking by panting in the same way that a normal chimpanzee responds to being tickled: there was no sign that Rob, as he was called, found the stimulus unpleasant. At McGill University, I made comparable observations with dogs. These dogs were kept away from harmful stimulation during early life, and at maturity they often showed no response to stimuli that would have produced strong emotional disturbance in normally reared dogs. They were clearly deficient in their capacity to perceive and respond to pain. For instance, when they were being groomed, the animal keeper could not make them stay still, so that they frequently banged their heads against the hairclippers, showing no more response to this than they would to a gentle pat. Two of these dogs were observed in a room which had low-lying water pipes. To our astonishment the dogs repeatedly hit their heads on the pipes. One dog, by actual count, knocked his head on the pipes more than thirty times in a single hour, again without showing any behavioural evidence of pain.

The meaning that we associate with a pain-producing situation is also extremely important in determining the degree and quality of pain that we feel. There are many every-day observations of this kind. Imaging a father playing with his young son. As the boy walks by, the father gives him a slap on the bottom. The son turns round quickly and looks at the father. If the father laughs, the child will probably laugh too. But if the father scowls, the boy will very likely cry bitterly at the 'punishment'. In this way, through learning, meanings become associated with pain, and patterns of perception and response are built up to injurious stimuli. These acquired meanings and associations may develop permanency in the individual's behaviour, and, as some writers have noted, 'parental influences may be decisive factors in determining the amount of pain their children will suffer from minor injuries throughout the rest of their lives'.

There are many more such examples. Most of us have felt pains that we thought might mean some terrible disease. But as soon as the physician assures us that the pain comes from a source that is not serious, the pain may vanish. On the other hand, if we know that the source of pain is a serious threat to our lives, the pain may become unbearable. The pain of a toothache may sometimes have a similar course. It may be most unbearable during the night, when we can do nothing about it, but in the morning, as we go to see the dentist, it may mysteriously disappear.

There is some striking recent evidence that bears our these everyday observations. Beecher, now at Harvard University, had the opportunity to study, during the last war, the amount of pain felt by soldiers who received wounds in battle. To his surprise, when the men were carried to the most forward hospital after having received terrible wounds, only one out of four claimed that they had enough pain to require a pain-killing drug. These men, Beecher carefully points out, were not in a state of shock but fully awake and responsive. Yet civilians in the hospital with very similar types of surgical wounds showed a reverse of the statistics: four out of five claimed they were in severe pain and demanded an appropriate drug.

Beecher concluded from his study that 'the common belief that wounds are inevitably associated with pain, that the more extensive the wound the worse the pain, was not supported by observations made as carefully as possible in the combat zone . . .' He goes on to say, speaking as an anaesthetist:

> The data state in numerical terms what is known to all thoughtful clinical observers: there is no simple direct relationship between the wound *per se* and the pain experienced. The pain is in very large part determined by other factors, and of great importance here is the significance of the wound . . . In the wounded soldier [the response to the injury] was relief, thankfulness at his escape alive from the battlefield, even euphoria; to the civilian his major surgery was a depressing calamitous event.

The importance of psychological factors in pain is further borne out by other fascinating observations made by Beecher. He found that, at times, severe pains can be relieved by giving the patient an inert substance in the place of morphine or other analgesic drugs. These substances, often sugar or salt, are called placebos or dummy pills. And fully a third of people have their pains made better by a placebo instead of a pain-killing drug. But, as Beecher points out, this in no way implies that these people do not have real pain; it is real pain. It is just that what we call pain is in large part a function of complex psychological factors. And the clinician may sometimes effectively treat pain by treating these factors as well as the irritating sources in the body.

It is clear from these observations that there is not always a one-to-one relationship between physical damage and the amount of pain experienced. Indeed, there may sometimes be terrible pain in the absence of any apparent stimulation. It is difficult to find a more convincing example of this than the unfortunate people with phantom-limb pain. This needs some explanation. After people lose a limb, the majority of them continue to feel it as though it were still there. What this phantom limb feels like has often been described as 'pins and needles': the feeling we have when our arm or leg has 'fallen asleep'. This is the painless phantom limb, and it occurs in more than ninety-five per cent of people who have lost an arm or leg; in other words, it is a completely normal occurrence. What it means is that even though the limb is lost, the neural activities (or, if you like, the memories) associated with it still continue to reside in the central nervous system. These memories, then, contribute to the perception of the phantom limb.

About thirty per cent of people who have a phantom limb also have the misfortune to get pains in it, and about five per cent of them have very severe pains. These pains may be occasional or continuous, but they are felt in definite parts of the phantom limb. For example, a young woman describes her phantom hand as being clenched, with her fingers bent over her thumb and digging into the palm of her hand, so that the hand becomes tired and painful. When she is able to open her phantom hand, as a result of her physician's treatments, the pain goes away. Just how vivid phantom-limb pain can be was noted as long ago as 1552 by Ambroise Paré. He wrote:

> Verily it is a thing wondrous strange and prodigious, and which will scarce be credited, unless by such as have seen with their eyes, and heard with their ears, the patients who have many months after the cutting away of the leg, grievously complained that they yet felt exceeding great pain of that leg so cut off.

Professors W. K. Livingston and F. P. Haugen, of the University of Oregon Medical School, have made a special study of cases with phantom-limb pain; and I had the privilege of meeting a number of their patients, over a period of years, as guest observer in their Pain Clinic. I recall one elderly lady particularly well. She had lost both legs, and had very painful phantom limbs. Still, she delighted in listening to music. When she heard intensely emotional music, such as Beethoven's 'Appassionata', she found that her pain got worse. But if she heard a quieting Chopin 'Nocturne', her pain would decrease in intensity and unpleasantness.

This is not at all uncommon, for there are many reports of severe increases in phantom-limb pain as a result of emotional upsets such as a disturbing film, or having an argument with a friend. So here, too, without a doubt, psychological factors make their contribution, along with the other ongoing physiological processes, in determining an increase or decrease in the severity of pain that is felt. And it is also obvious that the pain of the phantom limb, both in its intensity and its long duration, cannot be attributed in any simple and direct fashion to an external stimulus.

I would like to point out strongly that these people with phantom-limb pain have real pain. They are not imagining it. And rarely can this pain be attributed simply to a neurosis. Indeed, most attempts to prove that phantom-limb pain is purely a neurotic condition have tended to show the opposite: it is not. We know that irritation of the nerves of the remaining part of the limb contribute to the pain process, since stimulation of these nerves can trigger off severe pain. But this is not the whole story. All the evidence suggests that the primary focus of physiological disturbance has somehow moved into the central nervous system itself.

All the observations I have described, taken together, indicate that the same injurious stimulus can have different effects on different people, or even on the same person at different times. A stimulus may be painful one day and not the next. Pain, then, is a personal experience which we must judge in terms of the behaviour of the person experiencing it, and not only in terms of the stimulus itself. It is an individual psychological experience, based on the unique past history of a particular person, the meaning the stimulus has to him or to her, the 'state of mind' at that moment, and other factors as well, all acting with the organic cause to produce the perception we call 'pain'. This is what I mean by 'the personal pain.'

Essays of Our Time I ● *Part* 7

ROGER BURLINGAME, *a* New York *writer, is the author of more than twenty books of verse, fiction, social history, and biography, including studies of Billy Mitchell and Henry Ford. "The Analyst's Couch and the Creative Mind" is from his recent book* I Have Known Many Worlds.

HENRY MILLER, *once a stormy petrel who has now settled in Big Sur, California, was born in Brooklyn and educated by the world. After working in an employment agency, he expatriated himself to Paris in 1930, where he wrote a series of books, many of which have been banned in the United States. He is considered by the beat-generation writers as a progenitor of their movement.*

AGNES DEMILLE, *at the age of eight, saw the great ballerina Pavlova and decided to become a dancer. After years of disappointment and failure, she won fame with her own* Rodeo *the first truly American ballet, and with her choreography for* Oklahoma *and* Carousel. *Her* Dance to the Piper *is an illuminating autobiography and commentary on the ballet.*

JEAN COCTEAU, *French playwright, novelist, poet, and movie director, is known chiefly for his iconoclastic writings and conduct and for his connection with the surrealist movement. His play* The Infernal Machine *was produced in New York, and his movies* Orpheus in the Underworld, Beauty and the Beast, *and* The Blood of a Poet *are frequently revived.*

WILLIAM BARRETT, *was among the first to introduce the European philosophy of existentialism to America.* The Irrational Man, *from which "Modern Art" is drawn, is the best introduction to existentialism available in English. Formerly an editor of* Partisan Review, *William Barrett is an associate professor of philosophy at New York University.*

The Analyst's Couch and the
Creative Mind

I HAVE NOT called myself an artist though in much of my writing I have worked with artist's materials and in the artist's framework. I believe, therefore, that I have what is known as a creative mind and though circumstances have not always permitted it, I like to write from the inside out. And, from my own long and kaleidoscopic experience and from the experiences of some true artists whom I have known closely I am convinced that, however much good it may do the business executive, the physician, the politician, or the housewife, the psychoanalyst's couch is not for the creative mind. In testimony I offer case history.

If, for instance, the theses of the psychiatrists and psychoanalysts are applicable to me, I should be, if not a gibbering idiot, at least a model of chronic maladjustment. According to late theory, my parents —indeed my entire family including my Irish Nanny—did everything wrong from the moment the doctor shook the breath into me.

First of all, I was an afterthought. I came along eleven years after my parents had apparently decided that enough was enough. Later, when it was supposed that I could understand such things, I was told that I was planned and I believe it. A year or so before my birth, the family's economic condition improved and this, added to Mother's nostalgia for babies, moved the uninstructed parental minds toward the belated impulse. And, in those primitive days, insufficient exploration had not yet proved how dangerous afterthoughts can be—especially when the progenitors are past forty.

During the fateful years zero to five, my nurse indoctrinated me with every variety of morbid fancy. She had, for example, a passion for funerals. Often when she took me walking in the city she would detect a funeral blocks away and seizing me by the hand would run me breathlessly to the scene so that she could count the carriages behind the hearse. I became so fascinated with the promp of death that once, when asked what I wanted for Christmas, I replied a toy cemetery, please, complete with plumed hearse, corpse, and practicable coffin.

Nanny also exploited my precarious constitution. Born in what was

181

known as "the grippe year," I was frequently on the threshold of death, from which I was saved by a series of miracles. In the intervals between the crises, Nanny surrounded me with fears. Everything that I must not do I must not do "for fear" of the consequences: bronchial pneumonia, for example, if I went out in the rain. Nanny was entranced by the long names of diseases and I too grew to mouth and love their resonant beauty. Starting with the sonorous "pneumonia," my sallies into the poetry of medicine have led me into rapture over the rhythm and melody of "insomnia," "arteriosclerosis," and, best of all, "electrocardiogram."

The "sentence of silence" so abundantly condemned in the paleo-Freudian days was strictly imposed upon me. Every scrap of information about sex was withheld from me notwithstanding my insistent questioning and the fact that my mind was, from my first consciousness, profoundly occupied with the subject.

Far from the teachings of "progressive" up-bringing, my behavior was geared to a set of absolutes. Reason rarely intervened between me and parental authority. I did things because they were right and they were right because Mother or Father or my grown-up brother or sisters or Holy Scripture said so. (Nanny also got in on this act.) In my consciousness, moral relativity was a stranger though I know now that it governed much of my father's thinking.

Finally, my strenuous religious training brought me into a vivid and daily awareness of sin. I don't think the reality of sin would have impinged much upon Mother's clean and extrovert mind except that her prayer book was so jam-packed with it. But to me the abstraction inherent in all the resounding Anglican prayers was troubling indeed and, in my introspective hours, as I grew older, I even became fearful that I might have sinned without knowing it. On my knees in church, my small head buried in my folded arms, I sometimes put the question to my Maker but I was never quite sure of any response.

My earliest memory is of weaving my way through a forest of legs. Unlike most children, I had five parents instead of two. All—even my still adolescent sister—had equal authority, at least when the others weren't around. They could all say Don't to me and they all did. Sometimes there were jurisdictional disputes conducted in whispers which I heard or in French which I understood. I hugely enjoyed the conflicts between my sisters, sometimes involving slammed doors or ending with that final thrust, "All right for you," which was so popular in those days among the young.

The only time no one said Don't to me was when I was sick. Then they hovered silently near my bedside so imbued with the belief that I was going to die, I wonder they did not kill me with their thoughts. I did, indeed, sometimes suspect the incidence of my demise. I was deeply impressed by that macabre prayer they used to teach children to say:

> If I should die before I wake
> I pray the Lord my soul to take . . .

I could see the Lord's hand coming through the darkness and grabbing my small soul. I then thought myself into a white coffin with my disembodied spirit hovering over my bereaved family and happily observing their tears.

When it wasn't too painful, I really enjoyed being sick. To lie in a darkened room with Mother's countless petticoats rustling about and a fragrant inhalant cooking over an alcohol lamp was quite pleasurable. I liked the taste of the paregoric—the universal remedy for everything that could not be cured by castor oil—the frequent doses of which, by another miracle, I survived. Nanny, in these times, was relegated to the background and Mother took full charge. Is it surprising, then, that I acquired that most devastating of all fixations for the growing male, a "silver cord" attachment?

Could a combination of Doctors Freud, Jung, and Adler—not to mention John Dewey and the progressive educationeers—imagine a more blighting background? Yet I have eluded breakdown, compulsive criminality, perversion, and the Death Wish. I have spasms of self-pity but so do my younger acquaintances whose psychiatrists are just around the corner. My suicidal impulses are rare and fleeting—subject to diversion by almost any bright object. Rape, homosexuality, and sadism have appeared interesting but not compelling. My impulses toward murder have usually had rational motivation. It is true that I often treat my wife with extreme mental cruelty but so do the graduates of the progressive schools.

I take no credit for having licked, with my heroic character, all of the grim conditioners I have described. Indeed, I have never wanted to lick them. On the contrary, I exult in every one. Far from frustrating me they have been largely responsible for every worthy thing I have done.

Take, for example, the reticence about the so-called facts of life. The silence was highly stimulating to what I like to think was my incipiently creative mind. Had I been told, I should have been deprived of the delight as well as the constructive exercise of discovering them for myself. Does the child from whom nothing is hidden get more fun out of life? Will the creativeness of new generations be enhanced by absence of mystery? Is the imaginative child whose stories are all told him on the television screen any better equipped than one who devises his own plots and people, albeit with a certain creative agony? No; I cherish the secrecy to which I was so early introduced and I have practiced it happily.

What I have withheld has given me more joy than what I have expressed because it has helped build a storehouse, a potential of great pregnancy. Secret after secret I can now give birth to in sublime pain. The confessional to priest or analyst is abhorrent to me. If you keep your hopes or fears, your chimeras, the tantrums of your conscience inside you, you can still make use of them; told, they leave you empty, sterile, and impotent. Confession, except in creation, is exceedingly bad for the creative soul.

And how about the other mental and emotional ingredients of my child life? To the artist, morbid thought is a pigment. To be there ready at any moment to be dipped into for the creation of a painting or a story it must be squeezed early on the palette of the child's mind. If the child is an incipient artist, it will not stand there alone. Brighter colors will probably be juxtaposed. The child need not be preoccupied by morbid thought but if he is to be an artist he must be aware of its existence. It is cruel to protect an imaginative child from the sense of death or the taste of grief. To an artist a Nanny with her funerals may be immensely useful.

Nor are the feminine pressures hurtful to the male artist. If he is a novelist he must be, in himself, man, woman, and child. The mother who runs frightened by the shadows of Oedipus had better consider carefully whether her son is a potential artist or bond broker.

As to the unreasoned dicta about right and wrong, these established a code like the multiplication table which catches you up when you make a mistake. Yet it may also, to change the metaphor, be a springboard from which to take off. Of course I have departed from some of the formulas but how could I have departed if there was nothing to depart from? The shore you leave stays in your mind however far you swim away, but how about the child who has known no shore, who has been taken out in a boat in the dark and dropped into an unbounded sea?

There is a truism which says you must know the rules in order to break them, and who breaks more rules than the writer unless it be the painter or composer?

I have left behind most of the religious concepts that were so important to my mother and I have sometimes said that my strict religious bringing up threw me, on maturity, into agnosticism, yet in my heart,

I also value that memory. Once the sin ingredient evaporated there was a residue of beauty. My doubts about a personal God cannot filter that out. But how constructive that knowledge of faith, of the faith of others if not my own, of the intellectual fact of God, however skeptical I may be of his tangible existence! The best book by far that I ever wrote was based on what I heard in those solemn hours when Mother prepared me for confirmation.

I once knew a true artist—a painter of transcendent talent—who had been brought up on an austere New England farm, a desire-under-the-elms sort of place where morbid thought abounded. His own ran to cows. For hours, as a child, he would sit on a fence and reflect on the sufferings of cows. The cow, to him, was a symbol of exploited femininity; her entire existence was by necessity dedicated to being a female. She was bred, gave birth, and began to nurse her child; then both child and milk were stolen from her. When the milk stopped, the whole sad sequence was repeated. What my friend supposed to be the other enterprises in which the cow might have engaged had she been relieved of the urgency imposed upon her was never quite clear to me or perhaps to him; the point was that the grief about the cows developed into other griefs as he matured and he became, so he said, an exceedingly unhappy man. Yet all this time he was painting pictures which were the wonder of the art world. Everything he did had the nostalgic trace essential to any real work of art.

One day he heard about a Swiss psychoanalyst who could treat those grim neuroses which were a legacy from a morbid childhood. So he laid his painting aside and spent a year in Zurich. I had lunch with him the day after he returned. "I am," he said, "completely happy. The nightmares are gone. I can look back on my obsessions and laugh at them. My slate has been washed clean."

Unfortunately his palette had also been washed clean. From that moment his pictures were commonplace or pretty. He lost his place in the top rank. Perhaps he would have been restored in time because I am inclined to believe that a true artist is, in the long run, indestructible, but not until he had put back some of the things that the doctor had erased. For that he died too soon.

But this is only one story. I could tell others as true and as sad of men and women who have confessed too much. Some have survived because, once on the couch, they have instinctively kicked and screamed or slyly, with tongue in check, defrauded their expensive doctor.

I am far from believing that there is pain in all creativity; I have touched the fringe often enough to be aware of its joys—even when they are merely the joys of cool sweat after fever, but I am certain that therapy designed to eliminate suffering from the creative mind is more often destructive than otherwise. I think certain honest analysts have become aware of this. At least two of them who are more interested in the truth than in their bank accounts told me that certain artists have so resisted the treatment—as if they were being robbed—that the doctors have had to abandon the cases.

Now if all this be true, why is it that psychoanalysis may still be good for the industrial executive, the lawyer, the government worker, or the secretary of the woman's club? It is, I think, because these people have no machinery for sublimating their childhood "disasters." They cannot *use* their traumas as the painter, the writer, or the composer may. Use is the great anodyne for these wounds. The use may be painful, but when the chagrin is painted or written it is often gone or its combination with its product mellows it. At any rate something has resulted, the rotary motion has ceased, a tangent has been struck. The frustration has been embodied in something which may partake of immortality; at least it may transfer the artist's hurt to the multitude of those who see or read it. A neurosis is better expressed, I think, than confessed.

But it has now become fashionable to turn adolescents or even children—whose talents may still be unsuspected—over to persons who practice under the general name of psychiatrist. "Send her to a psychiatrist," or, "Let Doctor X see him," say parents at the drop of a tantrum. In many cases neither parent nor child knows what creative potentials may be in Dick's or Mary's make-up.

My advice to parents would be: Try to find out if your child has leanings toward graphic or literary or musical creation before you call in the doctor. And to the doctor, I would say, impertinently, make sure you are not removing something valuable in your attempt to ease your patient's pain or his family's inconvenience. If you detect a foreshadowing of the art that may come, forego your fee and send the patient home. Usually even the child, if he be an embryonic artist, will quickly show his allergy to the analyst's methods.

In days past, there was a synthetic treatment of non-creative patients which was known as occupational therapy. This is still practiced, I believe, in the rehabilitation of mentally wounded veterans and in various old-fashioned establishments. Here, patients are made to express their troubles in some medium of art if it be only a string of beads. This, I am told, is looked down upon by "modern" practitioners. Yet does it not suggest that the man or woman dedicated—one might almost say addicted—to some all-absorbing creative endeavor is in little danger from his neurosis and, perhaps, even cannot do without it?

The Creative Life

WORK, IT SEEMED to me even at the threshold of life, is an activity reserved for the dullard. It is the very opposite of creation, which is play, and which just because it has no raison d'être other than itself is the supreme motivating power in life. Has any one ever said that God created the universe in order to provide work for Himself? By a chain of circumstances having nothing to do with reason or intelligence I had become like the others—a drudge. I had the comfortless excuse that by my labors I was supporting a wife and child. That it was a flimsy excuse I knew, because if I were to drop dead on the morrow they would go on living somehow or other. To stop everything, and play at being myself, why not? The part of me which was given up to work, which enabled my wife and child to live in the manner they unthinkingly demanded, this part of me which kept the wheel turning—a completely fatuous, egocentric notion!—was the least part of me. I gave nothing to the world in fulfilling the function of breadwinner; the world exacted its tribute of me, that was all.

The world would only begin to get something of value from me the moment I stopped being a serious member of society and became—*myself*. The State, the nation, the united nations of the world, were nothing but one great aggregation of individuals who repeated the mistakes of their forefathers. They were caught in the wheel from birth and they kept at it till death—and this treadmill they tried to dignify by calling it "life." If you asked any one to explain or define life, what was the be all and the end all, you got a blank look for answer. Life was something which philosophers dealt with in books that no one read. Those in the thick of life, "the plugs in harness," had no time for such idle questions. *"You've got to eat, haven't you?"* This query, which was supposed to be a stop-gap, and which had already been answered, if not in the absolute negative at least in a disturbingly relative negative by those who knew, was a clue to all the other questions which followed in a veritable Euclidian suite. From the little reading I had done I had observed that the men who were most *in* life, who were moulding life, who were life itself, ate little, slept little, owned little or nothing. They had no illusions about duty, or the perpetuation of their kith and kin, or the preservation of the State. They were interested in truth and in

187

truth alone. They recognized only one kind of activity—*creation*. Nobody could command their services because they had of their own pledged themselves to give all. They gave gratuitously, because that is the only way to give. This was the way of life which appealed to me: it made sound sense. It *was* life—not the simulacrum which those about me worshipped.

I had understood all this—with my mind at the very brink of manhood. But there was a great comedy of life to be gone through before this vision of reality could become the motivating force. The tremendous hunger for life which others sensed in me acted like a magnet; it attracted those who needed my particular kind of hunger. The hunger was magnified a thousand times. It was as if those who clung to me (like iron filings) became sensitized and attracted others in turn. Sensation ripens into experience and experience engenders experience.

What I secretly longed for was to disentangle myself of all those lives which had woven themselves into the pattern of my own life and were making my destiny a part of theirs. To shake myself free of these accumulating experiences which were mine only by force of inertia required a violent effort. Now and then I lunged and tore at the net, but only to become more enmeshed. My liberation seemed to involve pain and suffering to those near and dear to me. Every move I made for my own private good brought about reproach and condemnation. I was a traitor a thousand times over. I had lost even the right to become ill—because "they" needed me. I wasn't *allowed* to remain inactive. Had I died I think they would have galvanized my corpse into a semblance of life.

"I stood before a mirror and said fearfully: 'I want to see how I look in the mirror with my eyes closed.'"

These words of Richter's, when I first came upon them, made an indescribable commotion in me. As did the following, which seems almost like a corollary of the above—from Novalis:

"The seat of the soul is where inner world and outer world touch each other. For nobody knows himself, if he is only himself and not also another one at the same time."

"To take possession of one's transcendental I, to be the I of one's I, at the same time," as Novalis expressed it again.

There is a time when ideas tyrannize over one, when one is just a hapless victim of another's thoughts. This "possession" by another seems to occur in periods of depersonalization, when the warring selves come unglued, as it were. Normally one is impervious to ideas; they come and go, are accepted or rejected, put on like shirts, taken off like dirty socks. But in those periods which we call crises, when the mind sunders and splinters like a diamond under the blows of a sledge-hammer, these innocent ideas of a dreamer take hold, lodge in the crevices of the brain, and by some subtle process of infiltration bring about a definite, irrevocable alteration of the personality. Outwardly no great change takes place; the individual affected does not suddenly behave differently; on the contrary, he may behave in more "normal" fashion than before. This seeming normality assumes more and more the quality of a protective device. From surface deception he passes to inner deception. With each new crisis, however, he becomes more strongly aware of a change which is no change, but rather an intensification of something hidden deep within. Now when he closes his eyes he can really look at himself. He no longer sees a mask. He sees without seeing, to be exact. Vision without sight, a fluid grasp of intangibles: the merging of sight and sound: the heart of the web. Here stream the distant personalities which evade the crude contact of the senses; here the overtones of recognition discreetly lap against one another in bright, vibrant harmonies. There is no language employed, no outlines delineated.

When a ship founders it settles slowly; the spars, the masts, the rigging float away. On the ocean floor of death the bleeding hull be-decks itself with jewels; remorselessly the anatomic life begins. What was ship becomes the nameless indestructible.

Like ships, men founder time and again. Only memory saves them from complete dispersion. Poets drop their stitches in the loom, straws for drowning men to grasp as they sink into extinction. Ghosts climb back on watery stairs, make imaginary ascents, vertiginous drops, memorize numbers, dates, events, in passing from gas to liquid and back again. There is no brain capable of registering the changing changes. Nothing happens in the brain, except the gradual rust and detrition of the cells. But in the mind, worlds unclassified, undenominated, unassimilated, form, break, unite, dissolve and harmonize ceaselessly. In the mind-world ideas are the indestructible elements which form the jewelled constellations of the interior life. We move within their orbits, freely if we follow their intricate patterns, enslaved or possessed if we try to subjugate them. Everything external is but a reflection projected by the mind machine.

Creation is the eternal play which takes place at the border-line; it is spontaneous and compulsive, obedient to law. One removes from the mirror and the curtain rises. *Séance permanente.* Only madmen are excluded. Only those who "have lost their mind," as we say. For these never cease to dream that they are dreaming. They stood before the mirror with eyes open and fell sound asleep; they sealed their shadow in the tomb of memory. In them the stars collapse to form what Hugo called "a blinding menagerie of suns which, through love, make themselves the poodles and the Newfoundlands of immensity."

The creative life! Ascension. Passing beyond oneself. Rocketing out into the blue, grasping at flying ladders, mounting, soaring, lifting the world up by the scalp, rousing the angels from their ethereal lairs, drowning in stellar depths, clinging to the tails of comets. Nietzche had written of it ecstatically—and then swooned forward into the mirror to die in root and flower. "Stairs and contradictory stairs," he wrote, and then suddenly there was no longer any bottom; the mind, like a splintered diamond, was pulverized by the hammer-blows of truth.

AGNES DE**MILLE**

The Milk of Paradise

ALL DURING THIS separation I told myself as I wrote my husband that later when he returned I wanted to quit the theater and rest. But deep in my heart I knew I wanted nothing of the sort. Was it likely that under the stimulus and joy of his return I would suddenly bank my fires? Men have always been able to experience family and work together. It has been assumed that because of the greater emotional demands made on women, they could not have both, and they have hitherto been constrained to choose. But I was in a new century and I was greedy. I wanted wifehood, motherhood and work. I wanted all.

There were two thousand years of domestic history dead against me and against me were the race memories and traditions I had myself inherited. But there was in my blood something else, another need, as deep and as old, and this urged without respite or peace. This would not let me be.

I had drunk the Milk of Paradise and known power. I could not think to give this up. I could forfeit my life, and my comfort, riches and convenience, for love—but not the magic release of work! This was my identity.

The fact that for millennia all such desires have been arbitrarily suppressed in women proves nothing but the brutality of convention. In primitive and ancient cultures women were thought, because they were women and because they gave birth, to have special powers and were the preferred celebrants vital to certain life and death occasions.

Mastery in any field is attained by practicing what is valued at times of recognized importance. No genius, no matter what the field, is an unprecedented accident. There must be a need, an expectation and trust. Behind Sappho was a long line of honored female poet-composers, the last supremely great female composers in the history of music. She was the culmination of a tradition* and it is instructive to note that Sappho was not only by contemporary accounts (which is all we have of her, since the music has been lost) the greatest of her profession but that she was a good wife and mother and that her social reputation within her community and during her lifetime was exemplary. It was a century later that the boys in Athens started a whispering campaign of personal defamation which reinforced a growing legend: that any woman who dedicated herself to art must be a freak, that artistic creativity was compensation for lack of creativity in more natural and suitable functions. This myth was not based on fact, or on any larger understanding of women's capacities or happiness, but directly on men's convenience. Women have at last, to their terrible cost, come to accept this view. It suited their men. And they understandably wanted to suit their men.

As the conviction took hold, and woman began to think of herself as not only different but inferior, she gradually lost her function of a necessary ritual voice in the community. Where is she, for instance, in the Christian Church? In the Hebraic? The Moslem, Hindu, or Shinto? On her knees with her head covered up and her mouth shut, removed at a prophylactic distance from the high altar and all sacred vessels. In our church women have been considered from Old Testament times unclean, a moral and ritualistic hazard. The very functions and powers that primitive religions cherished here betray her. Women from the end of the first century A.D. have not been allowed to officiate in the church, build or design the church, compose or write for the church, perform in the church, nor even for some hundreds of years sing as lay members of the congregation.† "Woman was represented [by the early Church Fathers]," writes Lecky, "as the door of hell, as the mother of all human ills. She should be ashamed at the very thought that she is a woman. She should live in continual penance, on account of the curses she had brought upon the world."‡

---

* There were similar priestess-musicians in Egypt, Assyria, Babylonia and India.

† Women have been admitted to Protestant choirs only within the last three hundred years.

‡ *History of European Morals,* Vol. II, pp. 357–358.

Consecrated women, that is, women whose every female function had been exorcized, neutralized and spayed, were permitted certain holy or clerical offices but always secretly, and behind bars. At one period the unsterilized were forbidden by papal edict to sing anywhere at all, even over their slop pails and washboards. But this restriction could not long prevail. Women's natural rejoicing while scrubbing floors and cleaning out the garbage was not to be restrained and they gave tongue to their enthusiasm. But only domestically. The church doors remained shut except at a most terrible price: the dedication of her entire life, private floorwashing and all.

And many thought the cost slight. For among other attractions the church provided the only art experience the average person, male or female, could know. During the Dark Ages its vast projects exploited all the talents available in any community. Throughout eight hundred years of endowed scholarship it developed the many arts it could use. But the arts it could not use—chiefly dancing—withered. No ecclesiastical or ritual choreography was composed nor was any method of dance notation evolved, as unquestionably would have been done had the holy fathers wished to preserve any visual ceremonial. The artists the church was permitted to use, that is, men, achieved great works. The artists it was not—what became of them? Barred up. Barred out. Wasted. Lost.

Stimulated by religious sanctions, the average husband and father placed even harder and more cruel blocks in the path of women's imaginative expression. By persuading themselves and their wives that no woman could devote time to anything but her husband and household without moral treason, they managed to discourage undomestic yearnings. Men wanted their wives womanly; by that was meant, we gather, they wanted them steadfast, attentive, enthusiastic, enduring—most certainly enduring—and serene; and by serene was meant that the women were to have no doubts about men's judgments and no disturbing inclinations of their own, a concept successfully implemented by a child a year—usually a convincer. Sixteen children without benefit of pediatrician, nursery school, or corner drugstore guaranteed attentiveness.

The women who were at the head of a great household were in a position of considerable influence: they administered battalions of servants; they supervised the many domestic industries which supplied virtually everything used in daily life, and which had to be made on the premises; they ran dispensaries for whatever medicine was needed; they arbitrated and organized and instructed. They did not, therefore, have much leisure and any free time there was they devoted to husband and children and not to idle flights of fancy.

The women had no doubt great satisfaction in being necessary and effective and may well have been both serene and content; we have not heard otherwise. The important point is that we have not heard. They were speechless. The experience of rearing up families, which was the universal lot of all lay women, did not find in seventeen centuries a single authentic female statement.

Nor did any of the men speak up. Men have sung about acres of pearly breasts, snowy throats and bee-bruised lips, but about the service, companionship and character of his helpmeet, not one word. Until the Victorian era the sharer of bed and bosom remained "my wife, poor wretch!" Consciously or unconsciously, women have lived for hundreds, for thousands of years with the belief that their happiness lay in serving God wholly or in serving husband and children wholly. Thus by religious sanction and matrimonial reinforcement the great taboo was fixed in our mores.

For over a thousand years woman's chief creative expression was restricted to the statements of saints and visionaries locked behind walls, special in nature, in no way representative of ordinary woman, her passions or fate.

Outside the safety of the church most transgressors against the social code paid dearly for their defiance with loss of caste and with cruel personal restrictions. Only lower-class women were permitted to embroider or paint, the two being considered of an equally artisan nature. Certain pretty outcasts were permitted to sing or act, although there were long periods of interdiction against even depraved women doing either. But within and without the cloister the usual price of self-expression for intellectual or well-born women was the forfeit of sexuality.

As late as the eighteenth and nineteenth centuries, when gentlewomen began to have what we would consider professional careers, the majority remained spinsters. The married few took husbands late when the pattern of their minds had been firmly set, like Elizabeth Barrett and George Eliot. The exception that leaps to mind is, of course, George Sand, but it must be remembered that if she had many lovers, she found by her own admission lasting happiness with no one; she remained ill-mated and lonely throughout.

And as one considers the great names of the last two centuries certain facts become apparent: many worked semisecretly under male pseudonyms; few married, fewer still bore children; very nearly all were sick, flat on their backs as often as not.

And what kind of art did these rebellious lonely people produce? Except in two fields, not the best. There were among them a few lyric poets not comparable to the greatest men, a few second-class painters, no architect, until very recently no sculptors, not one single first-rate composer excepting the nuns Kassia, Mechtild, and Hildegarde, whose work their church did not think fit to preserve but who left a tremendous contemporary reputation.

This is a fairly frightening history. It matters not a whit how you educate a girl, what techniques or attitudes you teach her. If she knows that her men will not welcome her talents she is going to proceed timidly. Put any gifted child at the keyboard, train her, exhort her six hours a day, but let it be borne in on her that there never has been in recorded music a first-rate female composer, that no man will consider her work without condescension, and, worst of all, that within herself she may provoke conflicts that she cannot hope to surmount, and you may get results, but they won't be Beethoven.*

This has been wasteful for art, cruel for the women, and unhelpful to the men because they have been persuaded to build up their pride of manhood on assumptions that were bound to give way the moment women found the restraints served no good purpose and need not be endured.

Today women know almost as much freedom as in pagan antiquity and turn eagerly to the arts, but to only three with promise of supreme success.

First, now as before, and always, to the performing careers, where in spite of long periods of interdiction and censor they have managed consistently to excel. Second, to creative storytelling and prose, in which they hold their own with the best. And third, to choreography. In this field they have practiced without restriction. No man ever barred the way here because no man thought highly enough of the business to keep women out, as he had done from so many august, holy, or honorable occupations.

The Christian Church had proscribed dancing and it was utterly without dignity, cut off from all serious motivation, the sources of ancient meaning and glory. The Christian Church was the first great church to do this. So strongly had dancing been involved in all previous worship that it took more than one thousand years to root it out of the Catholic service (a good deal longer than it took to root women out). But it was at last eradicated and there remain now only vestigial remnants in the Mass. The church is poorer for the loss; the effect on

---

* It is interesting in this connection to consider what educators have found in regard to the schooling of Negro children: that they show no inferiority of endowment or application until about the eighth year when the full realization of their social status and lack of opportunity becomes clear to them. Trauma frequently cripples further development.

dancing has been disastrous. For two thousand years dancing and dancers have struggled under religious and social censure more formidable than that placed on any activity, except sin itself—and sex.

Dancing nevertheless remains the germinal art, the mother of theater and all other arts, in an anthropological sense the mother of the church. And it is in this ancient medium that those members of the community debased from proper participation in more honored practices have served a quickening purpose. The rejected art and the rejected artist meet here in apt congress. Here woman is despised for her trade and not for her sex, and there is all the margin between success and failure in this differentiation. It has been the women who have transfigured not only the art, but the point of view and purpose of its practitioners, its status and relation to other arts and to the community. Dancing is the only art where women have functioned to such crucial purpose, but it is the only art where they have not worked in the teeth of universal doubt.

There have been great male choreographers—Noverre, Bournonville, Petipas, Fokine, Massine, Balanchine, Ashton, Tudor. I think one must truthfully report that the greatest have been men. But there has been no artist in a class with Michelangelo, Shakespeare, Goethe, or Bach. Indeed, to rank any choreographer with these seems like impertinent hyperbole. Nor have there been any male figures comparable in dynamism and originality to Isadora Duncan, Martha Graham, or Mary Wigman.

The very handicaps and limitations which have frightened away gifted men work to woman's advantage. Here her training and habits stand her in good stead. Here even her body is helpful. Anonymity has been her history. She is at home in an art without literature, without past or future. She has never hoped beyond today and tomorrow— or much beyond the door of her house. Are not her daily efforts spent on evanescence? Cooking, washing, watching, caring, each day erasing the labors of the day before as each gesture erases from the air its precedent? And as every day's work must start afresh in endless repetition, so each dance begins clean with no record. The dancer enters space without a guiding mark and the pattern is rehearsed and leaves no sign—no sign except the exchange between living people, the relationship established, if only once and never again. The patience for this is woman's special endowment. She is aware that there is no substitute for the breath of life; that it is unique and personal; that the unduplicated action, the unrepeated speech, the gesture or word thrown away or heard by few or only once may be as important as any public message. She remembers that the source is inexhaustible; that it is the moment of life that counts, the rebirth; that again and again and again the dancer jumps and runs, and when he falls, another, by vital invitation, leaps out. This, woman understands. This is the stuff of her life.

Women today comprise nearly one third of our total working force —many thousands of them in the arts—but the ones that turn to dancing do so still for the antique reasons—power and Dionysian release on their own terms.

Dancing ranks with women's oldest professional careers, religious dedication and prostitution. It is inextricably related to both. First as priestess, then as prostitute, then as theater performer the dancer found a way of winning fortune, an excuse from household slavery and enforced seclusion.

Dancing has always been fruitful in its effects of direct fulfillment and satisfaction, and today the appeal is, as before, spell-binding through the body. It is not the concomitants of theatrical success that draw young girls so much as the vision of becoming generically DANCER in the permitted dress, exposed legs, free and floating arms, aerial skirt. I think they want this because it produces effects of transformation as recompense for all they find insupportable in woman's traditional lot.

Dancing inflames and exercises the senses of the viewer (hence its long connection with prostitution) and of the performer (hence its long connection with religion). It is a physical release as no other performing art can be, because it is practiced on the whole body; the body is the instrument, the medium itself, and the exposure is total and voluptuous. Therein lies the clue to its compulsive lifelong hold. It can become more frequently than not a substitute for physical sex and it has all too often been chosen as a vocation because woman's life, sexually speaking, has become in our civilization unsatisfactory, uncertain and expensive to the individual.

In what way, then, is dancing a solution? Briefly, it guarantees satisfaction and control to people who are afraid they will not otherwise know them. A dancer can do more than pray or hope; she takes matters into her own hands.

Every girl has known from time immemorial that she had better have a dowry or looks, and if she possessed neither, there was usually nothing for her but to be family drudge or enter the church, where God could be counted on to overlook what husbands would not. On her appearance still depends in large measure her chance for a good marriage and children, for a continuing sex life, for a high income. Numbers of ill-favored women have succeeded to the physical rewards of life, it is true, but it is in spite of handicap and by exercising faculties not demanded of the more handsomely endowed. Age and appearance, therefore, are important, particularly in any situation where women out-number men.

Doctors assure us that any feeling of inferiority induced by physical appearance, short of mutilation, is in reality a symptom of a deeper conflict, and that the truly beautiful are as capable of self-doubt as the plain. This may be so, but it is not the prevailing popular understanding.

A woman's age has always been important because her value has been reckoned chiefly as a breeding animal and fecundity determined her economic status. This is happily no longer so.

Youth and physical beauty, nevertheless, are still held up before us as a promise, and have been in legend, story and song. We are told, and we believe, women more than men, that to win love, but, more imperatively, to retain love, we must be beautiful. It is a terrifying threat. And it faces us on every billboard, magazine page, screen, stage, shopwindow and, yes, even on the pages of every nursery picture book, because the princess was always beautiful or became so. And as we grew up, we accepted the idea more and more. Mother's friends always spoke of "the fine little boy" or "the son," but it was "the pretty little girl," and if that adjective was omitted and the word "dear" substituted, we became sensible of something hurt or slightly damaged and needing special tenderness.

Woman's best approach to happiness, we learn on all sides, is the quick rousing of men's erotic interest, and the advertisements are ex-plicit as to what rouses men. It can be bought in a bottle—and it is quite expensive but well worth the price. Five of the largest businesses in the United States—cosmetics, ladies' clothing and accessories, furs, jewelry, both real and false, women's magazines—have sprung from the premise that romance follows beauty and that beauty can be purchased. The young woman is advised to make herself lovely and then lie around like a kind of bait, and she is warned that only after the trap has suc-cessfully sprung can she satisfy her own inclinations.

Now, for many young people this is a dismaying proposition. A girl may very well feel she cannot make the grade; she may also feel fundamentally outraged in having her life controlled by someone else's tastes, implying, as it does, a passivity which she may interpret as help-lessness.

The fact is many women do not favor being passive, are downright frightened by it, having witnessed centuries of results. Young girls see quite a lot of women, particularly mothers, and often they are not enchanted. They see mothers tied to housework who would prefer not to spend their days sweeping and cooking. They see mothers and older sisters doing jobs and chores which are considered more menial and

less important than fathers' jobs and that bring in no money. It is
father who has the cash for his freedom; mother must ask. Indeed,
mother has almost no freedom at all to speak of. Mothers are always at
the call of other people's needs and desires. Their daughters find little
charm in the pattern. They would like to be free to please themselves,
forever children, unless they might grow up to some of the freedom of
father. But growing up for a woman, as they observe, seems to mean
less freedom, and no guarantee of happiness. And so some of them, the
dancers, never grow up.

Very few dancers develop the bodies of mature women; they keep
lean in the hips and flat-breasted, a phenomenon remarked on by all
costume designers. It is also a fact that the greatest performers, the
women best capable of communicating sensuous satisfaction, are in
their bodies least sensual. In effect they have sacrificed all organs of
personal fulfillment and maintain and cherish only the means for public
satisfaction, the system of bones and sinews for levitation and propul-
sion. The ballet foot and leg, which when used to its full capacity can
evoke an almost physical response, is in repose as tight and straight as
the leg of a mule. Certain great soloists have been lacking in even
primary sexual functions and are known to have menstruated rarely in
their lives. For the rest, very many, possibly a majority, are partially
frigid and most tend to be, in spite of legend, more chaste than otherwise. I do not mean to imply that they are not passionate and gallant,
but that certain deep rejections and fears prevent easy sexual release.
The majority of American women are, it is claimed by medical statistics,
partially frigid, and perhaps dancers no more than others. In any case,
the dancers have evolved a substitute expression and do not mind the
state so bitterly. This, of course, is no good answer to the fear of life.
But it is an instinctive and practical one.

Even Isadora Duncan, who clamored the loudest for love, was no
exception. She was a true sensualist and she seems to belie in the richness of her experience all I have argued about women's substitution of
dancing for life. But consider her point of view repeatedly expressed:
she vowed when very young never to submit to woman's usual fate,
never to marry, that is, never to put herself or her fortune into any
man's keeping, to bear children if and when she pleased, to leave them
or look after them at whim, to be absolutely free and to remain so. She
wished to have the freedom of a pagan as she imagined it, for she
recognized love as a transient ecstasy. The communion on which marriage is built she never, I believe, envisaged, nor constancy, security,
fruition, these being the rewards of the female life she scorned. She
followed a dream, power without responsibility, release without cost.

And her way of attainment was the cultivation of her body. The littlest ballet pupil in first position before the mirror is starting on the same historic path.*

For in dancing the face matters least and the body is beautiful if it functions beautifully. It is not the shape of the leg, but the use of the leg that tells. Furthermore, and most felicitously, the beautiful use changes the flesh and corrects all manner of imperfections. Contrary to maxims, one can by taking thought add a cubit to stature. When a dancer stands before a mirror, she no longer sees what her big brothers see, but a promise. If her nose turns up or down, no matter: men will gasp at the carriage of her head. If she is fat, she will get thin. If she is thin, the muscles of her back and thighs will enable her to move like a voluptuary. And who is to say or who cares what she is, whether this or that, if she stands in the center of a stage in the revealing and beautiful uniform of her trade, escorted by the best cavalier in the business, who has forfeited the right to refuse her and must take her if she is the best, not the prettiest, mind you, but the best and the most skillful. And there for all to see, in public, she will perform with him the ritual of romantic courtship. More than in any other art, there are enormous rewards as regards direct attention, admiration, emotional release, and they remain always under the performer's command. She never surrenders her will. She gets her rewards directly by her own effort. There need be no intermediary—and for any female who doubts her powers this is a temptation of frightening persuasiveness.

Dancing represents sex in its least costly form, free from imprisonment and free to a great extent from emotional responsibility, and, above all, as a sure thing, independent of someone else's pleasure. In other words, it means freedom *from* sex. The forces which impelled women to the austerity of the church operate to form the great dancer. In a strange transmutation dancing is a form of asceticism—almost a form of celibacy.

Is, then, the aesthetic impulse rooted in neurosis and unable to develop except under the compulsion of pain? Are these brutal disciplines and forfeits necessary to creative effort? The ancients did not rely on any such goads and, notwithstanding, their art flourished. The restraints we place on women creators could well be accidental to our culture, of no great profit to the individual or the work, but, rather, destructive to both. I believe this to be the case and that the genius

---

* I would like to interject that very few daughters of contented mothers have become ballerinas. I cannot name a father who urged a dancing career on his girl unless he was himself a dancer and looked upon the matter as one of natural succession.

with which certain women write or paint or compose or choreograph derives from faculties and needs beyond any mere act of compensation. I believe that talent is compounded of the entire personality and is as much a sign of exuberant health as of sickness. But the bewitchment of hundreds of thousands, of millions of girls by the dream, by even the discipline of dancing cannot be called creativity, nor even vocation. It is escape, it is protest, and it is, in large part, hysterical protest.

For a time it serves the art form well, but only for a time. In the working conditions of our world and theater the dedicated ones are forced under emotional whips to greater and greater effort. But there is a limit. The personality ceases to expand, ceases to breathe, in certain aspects it withers and this is reflected in a stunting of the art. The audience is always aware.

An act of suppression that cancels out emotional or imaginative life, the one at the cost of the other, is obviously wasteful. With either choice a major section of the personality is wrecked and all human relations, in marriage and out, must suffer.

A dancer's release, like most magic, is transient and won each time by renewed and arduous effort. Dancing has become consequently a kind of sexual limbo whose inhabitants identify their own flesh with their purpose, a confusion not equally true for women artists whose bodies are not their lifework. Dancing is, in a deep sense, the only physical union many of these women know, a sort of automarriage. And as with all such narcissistic unions, there develops an aura of melancholy and the promise of death. Many a young dancer has drowned in the mirrors before which she spends her life. The others live only when the reflection from the audience fans breath back into their emptying spirits.

Whatever rewards the dancer knows in place of the usual emotional and sexual associations, she is frequently assailed by doubts in her late twenties or early thirties. Even the very great know these morbid spells. The needs of the heart cannot be cheated forever. The dancer grows frightened. The dancer realizes suddenly she is a spinster and aging, no matter how fast she gets around the room. The life of merciless effort, the dimming chances of permanent fame, exhaustion and the growing comprehension of what old age means to a fading athlete without family or home suddenly terrify even the stanchest. The conviction grows that the sacrifice has been too much and perhaps not necessary. There is many a *volte-face* at this point and a marriage with at least one child in a frantic effort to put life back on balance.

But our theater is not set up for family life; dancing in particular is conditioned by world-wide touring, uncertain irregular seasons and precarious pay. Dancers today do not inherit the career dynastically as they used to, like the Vestris, the Taglioni (five distinguished members and three generations in this family), the Grisi, Elssler, Karsavin clans. Our dancers are not protected wards of the state with guaranteed salaries and pensions. The married dancer is called upon to relinquish jobs that would further her career and settle for domesticity against professional interest. Many do this serenely and good-naturedly; this is nothing more than the problem of reconciling life and art, which is present with all workers, but in a dancer's case, particularly for women, it is final. She may consider the exchange worth the price either way. She may not and live in perpetual conflict.

It is astonishing under the circumstances that none of these factors deters young girls one whit. Five million of them in this country alone are studying to be professional dancers.

Perhaps this is so because women today, even dancers, cannot bring themselves to accept these conditions as permanent. They see no reason why they should not have both work and family, what with Deepfreeze, Waring mixers and diaper service. They believe also with all their hearts and hopes—because it suits them so to believe—that sweet reasonableness and a sense of fair play will dissolve the major block to the double life: their husbands' attitude.

Marriage is difficult with any artist. "A man does not love a woman for her genius; he loves her in spite of her genius," writes Maurice Goudeket, the husband of Colette. Marriage is perhaps hardest of all with a theater personality because the work is not wholly under the control of the individual. Dancers above all do not make easy wives. The union has to run a gamut of conflicting loyalties. A dancer's husband has to share his wife's discipline. His life is as curtailed as hers and quite literally by hers. Most men, particularly men outside of the profession, find such conditions onerous.

But the unrest is general and pertains to all careers and all classes of society. Preachers, doctors and teachers warn; magazine and newspaper editorialize. The women's magazines are particularly explicit: if the wife has to work outside the home she must never let it impinge on her husband's schedule, and if inside the home she must see that it is finished and put away before he comes back from his own work and she must never for one moment let him think that hers is important compared with his, or his interests and hobbies and needs. And for this reason and because it will be construed as a direct reflection on his virility, she must not earn more money. He will develop ulcers, sinuses, abscesses, tuberculosis. He will borrow the classic symptom of women's frustration, the bitter, black headache, and although women's magazines do not care to name this, he will add one of his own, partial or total impotence, which is a form of suicide and just as unanswerable. He may in the end leave her.

If the women do not depend on their men as their grandmothers did, the men similarly manage to do without them. It has become a game of mutual attrition played out on a level where both are pitifully defenseless. Medical statistics and divorce courts list the ruin. The suicide rate among men, the alcoholism, the excesses of sedation and narcotics, the growing overt homosexuality, the juvenile neuroticism and delinquency attest to the monumental cost of the emotional adjustment. This is the "furious and lamentable region" that Conrad speaks of, "the dwelling place of unveiled hearts" where there is neither right nor wrong but only human suffering.

Woman has always accepted with grace, with pride and satisfaction, her husband's interests and achievements, taking joy, taking not in any way a sense of diminution and shame. Can the husband endure to learn this? Does he wish to? Will he not rather attempt to put things back as they were, stuffing all hopes, ambitions and zests not centered on himself into the family cupboard and setting his back to the door? Indeed, indeed, things cannot go back. Pandora's box is opened. The girls are earning money.

It is of no consequence who works better—men or women; it is important that each work differently and that each be allowed to try without penalties. "Never destroy any aspect of personality," said my grandmother George, who had no career except caring for her family, "for what you think is the wild branch may be the heart of the tree." Not all women want a double life. But those who do should not be denied on the grounds of sex. It is not easy to be a devoted wife and mother and a first-class artist; it is equally hard to be an artist with no root experience in life. It is impossible to be a good wife or a wise mother, embittered, balked and devoured by inner energies. Creative exercise can be disciplined to a household schedule—not easily, but women everywhere prove it can be done. For when all faculties are exercised the enormous releases of strength and satisfaction more than make up for the extra attention demanded. Extra attention? No, rather, elimination of waste and repining. The alternation of diaper washing and composing spell one another in mutual refreshment. Ask any responsible working mother. And the children will reflect the zest and energy of the parent's life—and as to the work, how it flourishes! How it flowers and expands! Even under discipline, perhaps particularly under discipline, because it is voluntary and joyful, because the sources of life are fulfilled and replenished and because, as in all things, the greater the range of accomplishment, the greater the capacity for more.

I think this is what Isadora Duncan meant when she spoke of founding a new religion: the total release of women's hearts, the total use of their gifts.

Women have bent to the yoke and the scars of their durance are upon their children. But with the lessening of all social and religious restrictions, with widening economic opportunities, with practical invention bringing ease and leisure, there stands between woman and whatever life she yearns for only one barrier: her husband's good will. Failing this, she fails all. She must have his blessing, his pride in her achievement. Let him dower her with this and there will come the great works for which we have waited so long. But beyond and beneath there will come happiness.

It is an act of recognition that is needed, an act of love.

JEAN COCTEAU

The Cat That Walks by Itself

THE SPIRIT STIRS, chafes at its bonds, exults, burns, and rises again from its ashes. This stationary motion ought to be studied, and the new science might well be called phoenixology. Nothing ever overtakes anything else. Vermeer of Delft does not overtake Piero della Francesca; Rembrandt does not overtake Vermeer; nor Renoir, Goya; nor Picasso, Van Gogh; and so on. These outstanding men burn with a light which sometimes casts deep shadows. But the age we live in, drunk with speed, or rather with what it takes to be speed, has invented a fashionable term—*dépassement*. We all hustle and bustle for the sake of overtaking the next man, of getting somewhere first. And what we do is to get held up at the traffic lights or end in a hospital bed.

The conspiracy of noise, which came after what used to be the conspiracy of silence, seeks to keep up a chaotic hubbub in which the secret values of the world are confused with its manifest and ephemeral values. The conspirators get hold of a poet, a painter, a musician, or a scholar, and push him on the platform with Miss Europe or the supersonic pilot. But Beau Brummel's remark applies to every rung of the spiritual ladder. 'I could not be elegant at Ascot', he said, 'because you had noticed how elegant I was'. Our real vocation is invisible, and there was a time when nobody tried to force into view what ought only to be seen at a distance in time, like starlight.

In 1954 Baudelaire would not be left in the wings, but dragged on to the stage on the pretence that he approved of the fashions of the day. He would have to take part in some benefit performance. This cruel and all-devouring passion for the up-to-date might even find it amusing to drag Toulouse-Lautrec out of the wings and make his poor crippled legs dance the cancan. So, since we are thrust on to the platform, we shall struggle hard to play the part of a false self, a fable, a legend, a double, and to hide our silence and our privacy beneath a protective shell of half-truths and tittle-tattle.

It is to defend our invisible world that we turn our visible selves into caricatures and scarecrows. The term *dépassement* is accompanied by another word, *engagement*. You overtake, you are overtaken, you commit yourself, or else this famous 'speed' will leave you standing, ignored, by the roadside. An artist must make his way on foot. He is the cat that walks by itself. He is visible and invisible, like smoke. And his road is all the harder because the cars rush by and splash him with mud and glare. He must keep on his legs and overcome his tiredness.

Unfortunately young artists find it hard to keep up the struggle. They keep stopping, lose heart, see the great arrogant cars going by and resign themselves to hitch-hiking. They jump into cars which are not theirs; they are 'committed'. They are delighted to be moving at speed, but the speed is not theirs either. They give up the great game of losing to win, and take to the modern game of winning to lose. So I was much amused by an article about myself which appeared in a London paper. This article accused me of being, as it were, too multifarious, of never settling on anything. The journalist who wrote the article had no inkling of a method of defence for the poet, which is a matter of preferring change to the uniformity of a literary school. This method bids us cover up our tracks and adopt a simple ruse to prevent the craze for the up-to-date from taking us up: the ruse which consists of never repeating ourselves; of taking care, when once a work has fallen from the tree, not to shake the tree to bring down others of the same kind— in short, as Stravinsky put it so strikingly, of 'always looking for a cool place on the pillow'.

For my own part, as I am the servant of the forces within that I only partly understand, I have always set out to baffle the critics and forestall their attempts to get a grip on me. For if they once got a grip on me I should no longer be able to live. I should die, and everybody knows that a poet does not die, but gives place to his work: that his chief function, for which he has made himself ready long before is, at the very end of his life, to *pretend* to die. I mean that the poet lives mainly after his death and gives place to his work, which does its best to get rid of him and which, when all is said, is his real self. The only death which is really frightening is the living death of those who submit to having a label pinned on them.

Poetry finds expression through many means. A play, a drawing, a painting, a tapestry, a film, a heroic deed—all these do its work as well as a poem. The artists who won honour for France all died in poverty—in the workhouse, in exile, or by suicide. Their example must never be forgotten. However hard the road, the artist must walk along the dark side, and keep to the edge of the great main roads, of the autostradas.

The theatre is theatrical. There has been a tendency to forget this. Perhaps the older actors, who had the vigour, could not go on playing young parts because of the cinema, where the actor must be as young as his role, and the load was too heavy for the youngsters to carry on their shoulders. Production and, later on, language of an undramatic kind took the place of direct action. Jean Giraudoux is an exception. His language is dramatic: and only his language. This stands out in 'Lucrèce'. There, the action of the play is inferior to the language, and an actress who is not particularly conversant with literature, like Madame Yvon de Bray, can make a hit by speaking a few lines, because an authentic human voice is suddenly heard in this wonderful puppet-theatre of which Giraudoux is the ventriloquist.

Alas, the theatre public tends to turn up its nose at dramatic action, to call it melodrama. In Giraudoux' case the language sanctifies the melodrama; but, on the other hand, the public has very little enthusiasm for such simple, close-packed language as Sartre uses in his adaptation of Dumas' 'Kean'. The public—I mean the *élite*—thinks that diverting action is unworthy of the audience, and turns away in disgust from the admirable theatrical contrivances which enchanted its members in childhood—turns away from Jules Verne's *Round the World in Eighty Days*, from *Michel Strogoff*, from *Peter Pan*. When I first put on *L'Aigle à deux têtes* in Paris—the English version, by the way, has no connection with my own play and is far too 'literary' (even the title is inexact, since it ought to be 'The Two-headed Eagle' and not 'The Eagle Has Two Heads')—what I had in mind was to give the pure theatre back its rights. This made the so-called *élite* flock to see the play and made it a success.

If one is as unfortunate as I have been, and becomes famous for things one has not done and words one has not uttered, one has to admit that legend is stronger than history, because history is truth which becomes false in the long run, and legend is falsehood which, in the long run, becomes truth. We must all go on walking on the dark side of the road, and leave the mirage of 'speed' to our double, the puppet who guards our freedom, like Leporello dressed in his master Don Juan's clothes; who braves all our perils for us and takes the beating that the critics aim at ourselves.

I have only one doctrine, and that is that poetry is a separate language and not, as is popularly supposed, a special way of using the language of common speech. The language of poetry is the highest form of expression given to man, and remains sublime, without ridicule. Shakespeare, Rimbaud, Goethe, Edgar Allan Poe, Pushkin, Gongora are the real England, the real France, the real Germany, the real America, the real Russia, the real Spain, whatever the political changes in these countries.

We must put up with being pushed aside by the craze for the up-to-date, for it has been proved, in politics as well as in art, that every significant and enduring achievement has seemed, in its own time, a failure. We must, I repeat, be burned to rise again, and every poet knows, alas, that, where his achievement is concerned, a successful issue is really a failure. Poetry is a religion without hope, but its martyrs guarantee the eternal truth of its dogma. What is the use of poetry? That is the question which the up-to-date mind asks the kind of out-of-date mind which, between ourselves, is really more up-to-date than its questioner. Answer: I know that poetry is indispensable but I do not know what for. If I knew, and told what I knew, I should be like a plant holding forth about gardening.

Here, then, are a few of the secrets of that moral beauty which has nothing to do with conventional morality and which is most exacting to pursue, for it is different for different people. But I think that when a pretty woman says she is anxious to 'keep her figure', the idea can be applied to artists, with the reservation that their beauty is an inner beauty and their beauty-parlours are for the soul—the soul which seems to regress in proportion to the mind's amazement at the triumphs of progress.

In Madrid, a little while ago, Salvador Dali was talking to me about *Tancredism*. Don Tancredo, in Spain, is the man in a white costume and white make-up who stands stock still on a table in the middle of the bull-ring. The bull rushes forward, stops, sniffs, and turns away. There is a good deal of *Tancredism* in art and politics. Standing stock still is one method of self-protection. But it just does not happen to be mine.

WILLIAM BARRETT

Modern Art

Now that my ladder's gone,
I must lie down where all ladders start,
In the foul rag-and-bone shop of the heart.
W. B. YEATS

ANYONE WHO ATTEMPTS to gain a unified understanding of modern art as a whole is bound to suffer the uncomfortable sensation of having fallen into a thicket of brambles. We ourselves are involved in the subject, and we can hardly achieve the detachment of the historian a few centuries hence. Modern art still provokes violent controversy, even after it has been on the scene a good half century and names like Picasso and Joyce have become almost household words. The Philistine still finds it shocking, scandalous, and foolish; and there is always a case to be made for the Philistine, and surely for the Philistine in ourselves without whom we could not carry on the drab business of ordinary living. Indeed, from the point of view we are taking here, the Philistine attitude, particularly in its irritation, may be just as revelatory historically as any other. But it is a case not only of the Philistine; sensitive observers still exist—directors of museums, connoisseurs, and historians —who find in modern art a disastrous falling away from the excellence of the art of the past. In a sense, all this controversy is pointless; so much of it has to do with the eventual historical rating of our own period, which is something we cannot even foresee. The century from Manet to Matisse may figure in future art histories as a period of impoverishment and decline, whose works cannot stand beside those of the old masters; or it may figure as a period of such abundant creativity that it can be matched only by the Renaissance during the fifteenth century. My own personal prejudice is toward the latter judgment, but I have no way of proving it; and such speculation, in any case, does not enter into my own experience of this art. We have simply got to give up the attempt to assess ourselves for posterity; the men of the future will form their own opinions without our help. What we so self-consciously call "modern art," after all, is nothing more nor less than the art of this time, *our* art; there is no other today. If we could have a different art, or a better, we would have it. As it is, we are lucky in this period to have any art at all. The Philistine rebukes the artist for being willful, as if all of modern art were a deliberate conspiracy against him,

207

the viewer; the artist can hardly hope to make this man understand that art is not a mere matter of conscious will and conscious contrivance, and that the artist, by changing his ideas (even by adopting the Philistine's), will not become a different person living at a different time and place. In the end the only authentic art is that which has about it the power of inevitability.

Nevertheless, the controversy, irritation, and bafflement to which modern art gives rise does provide us a very effective handle with which to take hold of it. Irritation usually arises when something touches a sore spot in ourselves, which most of the time we would like desperately to hide; rarely if ever does the fault lie totally with the provoking object. Modern art touches a sore spot, or several sore spots, in the ordinary citizen of which he is totally unaware. The more irritated he becomes at modern art the more he betrays the fact that he himself, and his civilization, are implicated in what the artist shows him. The ordinary citizen objects to modern art because it is difficult and obscure. Is it so certain that the world the ordinary citizen takes for granted, the values upon which his civilization rests are so clear, either to him or in themselves? Sometimes the artist's image is very clear (in general, modern art is *simpler* than academic art), but it goes against the grain of the ordinary man because secretly he understands its intent all too well; and besides, he has already limited "understanding" to the habitual pigeonholes into which he slips every experience. The ordinary man is uncomfortable, angry, or derisive before the dislocation of forms in modern art, before its bold distortions, or arbitrary manipulations of objects. The painter puts three or more eyes in the face, or several noses, or twists and elongates the body at the expense of photographic resemblance in order to build up his own inner image. Has the contrary attitude of strict and literal attachment to objects succeeded in resolving all the anxieties of the ordinary man, and has not in fact the rampant extroversion of modern civilization brought it to the brink of the abyss? Finally, the ordinary man—and in this respect the ordinary man is joined by the learned and sensitive traditionalist in art—objects to the content of modern art: it is too bare and bleak, too negative or "nihilistic," too shocking or scandalous; it dishes out unpalatable truths. But have the traditional ideals worked so well in this century that we can afford to neglect the unpalatable truths about human life that those ideals have chosen to ignore? Does the aesthete who extols the greatness of the past as an argument against modern art have any idea of how pallid his own response to, say, the Virgin of Chartres appears beside the medieval man's response? Or that his own aestheticism, however cultured, is in fact a form of sentimentality—since sentimentality, at bottom, is nothing but false feeling, feeling that is untrue to its object, whether by being excessive or watered down?

In a famous passage in *A Farewell to Arms* Ernest Hemingway writes:

> I was always embarrassed by the words sacred, glorious, and sacrifice and the expression in vain. We had heard them, sometimes standing in the rain almost out of earshot, so that only the shouted words came through, and had read them, on proclamations that were slapped up by billposters over other proclamations, now for a long time, and I had seen nothing sacred, and the things that were glorious had no glory and the sacrifices were like the stockyards at Chicago if nothing was done with the meat except to bury it. There were many words that you could not stand to hear and finally only the names of places had dignity. Certain numbers were the same way and certain dates and these with the names of places were all you could say and have them mean anything. Abstract words such as glory, honor, courage, or hallow were obscene beside the concrete names of villages, the numbers of roads, the names of rivers, the numbers of regiments and the dates.

For a whole generation that was the great statement of protest against the butchery of the First World War. But it has a greater historical significance than that: it can be taken as a kind of manifesto of modern art and literature, an incitement to break through empty abstractions of whatever kind, to destroy sentimentality even if the real feelings exposed should appear humble and impoverished—the names of places and dates; and even if in stripping himself naked the artist seems to be left with Nothing. Modern art thus begins, and sometimes ends, as a confession of spiritual poverty. That is its greatness and its triumph, but also the needle it jabs into the Philistine's sore spot, for the last thing he wants to be reminded of is his spiritual poverty. In fact, his greatest poverty is not to know how impoverished he is, and so long as he mouths the empty ideals or religious phrases of the past he is but as tinkling brass. In matters of the spirit, poverty and riches are sometimes closer than identical twins: the man who struts with borrowed feathers may be poor as a church mouse within, while a work that seems stark and bleak can, if genuine, speak with all the inexhaustible richness of the world. The triumph of Hemingway's style is its ability to break through abstractions to see what it is one really senses and feels. When the modern sculptor disdains the pomp of marble and uses industrial materials, steel wire, or bolts, or even rejected materials like old board, rope, or nails, he is perhaps showing himself to be impoverished next to the heroic grandeur of a Michelangelo, but he is also bringing us back to the inexhaustible brute world that surrounds us. Sometimes the confession of poverty takes a violent and aggressive tone, as when the Dadaists drew a mustache on the Mona Lisa. Dada itself, like Hemingway, came out of the revolt against the First World War, and despite its clowning must now be regarded as one of the *valid* eruptions of the irrational in this century. The generation of the First World War could hardly be expected to view Western culture as sacrosanct, since they perceived—and rightly—that it was bound up with the civilization that had ended in that ghastly butchery. Better then to reject the trappings of that culture, even art itself, if that would leave one a little more honest in one's nakedness. To discover one's own spiritual poverty is to achieve a positive conquest by the spirit.

Modern art has been an immense movement toward the destruction of forms—of received and traditional forms. The positive side of this has been an immense expansion of the possibilities of art and an almost greedy acquisition of new forms from all over the globe. Around 1900 French painters became interested in African sculpture. (The introduction of Japanese prints into Europe in the nineteenth century had already brought with it a profound shift in the sensibility of Western painters.) And these borrowings were only the beginning: by now we have become accustomed to painters and sculptors drawing their forms from Oriental and primitive art of every culture. This century in art, André Malraux has said, will go down in history not as the period of abstract art but as the period in which all the art of the past, and from every quarter of the globe, became available to the painter and sculptor, and through them became a part of our modern taste. Certainly, we can no longer look upon the canon of Western art—Greco-Roman art as revived, extended, and graced by the Renaissance—as *the* tradition in art, or even any longer as distinctly and uniquely *ours*. That canon is in fact only one tradition among many, and indeed in its strict adherence to representational form is rather the exception in the whole gallery of *human* art. Such an extension of the resources of the past, for the modern artist, implies a different and more comprehensive understanding of the term "human" itself: a Sumerian figure of a fertility goddess is as "human" to us as a Greek Aphrodite. When the sensibility of an age can accommodate the alien "inhuman" forms of primitive art side by side with the classic "human" figures of Greece or the Renaissance, it should be obvious that the attitude toward man that we call classical humanism—which is the intellectual expression of the spirit that informs the classical canon of Western art—has also gone by the boards. This is an historical fact the most immediate evidence of which is the whole body of modern art itself. Even if existential philosophy had not been formulated, we would know from modern art that a new and radical conception of man was at work in this period.

It would be a mistake to construe this breaking out on the part of Western artists from the confinement of what had been their tradition as mere expansion or a spiritually imperialistic act of acquisition. It is not simply an external and quantitative change in the number of forms the artist can assimilate, it is also, and more profoundly, an internal and qualitative change in the spirit with which the artist appropriates these forms. This breaking out of the tradition is in fact also a breakdown within the Western tradition. On this point the artistic conservative who rejects modern art, seeing it as a scandal and a departure from the tradition, sees rightly, however he may turn what he sees to his own purposes. That Western painters and sculptors have in this century gone outside their own tradition to nourish themselves on the art of the rest of the world—Oriental, African, Melanesian—signifies that what we have known as *the* tradition is no longer able to nourish its most creative members: the confining mold of this tradition has broken, under pressures both from within and without. It would be possible to avoid this painful conclusion and to dismiss this group of artists as mere irresponsibles, and skillful renegades from the tradition, if there were any artists of comparable achievement whose work the anti-modernist could set over against theirs. But what is equally sure—and this negative evidence is strong or even stronger on the side of the moderns—is that the academic art of this period is as dead as mutton. It excites no one, depresses no one, and does not even really soothe anyone. It simply does not live; it is outside the time.

If we turn to the internal and formal characteristics of modern art, without reference to its external inspirations in African or primitive or Oriental art, we find the same indications of a radical transformation of the Western spirit. Cubism is the classicism of modern art: that is, the one formally perfected style which modern art has elaborated and from which all modern abstract art that is valid has derived. A great deal of nonsense has been written about the creation of Cubism, connecting it with relativity physics, psychoanalysis, and heaven knows how many other complex and remote things. The fact is that the painters who created Cubism were creating paintings and nothing else—certainly they were not dealing in ideologies. Cubism evolved in a succession of perfectly logical steps out of previous stages of painting, out of the Impressionists and Cézanne, and it raised a series of pictorial problems that had to be solved within the medium of painting and by painters working strictly as painters—that is, upon the visual image as such.

Yet a great formal style in painting has never been created that did not draw upon the depths of the human spirit, and that did not, in its newness, express a fresh mutation of the human spirit. Cubism achieved a radical flattening of space by insisting on the two-dimensional fact of the canvas. This flattening out of space would seem not to be a negligible fact historically if we reflect that when, once before in history, such a development occurred but in the opposite direction—when the flatness of the Gothic of primitive painters passed over into the solidity, perspective, and three-dimensional style of early Renaissance painting— it was a mark that man was turning outward, into space, after the long period of introspection of the Middle Ages. Western man moved out into space in his painting, in the fourteenth century, before he set forth into actual physical space in the age of exploration that was to follow. Thus painting was prophetic of the new turn of the human spirit which was eventually to find expression in the conquest of the whole globe. Have we the right, then, to suggest that the flattening of painting in our own century portends a turning inward of the human spirit, or at any rate a turning away from that outer world of space which has hitherto been the ultimate arena of Western man's extroversion? With Cubism begins that process of detachment from the object which has become the hallmark of modern art. Even though Cubism is a classical and formal style, the artist nevertheless asserts his own subjectivity by the freedom with which he cuts up and dislocates objects—bottles, pitchers, guitars—as it pleases him for the sake of the picture, which is now no longer held up to us as a representation of those objects but as a visual image with its own independent value alongside that of nature. The subjectivity that is generally present in modern art is a psychological compensation for, sometimes a violent revolt against, the gigantic externalization of life within modern society. The world pictured by the modern artist is, like the world meditated upon by the existential philosopher, a world where man is a stranger.

When mankind no longer lives spontaneously turned toward God or the supersensible world—when, to echo the words of Yeats, the ladder is gone by which we would climb to a higher reality—the artist too must stand face to face with a flat and inexplicable world. This shows itself even in the formal structures of modern art. Where the movement of the spirit is no longer vertical but only horizontal, the climactic elements in art are in general leveled out, flattened. The flattening of pictorial space that is achieved in Cubism is not an isolated fact, true only of painting, but is paralleled by similar changes in literary techniques. There is a general process of flattening, three chief aspects of which may be noted:

(1) *The flattening out of all planes* upon the plane of the picture. Near and far are pushed together. So in certain works of modern literature time, instead of space, is flattened out upon one plane. Past and present are represented as occurring simultaneously, upon a single plane of time. James Joyce's *Ulysses,* T. S. Eliot's *The Waste Land,* and Ezra Pound's *Cantos* are examples; and perhaps the most powerful use of the device was made by Faulkner in his early novel *The Sound and the Fury.*

(2) More important perhaps is the *flattening out of climaxes,* which occurs both in painting and literature. In traditional Western painting there is a central subject, located at or near the center of the picture, and the surrounding space in the picture is subordinate to this. In a portrait the figure is placed near the center, and the background becomes secondary to it, something to be blended as harmoniously as possible with the figure. Cubism abolished this idea of the pictorial climax: the whole space of the picture became of equal importance. Negative spaces (in which there are no objects) are as important as positive spaces (the contours of physical objects). If a human figure is treated, it may be broken up and distributed over various parts of the canvas. Formally speaking, the spirit of this art is anticlimatic.

When we turn to observe this same deflation or flattening of climaxes in literature, the broader human and philosophic questions involved become much clearer. The classical tradition in literature, deriving from Aristotle's *Poetics,* tells us that a drama (and consequently any other literary work) must have a beginning, middle, and end. The action begins at a certain point, rises toward a climax, and then falls to a denouement. One can diagram a classical plot of this kind by means of a triangle whose apex represents the climax with which everything in the play has some logical and necessary connection. The author subordinates himself to the requirements of logic, necessity, probability. His structure must be an intelligible whole in which each part develops logically out of what went before. If our existence itself is never quite like this, no matter; art is a selection from life, and the poet is required to be selective. However, it is important to note that this canon of intelligible literary structure—beginning, middle, and end, with a well-defined climax—arose in a culture in which the universe too was believed to be an ordered structure, a rational and intelligible whole.

What happens if we try to apply this classical Aristotelian canon to a modern work like Joyce's *Ulysses,* 734 pages of power and dullness, beauty and sordidness, comedy and pathos, where the movement is always horizontal, never ascending toward any crisis, and where we detect not the shadow of anything like a climax, in the traditional sense of that term? If Joyce's had been a disordered mind, we could dismiss all this as a sprawling chaos; but he was in fact an artist in superb control of his material, so that the disorder has to be attributed to his material, to life itself. It is, in fact, the banal gritty thing that we live that Joyce gives us, in comparison with which most other fiction is indeed fiction. This world is dense, opaque, unintelligible; that is the datum from which the modern artist always starts. The formal dictates of the well-made play or the well-made novel, which were the logical outcome of thoroughly rational preconceptions about reality, we can no longer hold to when we become attentive "to the things themselves," to the facts, to existence in the mode in which we do exist. If our epoch still held to the idea, as Western man once did, that the whole of reality is a system in which each detail providentially and rationally is subordinated to others and ultimately to the whole itself, we could demand of the artist that his form imitate this idea of reality, and give us coherence, logic, and the picture of a world with no loose ends. But to make such a demand nowadays is worse than an impertinence: it is a travesty upon the historical being of the artist.

Even where the writer has more of a story, in the traditional sense, to tell, he may prefer not to tell it in the traditional way. In *The Sound and the Fury* Faulkner has much more of a novelistic narrative than Joyce in *Ulysses*—the decline of a family, a suicide, the elopement of a girl, and so on—but he chooses not to present these events in the form of the well-made novel. And the choice is wise, for the power of the novel is increased immeasurably thereby. The brute, irrational, given quality of the world comes through so strongly in Faulkner's peculiar technique that he actually shows, and does not merely state, the meaning of the quotation from which his title is derived:

> *[Life] is a tale,*
> *Told by an idiot, full of sound and fury,*
> *Signifying nothing.*

Shakespeare places these lines in the context of a fairly well-made tragedy in which evil is destroyed and good triumphs; but Faulkner shows us the world of which Shakespeare's statement would be true: a world opaque, dense, and irrational, that could not have existed for Shakespeare, close as he was still to medieval Christianity. Even where a purposeful human action is planned, in the novel, and the necessary steps taken to carry it through—as in the section on the day Quentin Compson commits suicide—what really happens has little to do with the traditional order, logic, sequence of events that normally accompany such an action. The day described shows us not the abstraction "Quentin Compson commits suicide" but, as the author turns his own and his reader's eye "to the things themselves," a process far more concrete and contingent: a sparrow chirps at the window, a watch breaks, the hero gets intangled in a perfectly absurd melee with a little runaway girl, there is a fist fight, etc.; and underneath all this is, but never mentioned, the slow blind surge moving forward like an underground river toward the sea, of a man's going to his death. This section, and the book itself, is a masterpiece, perhaps as great as anything yet written by an American; and is to be recommended to anyone who wants to know the concrete feel of that world.

In the course of the brute random flow of detail that is that last day of his life, Quentin Compson breaks the crystal of his watch. He twists off the two hands and thereafter, throughout the day, the watch continues to tick loudly but cannot, with its faceless dial, indicate the time. Faulkner could not have hit on a better image to convey the sense of time which permeates the whole book. The normal reckonable sequence of time—one moment after another—has been broken, has disappeared; but as the watch pounds on, time is all the more urgent and real for Quentin Compson. He cannot escape time, he is in it, it is the time of his fate and his decision; and the watch has no hands to reassure him of that normal, calculable progression of minutes and hours in which our ordinary day-to-day life is passed. Time is no longer a reckonable sequence, then, for him, but an inexhaustible inescapable presence. We are close here—as we shall see later—to the thought of Heidegger. (Faulkner certainly never read Heidegger; he may never even have heard of him. So much the better; for the testimony of the artist, the poet, is all the more valid when it is not contaminated by any intellectual preconceptions.) Real time, the time that makes up the dramatic substance of our life, is something deeper and more primordial than watches, clocks, and calendars. Time is the dense medium in which Faulkner's characters move about as if dragging their feet through water: it is their substance or Being, as Heidegger would put it. The abolition of clock time does not mean a retreat into the world of the timeless; quite the contrary: the timeless world, the eternal, has disappeared from the horizon of the modern writer as it has from the horizon of modern Existentialists like Sartre and Heidegger, and from the horizon of our own everyday life; and time thereby becomes all the more inexorable and absolute a reality. The temporal is the horizon of modern man, as the eternal was the horizon of the man of the Middle Ages. That modern writers have been so preoccupied with the reality of time, handling it with radically new techniques and from radically new points of view, is evidence that the philosophers in our age who have attempted a new understanding of time are responding to the same hidden historical concerns, and are not merely elaborating some new conceptual novelty out of their heads.

These details about art, it should be apparent to the reader, are not dragged in by the heels. Nor are they the elaborate constructions which it has become the critical fashion in this country to force upon works of art. On the contrary, the features we have mentioned lie open and accessible—on the very surface, so to speak, of the works of art themselves; and to see them requires only that we take art seriously, which means to take it as a revelation: a revelation of its time and of the being of man, and of the two together, the being of man in his time.

No beginning, middle, end—such is the structureless structure that some modern literary works struggle toward; and analogously in painting, no clearly demarcated foreground, middleground, and background. To the traditionalist, immersed in the classical Western tradition, all this will appear negative, purely destructive. But if we do not keep our gaze narrowly riveted on the tradition of the West (and in any case this classical canon is only one of the traditions that have arisen in the course of the whole history of the West), we find that these requirements of logical and rational form do not hold for other traditions of art in other cultures. Oriental art, for example, is much more formless, organic, and sprawling than classical Western art. It has form, but a different form from that of the West. Why is this? The question is not a trivial one; it is perhaps as profound as any the West can ask these days, for this difference in art is not mere happenstance but the inevitable concomitant of a different attitude toward the world.

One of the best indications of this peculiar (to us) sense of artistic form among Orientals is given by E. M. Forster in his novel *A Passage to India*. A mixed group, English and Indians, are at tea, and Professor Godbole, a Hindu, has been asked to sing, but has let the occasion go by; then, as all are leaving, the Hindu says, "I may sing now," quite unexpectedly. (This unexpectedness is significant for the song is not to be given a formal setting, but to drop upon their ears as casually and contingently as life itself.) Forster's description of the song makes our point so beautifully that it is worth quoting in its entirety:

> His thin voice rose, and gave out one sound after another. At times there seemed rhythm, at times there was the illusion of a Western melody. But the ear, baffled repeatedly, soon lost any clue, and wandered in a maze of noises, none harsh or unpleasant, none intelligible. It was the song of an unknown bird. Only the servants

understood it. They began to whisper to one another. The man who was gathering water chestnuts came naked out of the tank, his lips parted with delight, disclosing his scarlet tongue. The sounds continued and ceased after a few moments as casually as they had begun—apparently half through a bar, and upon the subdominant.

The song begins, goes on, suddenly stops; but there is not the least trace of an Aristotelian beginning, middle, or end. Compare Godbole's song with the structure of an aria from an Italian opera. In the latter we have a beginning, a development through certain predictable phases toward the inevitable climax of the high note, and then the falling away or denouement, tying up the whole thing in a neat package: here is Aristotelian and rational form in music. But the Oriental song baffles the ear of the Westerner; it appears unintelligible. The reason is that the Westerner demands (or, let us say, used to demand) an intelligibility that the Easterner does not. If the Westerner finds the Oriental music "meaningless," the Oriental might very well reply that this is the meaninglessness of nature itself which goes on endlessly without beginning, middle, or end.

The real reason for the difference between the sense of artistic form in the East and in the West is thus ultimately a difference in philosophic outlook. Since the Greeks, Western man has believed that Being, all Being, is intelligible, that there is a reason for everything (at least, the central tradition that runs from Aristotle through St. Thomas Aquinas into the beginning of the modern period has held this), and that the cosmos is, finally, intelligible. The Oriental, on the other hand, has accepted his existence within a universe that would appear to be meaningless, to the rational Western mind, and has lived with this meaninglessness. Hence the artistic form that seems natural to the Oriental is one that is just as formless or formal, as irrational, as life itself. That the Western artist now finds his own inherited classical form unconvincing and indeed almost intolerable is because of a profound change in his total attitude toward the world—a change that is no less true even when the artist himself has not been able to bring it to conceptual expression. The final intelligibility of the world is no longer accepted. Our existence, as we know it, is no longer transparent and understandable by reason, bound together into a tight, coherent structure. The world that we are shown in the work of the modern painters and writers is opaque and dense. Their vision is not inspired primarily by intellectual premises; it is a spontaneous revelation of the kind of which perhaps only art is capable: it shows us where we stand, whether or not we choose to understand it. If we really open ourselves to the experience of two works of art as widely separated in time as Dante's *Divine Comedy* and Faulkner's *The Sound and the Fury*, the distance that Western man has traveled in the intervening centuries is revealed to us more clearly than through any number of abstract arguments. And the road that has been traveled is irreversible.

(3) The last and most important aspect of what we have called the process of flattening in modern art is *the flattening out of values*. To understand this one can begin at the simplest level in painting, where it means merely that large and small objects are treated as of equal value. Cézanne paints apples with the same passionate concentration as he paints mountains, and each apple is as monumental as a mountain. Indeed, in some of Cézanne's still lifes, if one covers up all of the picture except a certain patch of folded tablecloth, one might very well be looking at the planes and peaks of his Mont St. Victoire. For Cézanne the painting dictates its own values: little and big, high and low, sublime and ordinary outside the paintings are of equal importance if in a given painting they play the same plastic role.

Now all this is quite contrary to the great tradition of Western art, which distinguishes sharply between the sublime and the banal and requires that the highest art treat the most sublime subjects. The mind of the West has always been hierarchical: the cosmos has been understood as a great chain of Being, from highest to lowest, which has at the same time operated as a scale of values, from lowest to highest. Painters were expected to portray the sublime scenes from the Gospel, great battles, or noble personages. The beginning of genre painting in the seventeenth century was the first step toward what we now think of as modern painting, but it was not until the present century that the reversal of Western values was really accomplished. By now, the hierarchical scheme has been abolished altogether. Following Cézanne, the Cubists took as subjects for their most monumental paintings ordinary objects like tables, bottles, glasses, guitars. Now the painter dispenses with objects altogether: the colored shape on his canvas is itself an absolute reality, perhaps more so than the imaginary scene, the great battle, which in a traditional canvas it might serve to depict. Thus we arrive at last at *l'art brut* (raw, crude, or brute art), which seeks to abolish not only the ironclad distinction between the sublime and the banal but that between the beautiful and the ugly as well. Says the painter Dubuffet, one of the more interesting cultivators of this style:

> The idea that there are beautiful objects and ugly objects, people endowed with beauty and others who cannot claim it, has surely

no other foundation than convention—old poppycock—and I declare that convention unhealthy. . . . People have seen that I intend to sweep away everything we have been taught to consider—without question—as grace and beauty; but have overlooked my work to substitute another and vaster beauty, touching all objects and beings, not excluding the most despised—and because of that, all the more exhilarating. . . . I would like people to look at my work as an enterprise for the rehabilitation of scorned values, and, in any case, make no mistake, a work of ardent celebration. . . .

I am convinced that any table can be for each of us a landscape as inexhaustible as the whole Andes range. . . .

I am struck by the high value, for a man, of a simple permanent fact, like the miserable vista on which the window of his room opens daily, that comes, with the passing of time, to have an important role in his life. I often think that the highest destination at which a painting can aim is to take on that function in someone's life.

Such ideas seem scandalous to the Western traditionalist; they undermine the time-honored canon of beauty, countenance the most disorderly elements in existence, and strike against art itself. Yet they are ideas that might be easily understood by an Oriental. For the Oriental, opposites have never been put into separate watertight compartments as with the Westerner: as it is above, so it is below, in the East; the small is equal to the great, for amid the endless expanse of countless universes, each individual universe is as but a grain of sand on the shores of the Ganges, and a grain of sand is the equal of a universe. The lotus blooms in the mud; and generally the Oriental is as willing, in his indifference, to accept the ugly dross of existence as he is its beauty, where the Westerner might very well gag at the taste. We are not concerned here with the question of whether the West is now moving toward forms of thinking and feeling that are closer to what were once those of the East. What is of concern to the philosopher is the fact that here, in art, we find so many signs of a break with the Western tradition, or at least with what had been thought to be *the* Western tradition; the philosopher must occupy himself with this break if he is to recast the meaning of this tradition.

The deflation, or flattening out, of values in Western art does not necessarily indicate an ethical nihilism. Quite the contrary; in opening our eyes to the rejected elements of existence, art may lead us to a more complete and less artificial celebration of the world. In literature, again, the crucial example is Joyce's *Ulysses*. It was not a literary critic but a psychologist, C. G. Jung, who perceived that this book was non-Western in spirit; he sees it as Oriental to such an extent that he recommends it as a much-needed bible to the white-skinned races. For *Ulysses* breaks with the whole tradition of Western sensibility and Western aesthetics in showing each small object of Bloom's day—even the objects in his pocket, like a cake of soap—as capable at certain moments of taking on a transcendental importance—or in being, at any rate, equal in value to those objects to which men usually attribute transcendental importance. Each grain of sand, Joyce seems to be saying (as the Oriental says), reflects the whole universe—and the Irish writer was not in the least a mystic; he simply takes experience as it comes, in the course of the single day he depicts in the novel. Any such break with tradition, where a serious reversal of values is involved, is of course dangerous, for the artist runs the risk of losing the safeguards that the experience of the past has erected for him. A good deal of modern art has clearly succumbed to this danger, and the result is disorder in the art and the artist; but the danger is the price that must be paid for any step forward by the human spirit.

Essays of Our Time I • *Part* 8

JULIAN HUXLEY, *brother of Aldous Huxley, followed the scientific tradition of the family and became a leading English biologist and writer on science with such books as* Man Stands Alone *and* Science and the Modern World. *Recently he served as Director-General of UNESCO, the cultural and educational arm of the United Nations.*

PERCY W. BRIDGMAN, *exponent of the "operational" approach in the sciences, retired recently as professor of physics at Harvard University. For such works as* The Logic of Modern Physics *he was awarded the Nobel Prize in 1946.*

I. I. RABI, *a lover of the theater and of travel, is a professor of physics at Columbia University. Educated at Cornell and at Columbia, he taught at the City College of New York before joining the faculty of Columbia. He has devoted his studies to the nucleus of the atom, and in 1944 was awarded the Nobel Prize in physics. Since 1957 he has served on the President's Science Advisory Committee.*

JOHN H. STEELE, *a Scot, was born in 1926 and graduated from London University with a degree in mathematics. At present, he resides in Aberdeen and works in oceanographic research. He has published scientific papers and short stories.*

JULIAN HUXLEY

What Do We Know about Love?

THE OPENING SCENE of that glorious satire, *Of Thee I Sing*, reveals a party caucus with an admirable presidential candidate but no ideas. They accordingly ask the hotel chambermaid, as representative of the People, what most people are most interested in, and are unhesitatingly answered "Love." And so love becomes the chief plank in their platform.

The first thing we know about love is what the chambermaid's answer implied—that for most people it is the most absorbing and interesting subject in existence. (In 1954 the Russians, at the Second Congress of Soviet Writers, officially rediscovered this important social fact.) Love can send young people eloping to Gretna Green, break up families, reduce strong men to love-sick slaves, even lead to murder or make kings lose their thrones; it can also energize human lives, induce the writing of a great deal of verse, including some of the finest poetry, induce states of ecstasy otherwise unattainable by the great majority of men and women, and provide the substance for most of our emotional dreaming.

This statement needs two qualifications. While it applies to contemporary Western peoples and doubtless to many others, it is not true for all cultures: sometimes war or hunting may take first place. Secondly, love as a plank in the chambermaid's personal platform and as an engrossing subject of popular interest means only one kind of love—the romantic sexual kind, the fact of "being in love."

It is almost impossible to give a formal definition of anything so complex and general as love. All I can do is to indicate some of the range of meanings comprised in this one little word. There is mother-love and self-love, father-love and grandmother-love, and children's love for their parents; there is brotherly love (which gave Philadelphia its name) and love of one's country; there is being in love, and making love; one can say that a man loves his food, though good manners dictates that he should not say it himself (when I as a small boy said I would love some chicken, my great-aunt rebuked me with the Victorian rhyme "You may love a screeching owl; you may not love a roasted fowl").

Many people love dancing; there are music-lovers, art-lovers, sport-lovers, dog-lovers, bird-lovers, sun-lovers, mountain-lovers; most of us have an intense and deep-rooted love of the surroundings in which we grew up; ministers assure us that God loves us and insist that we should love God, while Jesus adjured us to love our enemies; and there is love of money and love of power. . . .

All these are legitimate and normal usage: in its comprehensive sense, love clearly includes all of them. But equally clearly, the love in which one can be or into which one can fall is for most of us somehow pre-eminent over all other kinds.

Being in love is a special case of love as a general human capacity. It is love at its most intense, and love personally focused and directed in a very special way. Our common speech reflects this fact. We talk of falling in love, as if it was something outside us, into which we are precipitated suddenly, accidentally and against our will, like falling into a pond. We say that X is infatuated with Y, or bewitched by her, or madly in love. Classical mythology expressed the suddenness and the sense of compulsion in the symbol of Cupid the blind archer, whose arrows inflict a magic wound on our emotional being.

Love at first sight (though of course not universal or indeed usual) is a frequent occurrence, surprising as a fact for scientific consideration as well as to those who experience it. But even when we are in love with someone we have known for months or years, the actual falling in love has been often, perhaps usually, not a gradual process but a sudden moment. Being in love, whether we fall suddenly or grow gradually into it, always has an element of compulsion, a sense of being possessed by some extraneous and magical power. Lovers are obsessed by an image of the loved one, to whom they ascribe every virtue and merit. Outside observers of the phenomenon speak of the lover's madness; and love is proverbially blind.

The lover experiences a sense of heightened vitality and finds a new significance in life. Mere contemplation of the beloved becomes a wellspring of the highest enjoyment. The lover seeks the presence of the beloved. Merely to see her (or him) from a distance is to feast the soul as well as the eyes; and to touch her is an inspiring bliss. But when, through two hands and two pairs of eyes, the two souls can interpenetrate, an even more magical state is achieved, as described in Donne's poem The Ecstasy.

> . . . Our hands were firmly cémented
> By a fast balm which thence did spring;
> Our eye-beams twisted, and did thread
> Our eyes upon one double string. . . .

As 'twixt two equal armies Fate
  Suspends uncertain victory,
Our souls—which to advance their state
  Were gone out—hung 'twixt her and me.

And whilst our souls negotiate there,
  We like sepulchral statues lay;
All day the same our postures were,
  And we said nothing, all the day.

Modern psychology has rightly abandoned the term *soul*, because of the philosophical and theological implications that have become attached to it; but we can translate it as meaning the unitary inner core of our conscious selves and this sense of the going out of our essential being and of its interpentrating or uniting with another being is one of the hall-marks of being in love.

This is embodied in one of the loveliest epigrams of the Greek Anthology:

Τὴν ψυχὴν 'Αγάθωνα φιλῶν ἐπὶ χείλεσω ἔσχον·
ἦλθε γὰρ ἡ τλήμων ὡς διαβησομένη.

As I kissed Agathon, I had my soul in my lips; for the rash creature came thither as if to pass across.

For true lovers, the act of physical union is actuated not merely or indeed mainly by the desire for pleasure but for the transcendent sense of total union which it can bring. William Blake rightly rebukes the puritans who

  Call a shame and sin
Love's temple that God dwelleth in . . .
And render that a lawless thing
On which the soul expands its wing.

And Robert Bridges reminds us how the lower is necessarily incorporated in the higher:—

We see Spiritual, Mental and Animal
To be gradations merged together in growth, . . .
. . . And that the animal pleasure
Runneth throughout all graces heartening all energies.

Even children may fall in sudden love, long before puberty and its hormones have actuated the full sexual urge. The classical example is Dante, who fell in love with Beatrice when she was just eight and he nearly nine. In his *Vita Nuova*—The New Life—he has left an immortal description of the event which coloured all his later existence. "At that instant, the spirit of life which dwells in the heart's most secret chamber began to tremble so violently that all the pulses of my body shook; and in trembling it said these words: 'Here is a god stronger than I, who is come to rule over me.'"

He only saw her a few more times, and she died at the age of twenty-five. But his love dominated the rest of his life, and inspired his great work. The distinction between love and sex is very obvious here. Dante reserved his fullest and highest love for a woman whose hand he had never even touched, but had four children by the excellent wife he later married. However, before dealing further with this question, I want to say something about the evolution and development of love— its evolution in nature apart from man, and its development in individual human beings.

People sometimes ask what purpose love serves in nature. But a biologist cannot answer a question framed in terms of purpose, for purpose implies deliberate design for a conscious end, and there is no evidence of that in the natural world. To be biologically answerable, the question should run, "What functions does love perform in living organisms?" Even so, the biologist cannot give a nice simple or single answer, for among animals there are various different kinds of love, expressed in various different ways, and manifested in different degrees of clarity and intensity. There has been an evolution of love, as of every other property of life, and we must supplement our question by asking how the different kinds of love have evolved.

In many young mammals, like kittens, some adult mammals, like otters, and various adult birds, like penguins and rooks and swifts, we find something closely akin to our love of play or sport—the enjoyment of bodily performance for its own sake, irrespective of its practical utility. Among birds there is the beginning of a love of beauty, manifested in the collection of bright objects by jackdaws and magpies, and in bowerbirds by a preference for certain colours and by their deliberate painting of their bowers. The roots of love of country are shown in the attachment of many kinds of birds and mammals to their home territory, and of love of nature in such rituals as the high aerial dawn-chorus of swallows and martins.

Finally, animals show several different types of love in the restricted sense—love focused on other individuals. There is parental love, of parent for offspring; there is offspring love, of offspring for parent; there is sexual love, between actual or potential mates; and there is social love, for other individuals of the same species. The roots of social love are found in gregarious animals, and are manifested in the distress caused by solitude and the impulse to seek the company of their fellows.

Parental love is in most species only maternal. In many mammals and in all polygamous birds, the mother alone is concerned about the young—think of bears or sheep or the domestic hen. But in some fish and toads and a few birds, like emus and phalaropes, it is the male alone that looks after eggs and young; and of course in all our familiar songbirds the cock bird helps to feed the young once they have been hatched by the hen, while in birds like grebes and gannets, auks and petrels and penguins, both cock and hen share equally in incubation too. Comparatively few insects show parental love (the female earwig is one), and in those where it is most developed, namely bees and ants, it is not strictly speaking parental love but maiden-aunt love (or nurse love if you like), for it is only the neuter females, the so-called workers, that have the instinct to look after the eggs and grubs.

This brings up an important point. In animals, parental (and nurse) love is purely instinctive; not only the urge to care for the young, but also the detailed ways in which it manifests itself, depend on inborn nervous mechanisms, and do not have to be learned. Furthermore, like all instincts, parental love, though doubtless associated with strong emotions, is blind and automatic. It is a psychological mechanism which works admirably in normal conditions, but is apt to go astray in abnormal ones. Thus a worker wasp which was kept from access to food for the young was seen to satisfy its nurse-instinct by biting off the hind end of a grub and offering it to the front end!

The same blind imprisonment of instinctive behaviour within a limited situation is seen even in birds and mammals. Thus song-birds only pay attention to their young so long as they are in the nest. When a cuckoo has ejected its foster-brothers and -sisters, the parents take no notice of their cries of distress, even if they are hanging on a twig just outside the nest. And even in normal circumstances it is not the sight of the young bird as an individual that impels the parents to feed it, but merely the colour and shape of its gaping mouth: they will feed an artificial gape of painted wood (if properly made) just as readily as their own nestlings. And a cow distressed by the removal of her calf can be comforted by its skin.

The same sort of thing holds for the sexual instinct. Certain orchids get pollinated by looking and perhaps smelling like female flies: the male flies try to mate with them, and in so doing transfers the fertilizing pollen from flower to flower. Similarly many birds will attempt to mate with a stuffed dead female as readily as with a real live one—provided that it is set up in a certain pose; and the sperm for artificial insemination in cattle and horses can be obtained because the mating urge of bulls and stallions is aroused by suitable dummies as well as by live cows or mares.

But the mental life of birds, for instance, is a curious mixture, in which some types of emotional behaviour are carried out blindly, crudely, and wholly instinctively, while others depend on detailed learning. A cock robin, for instance (not the fat American robin, which is really a thrush, but our little European robin redbreast), will be automatically and irrationally stimulated to his threat-display by the sight of a red breast, whether on a live rival, a stuffed bird, or a headless and tailless dummy; but he learns the difference between his mate and all other hen robins and can recognize her individually afar off.

The robin's red breast and the gape of nestling birds are examples of what are called *releasers*—they are visual sign-stimuli which release the action of innate impulses and chains of activity, in the one case of hostility or aggression, in the other of service or affection—the beginnings of hate and of love.

In polygamous-promiscuous species like ruff and sage-grouse and blackcock, the sexes never meet except on a communal display-ground, and the males' sexual "love" is merely the urge to physical mating, expressed in violent antics serving to intimidate rivals or stimulate mates by showing off the exaggerated masculine display-plumage.

In most birds, however, there is an emotional bond between mates, and the pair stays together, either for the brood, or for the season, or, in a number of species, for life. Life-mates like to be close together even in the winter, as you may see with jackdaws. This emotional bond is clearly one of the forerunners of human married love.

In some water-birds, such as grebes, where male and female share equally the duties of incubating the eggs and feeding the young, there are elaborate ceremonies of mutual display, participated in by both mates together, and obviously highly stimulating to the emotions. What is more, some displays are not confined to the period of courtship or physical mating, but continue right through the breeding season, until the young are full-grown. Here I would say the rituals of animal love find their fullest expression.

Though from the standpoint of the species this emotional bond has been evolved for the utilitarian function of keeping the mated pair together while their joint efforts are needed for the successful rearing of their young, from that of the individual birds the ceremonies are clearly very satisfying and have emotional value in themselves.

Emotional life in animals is essentially a patchwork. Particular urges or emotions arise in particular circumstances, and usually stay in separate channels. Fear may dictate behaviour for a period, then suddenly hunger steps in, then perhaps sexual desire. Animals lack man's capacity to bring together many different urges and emotions, memories and hopes, into a single continuity of conscious life. The main exception to this, interestingly enough, concerns love. Both in the parent-offspring relation and in that between the two sexes, attraction and hostility are often combined. The primary reaction of a nestling or a brooding heron to the appearance of an adult at the nest is fear and hostility: before the arriving bird is accepted as parent or as mate, it must be recognized as such; and recognition is effected by a special "appeasing" display. This in turn forms the basis for the elaborate ceremony of nest-relief, which finally serves as an emotional bond between the mated pair.

In many birds' species, during the "courtship" period, the sight of a bird of the opposite sex often acts as a sign-stimulus releasing both hostility (as an alien intruding individual) and attraction (as a potential mate). Thus the unmated male house-sparrow in possession of a nest-site endeavours to attract passing females, but if one tries to enter the nest he will attack her, and even after they have accepted each other as mates, it may be two or three days before she is allowed into her future home.

The courtship-displays of many species turn out to be ritualizations of this ambivalent emotion compounded of attraction and either hostility or fear (and show many parallels with human courtship, especially in young people). The male bird's aggressivity may be transformed into a stimulating display of masculinity and desire, and female timidity often expresses itself by reverting to infantile dependence, with adoption of the nestling's food-begging attitude.

Thus love, in the sense of positive attraction between individuals, has arisen during biological evolution in the form of a patchwork of distinct urges or drives, each serving a distinct biological function. The mechanism of each separate kind of love is largely built in to the species by heredity. For the most part, each drive is automatically activated by a sign-stimulus functioning as a releaser, a distinctive pattern of sight or sound (like the gape of the nestling for stimulating the parental feeding drive of its parents, or the "song" of male grasshoppers for the sexual approach of the female); and is expressed in a genetically predetermined set of actions (like the displays of amorous male birds). Learning by experience plays only a secondary role, or sometimes no role at all.

Further, there is little synthesis of the separate drives into a coherent or continuous mental life. However, desire is often frustrated, and attraction often compounded with hostility or fear, and the resultant conflict is reconciled in the performance of some ritualized ceremony of display. This may then be further specialized during subsequent evolution to provide more effective stimulation of the female, or be converted

into a mutual ceremony serving as a bond to keep the mated pair together; and such ceremonies, especially the mutual ones, may come to
have emotional value in themselves.

"'Tis love, 'tis love that makes the world go round," sang the
anonymous ballad-monger. And certainly love, in its dawning manifestations among animals, secures the perpetuation of the species and the
care of offspring, lays the foundations of more or less permanent marriage unions, and may even emerge as a value in itself.

When we come to our own species, we find a certain general
parallel between the process of individual development of love in man
and that of its evolution in animals, but also many important differences. There is more reliance on learning by experience, less on inborn
genetic mechanisms. However, two or three inborn sign-stimuli do seem
to exist. One is the smile. Even a crudely grimacing model of a smiling
face will elicit from an infant a smile (and the positive mood which
goes with smiling and is one of the bases of enjoying and loving). And
women's breasts (though, as Dr. Johnson pointed out, not feeding-
bottles) will act as a powerful sign-stimulus to male sexual love.

Non-sexual loves of many kinds appear and develop in the growing child. At the outset are the simple basic desires for food and warmth
and protection, soon transmuted into love of enjoyment and content-
ment, general satisfaction and fulfilment. Then the personal focusing
of love on to the individuals that provide what is desired—first mother
or nurse, then father, brothers and sisters, and other children. Then the
widening of the circle of love and of personal attachment (Walt Whit-
man speaks of the "fluid and attaching character" that some people
seem to exude); and finally, love for the beautiful or the strange, the
thrilling or the significant.

These more complex loves may sometimes attain the intensity of
passions. The full force of a child's emotions may be bound up with
some shell or curious stone that he has found: or the experience of
beauty may change his whole emotional attitude to life. Let Wordsworth speak:

My heart leaps up when I behold
    A rainbow in the sky:
So was it when my life began;
So is it now I am a man;
So be it when I shall grow old,
    Or let me die!
The Child is father of the Man;
And I could wish my days to be
Bound each to each by natural piety.

Or again, in his famous Ode:

> There was a time when meadow, grove and stream,
> The earth, and every common sight,
>   To me did seem
>   Apparell'd in celestial light,
> The glory and the freshness of a dream.

"The hour of splendour in the grass, of glory in the flower" may pass and fade, but the experience of love for natural beauty, of enhanced vitality and the upleaping heart, of self-transcendence in loving union with something outside oneself, may change a growing human being permanently, and can enter later into his love for God, for someone of the other sex, for ideals. As one of Truman Capote's characters says, apropos of a jay's lovely blue egg that she had kept from childhood, "love is a chain of love. . . . Because you can love one thing, you can love another."

The growing child comes to love many different kinds of things in many different ways—sometimes with the self-centered desire for possession; sometimes with the self-transcending desire for unity with the object of desire, or the outgoing sense of communion in the act of experience, as with Richard Jefferies' or Thomas Traherne's mystical experiences of the beauty and wonder of nature; sometimes with the enriching of enjoyment in the full and free exercise of his faculties, physical or psychological.

And then, at puberty, there is the intrusion of the sexual impulse. The sex impulse appears as an alien power, strong, new and often frightening. The experience is all the more upsetting because the new power, though alien to our past life or present make-up, is yet within us, a part of ourselves. The central problem of adolescence is, in general, how to incorporate this intruding force into the developing personality; and in particular, how to integrate sex and love. This is especially acute because of the disharmony between man's biological nature and his social arrangements, the fact that there is a gap of years between the time when the sexual impulse emerges (and emerges at maximum strength, at least in boys, as Dr. Kinsey has shown) and the time when marriage is possible.

Adolescence is also the time when love, as distinct from sexual desire, alters its character. At puberty romantic idealism raises its head as well as sex: and another problem of adolescence is how to integrate this idealism with the hard facts of existence, and romance with the practical business of living.

Man, however, differs from all other animals in having a brain which can and largely does bring all the various elements of experience into contact, instead of keeping them in a series of wholly or largely separate compartments or channels. This not only provides the basis for conceptual thought, and so for all man's ideas and philosophic systems, ideals and works of art and creative imagination, but also for his battery of complex sentiments unknown in animals, such as reverence and religious awe, moral feelings (including hate and contempt arising from moral abhorrence), and love in its developed form.

It also, however, provides the basis for emotional or psychological conflict on a scale unknown in animals. One of the unique characters of man is his constant subjection to mental conflict, with the resultant necessity for making moral decisions. Man's morality, indeed, is a necessary consequence of his inner conflicts.

Nowhere is this better illustrated than in love. Strong sexual desire, as well as the reverent worship of beauty, self-fulfilment, and ideal aspiration, plays a part in human love. But crude sexual desire in itself is merely lust and is universally regarded as immoral, and to many people the sexual act appears as something dirty or disgusting.

However, love at its truest and fullest and most intense can include in its single embrace an enormous range of emotions and sentiments, and fuse them all, even those of baser metal, in its crucible. It can combine humility with pride, passion with peace, self-assertion with self-surrender; it can reconcile violence of feeling with tenderness, can swallow up disgust in beauty and imperfection in fulfilment, and sublimate sexual desire into joy and fuller life.

It can, but it does not always do so. Sometimes the inhibitions of morality or romantic idealism are too strong, and the fusion is imperfect, the reconciliation remains incomplete. This is especially so in puritan cultures and religions imbued with a sense of sin. St. Paul's attitude to sexual love is expressed in his dictum that it is better to marry than to burn: tormented souls like St. Augustine and Tolstoy came to regard sexual love not as fulfilment but as sin, and Gandhi's autobiography tells us how his early indulgences drove him later to prescribe—for others!—self-control and abstinence instead of the ideal of pure enjoyment, of joy disciplined and transformed by tenderness, reverence, and beauty.

Sometimes, indeed, love involves contradictory and unreconciled emotions. In one of his most famous poems, Catullus wrote

Odi et amo: quare id faciam, fortasse requiris.
Nescio, sed fieri sentio et excrucior.

"I hate and love: how can that be, perhaps you ask? I know not, but so I feel, and am in torment." The hero of Somerset Maugham's *Of Human Bondage* is intellectually aware of the imperfections and indeed the unattractiveness of the girl he is in love with, but remains emotionally enslaved by her.

In love, indeed, the conflict between reason and emotion is often at highest pitch. However, though falling in love is irrational, or at least non-rational, yet love can be (though it is not always) later influenced by reason and guided by experience. Emotion in general is non-rational; it tends to all-or-nothing manifestations and is naturally resistant to the critical and balanced spirit of reason. And the emotions involved in love are so violent that this uncritical or anticritical tendency readily overrides reason. That is why love is called blind, why it may become a kind of madness or sickness. But reason can play a part later. With time, as the emotional violence of love diminishes and rational experience accumulates, a point may suddenly be reached at which reason gains the upper hand, the deluded lover's eyes are opened, he realizes that he has been blind, and he falls out of love as he once fell in. Such experiences are useful though harsh reminders of the sad fact that emotional certitude alone is never a guarantee of rightness or truth, in religious or moral belief any more than in love: sudden religious conversion resembles falling in love in many ways, including its non-rationality.

Luckily for the human race, love often chooses aright. And then reason and emotional experience may give it eyes to see and may transform a transient madness into the highest and most enduring sanity. This rationally guided transformation and development of love has been immortally described by Wordsworth in his poem, *Perfect Woman*. It is too long for me to quote in its entirety, but you will recall how it begins with a magical, altogether non-rational moment—

> *She was a Phantom of delight*
> *When first she gleam'd upon my sight;*

how experience altered the vision—

> *I saw her upon nearer view,*
> *A Spirit, yet a Woman too!*

and how it finally transformed sudden magic into permanent serenity—

> *And now I see with eye serene*
> *The very pulse of the machine . . .*
> *A perfect Woman, nobly planned,*

234

To warn, to comfort, and command;
And yet a Spirit still, and bright
With something of angelic light.

Often, however, love does not choose right the first time. I should rather say, first love often does not choose permanently right. Many teen-age "pashes" and "crushes," however violent at the time, and many cases of adolescent calf-love, though often valuable and indeed "right" in the sense of providing necessary experience to the callow personality, are soon outgrown.

Even when it comes to marriage, many first choices are wrong, and later ones may be much more right. The relation between love and marriage urgently needs reconsideration. For one thing, in our Western societies, we have become too credulous about romantic love, just as earlier ages were too credulous about religious faith. Both can often be blind, and then both can mislead us. For another, we have become obsessed with the rigid moralists' stern insistence on the inviolability and indissolubility of marriage—a religious doctrine imposed on a social bond.

The emotional certitude of being in love with someone does not guarantee either its rightness, or its uniqueness, or its permanence, any more than it ensures that the love shall be reciprocated. And the undoubted general desirability, both social and personal, of long-enduring monogamous marriage does not preclude the occasional desirability of divorce and change of marriage-partner, nor justify the branding of any extra-marital love as a grave social immorality or personal sin.

Our reconsideration should be related to the idea of greater fulfilment. Of course conflicts will inevitably arise between greater fulfilment for oneself, for one's partner, one's children, and one's community; but they will then be better illuminated and more readily soluble than in the light of romantic illusion, religious dogma, or static and absolute morality.

It must be remembered that love and its manifestations differ in different societies and cultures. We find a differentiation and development of love as part of the general cultural evolution of man. Margaret Mead and other anthropologists have shown to what a surprising extent cultures may differ in their general attitude to love, both sexual and parental, and in their expression of it. Masculinity may be valued either higher or lower than femininity, ardour and passion higher or lower than coolness and acceptance; parental love may be either indulgent or strict to children, or its expression, warm and full in early years, may be suddenly withdrawn from the child at a certain age; the attitude of society both to pre-marital love-making and post-marital love-affairs may differ enormously.

A striking example of the evolution of love is the rise of the idea of romantic love in medieval Europe. This found an exaggerated expression in the ballads of the troubadours and the rituals of chivalry, but has left a permanent mark on our Western civilization.

Love presents, in intensive form, man's central and perennial problem—how to reconcile the claims of the individual and of society, personal desires with social aims. The problem is perhaps most acute in adolescence, for this involves a disharmony of timing: our sexual desires arise, and in males arise in fullest force, several years before marriage is desirable or possible. Different cultures have met this problem in very different ways. Thus in eighteenth-century England and nineteenth-century France it was the acknowledged thing for upper-class young men to take a mistress, while this was frowned on in Geneva and New England. In twentieth-century America, dating and petting have superseded "bundling" as the recognized formula.

Many primitive societies go further, and institutionalize adolescent love. Thus among the Masai of East Africa the boys after initiation become Moran or Warriors and live in communities with the initiated girls, sharing what seems to be a very agreeable love-life. Only after some years do they marry, and from then on, extra-marital love is severely frowned on. Their neighbours, the Kikuyu, had a somewhat similar system, in which, however, full sexual intercourse was not permitted. The same sort of arrangement prevails among the Bontocs of the Philippines, as recorded by Stewart Kilton in his *Dream Giants and Pygmies*. Here, as among country-folk in England until quite recently, adolescent love-making serves also as a try-out of fertility. A girl can only marry if she conceives; and sterile girls become "a sort of educational institution" for young boys.

In modern civilization the problem is very real and very serious. On the one hand, clearly both undisciplined indulgence and complete promiscuity in love are individually damaging, or anti-social, or both; but on the other hand, complete repression of this most powerful of impulses is equally damaging, and so is the self-reproach that the indulgence or even the mere manifestation of the impulse arouses in sensitive adolescents who have had an exaggerated sense of sin imposed on them. From another angle, it is tragic to think of millions of human beings denied the full beauty and exaltation of love precisely while their impulses are strongest and their sensibilities at their highest pitch.

No civilization has yet adequately harmonized the disharmony or provided satisfactory means of resolving the conflict. Indeed there can be no solution in the sense that there is a single definite solution to a mechanical puzzle or a mathematical problem. The problem of love, as of any other aspect of life, must be solved *ambulando,* or rather *vivendo,* in living; and the correctness of the solution is only to be measured by the fulfilment achieved, the degree to which desirable possibilities are realized and conflicting elements and interests harmonized. What is more, we can rarely expect to arrive at a satisfactory solution at the first shot: fulfilment is a process, and we have to learn it, to achieve it step by step, often making mistakes, often precipitated into new and unforeseen problems or conflicts by the solution of previous ones.

Love between the sexes can provide some of the highest fulfilments of life. It also provides an important means for the development of personality: through it we learn many necessary things about ourselves, about others, about society, and about human ideals. We must, I think, aim at a moral and religious climate of society in which the adolescent experiments of love, instead of being branded as wicked or relegated to furtive and illicit gropings, or repressed until they collapse in neurosis or explode in lust, or merely tolerated as an unpleasing necessity, are socially sanctioned and religiously sanctified, in the same sort of way as marriage is now. Adolescent affairs of the heart could be regarded as reverent experiments in love, or as trial marriages, desirable preparations for the more enduring adventure of adult marriage. Young people would assuredly continue to make mistakes, to be selfish or lustful or otherwise immoral; but matters would I am sure be better than they are now, and could not well be much worse.

In considering love we must not leave out hate, for in one sense love and hate are the positive and negative aspects of the same thing, the primary emotional reaction to another individual. This can either be one of attraction, desire, or tenderness, or one of repulsion, fear, or hostility. In this light it is easy to understand how love, especially when ardent and blind, can so readily turn into equally uncritical hate.

From the evolutionary angle, however, love and hate must be thought of as distinct. They have independent origins and are canalized and expressed in different ways. As we have seen, love in animals may have a number of separate and specific manifestations—parental, sexual, and social. The same holds for hate; it may manifest itself in fear, in avoidance, or in aggression. We have also seen how love and hate may be simultaneously aroused, as in the combination of desire and hostility in the sexual life of birds, and may then be compounded and the conflict reconciled in a new expression, in the form of a ritual display.

For the most part, however, psychological conflict is avoided in animals by means of an automatic nervous mechanism similar to that which prevents conflicting muscles from coming into action simultaneously. When, for instance, a nervous message is sent to the flexor muscles to contract and bend our arm, it is accompanied by a second message inhibiting and relaxing the extensor muscles which would straighten it. The same sort of thing often happens with more complicated reflex activities, and, as already mentioned, with animal instincts: when the fear instinct is switched into action, the hunger or the sex instinct is switched out.

It may also operate in man's emotional conflicts: one of two conflicting patterns of feeling and thought may be either voluntarily and temporarily suppressed into the sub-conscious, or wholly and permanently repressed into the unconscious. There, however, as Freud discovered, it can still continue its nagging and produce a sense of guilt. Total and unremembered repression naturally occurs most often in infancy and early life, before experience and reason have had time to begin coping with the paralysing conflict between contradictory emotions and impulses.

The primal conflict which besets the human infant is between love and hate. He (or she) inevitably loves his mother (or mother-surrogate) as the fountainhead of his satisfactions, his security, comfort, and peace. But at times he is also angry with her, as the power which arbitrarily, it seems to him, denies him satisfaction and thwarts his impulses: and his anger calls into play what the psychologists call aggression—his battery of magic hate-phantasies and death-wishes and destructive rage-impulses.

But his hate soon comes into paralysing conflict with his love, and must be repressed. It also gives him a sense of guilt or wrongness, even from its lair in the unconscious; and this charge of primal guilt continues to exist and is built into his developing personality. When an action or impulse arouses this sense of guilt, it is automatically felt as wrong. Thus the infantile conflict between love and hate generates what we may call the individual's proto-ethical mechanism, the rudiment around which his conscience and his truly ethical sense of right and wrong are later built, rather as his embryonic notochord provided the basis for the future development of his backbone.

Of course, reason and experience, imagination and ideals also make their contributions. But the basis of conscience and ethics remains irrational and largely unconscious, as shown by the terrifying sense of sin and unworthiness which besets those unfortunates on whom a too-heavy burden of personal guilt has been imposed.

Consciences, in fact, are not genetically predetermined and do not grow automatically like backbones, but need the infantile conflict between love and hate for their origination. This is demonstrated by recent studies like those of John Bowlby and Spitz, on children who have been brought up in impersonal institutions or otherwise deprived of the care of a mother or personal mother-substitute, during a critical period between one and three years old. Many of them never develop a conscience, and grow up as amoral beings, creatures without ethics.

The mother is thus the central figure in the evolution of love. For one thing, maternal love always involves tenderness and devoted care, which sexual love does not. Only when the different kinds or components of love become blended, as they do most thoroughly in man, though to some extent in some birds and mammals, does sexual love come to involve tenderness as well as desire. As Robert Bridges writes in his *Testament of Beauty,* "In man this blind motherly attachment is the spring of his purest affection, and of all compassion." And again, "Through motherhood it [self-hood] came in animals to altruistic feeling, and thence-after in man rose to spiritual affection."

But the mother also provides the focus for the human infant's personal emotions, both of love and hate, and in so doing unwittingly lays the foundations of conscience, and starts the child on its course towards high morality and spiritual ideals.

I have no space to discuss many other aspects of love—the problem of homosexual love, for instance; or the interesting differences found by Dr. Kinsey between the development of sexual love in men and in women; or the relations between married love and conjugal fidelity.

But I would like to close with an affirmation of the unique importance of love in human life—an affirmation which seems to me essential in a tormented age like ours, where violence and disillusion have joined forces with undigested technological advance to produce an atmosphere of cynicism and crude materialism.

Mother-love is indispensable not only for the healthy and happy physical growth of young human beings, but for their healthy and happy moral and spiritual growth as well. Personal love between the sexes is not only indispensable for the physical continuance of the race, but for the full development of the human personality. It is part of education: through love, the self learns to grow. Love of beauty and of all lovely and wonderful things is equally indispensable for our mental growth and the realization of our possibilities. It brings reverence and a sense of transcendence into sexual and personal love, and indeed into all of life. In general, love is a positive emotion, an enlargement of life leading on towards greater fulfilment and capable of counteracting human hate and destructive impulses.

Let the final word be that of a poet who was also a man of science —Robert Bridges.

He [Aristotle] hath made Desire to be the prime mover of all.
I see the emotion of saints, lovers and poets all
To be the kindling of some personality
By an eternizing passion; and that God's worshipper
Looking on any beauty falleth straightway in love;
And that love is a fire in whose devouring flames
All earthly ills are consumed.

PERCY W. BRIDGMAN

Science and Common Sense

I SHALL HAVE TO BEGIN by recalling some matters that have been said so many times that I can expect only to bore you, but this is a risk that I can see no way to avoid if I am to make my main point. You all know that, since the turn of the century, discoveries have been made in physics, culminating in the unlocking of nuclear energy in the atomic bomb, which have entirely revolutionized our outlook, not only our outlook with regard to the construction of the world around us, but our philosophical ideas as well with regard to our relationship to the world. It is the latter to which I would like to direct your attention.

The new discoveries that have forced the revolution were in the realms of relativity and quantum phenomena. We shall see later that the quantum phenomena were more revolutionary in their implications than the relativity phenomena, but historically it is probable that the relativity phenomena played the more important role at first. The new relativity phenomena were highly paradoxical and included such effects as meter sticks whose length changed when they were set in motion, clocks that ran slow when moving, and weights that became heavier when moving. In fact, these effects were so paradoxical and contrary to common sense that some physicists and most men in the street refused to accept them and even sought to throw them out of court by ridicule.

But the facts refused to be thrown out of court, and the paradoxes were resolved by Einstein's theory of restricted relativity. This theory embraced, in the first place, the mathematical machinery by which all the experimental facts were correlated into a single mathematical structure. But no less notable as an intellectual achievement and equally essential to the removal of paradox was Einstein's handling of the physical concepts that entered the mathematical edifice. It is this latter that is our concern.

There are two aspects of Einstein's handling of the physical concepts. There is, in the first place, a realization that the paradoxes involved primarily questions of meaning and that the common-sense meanings of such terms as *length* and *time* were not sharp enough to serve in the situations presented by the new facts. In the second place, there was the method by which the necessary increased sharpness was imparted to the meanings. This method was to specify the operations that were involved in concrete instances in applying the term whose meaning was in question. For example, what do we mean when we say that two events are simultaneous? Einstein insisted that we do not know what we mean unless we can give some concrete procedure by which we may determine whether or not any two specific events are simultaneous. Analysis of the concrete procedures that we might use brings out the fact, not noticed before, that what we do to determine whether or not two events are simultaneous depends to a certain extent on the events themselves and is different and more complicated if the two events take place at different places than if they take place here. Furthermore, this analysis disclosed that what an observer does to determine whether two distant events are simultaneous is different from what another observer does who is in motion with respect to him. Simultaneity of two distant events is, therefore, not an absolute property of the events, the same for all observers, but is relative to the observers.

It is the same with length. What do we mean when we ask what the length of a moving object is? Applying the operational criterion of meaning, the meaning is to be sought in what we do when we measure the length of the moving object. When we analyze what we might do, we discover that there are several different possible procedures, equally acceptable to common sense. Thus, if we are asked to measure the length of a moving street-car, we might take an instantaneous photograph of it and measure the length of the photograph, or we might board the car, meter stick in hand, and proceed to measure it as we would any ordinary stationary object. If we get the same answer by the two procedures, we shall doubtless be satisfied and think that our catechizer was unnecessarily fussy in insisting that we tell exactly what we do to measure the length.

But here is where the new experimental facts come in that were not suspected before relativity theory. For it turns out that when we make our measurements with extreme precision, or when the street-car is moving with very great velocity, the results of the two methods are not the same, so that the precise method must be specified if we want to talk exactly about the length of the moving car. In other words, it is ambiguous to talk about the "length" of a moving object until we have specified exactly how the length is to be measured; and when we have specified the exact procedure, the results we get are generally different, depending on what the exact procedure is. In particular, by one of the two procedures just indicated, the length of the moving car would be the same as when it is stationary; and, by the other, it would be less. We see at once that we cannot treat this situation by the methods of common sense and say that it is absurd that the length should change when the car moves, because it *must* change according to at least one of our possible definitions. Realization of this at once removes the atmosphere of paradox from the statement that the length changes when the object is set in motion.

The precise way that we define length when the body moves is a matter of choice, and we will make our choice in the way most convenient for us in the light of all the experimental facts. It would take us much too deeply into relativity theory to attempt to see why the method that Einstein chose for defining the length of a moving object is, all things considered, the most convenient for the physicist. Suffice it to say that the method chosen was not the method that leaves the length unchanged by the motion, although such a method is possible and, for certain restricted purposes, might be considered more convenient.

Relativity theory has thus shown the importance of precision of meanings. It has disclosed that some of the apparently simple terms of common sense are actually complex when we attempt to apply them in situations beyond the bounds of ordinary experience. In these new situations, we are forced to make a choice between procedures that are equivalent in the ordinary range. The account we give of the new situation depends on the procedure that we choose—that is, on the meaning we give our terms. In discovering that in fact we do need to make distinctions of which we have never thought and which to a naive first impression appear a matter of indifference, we are discovering that in fact the world is not constructed according to the preconceptions of common sense.

The sort of phenomena with which quantum theory is concerned teach the same lesson as relativity theory, namely, that the world is not constructed according to the principles of common sense. However, the way in which common sense fails is somewhat different in the case of quantum phenomena. The unfamiliar world of relativity theory was the world of high velocities; the new world of quantum theory is the world of the very small.

Quantum theory began modestly enough with the discovery that some of the most familiar facts of daily life cannot be understood on the basis of the common-sense views of matter prevalent at the end of the last century. For example, it was impossible to understand why we cannot see a kettle full of boiling water in the dark. Common sense, when translated into mathematics, said that we should see it, but every burned child knows that we cannot. The paradox has now been removed from this and other related effects, so that we now understand, in a way that would have been incredible 25 years ago, most of the phenomena displayed by ordinary matter. This understanding has been provided by quantum theory. The theory is highly mathematical and it is well-nigh impossible to give an adequate outline of it in nontechnical language, but the one simple crude idea back of it all is that when we deal with very small things, such as atoms or electrons, the ordinary common-sense conception of *things* is no longer valid. The renunciation of common sense thus demanded by quantum theory is more drastic than that demanded by relativity theory. For now we get ourselves into *logical inconsistencies* if we try to think of things in the microscopic domain in the same way that we think of the objects of ordinary experience.

Suppose, for example, that I have a box with a partition in the middle and one electron on each side of the partition. I remove the partition for a moment, so that the electrons have an opportunity to exchange positions. I now find when I replace the partition that I again have one electron on each side of the partition. It now involves me in logical contradiction to ask whether the electron that is on the right side of the partition is the same electron that in the beginning was on the right side, or vice versa. Neither can I ask exactly how fast is the right-hand electron moving. Knowing that the electron is on the right of the partition makes it logically contradictory to know how fast it is moving. These are indeed revolutionary restrictions. Not to be able to ask which electron is which means that the electron does not have identity, and not being able to ask how fast it is moving means that the common-sense categories of space and time do not completely apply to it.

Consider another example. It is possible to make a so-called electron gun with which a stream of electrons may be fired at a target. If we start with a comparatively crude gun firing a coarse stream of electrons, we find the stream of electrons behaves much like a stream of water from a hose, so that we cannot hit with it a single sharp point of the target, but there is more or less scattering. Now common sense might lead us to expect that our marksmanship would become better as we refined the apparatus by making it more and more delicate and capable of dealing with a finer and finer stream of electrons. Experiment shows, however, that our common-sense expectations are entirely wrong, and that matters get worse instead of better as we refine the apparatus. In the end, when we have, at great pains, constructed a gun capable of firing single electrons, we find that we have almost completely lost control of the situation. No two shots ever come alike despite the best we can do, and we might as well spin a roulette wheel to find what part of the target any electron will hit.

The electron gun illustrates the general principle that, in the microscopic domain, events cannot be made to repeat. The situation thus disclosed is bad enough from the practical point of view, but I believe that it is even more upsetting from the conceptual point of view. For the one intellectual lesson that science has perhaps most insistently underlined is that our mental machinery is capable of making mistakes and that we continually have to verify and check what we are doing. The fundamental method of verification is repetition; the repeatable experiment has come to occupy such a position that the very definition of truth is often framed in terms of verification by repetition. It looks as though it does not mean anything in the quantum domain to ask for the truth about any specific event, yet how can I get along without the concept of truth? You may try to extricate yourself from the dilemma by saying that, although *I* may not verify the occurrence of some event by repeating the experiment, I *can* verify it by getting confirmation from some other observer who has also witnessed it. But this, unfortunately, is not a way out, because here we encounter another of those baffling properties of the microscopic world, namely, that an elementary event may be observed by only one observer. Confirmation by public report thus becomes impossible. To many, it might seem that thereby science is made impossible, science sometimes being defined in terms of publicity. However, if you are willing to grant that quantum theory is part of science, you see that matters are at least not quite as bad as this. Whatever the method by which eventually we get intellectual order into this situation, I think you can see that the observer must play a quite different role in the quantum domain than in the world of everyday life.

All these considerations mean that the conventional forms of thought are no longer applicable in the realm of the very small. I think you will agree that my foregoing statement is justified, namely, that the failure of common sense disclosed by quantum theory is more drastic than that disclosed by relativity theory. For, when in relativity theory we go to very high velocities, we merely encounter properties of matter that are strange to common experience, whereas when we go far enough in the direction of the very small, quantum theory says that our forms of thought fail, so that it is questionable whether we can properly think at all. One can imagine the consternation of our old philosophical friend Immanuel Kant who declared that space and time are *necessary* forms of thought.

What is the answer to the dilemma with which quantum theory confronts us, and where do the roots of the difficulty lie? Are we faced with the necessity of devising new ways of thinking? It does seem to me that eventually we shall have to find better ways of thinking, but I suspect that any improved method of thinking that we are capable of devising will eventually come up against essential limitations of some sort that will prevent its unlimited application. In the meantime, no agreement can be discerned at present among the experts with regard to the details of any way in which we might reform our thinking. As an example, there is the irreconcilable schism between the views of Einstein and Bohr on quantum phenomena. Whatever the eventual solution, I think we can at least be sure that it will be outside the realm of common sense. Furthermore, I believe the experts would at present agree that whatever new way we devise to think about the microscopic universe, the meaning of our new concepts will have to be found back at the level of the large-scale events of daily life, because this is the scale on which we live our lives, and it is we who are formulating the new concepts. This recognition and agreement entails, I believe, a consequence that is not commonly appreciated, namely, that the seeds and sources of the ineptness of our thinking in the microscopic range are already contained in our present thinking in the large-scale region and should have been capable of discovery by sufficiently acute analysis of our ordinary common-sense thinking.

I would now like to direct your attention to some qualities of our ordinary everyday thinking that are commonly overlooked but seem to be beginning to attract more attention and, I believe, may eventually give us truer understanding of the nature of our thinking process and its limitations. What I shall now say must be taken as strictly my own opinions. I have no professional philosophical competence to speak on these matters, and it is even probable that many of my fellow-physicists would not agree with me, if indeed they have any opinion on these matters at all.

You have all doubtless had some acquaintance with cybernetics, a subject named and largely created by Professor Norbert Wiener at Massachusetts Institute of Technology, and you know how much attention this subject is attracting and how many people are working at it.

Apart from any specific results that may come out of all this activity, such for example as discovering how to make bigger and better robots that will continually usurp more and more of the functions of human intelligence, it seems to me that the mere fact that so many people are concerning themselves with this subject is going to have important repercussions. For when so many people try so hard to make a machine that functions like the human brain, the point of view will gradually spread that the human brain is itself a machine of sorts. It will also be recognized that this machine must have limitations inherent in its structure, and that the things which the machine can do, including in particular thinking, is in consequence also subject to limitations. Thinking is done by the brain, and the presumption is that thought has characteristics imposed by the character of the brain. At any rate, we will come to see that we may not expect to understand the nature of thought at least until we understand the nature of the brain. If you ask why we should be concerned with the nature of thought, I would reply: the realization that the nature of thought is something which cannot be merely taken for granted is a realization that seems to be gradually dawning on us as we ponder the significance of our failures in the fields of relativity and quantum theory.

You will not, I think, ponder for long what limitations are imposed on thought by the structure of the brain until it will suddenly strike you that what is really happening here is that the brain is trying to understand itself. But is not this a brash thing for the brain to try to do, for how can the brain analyze its own action, when any conclusions at which it arrives are themselves activities of the very brain that was the original problem to understand? At the very best, the situation would seem to be somewhat strained and artificial, and you may perhaps anticipate that any conclusions at which we may arrive cannot have as simple and straightforward a significance as we had perhaps hoped. This does indeed seem to be the case. What we are encountering here is a special case of a system trying to deal with itself. Such situations occur not infrequently, and it seems to be the general rule that such situations present special difficulties and infelicities.

Many of the well-known paradoxes of logic arise when a system tries to deal with itself. A stock example is the ostensibly complete map of the city in which the map itself is located. If the map is complete, it must contain a map of itself; that is, the map must have a map of the map, and this in turn demands a map of the map of the map, and you are off on a chase that has no end. Within the last few years, a theorem with regard to such a system has been proved, a theorem that has been hailed among logicians as a truly epoch-making discovery in logic. This theorem was enunciated by Gödel, at the Institute for Advanced Study at Princeton. In very crude language, the theorem states that no logical system can ever prove that it itself is a perfect system in the sense that it may not contain concealed self-contradictions. This theorem, at one stroke, stultified the endeavors of some of the ablest mathematicians, just as earlier the discovery of new mathematical theorems had stultified the efforts of the circle-squarers and the angle-trisectors. Mathematicians had long been trying to prove by the principles of mathematics that mathematics contains no hidden inconsistencies, inconsistencies that some day might be discovered and bring down the whole imposing mathematical edifice in ruins. But Gödel's theorem showed that this is an impossible sort of thing to prove. The conclusion is that, if one wants to prove that mathematics is free from concealed self-contradictions, one has to use principles outside mathematics to prove it. If one then wants to prove that the new principles are free from contradiction, one must use other principles beyond and over those in question. We here encounter a regress that has no logical end and, humanly, ends in human weariness and the finite length of human life. This means that the human intelligence can never be sure of itself; it is not a tool capable of unlimited perfectibility, as is so often fondly imagined. All we can ever say is that, up to the present, we have found no inconsistencies where we have looked.

There is one other recent development that tends to make us more self-conscious of our intellectual limitations. In Hanover, New Hampshire, Adelbert Ames, Jr., with a number of collaborators, especially A. Hadley Cantril, of the department of psychology of Princeton University, has been studying in recent years how the perceptions of different people adapt themselves to situations that have been purposely devised to differ from the situations ordinarily encountered in daily life. For example, one can play tricks with perception by making lines converge or diverge which ordinary experience leads one to expect must be parallel. By combining various kinds of motion with curiosities of perspective, one can produce sensations completely foreign to ordinary experience, which the unaccustomed brain fits into its perceptual scheme in forced and unnatural ways. A striking example is the so-called trapezoidal window. A wooden frame like an ordinary window frame, except that the top and bottom sashes are not parallel, is rotated uniformly about a vertical axis. When the narrower end of the frame approaches the observer, the converging lines, associated ordinarily with greater distance, present the observer with an unaccustomed dilemma. Most observers resolve the dilemma by seeing the window frame in oscillating motion, back and forth, rather than in uniform rotation. In general, the way in which the observer perceives this and other strange situations varies with different persons and even varies with the same person, depending on what has been happening to him in the immediate past. This means that what a person sees in a given situation may, to a certain extent, be manipulated and controlled by another person.

Of course, there is nothing new in illusions. At Hanover, however, the study of such effects is being elaborated into a systematic technique for finding out about the nature of our perceptual processes. I think that most people, once they have seen the demonstrations, would be convinced that such studies cannot help being of great value in revealing details of the ways in which our perceptual machinery works.

Personally, however, I find these studies tremendously suggestive and stimulating from a point of view of greater generality, namely, in emphasizing the significance of the mere fact that we perceive at all. This is one of those things that are so universal we never think of them unless our attention is forced by some dramatic situation. Perception we have always had with us and we take it completely for granted. We *see things* out there in space moving about, and that is all there is to it. We accept these perceptions at their face value and, on them as a foundation, we build the pattern of our "reality." To this reality, we ascribe an absolute existence transcending its origin and ask ourselves how it is that the human brain can be capable of apprehending the absolute. By asking this question, we disclose our hazy feeling that what a brain can do is probably limited in some way. But except for this hazy feeling, it seems to me that the question is improperly put, and the fact that we ask it discloses an improper attitude on our part. Instead of asking how human brains can apprehend "reality," we should ask what sort of thing it is that the human brain can fashion to call reality. It was, I believe, Suzanne Langer who remarked that philosophy advances, not by finding the answers to the questions of preceding generations, but by finding that those questions were improperly put. Here it seems to me is obviously a question that has been improperly put. The perception of time and space have been furnished to us by the machinery of our nervous systems. This machinery is a terribly complicated thing, which in spite of its complication does not give rise to perception until it has received a long course of preparation and education. Anyone who has watched a small infant trying to coordinate its visual and tactual sensations recognizes that we acquire our perceptual abilities only by arduous practice. Yet we take our space and time with a deadly seriousness. Even so great a scientist as Sir Isaac Newton could say that space is the sensorium of God, and nearly every philosopher treats thought as in some way transcending the machine that thinks. It will doubtless be disturbing to many to give up our transcendentally fundamental time and space, but I think there is perhaps something to be gained also. Perhaps when we learn to take them less seriously we will not be so bedeviled by the logical contradictions in which they sometimes now involve us, as when we ask questions about the beginning or end of time or the boundaries of space.

There is another respect in which I have found the experiments of Ames most stimulating, namely, in disclosing details of our mental processes of which we are ordinarily completely unaware. For example, as one watches the rotating trapezoidal window, one's perceptions are in a continual state of flux, melting and forming and metamorphosing into one another in a way quite unfamiliar. How can one find words to describe such unfamiliar happenings, or how can one catch and hold such things? How can one even store in memory what he has experienced so that he may be sure that the manner of fusion of two perceptions which he has just experienced is the same as the manner of fusion which he experienced yesterday?

Of course, ever since psychoanalysis started, we have known that there are processes occurring in the brain that never get to the level of consciousness, but here it seems to me that we have something different, because here we are encountering new sorts of conscious experience. Among these, there are *transient* mental phenomena, accessible to sufficiently acute introspection. For example, as we listen to our fellow, the meaning that he is trying to convey grows before it is complete. Meanings do not spring full grown into our minds but pass through a stage of development that is seldom, if ever, the subject of analysis. It seems to be a general characteristic of our mental processes that we like to operate with static and complete things—we want our words to have fixed meanings and we analyze space into points and time into instants. But to sufficiently acute analysis, the fixed and static does not occur—it is something that we have constructed, and in so doing we have constructed away a whole world of mental phenomena.

It would seem not impossible that this world of transient phenomena and fine structure could be recovered and opened to us by deliberate cultivation and invention. What is needed is the invention of an introspectional microscope. Not until we have amassed a considerable experience of this world will we be able to talk about it or even remember our experiences. Gaining mastery of the microscopic world of introspection will involve much the same sort of thing that happens to a baby or to a kitten when its eyes are opened. Study of the process of gaining mastery of the new introspectional world may help us to reconstruct imaginatively what happened to us in our own babyhood.

It does not yet appear what the final method will be for dealing with all these considerations. I believe that the final solution will have to carry further the consequences of the insight that quantum theory has partially glimpsed, namely, that the observer must somehow be included in the system. The point of view of classical physics, and I believe also of all orthodox human thinking up to the present, was that the observer is a passive spectator, expressed sometimes by saying that what he observes would be the same whether he were watching or not. Quantum theory points out that this is only an approximation valid in the realm of large objects. The very act of observing a small object involves a reaction between the object and the observer, a reaction that must be allowed for in reconstructing the system from observation. To which we now add the insight that the relationship between the observed and the observer is a much more intimate relationship than these quantum considerations would suggest, and that it is in fact meaningless to try to separate observer and observed, or to speak of an object independent of an observer or, for that matter, of an observer in the absence of objects of observation.

It seems to me that our eyes are gradually opening. We are coming to recognize that it is a simple matter of observation that the observer is part of what he observes and that the thinker is part of what he thinks. We do not passively observe the universe from the outside, but we are all in it up to our necks, and there is no escape. It would be difficult to imagine anything more contrary to the tenets of common sense or to the attitude of the human race since it has begun to think. The common-sense way of handling our minds has, without doubt, been of decisive importance, and the discovery of the common-sense way of thinking was, doubtless, in the beginning a bit of an invention, perhaps the most important invention ever made. One of the things that we are in fact doing in accepting the common-sense way of thinking is to declare that, for our purposes, we do not need to complicate our thinking by continually holding ourselves to an awareness that the thinker cannot be divorced from what he thinks. We have thus brought about a tremendous simplification in our intellectual processes, and in the history of the human race the common-sense attitude has been more than justified. It seems to me, however, that we are approaching a position where we can recognize the limit of usefulness of this way of thinking. Common sense evolved in the comparatively simple situations of the primitive experiences of the human race, and although it may have been an invention, we may be sure that it was an unconscious invention, adopted with no due consideration of its limitations or possible alternatives.

The world with which common sense was evolved to cope was

simple with respect to the range of physical phenomena that it embraced, and simple also with respect to the social organization of the communities in which common sense was practiced. In the last 50 years, we have drastically extended our physical range toward high velocities and toward the microscopic and have been able to retain our command of the situation only by discarding those common-sense methods of thinking about physical things which had served the human race from the beginning. We may well ask ourselves whether something analogous may not be expected to occur, or is not in fact already occurring, when we pass from the simple to the complex in phenomena other than those of the physical world, using *physical* in its narrower sense. There are at least two other classes of nonphysical situations. These are social situations and the situations presented by the creation of abstractions or by abstract thinking. Consider first the social situations.

There will be, I suppose, no disagreement with contention that, in the last few generations, the complexity of our social environment has tremendously increased. With modern methods of communication with the speed of light and of transportation with more than the speed of sound, the social environment of each person is becoming effectively the whole world. Plain analogy with what has happened in physics suggests the question of whether we are not here encountering an extension of range in our social experience that will demand an analogous abandonment of common-sense methods of social thinking. By common-sense methods of social thinking, I mean those methods that developed in small communities and are fitted to deal with nothing more complex than the social situations presented by small communities. From this point of view, most of our social thinking would seem to be of the common-sense variety. One characteristic social attitude springing from such an origin is the conviction that there is one and only one "correct" or "right" social philosophy or world-view, or one line of conduct that one "ought" to follow. Such a point of view could be pretty well maintained in a community small enough to offer a background of uniform social experience to all its members and able to enforce conformity on all dissenters. But the impossibility of any such view has become amply apparent when the community has become the whole world, and we are forced to revise the very meanings that we attach to *truth* or *right* or *ought*. It would appear that there is a moral perception analogous to our physical perception of objects in space and time and, like our physical perceptions, dependent on our past experience. We may suppose that the savage, who has never seen a civilized window frame, when confronted for the first time with the rotating trapezoidal window, will see it, not in oscillating motion as we do, but in uniform rotation.

Analogously, the Hindu, brought up in the religious traditions of his group, perceives as a moral imperative that he must not kill the mosquito that annoys him. The realization of this is not new; the anthropologist has been dinning it into our ears for some time. The anthropologist, however, could point his moral only in somewhat academic terms and mostly from the record of the past by presenting us with the divergent practices of different peoples in different epochs. The lesson is now pointed with incomparably more dramatic force in our endeavors to find a basis for the harmonious living together of the entire world, a problem that demands the simultaneous reconciliation of so many divergent outlooks. At the very least, we shall have to evolve a new social philosophy and discover some method of getting rid of the provincialism that seems so right to common sense.

In addition to the social situations, a second nonphysical factor in our lives is afforded by our abstract thinking. How long the human race has been thinking and talking abstractly I suppose even the anthropologist cannot tell us, but it appeals to me as a good guess that we developed our common-sense method of handling the situations of daily life before we began abstracting. It is known that there are primitive peoples that have not yet formed as simple abstractions as "tree." The extension of thinking from concrete objects to abstractions constituted an extension of range sufficiently great to suggest the question, inspired by our experience with relativity and quantum theory, of whether the methods adequate to deal with the world of concrete objects continue to be adequate to deal with abstractions. To put the question is to suggest the answer. In the answer, I believe we can glimpse the solution to a riddle that has long baffled us. There is a class of people whose profession is to deal with abstractions—that is, the philosophers. By long tradition, philosophical thinking has come to be regarded by most people as the most exalted of all thinking, and the philosopher is often regarded with an approach to veneration. But along with this veneration most people are disillusioned and feel the futility of the whole philosophical enterprise, because after 2000 years of argument philosophy has settled no questions and no two philosophers agree. This situation can be understood in a measure when we recognize that the philosopher essentially is applying to abstractions the same common-sense methods that are applicable in the realm of concrete objects. I think simple observation of any conventional philosophical system will justify this statement, or, if one wishes, one can find a formal argument by Philipp Frank to show that the theses of philosophy are essentially the theses of common sense extended into the realm of abstractions. For example, Plato ascribes to ideas a reality like the reality of the objects of common sense. But ideas are not like things, and to treat them like things is only a kind of poetry. The cure for the common-sense attitude toward abstractions is to seek the meaning of our abstract terms by an analysis at least as searching as the analysis that we have been forced to apply to such simple physical terms as *length* or *time*. Such an analysis is seldom applied to abstractions, but the common-sense implications in our verbal habits are uncritically accepted. For example, one of the great abstractions is truth. In talking about truth, one uses such expressions as *the* truth, or thinks of truth as eternal in the heavens, which all may know and on which all can agree. But just as in physics we have been forced to recognize that there is not the one length of common sense but different kinds of length, such as optical length or tactual length, depending on our choice of method of measurement, so analysis will disclose that there is not just the one truth of common sense but different kinds of truth, depending on the method used for establishing "truth." For example, scientific truth is not the same as theological truth, and we must not talk about them as if they were and as common sense wants us to. Since truth is such a frequent topic for discussion in philosophy, this one example will suggest the modifications in conventional philosophical thought that might follow the abandonment of the common-sense attitude toward truth. Perhaps the philosophers might even agree. Even if the philosophers prove unregenerate, outside the realm of philosophy abandonment of the common-sense attitude toward truth will go far toward eliminating bigotry and intolerance.

In conclusion, the problem of devising successful substitutes for common sense has not yet been solved, and we are standing only on the threshold of a new era in human thought. Although the final solution is not in sight, there are certain lessons that we can take to heart at present in the expectation that we shall not have to retreat. It seems to me that, as a minimum, we henceforth cannot regard a man as well educated who does not intuitively recognize that common sense is not to be taken for granted, or who does not handle his thinking as a tool in the awareness that every tool has limitations built into it. Such a man, looking to the past, can only be amazed that the human brain has, by cut-and-try methods, evolved procedures as effective as it has for dealing with the world around us; looking to the present, sees perhaps the most important reason for the present internal social difficulties of the human race in its uncritical use of traditional habits of thought; and looking to the future, can feel only optimism for the time when we shall have learned how to substitute consciously directed control of our thinking for the blind procedures of common sense.

I. I. RABI

Scientist and Humanist

FOR MORE THAN half a century, from the period of the Darwinian controversy till the end of the 1930s, science remained almost unchallenged as the source of enlightenment, understanding, and hope for a better, healthier, and safer world. The benefits brought by science were and are still visible everywhere one looks. Human ills are being overcome; food supplies are becoming more abundant; travel and communication are quick and easy; and the comforts of life, especially for the common man, are vastly increased. In the person of Albert Einstein science enjoyed a world-wide respect almost akin to reverence and hardly equaled since the time of Isaac Newton.

In the last decade or so we have begun to detect signs of significant change. The knowledge and techniques developed through science for the illumination of the mind and the elevation of the spirit, for the prolongation and the amelioration of life, have been used for the destruction of life and the degradation of the human spirit. Technological warfare, biological warfare, psychological warfare, brainwashing, all make use of science with frightening results.

I do not suggest that warfare and its attendant horror is a result of modern science. Ancient Greece, at the zenith of that remarkable civilization, in a land united by a common culture and a common religion, destroyed itself in a bitter and useless war more thoroughly than Europe has done in the present century even with the aid of electronics, aviation, and high explosives. What I mean is that our epoch in history, which has produced one of the greatest achievements of the human race, may be passing into a twilight that does not precede the dawn.

Science, the triumph of the intellect and the rational faculties, has resulted in the hydrogen bomb. The glib conclusion is that science and the intellect are therefore false guides. We must seek elsewhere, some people say, for hope and salvation; but, say the same people, while doing so we must keep ahead of the Russians in technology and in the armaments race. Keep the fearsome fruits but reject the spirit of science. Such is the growing mood of some people at the present time. It is a mood of anti-intellectualism which can only hasten the destruction which these people fear. Anti-intellectualism has always been endemic in every society, perhaps in the heart of every human being. In times of

253

stress this attitude is stimulated and people tend to become impatient and yield to prejudice and emotion just when coolness, subtlety, and reason are most needed.

We are told, and most of us believe, that we are living in a period of crisis unequaled in history. To be cheerful and proud of our accomplishment and optimistic of the future is almost akin to subversion. To be considered objective and realistic, one must view with alarm. Yet we are not living in a period of hard times and unemployment! We have, I cannot say enjoyed but, rather, bemoaned, a period of prosperity and world-wide influence for good unequaled in history. Nevertheless, despite all, we seem to be acquiring a complacency of despair. In this mood, unable to adjust to new values, we hark back to a past which now looks so bright in retrospect, and we raise the banner of "Back to the Humanities."

What is meant by the slogan "Back to the Humanities"? What are people really looking for? What knowledge, what guidance, what hope for salvation, what inspiration, or what relief from anxiety does a practical-minded people like ours expect from a knowledge of the humanities? They do not wish to re-establish the study of the Greek and Roman classics in their original tongues, or to re-create the Greek city-state in Metropolitan Boston.

I venture to suggest that what they mean is something quite different from what is meant by the humanities. The progress of civilization in the modern age, especially in our own century, has brought with it an immense increase of knowledge of every kind, from archaeology to zoology. More is known of the history of antiquity than was known to Herodotus. We have penetrated farther into the heavens and into the innermost secrets of the structure of matter than anyone could have dreamt of in previous generations. We have run through the satisfactions of representational art to the puzzling outlines of abstract art. The increase in physical comfort and in communication has brought with it a whole set of new problems. The great increase in population necessarily means further crowding and additional social and cultural adjustment. Under these circumstances, it is natural for people to look for guidance toward a balanced adjustment.

What people are really looking for is wisdom. To our great store of knowledge we need the added quality of wisdom.

Wisdom is inseparable from knowledge; it is knowledge plus a quality which is within the human being. Without it knowledge is dry, almost unfit for human consumption, and dangerous in application. The absence of wisdom is clearly noticeable; the learned fool and the educated bore have been with us since the beginnings of recorded history. Wisdom adds flavor, order, and measure to knowledge. Wisdom makes itself most manifest in the application of knowledge to human needs.

Every generation of mankind has to remake its culture, its values, and its goals. Changing circumstances make older habits and customs valueless or obsolete. New knowledge exposes the limitations and the contingent nature of older philosophies and of previously accepted guides to action. Wisdom does not come in formulas, proverbs, or wise saws, but out of the living actuality. The past is important for understanding the present, but it is not the present. It is in a real sense created in the present, and changes from the point of view of every generation.

When change is slow, the new is gradually assimiliated, and only after a number of generations is it noticeable that the world is really different. In our century enormous changes in the circumstances of our lives and in our knowledge have occurred rapidly—in every decade. It is therefore not at all surprising that our intellectual, our social, and our political processes have failed to keep abreast of contemporary problems. It is not surprising that we become confused in the choice of our goals and the paths which we must take to reach them.

Clearly a study of the Greek and Roman classics in their original tongues or even in a good translation is a most rewarding venture in itself. This literature has never been surpassed in any age. And in reading this literature one is struck by how applicable the situations are to the present day. The fact that we can still be moved strongly by this literature is an illustration not merely of the constancy of structure of the human nervous system but also of the fact that great art and profound insights have a character which is independent of any age.

The humanities preserve and create values; even more they express the symbolic, poetic, and prophetic qualities of the human spirit. Without the humanities we would not be conscious of our history; we would lose many of our aspirations and the graces of expression that move men's hearts. Withal the humanities discern but a part of the life of man—true, a vital part but only a part.

It has often been claimed that the chief justification for the study of the humanities is that it teaches us values. In fact some people go even further and claim that the humanities, in which literature, parts of philosophy, and the history and appreciation of the fine arts are included, are the *only* sources of values other than the more spiritual values of religion.

This claim cannot pass without challenge. It cannot be said that it is absurd, but rather that it is a symptom of our failure in the present age to achieve a unity and balance of knowledge which is imbued with wisdom. It is a symptom of both ignorance and a certain anti-rational attitude which has been the curse of our century. It betrays a lack of self-confidence and faith in the greatness of the human spirit in contemporary man. It is the expression of a form of self-hatred which is rationally unjustifiable although deeply rooted.

Man is made of dust and to dust returneth; he lives in a universe of which he is also a part. He is free only in a symbolic sense; his nature is conditioned by the dust out of which he is made. To learn to understand himself he must learn to understand the universe in which he lives. There is more than enough in this enterprise to engage the boldest, the most imaginative, and the keenest minds and spirits of every generation. The universe is not given to us in the form of a map or guide. It is made by human minds and imaginations out of slight hints which come from acute observation and from the profound stratagems of experiments.

How can we hope to obtain wisdom, the wisdom which is meaningful in our own time? We certainly cannot attain it as long as the two great branches of human knowledge, the sciences and the humanities, remain separate and even warring disciplines.

Why is science, even more than the humanities, as a living component of our society so misunderstood? A glance at a current dictionary definition may give us a clue.

Science: "A branch of knowledge dealing with facts or truths systematically arranged and showing the operation of general law."

This definition brings to my mind a solitaire player or head bookkeeper for a mail-order concern. It is a partial truth which is also a caricature. It is out of harmony with the picture of Archimedes jumping out of his bath crying Eureka! or Galileo in misery and degradation during his trial and recantation, or Einstein creating the universe out of one or two deductions from observation and a profound aesthetic feeling for symmetry. Nor does this definition account for the violence of the opposition to scientific discovery which still exists in the same quarters in our own age.

It is often argued that physical science is inherently simple, whereas the study of man is inherently complicated. Yet a great deal is known of man's nature. Wise laws for government and personal conduct were known in remotest antiquity. The literature of antiquity shows a profound understanding of human natures and emotions. Not man but the external world was bewildering. The world of nature instead of seeming simple was infinitely complex and possessed of spirits and demons. Nature had to be worshiped and propitiated by offerings, cere-

monies, and prayers. Fundamentally nature was unpredictable, antago-
nistic to human aspiration, full of significance and purpose, and generally evil. Knowledge of nature was suspect because of the power
which it brought, a power which was somehow allied with evil. There
were of course always men who had insights far beyond these seemingly naïve notions, but they did not prevail over what seemed to be the
evidence of the senses and of practical experience.

It was therefore not until late in the history of mankind, not until
a few seconds ago so to speak, that it was recognized that nature is
understandable and that a knowledge of nature is good and can be used
with benefit; that it does not involve witchcraft or a compact with the
devil. What is more, any person of intelligence can understand the
ideas involved and with sufficient skill learn the necessary techniques,
intellectual and manual.

This idea which is now so commonplace represents an almost complete break with the past. To revere and trust the rational faculty of
the mind—to allow no taboo to interfere in its operation, to have nothing immune from its examination—is a new value which has been
introduced into the world. The progress of science has been the chief
agent in demonstrating its importance and riveting it into the consciousness of mankind. This value does not yet have universal acceptance in
this country or in any other country. But in spite of all obstacles it will
become one of the most treasured possessions of all mankind because
we can no longer live without it. We have gone too far along the direction which it implies ever to turn back without unimaginable disaster.

The last world war was started in an attempt to turn back to dark
reaction against the rational faculty and to introduce a new demonology
into the world. It failed as will every other such attempt. Once the mind
is free it will be destroyed rather than be put back in chains.

To my mind the value content of science or literary scholarship
lies not in the subject matter alone; it lies chiefly in the spirit and living
tradition in which these disciplines are pursued. The spirit is almost
always conditioned by the subject. Science and the humanities are not
the same thing; the subject matter is different and the spirit and tradition are different. Our problem in our search for wisdom is to blend
these two traditions in the minds of individual men and women.

Many colleges and universities are trying to do just this, but there
is one serious defect in the method. We pour a little of this and a little
of that into the student's mind in proportions which result from mediation between the departments and from the particular predilections of
the deans and the president. We then hope that these ingredients will
combine through some mysterious alchemy and the result will be a

man educated, well-rounded, and wise. Most often, however, these ingredients remain well separated in the compartmentalized mind, or they may form an indigestible precipitate which is not only useless but positively harmful, until time the healer washes it all away.

Wisdom is by its nature an interdisciplinary quality and not the product of a collection of specialists. Although the colleges do indeed try to mold the student toward a certain ideal of the educated man of the twentieth century, it is too often a broad education administered by specialists. The approximate counterpart to this ideal of the educated man, embodied in a real living person, is a rare being on any college faculty. Indeed, in most colleges and universities the student is the only really active connecting link between the different departments. In a certain paradoxical sense the students are the only broadly educated body in the university community, at least in principle.

The affairs of this country—indeed of almost every country— whether in government, education, industry, or business, are controlled by people of broad experience. However, this broad experience rarely includes the field of science. How can our leaders make wise decisions now in the middle of the twentieth century without a deep understanding of scientific thought and feeling for scientific traditions? The answer is clear in the sad course that events have taken.

This anguished thought has impelled many scientists, often to their own personal peril, to concern themselves with matters which in the past were the exclusive domain of statesmen and military leaders. They have tried to advise, importune, and even cajole our leaders to include the scientific factor in our fateful policy decisions. They have been successful, but only in special instances.

I am not making a plea for the scientist statesman comparable to the philosopher king. The scientist rarely has this kind of ambition. The study of nature in its profundity, beauty, and subtlety is too attractive for him to wish to forsake his own creative and rewarding activity. The scientist away from his science is like an exile who longs for the sights and sounds of his native land. What the scientist really desires is for his science to be understood, to become an integral part of our general culture, to be given proper weight in the cultural and practical affairs of the world.

The greatest difficulty which stands in the way of a meeting of the minds of the scientist and the non-scientist is the difficulty of communication, a difficulty which stems from some of the defects of education to which I have alluded. The mature scientist, if he has any taste in these directions, can listen with pleasure to the philosopher, the historian, the literary man, or even to the art critic. There is little difficulty from that side because the scientist has been educated in our general culture and lives in it on a day-to-day basis. He reads newspapers, magazines, books, listens to music, debates politics, and participates in the general activities of an educated citizen.

Unfortunately this channel of communication is often a one-way street. The non-scientist cannot listen to the scientist with pleasure and understanding. Despite its universal outlook and its unifying principle, its splendid tradition, science seems to be no longer communicable to the great majority of educated laymen. They simply do not possess the background of the science of today and the intellectual tool necessary for them to understand what effects science will have on them and on the world. Instead of understanding, they have only a naïve awe mixed with fear and scorn. To his colleagues in the university the scientist tends to seem more and more like a man from another planet, a creature scattering antibiotics with one hand and atomic bombs with the other.

The problems to which I have addressed myself are not particularly American. The same condition exists in England, France, and indeed in all other countries. From my observation we are perhaps better off than most. Our American colleges and universities, since they are fairly recent and are rapidly expanding, have not settled into complacency. They are quite ready to experiment to achieve desired ends. Our experimental methods have taught us how to impart the most diverse forms of knowledge. Although wisdom is more elusive, once the objective is clear that the ultimate end of education is knowledge imbedded in wisdom we shall find ways to move toward that ideal. The ideal of the well-rounded man is a meaningless ideal unless this sphericity means a fusion of knowledge to achieve balanced judgment and understanding, which are qualities of wisdom.

The problems are, of course, depressingly difficult. In the secondary schools—with their overcrowding, their teachers overworked and inadequately trained, the school boards, and, not least, the powerful clique of professional educators who form a society within our society—all that is unique and characteristic of science and mathematics is being crowded out of the curriculum and replaced by a fairy tale known as general science. The colleges and universities are in much better shape, although the great population increase is about to hit them with masses of inadequately prepared students. Most people would be quite content with a holding operation in which we could maintain the quality that is already possessed.

However, it seems to me that something could be done even now with the faculty members of the colleges and the universities. Wisdom can achieve a hybrid vigor by crossing the scientist and the humanist through a more extensive and intensive interaction within the faculty. Why should not the professor of physics be expected to refresh himself periodically by taking a course in aesthetics or comparative literature or in the Greek drama? Why shouldn't the professor of medieval philosophy or the professor of ancient history take a course in modern physics and become acquainted with the profound thoughts underlying relativity and quantum mechanics? It would let in some fresh air, or at least different air, to blow away some of the cobwebs which grow in the unventilated ivory towers.

Somewhere a beginning has to be made to achieve a more architectural quality in our culture, a quality of proportion and of organic unity, and it is reasonable to start with the members of the faculties of our institutions of higher learning. Here are all the strands of the tapestry which is to represent our culture, living in close proximity but separate, adding up to nothing more than the sum of the parts. The scientists must learn to teach science in the spirit of wisdom and in the light of the history of human thought and human effort, rather than as the geography of a universe uninhabited by mankind. Our colleagues in the non-scientific faculties must understand that if their teachings ignore the great scientific tradition and its accomplishments, their words, however eloquent and elegant, will lose meaning for this generation and be barren of fruit.

Only with a united effort of science and the humanities can we hope to succeed in discovering a community of thought which can lead us out of the darkness and the confusion which oppress all mankind.

JOHN H. STEELE

The Fiction of Science

PEOPLE OFTEN TALK about science being objective. They think of it as something logical and rather inhuman, with an attitude to life symbolised by the cold neutral colours of its apparatus. I sometimes wonder how true this is. I work in a laboratory. There is chemical apparatus on my bench and a calculating machine on my desk. The scientific journals are prepared to publish my results, so I suppose I can call myself a scientist. But does this job of mine deserve these attributes which people give to 'science'? For example, Kathleen Nott says 'progress for the whole human race would be, if not inevitable, at least highly probable, if a sufficient majority of people were trained to use their reasoning power on their general experience as a scientist is trained to use his reasoning power on his special experiences'. This blunt instrument of the analogy with science is also used frequently by literary men. Irving Singer wrote:

> Science is based on observations that are not affected by the idiosyncrasies of time and space, but critical evaluation depends on interpretations which vary from observer to observer; scientific statements are true or false, but statements in art criticism are neither one nor the other and can only be accepted or rejected.

It is this sort of thing that worries me. Is science—or, to put it simply, am I—'not affected by the idiosyncrasies of time and space'? Am I a machine with observations going in one end and scientific papers coming out the other; an automatically recording angel in a white coat? If that is science, then I must find another name for my job. What I know as science is not so objective, so neutral, nor so inhuman as these descriptions suggest. What are these supposedly neutral, objective 'facts' and 'observations'? Probably the commonest image is a young man noting the reading on a dial. In photographs he wears a laboratory coat and spectacles and looks suitably anonymous. He could be anyone; it is the foreground which counts.

Yet it need not be as simple as that. Niko Tinbergen has worked for many years on the instinctive acts of animals. He believes that the patterns of behaviour which an animal inherits are much more complex than was once thought possible. To prove this he has watched the reactions of different animals in widely varying situations, natural and artificial. But what are his observations? Which movements of a continuously moving animal are to be considered relevant to his theory? There is a film taken by Dr. Tinbergen of a colony of herring gulls showing how impossible it is for a casual observer to separate particular recurrent gestures from all the other acts which the birds make. But Dr. Tinbergen has watched gulls for many years and his facts, his observations, are chosen typical gestures which he considers relevant to his theories. The whole complex pattern of such a piece of work is highly individual; it is reasonable to say that it could not have been done by anyone else.

Yet it is not only in the biological sciences that this kind of individual judgement is required. It occurs in any study of natural events. Often it is impossible to ensure that every observation is correctly made and often they cannot be repeated—we must decide which to accept.

In physical oceanography, for example, the data are collected at sea in difficult circumstances and not until later will it be noticed that certain observations 'look wrong'. It is possible to think of explanations of these in terms of faulty equipment. It is possible to make special experiments to show that such things occasionally happen. But, finally, for the routine data, the scientist has to make his own decision to ignore certain values, to interpret a curve in a certain way.

These, then, are the situations in which the facts themselves are difficult, where the scientist is forced to make his own judgements on what is important or unimportant, right or wrong. Like all judgements they are based on experience, but also like all judgements they have no final justification. The answer is that these difficulties merely illustrate the shortcomings of this type of scientific work. They show how far it is from the ideal of science; an ideal more closely approached by theoretical physics. It is for this reason that physics is so often taken as the example by all the writers who wish to compare science with their own bit of the world.

Yet even if this were true, physics does not necessarily make the best model for comparison with, say, the criticism of poetry. Surely it would be better, if rather less imposing, to compare the critic Dr. Leavis studying a group of poems with Dr. Tinbergen watching a colony of herring gulls. There are differences but the similarities are just as interesting. Both must continuously decide what is important and what is unimportant, and they must convince us that their decisions are the right ones. But the main thing which they have in common is their strong individuality separating them from other critics or other scientists. Still the hankering after the ideal remains. There is the criticism of criticism; no longer the struggle with detail, the problems in one stanza; the concern now is with poetry itself, so now surely the comparison is with what science ought to be.

But what is this world of physics like, this place of controlled observation, of tame facts? It is the world of theory. A hypothesis is set up and it is deduced from it that a certain event should occur in certain circumstances. An experiment is performed to see if this happens. If it does not, then the hypothesis is disproved; if it does, then it is evidence in its favour. But how decisive is the experiment? To what extent does it help to establish the hypothesis? Is it possible there are other unthought-of explanations of this result.

The more general, and thus the more important, the theory is, the more it tries to explain. But this means there are more possibilities to be considered, more chance of something being neglected, a greater need for further experiment. It is here that we have arguments and disagreements; people have ideas which they cannot see how to prove; or they disagree about the interpretations of experiments. Now where are we with the statement, 'scientific laws are true or false but literary criticism is only a matter of emotion or opinion'? Surely it is obvious that while it is science, while the experiments are being made, it is only the results of these experiments which exist. They are part of the world just as a poem is. We argue about them, we interpret them and disagree about our interpretations. Afterwards when we have made a number of experiments we have learned something. We can make 'planes fly faster than sound and we can stop them with guided missiles that have atomic warheads. But this is no longer science, it is engineering or technology. The scientists are arguing now about something else, the theory of the 'heat barrier', perhaps, or the possibility of a new bomb. The usefulness is a by-product of science. It provides money to go further, just as a packed theatre or a third edition helps the writer. But these, so we are told, are not the definition of art.

How has this illusion come about? How is it that science is considered an impersonal activity, a kind of automation? Perhaps scientists themselves are to blame. In conversation one of them might say: 'I felt such-and-such might be the right way of looking at things, so I did this experiment. I was unlucky though, it turned out to be quite the opposite to what I had expected, but I made a better guess the next time'. However when he comes to make it public, he will write up his second guess (the first being quietly ignored) in this way: 'It can be deduced mathematically from this theory that an experiment should show . . .', and you may be sure it does. It is all done in the traditional manner; the personality, if there were any signs of it, has been removed by the editor. Sometimes a little emotion may creep in among the letters at the back of a journal; an opponent's arguments considered to be 'as violent as they are empty'. It could almost be a literary magazine—but it is soon hushed up.

Have I been exaggerating? I suppose so. Being a scientist is very different from being a literary critic, and both are unlike the job of a stockbroker. It is unusual to be successful at any two of these but it is not *a priori* impossible, for they are all ways of living. Stockbrokers would not try to prove that their job was not worldly, and the same attempt with literature has never been noticeably successful. It is only with science that the illusion exists; the illusion of a neutral, inhuman activity separate from the world of 'telegrams and anger'. Perhaps scientists are to blame for their part in creating it, but it would not last if it were not bolstered up by every writer who wishes to use this 'objectivity' to beat up his opponents for being emotional and opinionated.

Does it matter, though, if the illusion is so widespread that both the public and the scientists themselves believe it? Perhaps it does no harm beyond creating confusion in the literary journals. I think its effects are more serious. If people believe that science is something objective, then they will try to use it like a term in an equation—such an equation as 'science plus money equals bigger bombs'. When, for a time, this equation did not work for the hydrogen bomb, they looked for a simple logical explanation, and investigated the loyalty of the scientist in charge, Robert Oppenheimer. But it is not as simple as that. The fallacy in the equation was not logical, it was human.

The problem of making a hydrogen bomb seemed purely technical. One man thought it could be made; another, Oppenheimer, thought it could not. The evidence which they had was not decisive. It was one of these occasions when there can be arguments, interpretations, opinions; just as there can be with the moral problems of creating such a weapon. These problems are different but they are not separate. They are linked by the fact that they both have to be worked out in the mind of one man, and in the attempt to understand them they become connected; connected, not by logic, but because they are both human activities. And the greater that man's mind the more important and more subtle are those connections.

To pretend that they can be kept separate, one in a world of facts, the other in a world of opinions, can lead to tragedy; to the tragedy of Robert Oppenheimer who tried to keep them apart. When he was cross-examined at the public enquiry into his loyalty, he said: 'I have always thought the hydrogen bomb was a dreadful weapon. Even though from a technical point of view it was a sweet and lovely and beautiful job, I have still thought it was a dreadful weapon'.

'But', he was asked, 'did you say so?'

'Yes', said Oppenheimer, 'I would assume that I've said so'.

'You mean that you had a moral revulsion against the production of such a dreadful weapon?'

'Oh that's too strong', replied Oppenheimer.

'What is too strong', said his questioner, 'the weapon or my expression?'

'Your expression', said Oppenheimer. 'I had a grave concern and anxiety'.

'You had moral qualms about it, is that accurate?'

'Let us', said Oppenheimer, 'leave the word "moral" out of it'.

Essays of Our Time I ● *Part* 9

WALTER KAUFMANN, *an associate professor of philosophy at* Princeton, *is the author of, among other works,* Critique of Religion and Philosophy, From Shakespeare to Existentialism, *and* Nietzsche: Philosopher, Psychologist, Antichrist. *Born in Germany, Kaufmann received his B.A. from Williams in 1941 and a few years later received his Ph.D. from Harvard.*

PHILIP SCHARPER, *born in Baltimore, attended Georgetown University and later Fordham. At present an editor with Sheed and Ward, he was at one time an assistant professor of English at Fordham, and a staff member of the liberal Catholic weekly* Commonweal.

ARTHUR COHEN *was graduated from the University of Chicago at eighteen in 1946. He continued his studies at Chicago, Columbia, the New School for Social Research, and the Jewish Theological Seminary. Now the publisher of Meridian books, he is also the author of* Martin Buber *and* The Making of the Jewish Mind.

WILLIAM WARREN BARTLEY, III, *descended from a family of clergymen on the maternal side of his family, studied at Harvard, and has been a Danforth fellow in philosophy. He was editorial chairman of the* Harvard Crimson *and recipient of the National Council of Churches of Christ in the United States Parshad Award and the World Council of Churches Fellowship.*

WALTER KAUFMANN

The Faith of a Heretic

WHEN I WAS ELEVEN, I asked my father: "What really is the Holy Ghost?" The articles of faith taught us in school—in Berlin, Germany —affirmed belief in God, Christ, and the Holy Ghost, and I explained to my father: "I don't believe that Jesus was God, and if I can't believe in the Holy Ghost either, then I am really not a Christian."

At twelve, I formally left the Protestant church to become a Jew. Having never heard of Unitarianism, I assumed that the religion for people who believed in God, but not in Christ or the Holy Ghost, was Judaism.

A few months after my conversation with my father, but before I left the church, Hitler came to power. Warned of the persecution that my decision might entail, I replied that one certainly could not change one's mind for a reason like that. I did not realize until a little later that all four of my grandparents had been Jewish; and none of us knew that this, and not one's own religion, would be decisive from the Nazis' point of view. My decision had been made independently of my descent and of Nazism, on religious grounds.

I took my new religion very seriously, explored it with enormous curiosity and growing love, and gradually became more and more orthodox. When I arrived in the United States in January 1939, I was planning to become a rabbi. A lot of things happened to me that winter, spring, and summer; and when the war broke out I had what, but for its contents, few would hesitate to call a mystical experience. In the most intense despair I suddenly saw that I had deceived myself for years: I had believed. At last the God of tradition joined the Holy Ghost and Christ.

Of course, I could maintain my old beliefs by merely giving them a new interpretation; but that struck me as dishonest. Ikhnaton, the monotheistic Pharaoh—as I explained in a letter to my family who were by now in England—could also have reinterpreted the traditional polytheism of Egypt, but was a fanatic for the truth. He taught his court sculptor to make life masks of people to see how they really looked, and in one of the heads which the sculptor had then done of Ikhnaton, his hunger for the truth had become stone. I had loved that head for years. Should I now do what I admired him for not doing?

267

You may say that Ikhnaton was wrong and that it is the essence of religion to pour new wine into old skins, reading one's current insights into ancient beliefs. But if you do this, disregarding Jesus' counsel not to do it, you should realize that you could do it with almost any religion. And it is less than honest to give one's own religion the benefit of every possible doubt while imposing unsympathetic readings on other religions. Yet this is what practically all religious people do. Witness the attitude of Protestants and Catholics toward each other.

In my remaining two years in college I took all the religion courses offered, while majoring in philosophy; and I continued to study and think about both subjects as a graduate student and in the army. Eventually I got my Ph. D. and a job teaching philosophy. For over ten years now I have taught, among other things, philosophy of religion.* In the process, my ideas developed—into a book: *Critique of Religion and Philosophy.*†

The ideas were not all there as a result of the few experiences alluded to here: there were hundreds of others. Profound experiences stimulate thoughts; but such thoughts do not look very adequate on paper. Writing can be a way of rethinking again and again.

In the process of teaching and writing one must constantly consider the thoughts of men with different ideas. And prolonged and ever-new exposure to a wide variety of outlooks—together with the criticism many professors seek from both their students and their colleagues—is a more profound experience than most people realize. It is a long-drawn-out trial by fire, marked by frequent disillusionment, discoveries, and despair, and by a growing regard for honesty, which is surely one of the most difficult of all the virtues to attain. What one comes up with in the end owes quite as much to this continual encounter as it does to any other experience.

---

* Lest this should create a misleading picture of Princeton, it should be added that in our popular Department of Religion Protestantism is championed vigorously by five full professors and a large staff, and ordained ministers are encountered in other departments, too. Until his recent retirement, Jacques Maritain was a member of the Philosophy Department. Great universities, like this magazine, assume that there is a virtue in confronting students and readers with a variety of responsible approaches.

† Harper & Brothers, 1958. Many ideas in this article are more fully developed and backed up in this book which also deals with the positive aspects of various religions and with many topics not even touched on in this article; *e.g.*, existentialism, Freud, mysticism, Bible criticism, the relation of religion to poetry, and Zen. Among the questions that are barely touched in this essay and treated more fully in my book is the inadequacy of such labels as theism and atheism. The contents of the present article, incidentally—which is in no sense a summary of my *Critique*—may greatly surprise many of my students, past and present.

A liberal education, and quite especially a training in philosophy, represents an attempt to introduce young people to this adventure. We have no wish to indoctrinate; we want to teach our students to resist indoctrination and not accept as authoritative the beliefs of other men or even the ideas that come to us as in a flash of illumination. Even if one has experiences that some men would call mystical—and I have no doubt that I have had many—it is a matter of integrity to question such experiences and any thoughts that were associated with them as closely and as honestly as we should question the "revelations" of others. To be sure, it is easier to grant others their "revelations" as "true for them" while insisting on one's own as "true for oneself." Such intellectual sluggishness parades as sophistication. But true tolerance does not consist in saying, "You may be right, but let us not make hard demands on ourselves: if you will put your critical intelligence to sleep, I'll put mine to bed, too." True tolerance remains mindful of the humanity of those who make things easy for themselves and welcomes and even loves honest and thoughtful opposition above less thoughtful agreement.

The autobiographical sketch with which I have begun may do more harm than good. Some amateur psychologists may try to explain "everything" in terms of one or two experiences; some Protestants may say, "If only he had come to *me* about the Holy Ghost!" while some Catholics may feel that it all shows once again how Protestantism is merely a way-station on the road to Hell.

This is the kind of gambit that the shut-ins pull on travelers. As if I had buried the Holy Ghost beyond recall when I was eleven, and God when I was eighteen! I merely started relatively early to concern myself with such questions—and have never stopped since. Let the shut-in explore Judaism and Protestantism, Catholicism and Buddhism, atheism and agnosticism, mysticism, existentialism, and psychology, Thomas and Tillich. Let him consult the lot and not just his own present prejudice; let him subject his thoughts about religion to the candid scrutiny of those who differ with him and to his own ever-new re-examination; let him have a host of deep experiences, religious and otherwise, and think about them. That is the ground on which a genuine conversation can take place: it need not make a show of erudition, if only it has grown out of a series of open-hearted encounters. But as long as one is content to gloat over the silver lining of one's own religion, one bars any serious conversation and merely makes the first move in a game of skill.

To an even moderately sophisticated and well-read person it should come as no surprise that any religion at all has its hidden as well as its obvious beauties and is capable of profound and impressive interpretations. What is deeply objectionable about most of these interpretations is that they allow the believer to say Yes while evading any No. The Hebrew prophets represent a notable exception. When interpreting their own religious heritage, they were emphatically not conformists who discovered subtle ways in which they could agree with the religion of their day. Nor was it their point that the cult was justifiable with just a little ingenuity. On the contrary.

Let those who like inspiring interpretations be no less forthright in telling us precisely where they stand on ritual and immortality, on the sacraments and Hell, on the Virgin Birth and Resurrection, on the Incarnation and the miracles, and on: "Resist not evil." And: "Let him who would sue you in court for your coat have your cloak, too." And: "No one comes to the Father but through Me."

If you must pour new wine into old skins, you should at least follow one of Jesus' other counsels and let your Yes be Yes, and your No, No.

When considering Christianity, it is easy to get lost in the changing fashions of thought that have been read into it or reconciled with it—from Neoplatonism (Augustine) and Aristotelianism (Aquinas) to romanticism (Schleiermacher), liberalism (Harnack), and extentialism (Tillich, Bultmann, and others). There is no room here to cross swords with a dozen apologists; in any case, dozens more would remain.

The central question about Christianity concerns Jesus Christ. If he was God in a sense in which no other man has been God, then Christianity is right in some important sense, however Christendom may have failed. To decide whether Jesus was God in some such unique sense, a philosopher cannot forbear to ask just what this claim might mean. If, for example, it does not mean that Jesus of Nazareth knew everything and was all-powerful, it is perplexing what is meant. But a large part of what most Christians mean is surely that Jesus was the best and wisest man of all time; and many Protestants mean no more than that.

Millions of Christians agree on this claim and back it up by citing Gospel passages they like; but different people pick different passages. To some, Jesus looks like St. Francis, to others like John Calvin, and to many more the way a man named Hofmann painted him. Pierre van Paassen's Jesus is a Socialist and Fosdick's a liberal, while according to Reinhold Niebuhr Jesus' ethic coincides, not surprisingly, with Niebuhr's. To use a political term: almost everybody gerrymanders, carving an idealized self-portrait from the Gospels and much less attractive straw men from the literatures of other faiths. A great deal of theology is like a jigsaw puzzle: the verses of Scripture are the pieces, and the finished picture is prescribed by each denomination, with a certain latitude allowed. What makes the game so pointless is that not all pieces have to be used, and any piece that does not fit may be reshaped, provided one says first, "this means." That is called exegesis.

In *The Literature of the Christian Movement,* Morton Scott Enslin, one of the outstanding New Testament scholars of our time, remarks that the Jesus of the Fourth Gospel is really not very attractive, and that if it were not for the other three Gospels and the fact that most readers create for themselves "a conflate," the Jesus of St. John would lose most of his charm. Surely, the same consideration applies to all four Gospels.

Those who consider Jesus the best and wisest of men should reread the Gospels and ponder at the very least these five points.

First: Are they prepared to maintain their claim regarding the Jesus of any one of the four Gospels—and, if so, which? Or is it their point that the evidence warrants the assumption that the historical Jesus, however inadequately understood by the Evangelists, was a wiser and better man than Socrates and Jeremiah, Isaiah and the Buddha, Lao-tze and Hillel?

Secondly: Although Jesus is widely considered mankind's greatest moral teacher, the greatest Christian, not to speak of scholars, have never been able to agree what his moral teachings were. Matthew, and he alone, reports that Jesus said: "Let your Yes be Yes, and your No, No." But the four Evangelists agree in ascribing to Jesus evasive and equivocal answers to plain questions, not only those of the high priest and Pilate; and quite generally the Jesus of the New Testament avoids straightforward statements, preferring parables and hyperboles. Some of the parables are so ambiguous that different Evangelists, not to speak of later theologians, offer different interpretations. Nor have Christians ever been able to agree on the import of the hyperboles of the Sermon on the Mount. Luther, for example, taught that Christ's commandments were intended to teach man his utter incapacity for doing good: man must throw himself on the mercy of God, believing that Christ died for our sins. On concrete moral issues, Jesus can be, and has been, cited on almost all sides. The Buddha and the Hebrew prophets were not so equivocal.

Third: One of the few things about Jesus' moral teachings that seems fairly clear is that he was not greatly concerned about social justice. This makes his ethic much less impressive than the prophets'.

Fourth: Albert Schweitzer has argued in considerable detail that this lack of concern was due to the fact that Jesus predicated his entire message on a false belief: namely, that the world was about to come to an end. If Schweitzer is right, as I think he is, Jesus was surely not the wisest of men. And can we call him the greatest moralist unless we accept his radical depreciation of *this* life and his belief in Heaven and Hell?

Finally, the Jesus of the New Testament believed, and was not greatly bothered by his belief, that God would damn and torment the mass of mankind in all eternity. According to all three Synoptic Gospels, he actually reassured his disciples:

"If any one will not receive you or listen to your words, shake off the dust from your feet as you leave that house or town. Truly, I say to you, it shall be more tolerable on the day of judgment for the land of Sodom and Gomorrha than for that town."

This is no isolated dictum; the Sermon on the Mount, for example, is also punctuated by threats of Hell.

Augustine, Aquinas, and Calvin stressed Hell, but many Christian apologists today simply ignore all such passages. A few insist that in a couple of inter-testamentary apocalypses we find far more detailed visions of Hell. They do not mention that these apocalypses would not be known today if it had not been for the esteem in which the early Christians held them. For the Jews rejected them while accepting the humane teachings of men like Hillel and Akiba. Rabbi Akiba, a contemporary of Paul and the Evangelists, taught that "only those who possess no good deeds at all will descend into the netherworld"; also that "the punishment of the wicked in Gehinnom lasts twelve months."

Of course, Jesus also stressed love, citing—or agreeing with a Pharisee who cited—Moses. But this as well as the fact that he said some lovely things and told some fine parables is hardly sufficient to establish the Christian claims about him: that much he has in common with Moses, Micah, and Hosea, with the Buddha, Confucius, and Lao-tze, to name a mere half-dozen teachers who preceded him by a few centuries.

It might be countered that the story of Jesus is the best possible symbol of love. But is it? Consider the story the way it looks to people not committed to, and prejudiced in favor of, Christianity: God caused a virgin, betrothed to Joseph, to conceive His Own Son, and this Son had to be betrayed, crucified, and resurrected in order that all those— and only those—might be saved who should both believe this story and be baptized and eat and drink on regular occasions what they themselves believe to be the flesh and blood of this Son (or, in some denominations, merely the symbols of His flesh and blood); meanwhile, the rest of mankind suffer eternal torment, and according to many Christian creeds and teachers, they were predestined for damnation by God Himself from the beginning.

One might choose to be a Christian in spite of all this if one could intensely admire the great Christians who came after Jesus. But Peter and Paul, Athanasius and Augustine, Luther and Calvin, seem far less admirable to me, for all their admitted virtues, than Hosea and Micah, Isaiah and Jeremiah, Hillel and Akiba; or the Buddha, Socrates, and Spinoza. Maimonides, unlike Aquinas whom he influenced, did not believe in eternal damnation or that heretics should be executed. Some recent Protestant writers have been wonderfully forthright about Luther's and Calvin's shortcomings; but for candid portraits of the saints one must on the whole turn to non-Catholic writers—with at least one notable exception. In 1950, Malcolm Hay, a Catholic, published one of the most moving books of our time, *The Foot of Pride,* which is admirably frank about some of the most celebrated saints.

In an essay published in Germany in 1939—or rather in a book seized barely before publication by the Gestapo and destroyed except for about half-a-dozen copies—Leo Baeck, probably the greatest rabbi of our time, said something profoundly relevant:

> A good deal of church history is the history of all the things which neither hurt nor encroached upon this piety, all the outrages and all the baseness which this piety was able to tolerate with an assured and undisturbed soul and an untroubled faith. And a spirit is characterized not only by what it does but, no less, by what it permits. . . . The Christian religion, very much including Protestantism, has been able to maintain silence about so much that it is difficult to say what has been more pernicious in the course of time: the intolerance which committed the wrongs or the indifference which beheld them unperturbed.*

This thought may diminish even one's affection for St. Francis, but not one's admiration for the prophets.

The world's other religions remain. If we apply the same criteria, only two issue a real challenge to us, or at least to me: Judaism and Buddhism. I admire Genesis and Job, the Book of Jonah and the Dhammapada far above any book in the New Testament. But popular Buddhism with its profuse idolatry, its relics, and its superstitions repels me, and I have reservations even about the teachings of the Buddha. I admire much of his profound analysis of man's condition: the world has no purpose; it is up to us to give our lives a purpose; and we cannot rely on any supernatural assistance. Life is full of suffering, suffering

---

* The essay, "Romantic Religion," is included in Baeck's *Judaism and Christianity,* translated with an introductory essay, by Walter Kaufmann, Jewish Publication Society, 1958.

is rooted in desire and attachment, and much desire and attachment are rooted in ignorance. By knowledge, especially of the Buddha's teachings, it is possible to develop a pervasive detachment, not incompatible with a mild, comprehensive compassion—and to cease to suffer. But consider the Old Testament and Sophocles, Michelangelo and Rembrandt, Shakespeare and Goethe: the price for the avoidance of all suffering is too high. Suffering and sacrifice can be experienced as worthwhile: one may find beauty in them and greatness through them.

Much of the appeal of Christianity is due to the fact that it contains at least intimations—but really no more than that—of this tragic ethos. But the story of Christ remains uncomfortably similar to the saga of the boss's son who works very briefly in the shop, where he makes a great point of his home and is cruelly beaten by some of his fellow workers, before he joins his father as co-chairman of the board and wreaks horrible revenge. This "happy" end makes most of the Christian martyrs, too, untragic figures. These observations may strike believers as blasphemous, but they might do well to reflect on the manner in which they pass judgment on other religions, and there may be some point in considering how one's own religion must strike those who don't accept it.

Probably the only great religion in which genuine self-sacrifice and tragedy have occupied a central place is Judaism, especially prior to the introduction of belief in any after life. Moses is the very incarnation of humane devotion, wearing himself out in the service of God and men, expecting, and receiving, no reward whatever, but finding his reward in his work. He asks God to destroy him rather than his people and intercedes for them again and again. In the prophets, from Hosea to the songs of the suffering servant, we find the same outlook.

Why, then, do I not accept Judaism? In view of all the things I do not believe, I have no wish to observe the six-hundred-odd commandments and prohibitions that define the traditional Jewish way of life, or to participate in religious services. With most so-called orthodox Jews I have much less in common than with all kinds of other people, Jews and Gentiles. Reform Judaism seems to me to involve compromise, conformism, and the wish to be innocuous. To that extent, it, too, stands opposed to the ethos of the prophets. And if a succession of great Jews should equal the boldness of the prophets, who repudiated the ritual of their day, and go a step further by also renouncing, and denouncing, all kinds of belief—would not this amount to giving up religion?

What remains if you give up the great religions? Many people think: only Communism, Nazism, and immorality. But the morality of Socrates, Spinoza, and Hume compares favorably with Augustine's,

Luther's, and Calvin's. And the evil deeds of Communism and Nazism are not due to their lack of belief but to their false beliefs, even as the evil deeds of the Crusaders, Inquisitors, and witch hunters, and Luther's exhortation to burn synagogues and Calvin's decision to burn Servetus, were due to *their* false beliefs. Christianity, like Islam, has caused more wars than it has prevented; and the Middle Ages, when Europe was Christian, were not a period of peace and good will among men. Does it make sense that those who refuse to let their Yes be Yes and their No, No—those who refuse to reject false beliefs, those who would rather stretch them and equivocate—should have a monopoly on being moral?

Renouncing false beliefs will not usher in the millennium. Few things about the strategy of contemporary apologists are more repellent than their frequent recourse to spurious alternatives. The lesser lights inform us that the alternative to Christianity is materialism, thus showing how little they have read, while the greater lights talk as if the alternative were bound to be a shallow and inane optimism. I don't believe that man will turn this earth into a bed of roses either with the aid of God or without it. Nor does life among the roses strike me as a dream from which one would not care to wake up after a very short time.

Some evils and some kinds of suffering can be abolished, but not all suffering can be eliminated; and the beauty, goodness, and greatness that redeem life on earth are inseparable from suffering. Nietzsche once said: "If you have an enemy, do not requite him evil with good, for that would put him to shame. Rather prove that he did you some good." If life hurts you, the manly thing is neither to whine nor to feel martyred, but to prove that it did you some good.

No one way is the best way of life for all. To me the *Apology* of Socrates, as immortalized by Plato in less than thirty pages, presents a challenge from which I cannot, and have no wish to, get away. Here is part of Socrates' answer to the charges of impiety and corruption of the Athenian youth, on which he was convicted and put to death:

I am better off than he is—for he knows nothing but thinks he knows, while I neither know nor think I know. . . . If you say to me, . . . you shall be let off, but upon one condition, that you are not to inquire . . . in this way any more, and that if you are caught doing so again you shall die—if this was the condition on which you let me go, I should reply: . . . while I have life and strength I shall never cease from the practice and teaching of philosophy, exhorting anyone whom I meet. . . . Are you not ashamed of heaping up the greatest amount of money and honor and reputation, and caring so little about wisdom and truth? . . . The unexamined life is not worth living. . . . If you suppose that there is no consciousness, but a sleep like the sleep of him that is undisturbed even by dreams, death will be an unspeakable gain. . . . Eternity is then only a single night.

It would be folly to wish to foist this outlook on everybody. Professors of philosophy discourage and fail a large percentage even of their graduate students and are assuredly not eager to turn all men into philosophers. In philosophy, as in religion, teaching usually involves a loss of dimension; and the Socratic fusion of philosophy and life, critical acumen and passion, laughter and tragic stature is almost unique.

One need not believe in Pallas Athena, the virgin goddess, to be overwhelmed by the Parthenon. Similarly, a man who rejects all dogmas, all theologies, and all religious formulations of beliefs may still find Genesis the sublime book *par excellence*. Experiences and aspirations of which intimations may be found in Plato, Nietzsche, and Spinoza have found their most evocative expression in some sacred books. Since the Renaissance, Shakespeare, Rembrandt, Mozart, and a host of others have shown that this religious dimension can be experienced and communicated apart from any religious context. But that is no reason for closing my heart to Job's cry, or to Jeremiah's, or to the Second Isaiah. I do not read them as mere literature; rather, I read Sophocles and Shakespeare with all my being, too.

Moreover, I am so far quite unable to justify one of my central convictions: that, even if it were possible to make all men happy by an operation or a drug that would stultify their development, this would somehow be an impious crime. This conviction is ultimately rooted in the Mosaic challenge: "You shall be holy; for I the Lord your God am holy."

To communicate to others some feeling for man's religious quest, to arouse an aspiration in them which nothing but death can quell, and to develop their critical powers—that is infinitely more important to me than persuading anybody that Shakespeare was right when he wrote these lines:

The cloud-capp'd towers, the gorgeous palaces,
The solemn temples, the great globe itself,
Yea, all which it inherit, shall dissolve;
And, like this insubstantial pageant faded,
Leave not a rack behind. We are such stuff

As dreams are made on, and our little life
Is rounded with a sleep.

I do not believe in any after life any more than the prophets did, but I don't mind living in a world in which people have different beliefs. Diversity helps to prevent stagnation and smugness; and a teacher should acquaint his students with diversity and prize careful criticism far above agreement. His noblest duty is to lead others to think for themselves.

Oddly, millions believe that lack of belief in God, Christ, and Hell leads to inhumanity and cruelty while those who have these beliefs have a monopoly on charity—and that people like myself will pay for their lack of belief by suffering in all eternity. I do not believe that anybody will suffer after death nor do I wish it.

Some scientists tell us that in our own galaxy alone there are probably hundreds of thousands of planets with living beings on them, more or less like those on the earth, and that there are about 100 million galaxies within the range of our telescopes. Man seems to play a very insignificant part in the universe, and my part is surely negligible. The question confronting me is not, except perhaps in idle moments, what part might be more amusing, but what I wish to make of my part. And what I want to do and would advise others to do is to make the most of it: put into it all you have got, and live and, if possible, die with some measure of nobility.

PHILIP SCHARPER

What a Modern Catholic Believes

I WAS A CATHOLIC until my fifteenth year because as an infant I had been carried to the Parish church and baptized. Later I went to a Catholic grade school, learned my religion by rote from the little paperbound catechism, and absorbed the rules of piety laid down by the nuns who taught me—frequent prayer, regular Confession and Communion, and penance for my sins. It was, if you will, a small religious world but a warm one.

When I was fifteen this little world of faith-by-formula, of small but smug religious practices, quite suddenly broke apart under the weight of some books in my father's library. One day I picked from the shelves a copy of the *Confessions* of Jean Jacques Rousseau which had slipped between the *Confessions* of St. Augustine and the *Apologia pro vita sua* of Cardinal Newman. I had some suspicion, I remember, that the confessions of this Frenchman whose name I could not pronounce would be more interesting than those of a Saint or a Cardinal of the Church.

And as it turned out they were. I was fascinated by Rousseau, read him closely, and soon felt that I was a very liberated young man indeed. I became more and more resentful of the Jesuit high-school teachers who were then in charge of my education. Their philosophy, needless to say, was based on a less optimistic view of man and boy than Rousseau's. He at least told me that I was innately noble, that I possessed enormous natural powers which only needed to be released. My Jesuit teachers merely warned me against lustful desires of the flesh, against the dangers of overbearing pride in body and mind. I much preferred Rousseau's estimate of me to theirs.

A footnote supplied by the helpful editor sent me to the *Life of Jesus* by Ernest Renan, the nineteenth-century philosopher, orientalist, and heretic who portrayed Christ as a young humanitarian going about Palestine preaching sermons on love. I sympathized with his romantic view of the Gospels as a series of beautiful legends and with his rejection of Catholic doctrine. During the summer I read him and Rousseau, I kept up the externals of Catholicism, but secretly I had my own private version of its fundamentals: Mary was the "Ideal Woman," the Mass a "moving drama," the Church itself the "protector of the poor." When I returned to school in the fall, I could feel only a smug and pitying superiority toward my Jesuit teachers: they were blind to the gross and insupportable superstitions to which they had dedicated their lives. I was free of all that.

But I soon found that I was quite miserable in my freedom. And no matter how much I tried to combat it, my sense of misery grew worse. Looking back—as I often have done since—I do not believe that this misery was caused by the pangs of guilt, by the nostalgia for the warmth of the nest to which a facile psychology might attribute it. It was caused, I believe, by one fact only: I had wrenched myself free from reality and felt that I was slipping into an aimless and incomplete world.

Without sensing the irony, I carried my doubts and my misery to one of my Jesuit teachers. When I told him of my reading, my loss of faith, my sense of pain, he did not, as I had expected, become furious or sorrowful. Instead, he gave me a book by a well known Jesuit who had not long ago left the Church; without scorn or sarcasm of any sort he told me that in it I would find better arguments for leaving the Church than in Renan or Rousseau. "When you have finished it," he said, "I suggest you read over the Gospels at least twice." I read the ex-priest's exposé and closed the book feeling profoundly sorry for him. I read the Gospels over three times and "re-entered" the Catholic Church.

My crisis of faith, then, was dealt with by a Catholic priest who gave me what most people would regard as Protestant or even rationalist advice: consider carefully the criticism of the Church and read carefully the Gospels.

I have gone over the incident at some length only because so many non-Catholics seem to think of our faith as frozen, passive, blind, unquestioning. Nothing could be further from the truth. The authoritarian structure of Catholicism cannot reach into the depths of a man's conscience and forbid him to consider alternatives. I cannot accept the Church's authority on the Church's authority. If ever I were to become convinced that Catholicism were false I would be obliged, *in conscience,* to leave the Church.

So, far from outgrowing the curiosity of my adolescence, I still study criticisms of the historical credibility of the Gospels, of the possibility of divine revelation, of the doctrines of the Church. Rousseau and Renan have been followed in my reading by the commentaries of modern positivists such as Bertrand Russell, existentialists such as Sartre, and the analyses of the Gospels which have been made by such theologians as Bultmann.

Many of these writers challenge the story of Christ's life in the Gospels and of course this is easy enough to do. There are few contemporary records which parallel the events of these books—although even pagan sources confirm some of them—and it is not difficult to label their rough-grained details as "myths" if one can relate them to pre-existing beliefs and if one does not believe them.

But I have never seen solid historical evidence which contradicts the essentials of the Gospels; if it were offered, I could not close my mind to it. Nor could I, or do I, close my mind to the differing interpretations of the message, the implications, the "consistencies" and "inconsistencies" of the Gospels that intelligent men have been making for hundreds of years.

My Catholic faith, then, is being tested almost daily, and every day, in a dozen little ways, I make up *my* mind about it. (Many of my non-Catholic friends act toward me as if I believed in my pastor, Bishop, and Pope—and *these* gentlemen believe in God.) In this constant testing of faith I have always arrived at the same answer: I believe in

A Person, Jesus Christ, who proclaimed himself to be true God and true man and founded a Church which was to proclaim his Gospel, a message of love to all men for all time. This belief of mine means that I accept divine revelations made to people nearly two thousand years ago. They said they saw Christ on Earth and heard his message. I have not, and yet believe the revelations to be true. Why do I?

There are many reasons for this faith but the most important one for me is contained in the word Person. For the Catholic the experience of Christ is an encounter with a Person. This fundamental element of Catholicism seems the most difficult one for the non-Catholic to understand. It is not an encounter of the human mind or heart with an abstract idea, or with an allegory, or with a series of historical events. The Mass, the great prayer of the Church, is not a symbolic rite. It is a renewal, not in symbol but in fact, of Christ's sacrifice for man.

The Church places so much importance upon this personal encounter of Christ and man that she insists that the Catholic face up to the encounter every Sunday, and makes it possible the other six days by the daily Masses in her Church. The climax and the consummation of the encounter, the Mass, takes place in the act called Communion. Here the priests and the people receive the total Christ, God and Man, present—not in metaphor, but in fact—within the small consecrated wafer called the Host.

But in what sense, the non-Catholic is likely to ask, does the encounter take place in fact? In what sense do Catholics mean that Christ is in fact present in a wafer the size of a half-dollar? Obviously it is not a fact in the sense of an observable or measurable phenomenon. St. Thomas Aquinas wrote of the Presence of Christ in the Host: "Sight, touch, taste, all fail; only hearing can be trusted." By "hearing," Aquinas meant both the promise of Christ in the Gospels that he would give to men his flesh and his blood, and the tradition of the Church which teaches that the promise was literal. For the Catholic, then, the encounter with the Person of Christ is not an impression of the senses but it *is* an experience he can feel with all his being; he cannot prove to a scientist that it takes place but it is one of the most profound facts of his life.

Of course, for the skeptic who demands hard physical evidence before acknowledging the reality of an experience, this encounter is a self-deception. But it might be recalled that it is an experience shared by millions of people all over the world, including many highly trained in discriminating the evidence of both the senses and the sensibilities—atomic physicists and psychoanalysts, secular college presidents and seismographers, Supreme Court Justices and novelists like Mauriac,

Greene, and Waugh. This is not proof that the encounter is "true" but simply a reason why it should not be glibly dismissed, as it so often is, as "false."

The experience of Christ as a Person stands at the center of all Catholicism, and for me the discovery of it, after the years of smug observance and the crisis of doubt I have described, was the beginning of real understanding of the Catholic faith, the divine revelations on which it is based, and the role of the Church in it. I began to understand that religion is the surrender of the human being to an invading God and the function of the Church is to make clear the terms of that surrender. The Church tries to insure that the worshiper is not panicked or scared into retreat by his religious feeling but shows him a way in which he can fully give himself to the Person he has come to know as all-loving.

What may seem to the non-Catholic to be a pile of stones, a hierarchy, an institution became for me the place which makes possible a profoundly meaningful personal encounter. There was little difficulty, then, for me to think of the Church as the "Bride of Christ" from whose womb, the baptismal font, I had been brought forth into life fifteen years before. The terms—bride, womb, birth—must, I fear, either offend or amuse many; but I have used them because they indicate the essential personalism of the Catholic vision, which is for me one of the abiding attractions of the Catholic faith.

Our own age, in its own way, has become intensely aware of the human personality, particularly of the dangers to it posed by the pressures, the machines, the organization, of modern industrial society. One of the most significant tasks of modern philosophers has been to distinguish between true and false encounters between persons. Gabriel Marcel's concept of "presence," Emmanuel Mournier's philosophy of "attention," for example, are both intended to describe the authentic encounter of persons in a world where they have become all too rare.

Perhaps the best known of these personalist thinkers is Martin Buber, the Jewish philosopher and storyteller who now teaches at the Hebrew University in Jerusalem. For Buber, true and direct communication between persons involves a relation between an "I" and a "Thou" and he uses the single word "I-Thou" to express the directness, the uniqueness, the awareness of oneself and the other upon which a genuine relationship is founded. In a recent essay, Jacob Trapp says of Buber's word "I-Thou": "The young child speaks it, the savage speaks it, before he even knows the words, by seizing the relationship in a flash and counter-flash of meaning . . . the separation into 'I' and 'Thou' comes later." But "I-Thou" relations may become degraded into "I-It"

relations which involve an encounter not of true persons but of objects
—or people who are considered as objects—and this, Buber thinks, is
especially true of our society. The modern crisis, he has said, "is the
tyranny of the exuberantly growing 'It.'" In a world mushrooming with
things and organization, as Trapp puts it, "the precious I-Thou moments seem rare, strange, lyric, and dramatic episodes and are the stuff
of Martin Buber's mystical and religious experience." God, to Buber, is
the "Eternal Thou."

For me, Buber's philosophical insights are no less profound and
relevant to today's religious dilemmas because he is not a Catholic.
But as a Catholic I have found that the relationship of persons he
describes has its fullest expression in the Holy Communion. I know
no union more intimate than this, in which the human person strives
to summon into unity all he is in order to meet the Divine Person who
has both sought and made possible this most incredible of personal
encounters.

One cannot—or at least I cannot—satisfactorily describe this union.
I have known human love, as a child, parent, friend, and husband, and
each of these unions is, in the end, ineffable. How much less subject
to description is the union wherein one believes that he holds within
himself Jesus Christ, God Incarnate.

But at first, it can be said, the encounter is usually distressing. I
am aware of my dullness and distraction and incapacity to love. But I
am also aware that God is within me and I try to respond to that fact.
In me, at this moment all history meets and whatever I know of reality
engulfs me—I have received Christ, "born of the Father before all ages,"
who "under Pilate was crucified" yet who "lives and reigns forever."
I feel that the ancient myths meet in me and are clarified. I have been
with Beowulf beneath the sea and gone with Orpheus beneath the
earth. I am aware of death, confront it, and invite the future that
includes it—not only actual death, but the metaphorical one, the daily
dying in which the "old man" of sin and self-will is crucified in order
that the "new man" of faith and justice might be born.

This union is not for the individual Catholic alone—just the opposite is true. I have known Christ, in deep, dark union; I must therefore
share his concerns and make his purposes my own as I leave the Church
and go into the community of men. One of the effects of Communion
upon the Catholic is to multiply his nerve ends, to make him more
aware of the sufferings and needs of his fellow men everywhere, in
whom he sees Christ and with whom he must try to establish a true
and loving encounter.

For Christ, the love of God was inseparable from the love of man.

It was of the outcast, the hungry, the imprisoned, the sick that he said: "If you have done it unto one of these—you have done it unto me." To cheat the butcher, calumniate the baker, or cuckold the candlestick maker is to sin against Christ. So the Catholic must try to see Christ everywhere; he must try to fill his being with the spirit of the Person he has come to know.

In stressing as I have the theme of persons within Catholicism, I would not imply for a moment that this theme was missing from either Judaism or Protestantism or indeed that agnostics, humanists, or other secular thinkers were unaware of it. But it is precisely the lack of emphasis on the personal and the intimate which makes the other faiths I know of untenable for me.

However courageous the secular creeds may be in confronting a world of suffering and despair, however optimistic they may be in hoping for men to "progress" toward some kind of brotherhood, they seem to me sadly incomplete and blind to the reality of the Person who purely embodies the values they generally agree upon. Clearly one of us is wrong.

But why can't I be a Protestant or a Jew? I have no expert knowledge of these religions and am aware how painfully little I know about them. But from what I know of them, I feel that both Protestantism and Judaism suffer from a cast of mind which I would call Grecian— an affinity for the abstract and a corresponding uneasiness in the presence of the definite, the felt, the experienced. When the Greeks tell of their Gods, the Gods generally become either man writ large, as in Homer, or an abstract idea written with a capital letter—Plato's Good or Aristotle's Mind. "When Athena was thought of as goddess of wisdom," we are told, "she soon ceased to be Athena and became Wisdom."

My own impression—and it is little more than that—is that contemporary American Judaism constantly threatens to freeze the God of Abraham, Isaac, and Jacob into an abstraction; the relation to God of many Jews I know does not seem an intimate one and sometimes seems uneasy and uncertain, however it may have been in the past.

Contemporary Protestantism seems to me to exhibit a similar drive toward the abstract or at least the partial. On the fundamental question of Christianity—"What Think Ye of Christ?"—the voices of my Protestant friends, their pastors, and their theologians are raised in a strong but a very dissonant chorus. The Protestant theology I read with interest and profit tells me of the "Jesus of History" of Albert Schweitzer, the "Christ of the Faith" of liberal Protestantism, the "achievement of authentic selfhood" of Bultmann, or the "man at his best" of some of the more popular preachers.

I cannot enter into personal union, an interchange of knowledge and love, with these partial Christs, nor can I wait until the theologians have arrived at a synthesis. Their art is long but my time is fleeting. Feeling with all my heart that God can be close to me, a part of me, I find time here and now made meaningful.

Because of this difference in the way we conceive God, then, I feel that time itself passes differently for the Catholic. For the Jew and the Protestant, it often seems as if God acted once—in making a Covenant with Israel, or in the individual Protestant's decision for Christ— and now their relation to him is established. Never by their words, but by their tones when they speak of God, and by their style of life, my Protestant and Jewish friends seem to tell me that their relation to God is secure, the issue of their lives assured. But for the Catholic, time is registered in the daily, hourly, and momentary possibility that man may turn away from God, may not live up to the enormous responsibilities that a close and personal relation with a loving God has imposed on him.

It is not enough for the Catholic to be aware of *man's* lack of perfection and his sinfulness. He is constantly aware of *his own* inadequacy, his own sin and need for repentance. He is encouraged to examine his conscience twice a day and go to Confession frequently.

This Catholic sense of intense personal relation—and intense obligation—to God may lead to a Christian experience more dominated by fear than by love. But it can also infuse otherwise commonplace problems in daily life with spiritual seriousness and vigor.

Perhaps a concrete example will illustrate what I mean: At a recent Catholic inter-racial conference, an examination of conscience was proposed covering such points as: "May a Catholic cast his vote for a racist candidate otherwise competent? May a Catholic college send its Negro players to a segregated contest? May a Catholic sit in a designated section of a segregated bus?"

These questions are not some kind of political poll; they are pressed against the moral conscience of the individual Catholic who is guided by the pulpit, catechism, and confessional, as well as by the example of Christ. I am not suggesting that Catholics are morally superior to any group. I see no evidence of that. They are all sinners but they are sinners with high—and explicit—moral principles.

I am much more aware of the role of the spirit within the Church than the role of authority, but I realize that when a non-Catholic looks at the Church he often tends to see a formidable authoritarian structure —an "It" in Buber's language. But for the Catholic the Church has a Divine Commission: to bring about the personal encounter I have described and to make clear its consequences. And she does. When a Catholic looks at the Church, he sees a "Thou."

The Church to me, therefore, cannot be the Pope, Cardinal Spellman, the Knights of Columbus, the Legion of Decency, nor that incredible Irish Monsignor who drives a Cadillac, golfs four days a week, and preaches against the Community Chest—he has to answer for his conscience and I for mine, and I am happy with that arrangement.

Nor can the Church be represented for me by the "wicked Popes" singly or in concert. I believe the Popes infallible in a very restricted area but I could never deem them perfect—how could I, when history shows some of them to have been spectacularly imperfect?

I do not defend the Spanish Inquisition, past or present; I accept the constitutional separation of Church and State (as does the American Catholic hierarchy); I welcomed the Supreme Court decisions in the "Miracle" and "La Ronde" cases (as many Catholics did not); I think only equitable the recent decision of the New York City hospitals which permits doctors to use birth-control therapy if the patient desires.

I am not alone in these views, nor am I in the least "suspected" for them. The *Commonweal*, a Catholic weekly paper (on which I was once an editor), has supported them all; and, without formal ecclesiastical objection, it has attacked McCarthyism, advocated aid to the Communist governments of Tito and Gomulka, deplored the treatment of Protestants in Spain, and called for increased federal aid to public schools.

All this may sound suspiciously like a Catholic campaigning for public office but I am simply trying to show something of the freedom an individual Catholic can enjoy vis-à-vis the authoritarian structure of the Church—a Church which, it might be noted, has canonized as Saints some of those Catholics who openly challenged its abuses of authority during their lifetimes. St. Joan, after all, was burned at the stake by that enduringly mischievous combination—a coalition of prelates and politicians. Catholics are not obliged to acquiesce in abuses that may be perpetrated by such a coalition today; on the contrary, they can and should, take a strong stand against them.

No matter how badly individual Catholics—lay or cleric—may betray the ideal of the Church, this ideal is not blind obedience, but devotion to Truth. For the Catholic, God is Truth and is mocked by feigning, rationalization, expediency, or the assertion of naked power in his name. As a Catholic I feel that I have encountered the truths of God within the Church and have come to know these truths only by a constant examination of my faith, myself, and the Church with all the reason at my command. In the Church, therefore, I have found the "perfect freedom of the sons of God" and I grieve to realize that in our time and place so many Catholics have distorted her image into that of an inhuman machine designed for the creation and conservation of power.

Far closer to the truth is the image once evoked by Gerard Manley Hopkins, the Jesuit poet. In a sermon which probably shocked his Victorian congregation he compared the Church to a cow with full udders, patiently waiting for the world to come and be fed.

In its very homeliness it says much that I should like to say, but have been unable to. At any rate, there she stands, brooding over time and history. And I stand with her because (if I may borrow a phrase from Martin Luther) God help me, I can do no other.

What are the alternatives? I have tried to show (all too sketchily) why I cannot consider secularism and do not accept Judaism or Protestantism, although I am grateful for the common history I share with each. What little I know of Oriental religions reminds me of persistent thrusts within the Catholic tradition which American Catholics are apt to forget—the primacy of contemplation, the attitude of reverence before the whole of God's reality, the realization that religion must not be conceived exclusively as either theology, ethics, or institution. I am grateful for these reminders of the rich complexity within my own tradition provided by Oriental religions, but I am not impelled to join the American devotees of them.

So I am still stuck with the Roman Catholic Church, the Sacred Cow of Gerard Manley Hopkins. She offers me life, now and forever. I have never been swayed much by philosophical arguments on either side regarding life after death. But I do most firmly believe it on the promise of Christ, which has been preserved for me by the Church.

It will be the deepest of all personal encounters—knowing and loving God for all eternity. The "I" with enlightened intellect and undistracted will, the "Thou" the unchanging God who has, I know, pursued me all my life and who will, I hope, catch up with me at the end.

ARTHUR A. COHEN

Why I Choose to Be a Jew

UNTIL THE PRESENT DAY, the Jew could not *choose* to be a Jew—history forced him to accept what his birth had already defined.

During the Middle Ages he was expected to live as a Jew. He could escape by surrendering to Islam or Christianity, but he could *not* choose to remain anonymous. In the nineteenth century, with the growth of nationalism, Christianity became the ally of patriotism. The Jews of Europe were compelled to prove that their religion did not compromise their loyalty to King, Emperor, Kaiser, or Tsar. But no matter how desperately they tried to allay suspicion by assimilation or conversion, the fact of their birth returned to plague them. Finally, in the Europe of Nazism and Communism, the Jew could not choose— on any terms—to exist at all.

In the United States today, it is at last possible to choose *not* to remain a Jew. The mass migrations of Jews from Europe have ended and the immigrant generation which was tied to the European pattern of poverty and voluntary segregation is dying off. Their children, the second generation, were as suspicious of the gentile American society in which they grew up as they were condescending toward the ghetto world of their parents. The second generation, however, made the Jewish community economically secure and fought anti-Semitism so effectively that, though still present, it is no longer severe. *Their* children—the third generation of Jews now in its twenties and thirties— are able to choose.

For this generation the old arguments no longer hold. It was once possible to appeal to history to prove that Jewish birth was inescapable, but history is no proof to those who are—as many Jews are—indifferent to its evidence. Loyalty to the Jewish people and pride in the State of Israel are no longer enough to justify the choice to be a Jew. The postwar American Jew no longer needs the securities which European Jewry found in Jewish Socialism, Jewish Nationalism, the revival of Hebrew, and the Zionist Movement. *Fear*—the fear of anti-Semitism— and *hope*—the hope for the restoration of Israel—are no longer effective reasons for holding onto Jewish identity. The fear has waned and the hope has been fulfilled.

The irresistible forces of history no longer *compel* the Jew to

287

choose Judaism. In many cases, moreover, he is choosing to repudiate Judaism or to embrace Christianity. I do not say the numbers are alarming. That they exist at all is, however, symptomatic. It is only the exceptional—those who are searching deeply or are moved profoundly, who ever reject or embrace. The majority tend more often to undramatic indifference—to slide into the routine of maturity without asking questions for which no meaningful answers have been offered.

Given the freedom to choose I have decided to embrace Judaism. I have not done so out of loyalty to the Jewish people or the Jewish state. My choice was religious. I chose to believe in the God of Abraham, Isaac, and Jacob; to acknowledge the law of Moses as the Word of God; to accept the people of Israel as the holy instrument of divine fulfillment; to await the coming of the Messiah and the redemption of history.

Many Jews will find my beliefs unfamiliar or unacceptable—perhaps outrageous. The manner in which I arrived at them is not very interesting in itself, but I think two aspects of my experience are worth noting because they are fairly common: I come from a fundamentally unobservant Jewish home and my first religious inclination was to become a Christian.

My parents are both second-generation American Jews whose own parents were moderately religious, but, newly come to America, lacked either the education or the opportunity, patience, and time to transmit to their children their own understanding of Judaism. My parents went to synagogue to observe the great Jewish holidays—Passover, the New Year, and the Day of Atonement—but worship at home, knowledge of the liturgy, familiarity with Hebrew, concern with religious thought and problems, did not occupy them. Their real concern—and they were not unique—was adjusting to American life, achieving security, and passing to their children and those less fortunate the rewards of their struggle.

It would be ungrateful to deny the accomplishments of my parents' generation. They managed to provide their children with secular education and security. But although the flesh was nourished, the spirit was left unattended. When I had finished high school and was ready to leave for college I took with me little sense of what my religion, or any religion, involved. I knew only that in these matters I would have to fend for myself.

When an American Jew studies at an American university it is difficult for him not to be overwhelmed—as I was at the University of Chicago—by the recognition that Western culture is a Christian culture, that Western values are rooted in the Greek and Christian tradition. He may hear such phrases as "Judaeo-Christian tradition" or "the Hebraic element in Western culture," but he cannot be deluded into thinking that this is more than a casual compliment. The University of Chicago, moreover, insisted that its students study seriously the philosophic sources of Western culture, which, if not outspokenly Christian, were surely non-Jewish. I soon found myself reading the classics of Christian theology and devotion—from St. Augustine and St. Anselm through the sermons of Meister Eckhart.

It was not long before my unreligious background, a growing and intense concern with religious problems, and the ready access to compelling Christian literature all combined to produce a crisis—or at least my parents and I flattered ourselves that this normal intellectual experience was a religious crisis. The possibility of being a Christian was, however, altogether real. I was rushed, not to a psychoanalyst, but to a Rabbi—the late Milton Steinberg, one of the most gifted and profound Jewish thinkers of recent years. Leading me gently, he retraced the path backwards through Christianity to Judaism, revealing the groundwork of Jewish thought and experience which supported what I have come to regard as the scaffolding of Christian "unreason."

It was extremely important to me to return to Judaism through the medium of Christianity—to choose after having first received the impress of Western education and Christian thought. Since it would have been possible to become a Christian—to accept Christian history as my history, to accept the Christian version of Judaism as the grounds of my own repudiation of Judaism, to believe that a Messiah had redeemed *me*—I could only conclude that Judaism was not an unavoidable fate, but a destiny to be chosen freely.

My own conversion and, I suspect, the conversion of many other Jews to Judaism, was effected, therefore, through study, reflection, and thought. What first seized my attention was not the day-to-day religious life of the Jewish community around me, but rather principles, concepts, and values. I had first to examine the pressing theological claims of a seemingly triumphant Christianity, before I could accept the ancient claims of a dispersed, tormented, and suffering Jewry.

This may sound reasonable enough to a gentile, but I must point out that it is an extremely unconventional attitude for a Jew. Historically, Judaism has often looked with disfavor upon theology. And today, despite the fact that traditional emotional ties can no longer be relied upon to bind the third generation to Jewish life, American Jewish leadership has not seen fit to encourage the examination of the theological bases of Jewish faith. In fact, the leading rabbinical seminaries teach little Jewish theology as such, give scant attention to Jewish philosophic literature, and have allowed the apologetic comparison of religious beliefs to become a moribund discipline. Even practical problems involving some theological insight—the nature of marriage, the Jewish attitude toward converts, the life of prayer—are dispatched with stratospheric platitudes, or not discussed at all.

Why this distrust of theology? I suspect that some Jewish leaders fear—perhaps not unjustifiably—that theological scrutiny of what they mean by God, Israel, and Law might reveal that they have no theology at all. Others no doubt fear—again not unjustifiably—that their unbending interpretations of Jewish Law and life might have to be revised and re-thought. Theology often produces a recognition of insufficiency, an awareness that valid doctrine is being held for the wrong reasons and that erroneous doctrine is being used to rationalize right action. But the major Jewish argument against Jewish theology is that it is a Christian pastime—that it may, by insinuation and subtle influence, Christianize Judaism. In this view, Christianity is a religion of faith, dogma, and theology and Judaism is a religion which emphasizes *observance* of God's Law, not speculation about it.

For me this argument is a vast oversimplification. Christianity is not without its own structure of discipline, requirements, and laws— the Roman sacraments and the Lutheran and Anglican liturgy, for example—and this structure does not move with the Holy Spirit as easily as St. Paul might have wished. Judaism, on the other hand, is not tied to the pure act. It has matured through the centuries a massive speculation and mystic tradition which attempts to explain the principles upon which right action are founded. Judaism need not, therefore, regret the renewal of theology. It already has one. It is merely a question of making what is now a minor chord in Jewish tradition sound a more commanding note.

As a "convert" who thinks that theology must come first, what do I believe?

The convert, I must point out, is unavoidably both a thinker and a believer—he thinks patiently and believes suddenly. Yet belief, by itself, cannot evict the demons of doubt and despair. As a believer I can communicate my beliefs, but as a thinker I cannot guarantee that they are certain or will never change. As all things that record the encounter of God and man, beliefs are subject to the conditions of time and history, and the pitiable limitation of our capacity to understand such enormous mysteries. As I shall try to show, however, the four beliefs which I have already set down lie at the center of my faith as a Jew. They depend upon one another; they form a whole; they differ profoundly from the substance of Christian belief.

First, I chose to believe in the God of Abraham, Isaac, and Jacob.

This is to affirm the reality of a God who acts in history and addresses man. Although this God may well be the same as the abstract gods formulated by philosophers, he is still more than these—he is the God who commanded Abraham to quit the land of the Chaldeans and who wrestled with Jacob throughout the night.

The philosopher and the believer must differ in their method. The philosopher begins by examining that portion of reality to which reason allows him access. The believer, however, must at some point move beyond the limits which reason has defined. He may rightly contend that reason points beyond itself, that the rational is real, but that much in human life—evil, suffering, guilt, and love—is terrifyingly real without ever being rationally comprehensible.

Reason may thus push a man to belief, and it is inaccurate to speak of the believer as though he had deserted or betrayed reason. Informed belief demands philosophic criticism and refinement. The believer is bound to uphold his faith in things he cannot see or verify; but he is foolish if he does not try to define what that belief is and clarify the unique ways in which it makes reality meaningful for him.

For me then to believe in the Biblical God, the God of the Patriarchs, the smoking mountain, the burning bush, was not to surrender reason, but to go beyond it. More than accepting the literal words of the Bible, it meant believing in the Lord of History—the God who creates and unfolds history, and observes its tragic rifts and displacements—from the Tower of Babel to the Cold War; who, in his disgust, once destroyed the world with flood and later repented his anger; who, forgoing anger, gave the world counsels of revelation, commencing with the gift of Torah to Moses and continuing through the inspired writings of the ancient rabbis; and who finally—through his involvement with the work of creation—prepares it for redemption.

It may seem difficult—indeed for many years it was—to consider the Bible, which is the source of this belief, as more than the unreliable account of an obscure Semitic tribe. But gradually I came to discover in it an authentic statement of the grandeur and misery of man's daily existence—a statement which I could accept only if I believed in a God who could be addressed as "Lord, Lord."

My second belief is an acknowledgment that *the Law of Moses is the Word of God.* The Bible tells us that the Word of God broke out over the six hundred thousand Hebrews who assembled at the foot of Sinai. That Word was heard by Moses—he who had been appointed to approach and receive. The Word became human—in its humanity, it undoubtedly suffers from the limitation of our understanding—but it lost none of its divinity.

The Law is always a paradox: it is both the free Word of God and the frozen formality of human laws. But the Law of Moses was vastly different from what we usually understand law to be. It is true that in the days before the Temple was destroyed by Titus in 70 A.D. divine law was the enforceable law of the judge and the court; but later the great rabbis who interpreted it conceived of the revelation of God to Israel, not as law in its common usage, but as *Torah*—teaching.

Torah is a fundamental concept for the Jew. Narrowly conceived, it refers to the Pentateuch—the first five books of the Bible which are the pristine source of all Jewish tradition. In them are the laws of the Sabbath and the festivals; the foundations of family and communal morality; and the essentials of Jewish faith—the unity of God, the election of Israel, and the definition of its special mission. But, broadly conceived, Torah refers to *any* teaching which brings man closer to the true God, who is the God of Israel and the Lord of History.

Torah has two aspects—the actual way of law and observance (the *halachah* as it is called in Hebrew) and the theology of the rabbis which interprets that way (called the *aggadah*). By means of both, according to Jewish tradition, God proposes to lead *all* of his creation to fulfillment, to perfect its imperfections, to mend the brokenness of his creatures. The Jewish people—the guardian of the *halachah* and the *aggadah*—has been elected to be pedagogue to all the nations of the world, to become on its behalf "a kingdom of priests and a holy people."

Jews can achieve holiness—the primary objective, I believe, of their religion—neither by prayer nor meditation alone. Judaism values prayer only in conjunction with the act; it praises study only in relation to life.

God does not propose or suggest ways to achieve holiness; he commands them. According to Torah, he lays upon each Jew "the yoke of the commandments." To observe the Sabbath is as much a commandment as is the obligation to daily prayer; the grace which accompanies eating as essential as the study of sacred literature. Although tradition distinguishes between practical and intellectual commandments, it considers both to be equally the expressed will of God. The arbitrary and the reasonable—the dietary laws and the prohibition of homosexuality for example—both proceed from God.

Judaism begins with an explicit fact: the revelation of Torah. Many of its commandments may seem trivial. But it should not be expected that God will leave the trivial to man and concern himself only with the broad, general, and universal. The corruption of man takes place not only in the province of principle, but in the small and petty routine of life. The Torah is therefore exalted and picayune, universal and particular, occupied equally with principle and the details of practice. It tolerates no separation between the holy and the profane —all that is secular must become sacred, all that is profane must be kept open to the transforming power of God.

The exact degree to which Jews should fulfill all the commandments of the Law is one of the most difficult and perplexing dilemmas for modern Jews. Orthodox Jews are in principle obligated to observe all of Jewish Law, Reform Jews have cut observance to a minimum (though there is a movement to increase it), Conservative Jews stand somewhere in between. I will not attempt it in this space, but I believe it is possible to show that the fundamental question is not whether the Jew performs the required acts of observance, but whether he is truly aware of the sacred intention of these acts. One can, for example, recite the blessings over the food one eats and feel nothing of the sanctity of food; on the other hand one can silently acknowledge the holiness of eating, and fulfill the command of God. Both are needed—the blessing and the inner acknowledgment, but the former is surely incomplete without the latter.

The third of my beliefs is, as I have indicated, simply an element of God's revelation in Torah—that *the Jewish people have been chosen as a special instrument of God.*

The Jews did not request the attentions of God. There is significant truth—truth moreover which the rabbis of the Talmud endorse— in the popular couplet: "How odd of God, to choose the Jews." Odd, and unsolicited. The ancient rabbis disclaim particular merit. If anyone possessed merit, they repeat, it was not the generation that fled Egypt and braved the wilderness for forty years, but the generations of the Biblical patriarchs—Abraham, Isaac, and Jacob. They had no organizer such as Moses, nor strength of numbers, nor the miracles of the well, manna, and quail. They made a covenant with God on sheer trust. The generation of Sinai was *compelled* to become the people of God or perish. A God of History grows impatient with delay. The God of Israel was profoundly impatient on Sinai.

This tradition of election should not be confused with racial pride or an attitude of arrogant exclusion toward others. The Jew believes neither that the truth flows in his blood nor that the gentile cannot come to possess it. Judaism is exclusive only in the sense that we affirm we possess important truth which is available to all—everyone can join but only on our terms.

The election of Israel is not a conclusion drawn from history—the survival and endurance of the Jews through twenty centuries of destructive persecution could be no more than blind accident. At best it could be construed as a compliment to the resiliency and stubbornness of the

Jewish people. Judaism has insisted, however—not as a declaration after the fact, but as a principle of its very existence—that it is both a holy nation chosen by God to be his own and a suffering nation destined to endure martyrdom for his sake. God announces not only that "Ye shall be holy unto me; for I the Lord am Holy, and have separated you from the people, that ye should be mine" (Leviticus 20:26) but that "You only have I known of all the families of the earth: therefore I will visit upon you all your iniquities" (Amos 3:2).

Israel is thus called not only to be the example to the nations, but, being the example, is tried all the more sorely for its transgressions. To be sure, this is not a doctrine for the uncourageous. No one even slightly familiar with the agonies of Jewish history could claim that the election of Israel has brought with it particular reward and security. It is, however, precisely the fact of Jewish suffering which makes its election and mission all the more pertinent to the modern world. To have believed and survived in spite of history is perhaps the only evidence which Judaism can offer to the accuracy of its conviction that it is called to be a holy community.

In the face of Christendom and the obvious success which its claims have enjoyed, it may seem foolish or presumptuous for Judaism —a small and insignificant community of believers—to assert my fourth belief: that *Jesus is not the Messiah of which the Bible speaks,* that Christianity has conceived but one more imperfect image of the end, and that *a Messiah is yet to come who will redeem history.*

But there are enduring reasons why Jews cannot accept Jesus as the Messiah. Both Christian and Jew begin with the conviction of the imperfection of man. The Christian argues, however, that creation has been so corrupted by man as to be saved only through the mediation of Jesus. The Jew considers creation imperfect but, rather than corrupt, he finds it rich with unfulfilled possibility. The role of man is to bring creation to that point at which the Messiah can come to glorify man by bringing him the praise of God—not to save him from self-destruction, as Christianity would have it. According to Jewish tradition, Moses died from the kiss of God. It would be fitting to conceive the advent of the Messiah and the Kingdom of God as the bestowal of a kiss.

This does not mean that God congratulates man for his good works but rather that he shares both in the agony of history and in its sanctification. Judaism does not imagine that every day we are getting better and better, and that finally we will reach a point where the Messiah will come. As likely as not, it seems to me, history is coming closer each day to suicide. The mission of Judaism is not to stave off disaster but to enlarge man's awareness of the Divine Presence.

Jews believe, if they are to remain Jews, that the Messiah has not come. They can accept Jesus of Nazareth as little more than a courageous witness to truths to which his own contemporaries in Pharisaic Judaism by and large subscribed. Jesus was, as Martin Buber has suggested, one in the line of "suffering servants" whom God sends forth to instruct the nations. It is to the dogmatizing work of St. Paul that one must ascribe the transformation of "prophet" into "Christ"—and it is therefore St. Paul who severs Jesus from the life of Israel. The rejection of Jesus must now stand to the end of time.

The role of Israel and Judaism, until the advent of the true Messiah, is to outlast the world and its solutions—to examine its complacencies, to deflate its securities, to put its principles to the test of prophetic judgment. This is an aristocratic and painful mission, for though Judaism may address the world and lay claim to it, it does not seek to convert it.

Judaism does not say "The world is not changed—therefore we do not believe in the Messiah." This is only partially true, for the coming of the Messiah will mean more than a reformed world in which the wolf and lamb shall share bread together and war shall cease. This social image of salvation is true as far as it goes, but it does not go far enough. The Messiah is not a handyman or a plumber—his task does not consist in "mending" a world that is temporarily faulty but is essentially perfect. The world is to be transformed—not reformed—by the Messiah.

This transformation will come to pass, Judaism believes, only when the world wishes it so deeply that it cannot abide itself more a single moment. At that moment the Messiah may come. This moment of expectancy has not yet arrived. The rabbis have taught us that I, and all of the House of Israel, prevent him from coming. Of this there is no question, but we cannot avoid concluding that he has not come.

For the Jew who comfortably repeats the rituals of his religion without confronting the principles of faith which they express, and for the Jew who was not aware that Judaism had any principles of faith at all, this personal statement may seem shocking. But I do not think my position or my background are by any means unique. If, as I have argued, the present generation of American Jews is indeed the first generation of Jews in centuries who are free to choose to believe as Jews, then, in my terms at least, my argument is important. Now as never before it will be possible for the Jewish people and the State of Israel to survive, but for Jewish *religion* to perish. For me, and for other believing Jews, it is crucial for mankind that Judaism survive. The mission of Judaism is not completed nor the task of the Jewish people fulfilled. If the Jewish people is an instrument sharpened by God for his own purposes, it must go on serving that purpose, sustaining its burden, and keeping that trust which alone can bring all men to redemption.

WILLIAM WARREN BARTLEY, III

I Call Myself a Protestant

IN 1880, THE RUSSIAN novelist Dostoevsky placed on the lips of Ivan Karamazov, the atheist, the famous legend of the Grand Inquisitor, Cardinal of Seville, who deceived his flock for their own sake.

According to Ivan's tale, Christ had reappeared in Seville and had been promptly imprisoned by the Inquisition. Late at night, the Cardinal—who Ivan describes as also an atheist—visits Christ in the dungeon and attempts to justify to Him his suppression of intellectual and religious freedom in Spain. Describing the believers whom he and those who shared his priestcraft had deceived, the Cardinal insists:

> All will be happy, all the millions of creatures except the hundred thousand sufferers who have taken upon themselves the curse of the knowledge of good and evil. Peacefully they will die, peacefully they will expire in Thy name and beyond the grave they will find nothing but death. But we shall keep the secret, and for their happiness we shall allure them with the reward of heaven and eternity. . . . Judge us if Thou canst and darest. . . . I too prized the freedom with which Thou hast blessed men. . . . But I awakened and would not serve madness. I turned back and joined the ranks of those who have corrected Thy work.

Four hundred years after the Grand Inquisitor, and three quarters of a century after Dostoevsky, a man who is often called the twentieth century's greatest Protestant theologian—Paul Tillich—has endorsed a similar kind of priestcraft. Like the Grand Inquisitor, Tillich does *not* believe in the popular "God of Theism," the God who answers prayer and offers men a life beyond the grave. Frequently he has emphasized the contrast between his own theology and faiths which hold to a more literal interpretation of the Biblical teachings. In his *Dynamics of Faith* (1957), for instance, Tillich writes [italics mine]:

The primitive period of individuals and groups consists in the inability to separate the creations of symbolic imagination from the facts which can be verified through observation and experiment. *This stage has a full right of its own and should not be disturbed, either in individuals or in groups, up to the moment when man's questioning mind breaks the natural acceptance of the mythological visions as literal.*

Tillich contrasts this stage with

the second stage of literalism, the conscious one, which is aware of the questions but represses them, half consciously, half unconsciously. The tool of repression is usually an acknowledged authority with sacred qualities like the Church or the Bible to which one owes unconditional surrender. *This stage is still justifiable, if the questioning power is very weak and can easily be answered.* It is unjustifiable if a mature mind is broken in its personal center by political or psychological methods, split in his unity, and hurt in his integrity.

Tillich and the Grand Inquisitor seem agreed on a number of points. Both believe that it is better to let *innocent* ignorance prevail. When doubts do arise in an individual, they leave it to his minister to decide whether his doubts are weak enough to be "refuted" or whether he must be made one of the "hundred thousand sufferers" who inhabit the inner circle of the broken myth. Where Tillich and the Inquisitor most clearly *disagree* is over a positive program of enforced ignorance: Tillich would never conduct an inquisition.

I have brought these two passages together neither to condemn Tillich nor to suggest that his motives are identical with those of the Inquisitor. Much as he hated the position championed by the Cardinal, Dostoevsky could not help portraying him sympathetically as one who "all his life loved humanity." At least as much must be said for Tillich. Indeed, it is ironical that such a comparison can be made at all, for in his intellectual autobiography Tillich specifically mentions his personal *fight* against the figure of the Grand Inquisitor as "a decisive element of my theological thought."

My aim, rather, has been to bring home two points which anyone who is to understand modern Protestantism must grasp. In Protestant Christendom today, as in Dostoevsky's Seville, the beliefs and religious expectations of those learned in theology are very often not only different from and more complex than those of the average man in the pew; *they contradict them.* Agreement is no longer over *beliefs,* but over *passwords,* passwords which one may take literally, symbolically, or in some other way, depending on one's theological sophistication.

Nor are the theologians at all eager—and in fact they are rather worried—about communicating their beliefs to the "believers." They have only added to the breakdown of real communication by using various circumlocutions which make their break with traditional Christianity seem less serious than it is: we get different kinds of "truth," different kinds of "belief," different kinds of "knowledge."

"Well, yes," the theologian nods when pressed, "I don't believe that there is an afterlife, but the notion of an afterlife is *symbolically true,* you know."

"Yes, Virginia, there is a God."

The church services which result are weird pantomimes. Kneeling before the same altar in the same service, saying the same creeds and singing the same hymns, one man worships the God who acts literally, another worships the God who acts metaphorically, a third worships the God who acts symbolically, and yet another worships the God who doesn't act at all.

Serious division among Protestants over matters of belief is, of course, nothing new. Rarely, however, has it been over such fundamental issues. Past arguments usually have focused on matters like evolution, the nature and number of the sacraments, the form of baptism, the organization of the clergy. Atheism was largely left to those outside the church. Today the disagreement *within* the churches is over whether the traditional God exists and whether there is an afterlife.

The new disagreement, unlike past disputes, is not one among the various sects and church groups. Closer interchurch co-operation on organizational and political levels has, in fact, accompanied the growth of the newer series of disputes. For a superficial agreement over formulas, words, and symbols has helped to make co-operation on such peripheral matters possible.

The personal tensions and anxieties hidden under this surface unity are widely known. It is no secret, for instance, that there has been a rising number of nervous problems among younger ministers. Many denominations now administer psychological tests beforehand to all ministerial candidates.

Whether such tests are directed at the root of the trouble is quite another question. Yale Professor Wesley Shrader has attributed ministerial high tension not primarily to the initial psychological troubles of the clergy, but to the multiple "roles" they are expected to play *after* ordination. His remarks about role-playing are supported by many recent reports. For example, former Congregational minister Thomas S. Vernon, now teaching at the University of Michigan, has sorrowfully described the churchly game of "Let's pretend." The church members confide to each other that they no longer believe their church's doctrines, but "would not dare to let their minister know they felt that way." And the minister tells *his* confidants (when he dares to have any) that he doesn't believe the doctrines either, but "would not dare to say so from the pulpit"!

It is due largely to situations like these that the leading question among the thinking young members of the church today has become this: If I believe that *the most fundamental doctrines* of a church which I deeply love are false, what shall be my policy in regard to that church? Shall I withdraw to the Unitarians, or to the somewhat troubled indifference of non-affiliation? Or shall I remain within the fold and play at believing?

This is certainly the question in terms of which my own religious development took place. And it is a question which was bound to arise with particularly compelling force in Protestantism rather than in one of the two other main religious divisions of the Western World. Roman Catholicism effectively retreated from the problem in 1907, when the papal encyclical *Pascendi Gregis* condemned "modernism." Within Judaism, which contains an old tradition stressing action and the religious way of the communal life more than credos, the question— although it bothers many Jews—has never reached the urgency with which it challenges and confuses the members of a doctrine-ridden and Bible-centered Protestantism.

There is no denying that the attitude I have described—a combination of a type of atheism with sympathetic membership in a religious body—exists among many young church members today. But it was not until last September that a personal experience forced me to realize vividly how widespread this attitude is, even within the most solid bastions of the church. I was attending—at a camp on Lake Michigan—the annual conference of a graduate fellowship program sponsored by one of America's great educational foundations. One of the main requirements for appointment to these fellowships is a conviction that the study of religion, and especially of the Christian tradition, is a vitally important element of a liberal education. Ninety-five per cent of the fellows are church members.

After one of the meetings a random group of eight of us gathered for an evening of conversation. Before it was over, we found (to the surprise, I think, of all of us) that each of us was an atheist in the traditional sense of the term—we denied the existence of "The Living God" of historic Christianity. We disagreed somewhat about whether the various "philosophers' Gods" of recent invention—such as Whitehead's "grounds of concreteness" or Tillich's "Being Itself"—existed or were even meaningful conceptions. But we were agreed that even if such things were more than definitions, and did "exist," they were not the Gods that were being worshiped by most of the people in Christian pews. Twice more during the conference I participated in similar discussions with altogether different groups. Each time the result was the same!

While I share this attitude, I doubt that I arrived at it in a typical way. It was much more difficult for me to accept this position because my strong religious background had *not* been a repressive one that I would have wished to react against.

I grew up in a devoutly religious home of traditional Protestant belief. By the end of the second grade I had finished reading the entire Bible for the first time. It seemed a splendid and exciting mystery story with which my Oz stories couldn't compare. Before finishing grammar school I had read the Bible another half-dozen times and was fetching books on theology from the library. I remember quarreling with my cousins over evolution in the fifth grade and lying awake nights over the problem of transubstantiation while in the eight grade. (I was *for* both evolution and transubstantiation.)

Throughout high school, the study and practice of religion were an exciting quest; I was left completely free to come to whatever conclusions I thought correct; no attempt was ever made to "correct" any erroneous belief. I stress this early development simply because during the past few years a number of people have insisted to me that my present rejection of traditional theology *must* be the result of a repressive religious upbringing against which I am revolting.

When I entered Harvard College I encountered all the Big Questions in the lecture hall and naturally faced new problems about religion. But my religious background was so strong that the common freshman and sophomore reaction to religion never touched me. I assumed that one should expect to modify and to develop one's religious beliefs, to grow in religion as one grew older. I assumed that any problem *I* might have was all explained in some theological system *somewhere*. I had learned very well the theologian's vivid warning that "one must not throw out the baby with the bathwater." Since then I have learned that one man's baby is another man's bathwater.

Having put away my doubts, I also gave up really active consideration of theological problems: there was too much else to do and to learn at Harvard College. One by one, however—and unconsciously—I was undermining the foundations of my belief. While majoring in history, I had become deeply challenged by certain problems in the methodology of history. In order to solve them, I found—much as I at first disliked the task—that I had to learn some philosophy, and to study contemporary analytical philosophy, especially philosophy of science. So, at the beginning of my senior year, I dropped my program in Renaissance and Reformation history in order to enter the department of philosophy, where I wrote my honors thesis on a problem in the logic of explanation in historical discourse.

During my senior year, however, my religious beliefs and my new acquaintance with philosophy remained in separate compartments. As on one level I became more and more the devotee of contemporary philosophy, so on another level my Episcopalianism was becoming more and more High Church.

Immediately after graduation from Harvard I had a chance to reread some of the theological writers who had interested me. Now, however, with some philosophy behind me, I began to see things in a different light. The more I read in the writings of Tillich, Niebuhr, Barth, and other leading contemporary theologians, the more exasperated I became. Repeatedly I found them missing the crux of the arguments they were trying to refute, distorting the positions of their opponents, or selecting the worst representatives of a viewpoint for examination. Many times, in exasperation, I cried out to myself, "What kind of people do they think we are?" On every side new problems about religion arose.

As I had once turned to philosophy to help me solve my problems about history, so I now turned again to philosophy to help me clarify and solve my problems about religion. After a while, I became aware that a great change had come over me. I had never simply rejected one or two of my old beliefs; I had begun to look at the world in an entirely new—and exciting—way.

Whether or not my own development is typical, intellectual considerations like the ones I encountered have brought many of my contemporaries to similar conclusions. I shall mention a few of these briefly in what follows.

Not long ago the *New Yorker* magazine printed a Whitney Darrow cartoon in which several Earth people, debarking from their space ship on a foreign star, find history about to repeat itself. As Adam and the Serpent watch, an interspace Eve is about to taste the Forbidden Apple which gives the knowledge of good and evil. The cry of the Earth people is "Miss! Oh, Miss! For God's sake, stop!"

The cartoon reflects an attitude which is influential among contemporary theologians and many other members of our society: Adam the Knower is a *sinner*, tasting forbidden fruits in defiance of God's will. But another powerful part of our tradition is better characterized by a very different tale. Prometheus, who defied the gods to bring fire to the Greeks, is regarded not as a sinner, but as a *hero*. In this tradition, discovery, knowledge, and criticism of authority—despite their dangers—are good things.

At the beginning of the present century, under the impact of science and Biblical research, the leading Protestant theologians were definitely thinking in terms of the second myth. One could no longer accept the words of Scripture literally; one was forced to pick and choose, to use one's mind to find what one could salvage. Many sermons and essays discussed "The Transient and the Permanent in Christianity," and evoked the "Christian ethic"—a vague and often inconsistent amalgam of the Sermon on the Mount, nineteenth-century liberal principles, the social gospel, and some strands of the "Protestant Ethic."

Most of these liberals shared two basic attitudes: (1) Christianity should be concerned primarily with building the Kingdom of God as quickly as possible *on earth;* (2) doctrinal differences were comparatively unimportant. What was more vital was a tolerant sharing of religious experience.

The movement which dominates Protestant thinking today—known as "neo-orthodoxy"—can be understood as a reaction to these attitudes. From the ultra-conservative followers of Karl Barth to the relatively liberal supporters of Tillich, the neo-orthodox share the warning that man *cannot* achieve salvation—either personal or social—by his own efforts, and the conviction that Christianity is in some sense the true religion.

The first neo-orthodox or "crisis" theologian seriously to connect certain weaknesses in liberal religion with the practice of modifying Biblical thought in the light of modern science and philosophy was the Swiss theologian Karl Barth, whose famous *Römerbrief,* a commentary on St. Paul's *Epistle to the Romans,* was published during the latter part of World War I. Men must not go to the Bible to pick and choose the words that will support their desires, Barth admonished. To do so is an example of prideful reliance on reason. Men—the descendants of Adam—should let the Bible speak to them and heed its authority in an attitude of awe, trust, and obedience—whatever the devilish promptings of contemporary thought. "It cannot be otherwise than that Dogmatics runs counter to every philosophy no matter what form it may have assumed," Barth warns in his *Credo*. If the philosophy and science of the past three hundred years seem to conflict with the Word, let the philosophy and science go. Kierkegaard has aptly called this a "crucifixion of the intellect."

As Barth "threw the Revelation at men," Reinhold Niebuhr, in America, began to try to fit them with catchers' mitts. As a young minister of the Evangelical Church (now a part of the newly-formed United Church of Christ) in Detroit, Niebuhr had been a social-gospel liberal, later supporting his thinking with a theoretical Marxism. Using certain Christian concepts, such as that of "Original Sin"—which taught the inevitable sinfulness and corruptibility of men, as illustrated in the story of Adam's original defiance of God's command—Niebuhr eventually came to abandon his hope for an earthly utopia. Without this hope, he had to leave his Marxism.

Niebuhr now began to launch violent polemics against simple Christian idealists, injecting into much of the wishy-washy social thinking of Protestants a healthy note of realism and self-criticism. His shrewd remarks on social ethics commanded the respect not only of Christians, but of politicians and political philosophers as well. Most of his criticisms were variations on the same, well-choosen theme: Christians could not expect to build a utopia on earth; nor could they expect to keep entirely innocent in the effort to construct such a paradise. Final justification, therefore, would have to wait for Eternity. The redemption of Man must come "beyond History," the work of a God who is also beyond History. And here, of course, is where Barth's supernatural theology fitted in.

I, for one, found this invitation to "forget" the thought of the past three hundred years, whose objections to Barth and Niebuhr's supernatural metaphysics have never been answered, both impossible and immoral. For ethics is surely not limited to questions of personal and social conduct. One's decisions on philosophical matters demand rigor and realism too. Here, however, Niebuhr's shrewdness comes to a dead halt: he has even admitted his "boredom" about such matters.

As a result, he is put in an extremely curious position—one paradox seems to have escaped him—he is willing to subject his *ethics* to worldly demands, but *not* his supernatural *metaphysics*.

Niebuhr would say my objection is an example of "prideful reliance on reason." I suppose he is right. But how humble is Niebuhr's request to reject the hard thinking of three centuries in order to embrace his particular interpretation of the "Word of God"? More than *one* apple has a worm at its core.

And the Devil did grin
For his darling sin
Is pride that apes humility.

For one who rejects the neo-orthodoxy of Niebuhr and Barth, as

I did, Protestantism's most popular alternative is an approach similar to Paul Tillich's. For two main reasons, Tillich's theology provided no alternative for me: I deplore his method of argument, and I question his Christianity.

Tillich is quite unable to accept the "supernatural." His aim is to "heal" the old Christian ideas and stories by calling attention to what is still *acceptable* in them and by disarming those aspects which are no longer tenable. His first step is to *redefine* the old terms, so as to eliminate their supernatural features, and to reinterpret them as myths and symbols. The system which results is a radical revision which retains the *appearance* of orthodoxy.

Following Tillich, it would be possible, for instance, to reinterpret Niebuhr's favorite doctrine of Original Sin somewhat as follows. The Genesis story of Adam's original sin—for which God is said to be punishing the following generations of men—can be understood as a primitive explanation of the fact that there is already evil in the world when any of us arrive here: evil that is "there," beyond our control. Each child that is born this year, for instance, will grow up in a world already torn by war, which he is in no way responsible for bringing about, but which will condition his daily life and perhaps even bring him to personal destruction.

Other children will inherit the diseases of their parents; still others, their economic plight or unhappy married life. Even when the original situation can be corrected externally, scars often remain in the form of psychological neuroses. We are unable by ourselves to cure all the ills we are born with. Where healing does occur it is often more a matter of luck—the theologian would say "grace"—than of our own efforts. The result of such a reinterpretation is, for Tillich, a "broken myth," symbolically true.

Tillich's practice up to this point has won him many admirers, and, thus far, I was able to accept his procedure. Right here, however, an extremely important problem arises for Christian apologetics. Other faiths—not to mention literature, such as Shakespeare and Greek tragedy—also possess symbols and myths embodying important truths about the way men should confront life. How then can Christianity preserve its claims to religious superiority?

Tillich tries to answer this question by defining "objectively true faith" in such a way that Christianity will be the only faith that satisfies the definition. Tillich decrees that the symbols of an "objectively true faith" will imply their own "lack of ultimacy." Briefly, this means that such symbols will indicate that they themselves are not permanently valid, and that what is most important is something beyond themselves to which they are "pointing." Jesus, for example, by sacrificing himself on the Cross, indicated his own "lack of ultimacy," as an historical figure. Hence, for Tillich, the religion whose central symbol is Christ's Cross is (when properly interpreted) the "objectively true" faith.

Any serious reader of Tillich must protest at this point, "How does Tillich *know* that the symbols of the objectively true faith will be the ones that imply their own 'lack of ultimacy'?" The answer is, "Tillich simply defines things that way."

But if this is so, *the whole issue of Christianity's "objective truth" rests on a very arbitrary verbal definition!* Tillich's gamesmanship is, admittedly, a way in which one can save a system. If the meanings of the terms of one's system of belief can always be redefined to meet any objection, then, of course, the system can never be refuted. Likewise, in a game of chess where one player is allowed to change the rules of the game any time he is in danger of checkmate, the second player is unlikely ever to win. And Tillich is hardly the only one who plays this way. Communists use similar gambits when they talk about "democracy."

It is a good measure of the intellectual shoddiness of Tillich's system that—even with this enormous advantage—he is still unable to win his game. His criterion, certainly, cannot validate Protestantism. It can be shown that the death of Socrates (a man who sacrificed his person for the Good beyond himself), the present Russian state, and many other things are "objectively true" symbols if we use Tillich's definition. Far from "healing" the Christian concepts, his cure seems more damaging than the disease.

But suppose for a moment that he had succeeded; that he had shown that Christ's Cross was an "objectively true" symbol. Would he then have proved the superiority of Christianity? I don't think so—for I believe Tillich's theology is Christian in name alone. Far from re-establishing the Christian symbols, he is asking us to accept *his* philosophy and *his* religion understood in terms of reinterpreted Biblical concepts. The result is not Christianity; it is a new religion.

Whatever new truth Tillich may be able to inject into the traditional Christian terms, they have a different history. Compared to his radical new proposals, Roman Catholicism and fundamentalist Protestantism, for all their differences, are really quite similar. For me, Roman Catholics and fundamentalists seem to be playing solitaire. But at least one expects that their cards are all on the table.

This has been a personal statement. What has been my personal solution? As I have indicated, my acquaintance with contemporary

WILLIAM WARREN BARTLEY, III 306

philosophy was a decisive influence in my rejection of contemporary Protestant theology. I do *not* believe, however, as did the early "logical positivists," that statements must be either scientific or "meaningless."

This view persuaded many philosophers and scientists in the 1920s, but it has since been shown to be sadly inadequate. Professor Karl Popper, of the University of London, gave the first thorough refutation of logical positivism in the early 1930s. Later on, even Ludwig Wittgenstein, one of its founders, came to abandon it.*

My own thinking has been more influenced by Popper's critical rationalism than by the thought of any other single philosopher. He has argued conclusively, I believe, that—on many philosophical questions—it is often necessary to make interpretations of the world which might be called metaphysical and cosmological.

How is it possible to *choose* one's "ultimate" metaphysical approach to the world? This is an area where there will always be room for argument. For philosophical theories, unlike scientific hypotheses, cannot be conclusively refuted by empirical test.

Such theories, however, *can* be discussed rationally. Popper's suggestion—which is the best I know—is that they be confronted with the problems they are supposed to solve. Then we can ask questions of a theory, such as: "Does it solve the problem? Or does it merely shift the problem? Does it solve it better than other theories? Does the theory contradict other philosophical theories needed for solving other problems?"

My opinion is that all contemporary philosophical expressions of Christianity raise far more problems than they solve, and that most of them ignore the most pressing problems. I recognize, however, that other people may evaluate the current Christian philosophies differently. For in any such situation where a free decision is involved, two people may remain at loggerheads.

None of us, for instance, can convince the neurotic that he's ill if he doesn't want to accept our diagnosis. I cannot prove that two plus two is four to the person who fervently believes that one is equal to zero. I cannot convince Hitler that murder is wrong. For we disagree about the value of human—or should I say "non-Aryan" life. And I am completely nonplused by the English canon who last summer urged that the people in the mental hospitals are not ill but are *really* possessed by evil spirits!

In the old story, the Pennsylvania Dutchman says to his wife,

* See Karl R. Popper, *The Logic of Scientific Discovery*, Basic Books, New York, 1959, and "The Status of Science and of Metaphysics," *Ratio*, December 1958; and Ludwig Wittgenstein, *The Blue and Brown Books*, Harper, New York, 1958.

"Everybody is crazy but me and thee, Hanna, and sometimes I wonder even about thee!"

Anybody, from the neurotic to Reinhold Niebuhr, can play Pennsylvania Dutchman and ask us to "take the leap of faith" to his position. And that position beyond the chasm may have its own consolations. But if we look before we leap, some of us will be unable to crucify our intellects without impaling our integrity.

Rationalists, however, make mistakes too. That is why—provided neither of the disputants is a Hitler—I think the best solution may be the one my former teacher at Harvard, Professor Morton White, once beautifully recommended by endorsing Hamlet's reply to the Queen:

> My pulse, as yours, doth temperately keep time,
> And makes as healthful music. It is not madness
> That I have uttered. . . .
>   Mother, for love of grace,
> Lay not that flattering unction to your soul,
> That not your trespass, but my madness speaks!

For each of us plays Pennsylvania Dutchman at some time of his life. And sometimes the Pennsylvania Dutchman is right.

But what has been my *religious* solution? Although my philosophical views are quite opposed to traditional and contemporary theology, I still love the church, appreciate the beauty of the personal lives of many of her members, and am awestruck before the moral genius of Christ. I am also able to appreciate the mystical confusion—as well as the urgency—of a feeling both philosophers, such as Wittgenstein, and theologians, such as Tillich, have spoken of: an amazement that anything at all should exist.

In this predicament, I have not taken the obvious step of leaving the church entirely. I decided to make the much more ambiguous—but I think reasonable—move of joining the Society of Friends. The Friends have, or try to have, two virtues in religious matters: the courage to think, and the ability to love. Although they hope that after re-examination of a moral issue one's personal decision will accord with the feeling of the group and the ethical injunctions of the Bible, the final criterion remains one's sense of personal integrity, not an outworn creed or symbolism.

This is, indeed, what many of the neo-orthodox theologians revolted against: a simple sharing of private religious experiences; but it is deliberately so. The Friends show their ability to love and their concern for this world not by wallowing in despair over its hopelessness, but by positive work to alleviate its troubles. As their general stand on warfare (a position I cannot agree with at all) shows, they are not interested in simply adjusting their ethic to the prevailing mores of the culture. They are often silly and naïve, but they are desperately honest. They are seekers after truth, not purveyors of the one true Truth, Church, Scripture, Symbol, or Country Club.

Membership in this society had the same attraction for me, I think, that Buddhist affiliation, less practically, has had for many of my more adventurous contemporaries. It is a society within which, with kindred spirits, I may carry on my personal quest for ever deeper understanding. And it provides a place where I may candidly discuss religious issues that concern me with those who are similarly concerned, and without those who already know all the answers.

Is this a solution I would recommend generally? Hardly. Each man must make his own decision after a good deal of excruciatingly difficult thought. Even for the person who shares many of my opinions there are many alternatives.

I did feel that in all integrity I would have to leave the Episcopal Church. And for similar reasons I knew the doors of the Lutheran, Presbyterian, Methodist, and other more confessional churches were closed. When I say "closed," I do not mean that I think these churches would have kept me out. I am completely sure that (at least as far as the creedal qualifications are concerned) I could be accepted into the ministry of any of them, if I were to employ Tillich's conception of truth and his reinterpretation of Christian statements when the time came for the creedal examination. The doors were closed by my own conviction that it would be wrong to use such misleading philosophical tools.

Twenty-five years ago my choice might have been for the Congregational Churches. Today—because of their new emphasis on centralization and organization and their efforts to force some of the member churches into an uncongenial merger with a confessional church—I am afraid they are going in a different direction. I am sure that I could have joined the Unitarians, the Universalists, or the Ethical Culturists, but personal experience brought me to prefer the Society of Friends. This choice is only one approach in one man's personal quest for philosophical health. It is one which is both possible and appealing for a person who combines sympathy for religion and just a touch of mysticism with rejection of traditional theology. It is also a choice which is compatible with profound resignation, hope for the best, and eagerness to work for the better.

The courage to think, and the ability to love. These gifts, plus a modicum of strength, are all I care to ask for in this life. And I do not believe that there is any other.